Terrorism, Inc.

Terrorism, Inc.

The Financing of Terrorism, Insurgency, and Irregular Warfare

COLIN P. CLARKE

Praeger Security International

 PRAEGER™

An Imprint of ABC-CLIO, LLC
Santa Barbara, California • Denver, Colorado

Library of Congress Cataloging-in-Publication Data

Clarke, Colin P.
    Terrorism, inc. : the financing of terrorism, insurgency, and irregular warfare / Colin P. Clarke.
        pages cm. — (Praeger security international)
    Includes bibliographical references and index.
    ISBN 978–1–4408–3103–4 (hard copy : alk. paper) — ISBN 978–1–4408–3104–1 (ebook)
1. Terrorism—Finance. 2. Insurgency—Finance. 3. Irregular warfare. I. Title.
HV6431.C52   2015
363.325—dc23   2015004931

ISBN: 978–1–4408–3103–4
EISBN: 978–1–4408–3104–1

19 18 17 16 15   1 2 3 4 5

This book is also available on the World Wide Web as an eBook.
Visit www.abc-clio.com for details.

Praeger
An Imprint of ABC-CLIO, LLC

ABC-CLIO, LLC
130 Cremona Drive, P.O. Box 1911
Santa Barbara, California 93116-1911

This book is printed on acid-free paper ∞

Manufactured in the United States of America

Contents

Preface

Terrorism, insurgency, and irregular warfare (IW) are defining features of conflict in the twenty-first century. These types of conflict are indicative of the harsh reality of both the current and future operating environments. As globalization accelerates unimpeded, a host of continuing trends reinforce the threats posed by violent non-state actors operating in a milieu that can be most aptly described as complex and unpredictable.

Although the United States eschewed more direct involvement in Syria (at least as of early 2015), her status as the world's preeminent global power will no doubt necessitate future involvement in various failed states, alternatively governed spaces and other zones of instability. Whether fighting against ethnically-based militias, warlord-led criminal gangs, or transnational terrorist and insurgent groups, combating how these entities are funded and financed will remain a critical challenge. This challenge is compounded by the globalization of banking and finance and the ubiquity of communications and information technology that facilitates the virtual movement of money.

In 2015, the international security landscape is as pernicious as ever. Despite a massive commitment of resources, the United States was never able to completely stabilize Iraq or Afghanistan, which still continue to battle overlapping insurgent groups and terrorist organizations. Iran continues to support myriad terrorist organizations throughout the Middle East, and Al-Qaida has evolved from an organization based in South Asia to a networked model of regional affiliates stretching from the Sahel to the Arabian Peninsula to the Horn of Africa. The threat from one of

Al-Qaida's spawn, the Islamic State of Iraq and Syria (ISIS) is as tangible as it is enduring.

This book will analyze seven terrorist and insurgent groups to determine how these groups fund their organizations, the various ways in which funding supports their operational and organizational capabilities, and how this funding could be disrupted. The groups covered are geographically diverse, rely on a wide range of tactics and sources of financing, and face a multitude of states and organizations seeking to disrupt and dismantle their activities and infrastructure. Historical lessons learned will inform policy recommendations for the cases still ongoing. This research should be interesting to a range of individuals and organizations, including academics and scholars, military leaders, policymakers and government officials, as well as banks, financial institutions and other multinational corporations concerned with the growing challenge of analyzing threat finance.

This book will proceed as follows:

CHAPTER 1. INTRODUCTION

Chapter one lays out the motivation for this book, introducing the analytic framework of the gray and dark economies. Next, chapter one reviews the various operational and organizational capabilities of terrorist and insurgent groups. Finally, the chapter provides a synopsis of the various means of combating the financing of terrorism, including both kinetic and non-kinetic efforts pursued by states and governments, as well as a brief history of the evolution of the effort to combat the financing of terrorism.

CHAPTER 2. THE PROVISIONAL IRISH REPUBLICAN ARMY (PIRA): "THE TROUBLES" IN NORTHERN IRELAND

Chapter 2 details how the PIRA relied on a range of activities to finance the insurgency in Northern Ireland over the course of 30 years, including diaspora donations from abroad (especially the United States), armed robbery, extortion, and coercing shopkeepers and business owners into paying protection money. Less lucrative but still valuable activities included income tax fraud, livestock smuggling (pigs, cattle, and bovine antibiotics), film piracy (including pornography), and automobile theft. The group also relied on legitimately owned businesses and has counted pubs, private security firms, taxi cab services, construction firms, and restaurants among its licit activities through which to both earn and launder money. These funds were used to purchase sophisticated weaponry, sustain its members, provide for the families of those members in prison, and develop a mature propaganda campaign. In time, the PIRA's funding stream afforded the group with the ability to transition to politics, embodied in its political wing, Sinn Fein. The British government relied on an extensive counterintelligence network to disrupt PIRA finances, while also targeting the group's leadership for kill, capture, arrest, prosecution, and imprisonment.

CHAPTER 3. THE LIBERATION TIGERS OF TAMIL EELAM (LTTE): A DIVERSIFIED FUNDING PORTFOLIO

Chapter 3 traces the rise and fall of the Tamil Tigers. Between its inception as an insurgent group in the mid-1970s and its demise in late 2009, the LTTE developed perhaps the most comprehensive array of military capabilities ever demonstrated by a terrorist group. Driving these capabilities was a diversified network of fundraising activities, ranging from extortion to human smuggling to armed robbery. The Tamil Tigers posed a truly asymmetric threat to the government of Sri Lanka and with the aid of its funding, boasted a navy, an air force, and an elite suicide commando unit used to assassinate heads of state and COIN force commanders. A transnational diaspora network provided propaganda, funding and weaponry to sustain the Tigers for most of the group's existence. The Sri Lankan government and its armed forces never effectively disrupted the LTTE's financing and only defeated the group through a scorched earth campaign that included mass atrocities against civilians.

CHAPTER 4. HEZBOLLAH: FINANCING THE PARTY OF GOD

Chapter 4 assesses Lebanese Hezbollah, a group that relies on support from Iran, a worldwide diaspora, and an extensive criminal portfolio to sustain its military capabilities and robust network of social services. Some of the larger services include Jihad al-Binaa (JAB), or Construction Jihad, the Islamic Health Committee (IHC), and the Relief Committee of Imam Khomenei (RCIK). The group's funding allows Hezbollah to maintain a vast arsenal of weaponry to expand its attack capability, sustain its operations over the long-term, inflict psychological damage on its adversaries, and diversify its methods and tactics. Multiple entities have attempted to combat Hezbollah, including the Lebanese government, the state of Israel, and the United States, although counter-threat finance efforts by each of the aforementioned have been met with mixed success. In turn, Hezbollah remains anchored in Beirut and its surrounding environs as perhaps the world's most capable hybrid actor—part terrorist group (with some conventional capabilities), part socio-political organization. The result has been a muddled response from those unsure of how to deal with this type of IW threat.

CHAPTER 5. HAMAS: GUNS AND GLORY IN GAZA

The analysis in Chapter 5 focuses on the Palestinian Hamas, a group that effectively balances its efforts to raise funds between gray market and dark market activities. The group's decision to dedicate more funding to its political activities may hint at a shift away from violence, yet its growing rocket arsenal suggests otherwise. Israel has enacted an array of policies, both kinetic and non-kinetic, that have affected the financial portfolio of Hamas. Similar to Hezbollah, Hamas presents a unique irregular warfare challenge to the Israelis, as well as to the broader Middle East. Hamas seems to have modeled itself on Hezbollah in some ways, as it has grown from a rag-tag terrorist group into a well-equipped hybrid threat. Countering Hamas will require a broad range of capabilities, likely to require both military and law enforcement measures, in addition to legal, civilian, diplomatic, and ministerial assistance.

CHAPTER 6. AFGHAN TALIBAN: FROM STRUGGLERS TO SMUGGLERS

In chapter six, the author examines the Afghan Taliban, a group that relies on donations from sympathizers abroad, as well as a growing involvement in the opium trade to fund its activities in Afghanistan and Pakistan. Still, a divide between the Taliban's leadership in Quetta and its mid-level commanders and foot soldiers in Afghanistan has been reflected in its fundraising activities. Different factions of the insurgency rely on different parts of the gray and dark economies, and the Taliban has ordered religious guidance specifically dealing with the trafficking of opium. While organizations like the Afghan Threat Finance Cell (ATFC) have made an impact by attenuating the Taliban's coffers, the international presence in Afghanistan is dwindling, so future efforts by the insurgency to raise funds will likely face fewer obstacles.

CHAPTER 7. AL-QAIDA: 9/11, FRANCHISE GROUPS, AND THE FUTURE AFTER BIN LADEN

Chapter 7 focuses on several important differences that exist between how Al-Qaida funds its organization now compared with how the group funded itself in the lead up to September 11, 2001. Al-Qaida central is far less relevant than it once was, having ceded autonomy to the fundraising committees of its affiliates in North Africa and the Arabian Peninsula. Determining the most effective way to counter the funding of a group that operates on such a transnational scale remains a continuous work in progress, but nevertheless retains significance for combating whatever the next iteration of this group ultimately morphs into over time. With its charismatic leader deceased, Al-Qaida has struggled to remain relevant, losing ground to the Islamic State of Iraq and Syria in the battle for the hearts and minds of aspiring jihadis throughout the Islamic world and the West. While some of the immediate laws enacted following the attacks of September 11, 2001, have been successful, many efforts have stalled or failed. This chapter addresses some of the successes, but also the failures, in order to discern best practices for countering this threat.

CHAPTER 8. THE ISLAMIC STATE OF IRAQ AND SYRIA (ISIS): BUILDING A CALIPHATE IN THE LEVANT

Chapter 8 examines the evolution of ISIS, which is the progeny of Al-Qaida in Iraq/Al-Qaida in the Land of the Two Rivers (which was originally known as Jama'at al-Tawhid wal-Jihad, or "Monotheism and Holy War Group") and is currently referred to as the Islamic State in Iraq and the Levant (ISIL)/the Islamic State in Iraq and al-Sham (ISIS), or the Islamic State (IS). ISIS has been labeled the richest terrorist group in history, flush with funds from robbery, extortion, and the smuggling and trafficking of oil. ISIS burst back onto the geopolitical radar following the withdrawal of U.S. troops from Iraq in 2011, coupled with the neighboring Syrian civil war and the marginalization of Iraqi Sunni Arabs by the sectarian government of Nouri al-Maliki. Since most of ISIS' funds are sourced locally, countering the financing of this group will be extremely challenging going forward and will require the cooperation of states in the region as well as the international community more broadly.

CHAPTER 9. CONCLUSION

This book concludes by analyzing, from a historical perspective, how terrorists and insurgents have funded their operations and organizations. Moreover, the concluding chapter revisits an examination of how terrorist and insurgent groups bankroll irregular warfare by dissecting the various ways they spend the money obtained from various revenue generating activities through the lens of a complementary set of operational and organizational tools. Next, Chapter 9 revisits what has worked and what has failed in the effort to combat terrorism financing, in addition to discussing the current limitations to countering insurgency and combating the financing of terrorism. The chapter concludes by discussing what obstacles lay ahead in the ever changing landscape of terrorism, insurgency, and irregular warfare and how some of these challenges can be managed effectively.

Acknowledgments

I am grateful to many people for contributing to this study and for their enduring support, without which this effort would not have been possible. I have been shaped by my education at many levels, including Chaminade High School, Loyola University in Maryland, the National University of Ireland Galway (NUIG), New York University (NYU) and above all, the University of Pittsburgh. At Pitt's Graduate School of Public and International Affairs (GSPIA), Phil Williams provided me with an intellectual safe haven at the Matthew B. Ridgway Center for International Security Studies. I am also thankful to Dennis Gormley, Forrest Morgan, and Donald Goldstein for shaping the research that evolved into my doctoral dissertation.

At the RAND Corporation, I would like to thank my friends and colleagues, Chad C. Serena, Christopher Paul, and Patrick B. Johnston for serving as a sounding board for my thoughts and ideas over the years, as well as for providing humor at times despite the grim nature of the subject matter we discuss.

At Carnegie Mellon University, I am thankful to several research assistants, including Max Goetschel and Christopher Skaggs, but especially Tiffany Tse.

I am particularly grateful for the opportunity to work with such dedicated and intelligent colleagues on Combined Joint Interagency Task Force Shafafiyat in Kabul Afghanistan in 2011. I am still close to several of those folks, you know who you are. That experience helped impress upon me exactly how difficult the challenge of countering the financing of terrorism and insurgency is and will continue to be in the future.

I would like to acknowledge the many named and unnamed scholars and practitioners who took time away from their busy schedules to avail me of their expertise and knowledge in this area. They include John Horgan, Peter Chalk, Louise Shelley, Gretchen Peters, Tom Keatinge, Matthew Levitt, and Jean-Marc Oppenheim, among others.

At Praeger Security International and ABC-CLIO, I would like to thank Steve Catalano, Suba Ramya, Nicole Azze, and Rebecca Matheson for their guidance throughout this process.

Most importantly, I would like to thank my family and friends, who provide me with the motivation to succeed and the humility to keep me grounded. Thanks and love to my mother Maureen, my father Philip, my brother Ryan, my sister Katie, my in-laws and my extended family, especially my cousins, SSgt Timmy Ledwith and SGT Sean Ledwith, who are *always faithful*. Lastly, I would like to thank my wife Colleen for her unconditional love, unwavering support and perhaps most of all, her limitless patience. LMB.

This book is dedicated to all of those affected by the tragic events of September 11, 2001 as well as to the men and women who defend freedom, both at home and abroad. Any and all mistakes contained here within are the sole responsibility of the author.

CHAPTER 1

Introduction

The lifeblood of any violent non-state organization is its ability to generate funds. In an irregular warfare environment, the importance of funding is magnified because unlike nation-states, terrorists and insurgents do not possess the ability to legally tax citizens in order to raise a standing military. On the contrary, terrorists, insurgents, warlords, and militias rely on both licit and illicit means to generate funds. These funds are then applied to build, consolidate and sustain the group's operational and organizational capabilities. The former augments a group's ability to successfully execute attacks, while the latter contributes to group cohesion. In turn, states and international organizations, those entities primarily tasked with countering these groups and their funding streams, rely on a range of kinetic and non-kinetic operations to disrupt and when possible, dismantle a malevolent group's ability to generate funds.

This book provides an overview of how terrorists and insurgents fund their activities, what these groups do with the revenue they generate, and how this funding can be disrupted. Terrorist financing—defined here as the process of raising, storing and moving funds obtained through legal or illegal means for the purpose of terrorist acts or sustaining the logistical structure of an insurgent organization—is an ongoing game of "cat and mouse."[1] Just as terrorists and insurgents are continually finding ways to adapt to evade law enforcement, security officials tasked with countering the financing of irregular warfare must rely on multiple countermeasures to deny, destroy, defend, detain, and disrupt a range of violent non-state actors. Nation-states and the international community rely on both military and law enforcement, in addition to efforts to build institutional capacity, establish norms, implement policies, and enforce laws as part of a broader combating the financing of terrorism (CFT) framework. This framework includes general crime fighting tools such as wiretaps and electronic surveillance, but also extends to sanctions and the freezing of funds and accounts.

In irregular warfare, violent non-state actors operate across the gray and dark economies and devote their finances to a range of asymmetric capabilities. By tracing the groups' patterns of financing, this research investigates terrorist and insurgent funding streams as well as the mechanisms in place to counter this funding. Increasingly, the international community has realized the importance of bringing all resources to bear. Rather than attacking terror finance with a single agency, nation-states and allied countries are collaborating to form combined joint interagency task forces (CJIATFs), which call upon the expertise of a diverse set of law enforcement professionals, from intelligence to treasury to legal experts and beyond.

While there is usually a clear distinction between terrorism and insurgency—the former is a tactic, while the latter is a movement—this distinction is not always recognized.[2] With the proliferation of research on both topics in the post-9/11 era, this problem became even more acute. Furthermore, discussions of civil war also potentially overlap the insurgency discourse, with distinctions between civil war, guerilla warfare, and insurgency occasionally hinging on a body count threshold (per year or throughout the duration of the conflict), tactics employed (low intensity versus conventional military), the actors involved (state versus nonstate, indigenous versus foreign), or other categorical distinctions that might classify conflicts as coups, countercoups, mutinies, insurrections, or other "revolutionary" activities. There is also no clear agreement on what differentiates irregular warfare from asymmetric warfare, or if a difference even exists between the two.[3]

There are many different ways to analyze terrorism and insurgency and to highlight differences and identify similarities. In their study of the role of airpower in counterinsurgency, Alan Vick et al. highlight the differences between the various targets, operations, and territory between terrorists and insurgents.[4] Insurgency is an armed political campaign while terrorism is a form of armed political communication. Insurgency uses mass mobilization by substate actors of a counter-state to challenge a national government for political power. Terrorism, on the other hand, is characterized by the use of violence by substate actors to attack innocent civilians in order to garner attention for their cause. While Vick et al. focus on territorial size, Byman et al. believe that the tactics used to gain and control territory are a more appropriate indication of whether the group is a terrorist or an insurgent group. Historically, several prominent groups—Provisional IRA, Hezbollah, LTTE, African National Congress (ANC)—were consistent practitioners of terrorism but also used a range of other tactics in their effort to control territory.[5] O'Neill finds that terrorism is merely a form of warfare in which violence is used primarily on civilians, while insurgent terrorism has a purpose. Unlike the former, the latter is used in the pursuance of a range of objectives, from short-term goals to intermediate and long-term.[6]

Definitions play a vital role in analysis. However, far too often academics and policymakers get tied up arguing over the definition of a term, rather than what the implications of that term might or might not be. In the end, a circuitous debate transpires amounting to little more than mere semantics. Meanwhile, the problem continues unabated until a more serious attempt at remedying the issue is addressed, with or without ever agreeing upon a single definition of the subject under consideration. At the end of the day, whether or not a group is labeled a terrorist or an insurgent is important because it has direct implications for strategy. Counterterrorism (CT) is different than counterinsurgency (COIN) and ISIS is not Al-Qaida, just as Hamas is different from Hezbollah. While it is essential to devote the resources necessary to counter non-state actors, it is a fool's errand to conceive of a grand strategy to combat non-state actors. To the extent that a strategy is formulated, it should be guided by specific principles, but tailored to each group individually in order to follow a nuanced and targeted approach on a case by case basis.

This research presents a comprehensive overview of the post–Cold War challenges associated with globalization, including the proliferation of failed and fragile states,[7] the ubiquity of porous borders, and the sanctuary offered by ungoverned/alternatively governed spaces. Moreover, it examines the rise of violent non-state actors in importance on the global security agenda and the struggles of nation-states (in the Westphalian sense) to deal with capacity gaps, functional holes, and legitimacy deficits.[8] "While there is ever-increasing literature on policy issues, strategies, and countermeasures, states must first understand their enemies before developing strategies to defeat them," notes threat finance scholar Michael Freeman.[9] This book is an attempt to begin understanding the range of threats, adversaries and enemies that seek to employ the tactics and strategies of terror against an international order firmly opposed to such violence, warfare, and criminality.

ANALYTIC FRAMEWORK AND ORGANIZING CONSTRUCT FOR THE CASE STUDIES

The first part of the framework is concerned with how terrorists and insurgents fund their organizations. To do this, each chapter analyzes what I term the *gray economy* of terrorist and insurgent groups, which is a combination of licit and illicit activities. The gray economy focuses on diaspora support, charities, fraud, legal businesses,[10] and money laundering. In addition to activities that blur the line of legality, insurgents and terrorists also depend on elements of the "dark economy," primarily focusing on various facets of transnational organized crime, including: human trafficking, narcotics smuggling, gun-running, money laundering,

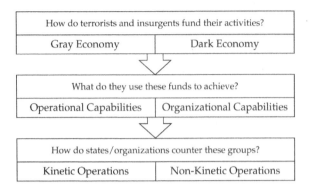

Figure 1.1

Analytic Framework

extortion, coercion/intimidation, kidnapping for ransom (KFR), corruption, and cybercrime.

The second part of the framework assesses what these organizations do with the funds gleaned from the gray and dark economies. After all, to conduct successful attacks, insurgents need money. Money is used to pay the salaries of insurgents, purchase weapons and equipment, bribe corrupt officials, provide for the families of killed or captured insurgents and social service provision. There are many sources of financing available to insurgent groups, especially those willing to commit crimes. Sometimes an external state sponsor is instrumental in helping to finance an insurgency, exemplified by the case of Hezbollah in Iran. Other times, as with the Tamil Tigers in Sri Lanka, a diaspora community is responsible for providing significant financial assistance to an insurgent group. Crime, whether drug trafficking, kidnapping, or armed robbery, is yet another avenue available to some insurgents. During the insurgency in Angola, the National Union for the Total Independence of Angola (UNITA) generated between $80 and $150 million a year from diamond smuggling and several other illicit activities.[11] Other groups rely on extortion, or "revolutionary taxes," as evidenced by cases in Peru, Colombia, Uruguay, Spain, Afghanistan, Pakistan, and Northern Ireland, to name just a few.[12]

The third and final piece of the framework looks at how these groups and their methods can be countered. For example, was the COIN force able to stop the insurgents from acquiring critical resources, or did factors like porous borders, sympathetic domestic and diaspora communities, and benevolent state sponsors continuously supply the insurgents with the resources necessary to prolong the insurgency and continue profiting from conflict? Although the United States has attempted to crack down on terror financing through Islamic charities since 9/11, charities linked to terrorist organizations have remained extremely resilient, displaying a penchant for adaptation that constrains the ability of the United States and the international community to make significant headway in this area, despite continued efforts.[13]

WHAT IS GRAY ECONOMY?

To properly explain what I mean by the term *gray economy*, I am referring to that combination of licit and illicit activities perpetrated by terrorist and insurgent groups for monetary gain. As a whole, the activities that comprise the gray economy are not entirely illegal. The gray economy encompasses, but is not limited to, diaspora funding, donations made through charities, fraud (including identity theft and cybercrime), legal businesses and front companies, and money laundering. The gray economy borders on the legal economy, interacts with the licit economy and intersects with ordinary business activities. All of this makes it difficult to counter. Diaspora communities *do* send legitimate remittances back to their countries of origins to help sustain their families. Honest individuals *do* contribute to a range of charities to help the less fortunate. Of course, funds bound for terrorists and insurgents travel through these same channels, so deciphering which are going to be used for good, and which will be used to kill and maim, is a difficult task for law enforcement and financial institutions. Terrorists and insurgents aim to take advantage of globalization by comingling their money with the voluminous amounts of capital transfers that total over $1 trillion a day.[14] Because terrorists and criminals combine their resources and profits with legitimate funds, this makes it difficult to detect where criminal funds end and legitimate funds begin.[15]

Diaspora Support

Diasporas are immigrant communities established in other countries. As Byman et al. have noted, significant diaspora support for terrorists and insurgents has occurred in every region of the world, with the exception of Latin America. Diaspora communities living abroad have sent support to insurgents in countries like Algeria, Azerbaijan, Egypt, India (Punjab and Kashmir), Indonesia (Aceh), Israel, Lebanon, Russia, Rwanda, Sri Lanka, Turkey, Northern Ireland, and Kosovo, to name just a few.[16] More recently, diaspora communities have played a role in insurgencies in Syria, Ukraine, Somalia, and Afghanistan. Several issues complicate counterthreat finance against diaspora movements. Chief among these, though, is that host-nation governments are challenged to discern between non-insurgent immigrants and pro-insurgent activities.[17]

There are different types of diasporas, including refugees and asylum seekers, migrants (both legal and illegal) comprised of guest workers and students, members of the anti-globalization movement, and organized trans-state ethno-national diasporas.[18] It is members of this last group, which can be either established or incipient, that have played the most significant role historically in funding terrorist and insurgent campaigns. In many of the cases discussed throughout this book, diasporas that have resulted from conflicts (e.g., Sri Lanka, Lebanon) are less compromising and serve to both "reinforce and exacerbate the protracted nature of conflicts by endorsing the most militant leaders in the homeland," which was the case with Prabhakaran and the Liberation Tigers of Tamil Eelam (LTTE) as well as with Nasrallah and Hezbollah.[19]

Charities

Financing terrorism through charity is a long-favored fund-raising technique, dating back to the Palestine Liberation Organization and the Provisional Irish Republican Army in the 1970s.[20] Charities are often, though not always, affiliated with religious support. This support, in turn, can fluctuate with the amount of media coverage of a particular conflict or movement. In Bosnia, Algeria, and Afghanistan, insurgents benefited from considerable support provided through religious charities, whose donations increased in the wake of publicized insurgent military success, or media-focused campaigns depicting civilian suffering in these countries.[21] In the ongoing Syrian conflict, charities from Kuwait and Qatar have allegedly funnelied money to Salafist jihadist organizations.[22] In what are known as syphoning transactions, funds raised by a nonprofit organization (NPO) are diverted to a terrorist organization for ulterior purposes.[23] Still, it is worth highlighting the skepticism that some scholars have in this regard, including Thomas Biersteker, who maintains that there is scant evidence that charities diversion remains a significant source of financing for core Al-Qaida.[24]

Fraud

Fraud is similar to larceny but defined distinctly as obtaining the property of another through trickery or deception.[25] Fraud comes in many forms and more recently identity theft and cybercrime have become popular (and lucrative) forms of fraud favored by criminals, terrorists, and insurgents. Often times, fraud is invisible to the untrained eye, but in fact, fraud is conducted frequently, and often surreptitiously. For terrorists, fraud is becoming a more popular way to raise funds because it is seen as a low-cost, low-risk method. Modern-day terrorists and criminals rely on intellectual property theft and skimming (theft of credit card information through cyber means) or phishing (false electronic mail solic-itations to trick an individual into divulging financial information) to pro-vide a high "bang-for-the-buck" ratio, and never involve face-to-face contact with the victims. The need for speed or agility is reduced because deception is prized over stealth.[26]

Legal Businesses

Legal businesses serve as front companies that allow terrorists and insurgents to conceal and launder the proceeds these groups make from their range of gray and dark activities. Terrorists and insurgents, or those closely connected to them, purchase and operate licit businesses in order to launder profits gained elsewhere through the business to make it seem as if the income was lawfully earned. For terrorists, front companies allow them to remain hidden within business activities while leveraging the funds in their possession to accomplish their objectives.[27] The type of business does not necessarily matter—but businesses that deal in high volumes of cash transactions are more conducive for laundering money. In Burma, a situation arose where insurgents involved in drug trafficking were allowed to continue their activities in return for a cessation of vio-lence. The result was that former insurgent drug lords like Lo Hsing Han and Khun Sa were able to invest drug proceeds into the Burmese economy and thus develop hotels, casinos, and various other businesses.[28]

Money Laundering

Money laundering is not an end in and of itself, but a method that is best conceived of, at least in the context of irregular warfare, as an illicit support activity. Just as terrorists and insurgents have learned to maintain a diverse funding portfolio, they have also acquired an appreciation for a diversification in the way funds are laundered. Terrorists and criminal organizations often launder money through the same channels, as was evidenced by the 2011 case of the Lebanese Canadian Bank, which has been accused of laundering money for a range of nefarious actors spanning South America, West Africa, and the Middle East.[29]

As a response to the threat posed by terrorists laundering proceeds from criminal activity to fund attacks, the United States has extended the anti-money laundering (AML) control regime beyond banks to include car dealers, casinos, jewelers, pawn shops, insurance companies and certain "corner shop money transmission businesses."[30] Never-theless, several of the most prominent international banks have been accused of rather egregious (and repeated) violations of the AML/CFT regime in countries where those regimes were previously thought to be effective, thus tempering expectations on progress and highlighting potential differences between the capability to prevent money laundering and the will to do so.[31]

In a simplified breakdown of money laundering, the act happens according to a three-step process. First, illicitly gained cash (which is generated through the gray or dark economy) is converted to monetary instruments or deposited into financial institution accounts. This is often referred to as placement. Second, the funds are moved through wire transfers, checks, money orders, and so on, into other financial institutions to obscure the original origins. This step is known as layering. Third, and finally, the funds are again moved through wire transfers, checks, money orders, and so forth and used to acquire legitimate assets or fund further activities.[32]

WHAT IS DARK ECONOMY?

While activities in the gray economy maintain some plausibility in the licit and legal domain, activities that occur in the dark economy are entirely illicit and illegal, with little room for interpretation. These activities usually, involve violence, or at least the threat of violence, and include kidnapping for ransom, armed robbery and theft, trafficking, smuggling and counterfeiting, extortion and protection, and external state support.

Some research suggests that as insurgent groups become more intimately involved with certain aspects of the dark economy (especially drug trafficking), their ideological commitment is enervated in direct relation to an increased interest in purely economic ends.[33] But this is not always true. Groups like the Provisional Irish Republican Army (PIRA), the Kurdistan Workers' Party (PKK), and the LTTE each engaged in forms of organized crime without deviating from their true role as insurgents.[34]

Both Makarenko's "model of terrorist-criminal relationships" and Cornell's "crime-rebellion nexus" suggest that the relationship between insurgency and organized crime should not be conceived of in terms of path analysis, but rather as a sliding scale on which groups can go back and forth between the extremes of crime and ideological insurgency, occupying any number of intermediate stages between these poles along the way.[35] The "mutative process" describes insurgents forced into criminality as a function of a dearth of financial support. In other words, some groups reach the conclusion that without the profits they obtain from the drug trade, they will be unable to continue fighting.[36]

Kidnapping for Ransom (KFR)

Kidnapping for ransom, or KFR, is a criminal tactic adopted by terrorist and insurgent groups for its dual purpose of simultaneously terrorizing the population while having the added benefit of funding these groups' activities. For decades, groups have relied on KFR as a method of raising funds. Today, groups like the Afghan Taliban, the Haqqani Network, Al-Qaida, and a range of criminal groups in Mexico all rely on KFR as a primary pillar of the dark economy.[37] In Southeast Asia, kidnapping for ransom by Abu Sayyaf Group (ASG) and the Moro Islamic Liberation Front (MILF) are further evidence of the blurred lines between criminality and terrorism.[38] In Colombia, both the FARC and the *Ejercito de Liberaicion Nacional* (National Liberation Army [ELN]) have relied on kidnapping, and in Central Asia, the Islamic Movement of Uzbekistan (IMU) has earned significant funding from this practice. Other groups have taken notice, as Chechen rebels and insurgents in Iraq also adopted the practice.[39]

Kidnapping can reap large sums of money. Examples of KFR payments that were particularly lucrative include the following:[40]

- Amir Aftab Malik, the son-in-law of a retired four-star army general and former chairman of Pakistan's Joint Chiefs of Staff, was freed after a ransom of approximately USD $3 million was paid to his captors, thought to be Lashkar-e-Jhangvi in North Waziristan.[41]
- In 2006, the Italian government reportedly paid the Taliban nearly $5 million to secure the release of two of its citizens kidnapped in Afghanistan.[42]
- A bus full of missionaries from South Korea was held captive in July 2007 in Ghazni province, Afghanistan. The Taliban reportedly received USD $5 million from Seoul to secure the release of the missionaries.[43]
- Johan Freckhaus, a French contractor working in Afghanistan, was kidnapped in June 2008 by the Taliban and released after French authorities paid roughly USD $1.5 million.[44]
- In February 2008, Pakistan's Ambassador to Afghanistan, Tariq Azizuddin was kidnapped. The Pakistani government allegedly released 55 militants from and paid USD $2.5 million to secure his release.[45]

More recently the Tehrik-i-Taliban Pakistan has extended its activities to major Pakistani cities, including Karachi, focusing largely on abductions of businessmen and entrepreneurs. Moreover, those businessmen who are not kidnapped might instead become victims of extortion, paying protection fees to avoid being abducted.

In 2007, more than 50 percent of the approximately 7,500 kidnappings worldwide occurred in Latin America.[46] As a crime, KFR is low risk, low cost, and high reward, making it the ideal criminal activity for terrorist groups.[47] In places like Iraq and Afghanistan, it should come as little surprise that insurgents and terrorists are engaged in KFR. Indeed, as Phil Williams notes, "with kidnapping gangs and insurgent and jihadi groups operating in the same space, some kind of relationship was inevitable."[48] Throughout the Middle East and North Africa, many Western tourists have been kidnapped over the past decade, with some national governments paying millions to save their citizens.[49] The risk is particularly high in conflict zones, including Afghanistan, Iraq, Syria, Somalia, Yemen and other failed states with large swaths of ungoverned territory. And while groups like Hezbollah do kidnap in order to use hostages as a bartering chip for possible future prisoner exchanges, the majority of kidnappings are driven by the desire for profit.[50]

Armed Robbery and Theft

Armed robbery and theft is one of the most basic forms of criminality used to obtain money. Robbing banks, businesses, and individuals can be a quick and reliable method of garnering a much-needed infusion of funds. Of course, there are risks of arrest, prosecution, or even death when engaging in such criminality. Both the PIRA and the LTTE earned a reputation for ruthless efficiency in armed robbery. That insurgents and terrorists engage in this type of activity should come as no surprise, especially if one thinks of organized crime as a lucrative fund-raising method. Indeed, according to Phil Williams, the defining characteristic of groups that commit such acts is not the activity itself, but the purpose of the group. In this sense, organized crime is an instrumental activity, and can be understood merely as a method or set of activities that groups employ to obtain funds. Like insurgents, these groups can have political ends, and may turn to organized crime methodologies to fund their political agendas.[51] (This includes funding the attacks and violence that may be instrumental in helping them further these ends and agendas.)

Smuggling, Trafficking, and Counterfeiting

The literature on transnational organized crime often uses the terms *smuggling* and *trafficking* interchangeably, except for human trafficking and human smuggling, where the first is a crime against the person and the second is a crime against the state. For the sake of clarity and precision, this research proceeds from the notion that smuggling is about the crossing of borders while trafficking refers to the broader process of moving illicit goods. Counterfeiting, while tangentially related to trafficking and smuggling, is clearly a separate category. The range of commodities that can be trafficked, smuggled, and/or counterfeited is broad. However, the most commonly smuggled and trafficked commodities are arms (weapons), drugs, humans, and natural resources. More recently, there have been reports that insurgents have profited from the smuggling of less traditional "commodities" like antiquities, human organs, and endangered animals. To be sure, legal commodities like cigarettes are also commonly smuggled, primarily to evade taxes in one state or country and obtain profits by evading these taxes by selling the cigarettes some-where else.

With the end of the Cold War, weaponry flooded the global arms mar-ket. AK-47s, rocket-propelled grenades, mines, and even nuclear com-ponents were bought and sold illicitly.[52] With the collapse of the Soviet Union, Eastern Bloc countries flooded the market with every-thing from small arms to missiles. Over time, different cities throughout the world have grown renowned for open air arms and weapons bazaars.[53] The Bakara Market in Mogadishu has been one of the world's busiest bazaars for the exchange in arms, weapons, and ammunition for more than two decades. Other cities include Bangkok in Thailand and Peshawar in Pakistan, during the 1970s and 1980s, respectively. In Colombia, post-Cold War arms stockpiles (along with demilitarized zones and state interference) contributed directly to the influx of arms into the country.[54]

During the brutal wars in West Africa during the 1990s, international arms traffickers from the former Soviet Union, Israel, and South Africa mingled with warlords, diamond merchants, and mercenaries. Due in part to ineffective arms embargos and regulations, as well as a growing black market, a large percentage of the population in this region has been heavily armed. Around this same time, the disintegration of the Federal Republic of Yugoslavia was driving demand on the global arms market. Reverting to its role as a clearinghouse for trafficked weapons during the Iran-Iraq War (1980–1988), the Balkans once again became a cross-roads for smuggled weaponry, including assault rifles, machineguns, small-arms rounds, antitank weapons, antitank rounds, mortar rounds, grenades, landmines, and an array of equipment, from boots to medical supplies and flak jackets.[55] Old networks were reinvigorated in an attempt to satisfy market shortages.[56] Weapons and ammunition were smuggled into the region using both traditional means, such as tunnels, and more ingenious methods, including empty metal cylinders of oxygen and in false bottoms of humanitarian aid containers.[57]

Due to high pecuniary value and the low volume to value ratio of smuggling and trafficking illicit narcotics (cocaine, ecstasy, heroin, hash-ish, marijuana, methamphetamine, opiates, etc.) and the chemical precur-sors required to manufacture some of these drugs, this criminal activity is an attractive one for criminals and terrorists.[58] In addition to money, the narcotics trade in drug-producing countries has the potential to provide terrorists with recruits and sympathizers among "impoverished, neglected, isolated farmers" who can help cultivate drug crops while also serving as a bulwark against pro-government groups and anti-drug campaigns.[59]

Involvement in the narcotics trade can bring together insurgent groups and drug cartels.[60] Furthermore, the demise of the latter could present opportunities for insurgents to fill the void, as in Colombia when FARC took over some of the territory previously controlled by the Medellin and Cali cartels in the 1990s. Other times, as with the PKK's drug trafficking activities in Europe, rather than cooperate with traditional criminal enterprises, insurgent groups seek to drive them out of the market to supplant them themselves.[61] Finally, as we have seen with the relationship between drug traffickers and Sendero Luminoso in Peru, the dominant party in the relationship can change over time. In the 1990s, a powerful (and brutal) Sendero held sway, while more recently, especially in the Valley of the Apurimac and Ene River (VRAE), the insurgents have been keen to play a more secondary role.[62]

Narcotics remain both the most common and most lucrative form of organized crime used by terrorist groups, including well-known traffickers like the Kosovo Liberation Army (KLA),[63] Basque Homeland and Liberty or ETA in Spain, and the IMU.[64] Profits derived from drug trafficking have enabled groups like FARC to obtain sophisticated weapons and communications technology.[65] More recently, an investigation in Australia uncovered 40 separate money laundering operations in that country, one of which delivered proceeds from drug trafficking to Hezbollah.[66] The cultivation of illicit crops like poppy or coca is labor-intensive and provides employment to hundreds of thousands to millions of people in particular countries, including Afghanistan and Colombia, respectively.[67] Producer countries are often the least profitable part of the process; the lion's share of earnings is garnered by those who refine and market the drugs.[68]

Humans

Each year, hundreds of thousands of women and children are trafficked and forced into prostitution, many of them traveling along the "pipeline of people and contraband" coming from Eastern Europe, Central Asia, the Middle East, Russia, and North Africa destined for Western Europe.[69] Indeed, prominent human trafficking routes from China and Nigeria into Europe are a cause for serious concern.[70] Human trafficking can include alien smuggling and it should be noted that although the global sex trade is a major driver in this regard, humans are trafficked for many reasons, include labor exploitation, which is increasingly common in agriculture, construction and forced domestic servitude.[71] The trafficking of humans not only provides funding for criminal and terrorist organizations, but also fuels worries of lone wolves and sleeper cells infiltrating states undetected and blending into everyday society before attacking. With the collapse of Libya during the Arab Spring, the countries flanking Europe's southern borders remain on high alert, especially Italy.

Natural Resources, Gems, and Precious Metals

In what have come to be known as resource insurgencies, insurgents do not seek so much to win control of the state or establish their own government as they fight to eliminate state interference with their exploitation of natural resources (e.g., diamonds, timber). During the brutal civil wars in West Africa throughout the 1990s, the Revolutionary United Front (RUF) acquired weapons either by raiding Sierra Leonean army forward supply posts or by trading diamonds with Liberian warlord Charles Taylor. As a border sanctuary, the insurgents relied on a forested boundary enclave near the Liberian side, which provided them with an ungoverned area to smuggle diamonds and engage in illegal logging.[72] Where precious gems or stones are unavailable, like in Somalia, non-state actors fighting to control territory throughout the Horn of Africa, including the Al-Qaida linked Al-Shabaab militant group, rely on a range of other criminal activities linked to the exploitation of natural resources, from the illicit ivory trade to the booming market for smuggled charcoal.[73]

Extortion and Protection Payments

Extortion is defined as "obtaining property from another due to future threats of physical injury, property damage, or exposure to ridicule or criminal charges."[74] Long a favored technique of organized crime, extortionists run protection rackets, which are payments made by victims in return for not being assaulted (or worse) or having their homes, businesses, or families threatened. Insurgents, terrorists, and criminals from Russia to Indonesia to Somalia have all employed extortion as a means of funding their campaigns of violence. For those non-state actors seeking to maintain the popular support of their constituencies, there is a fine line between protecting and preying on the local population.

Just as with violent criminals who rob drug dealers, terrorists and insurgents prey upon narcotics traffickers as a frequent source of extortion, since they are unable to go to law enforcement authorities. Sometimes, this can be a slippery slope toward trafficking themselves, while other times it can be a way for those who want little to do with trafficking narcotics, but still want to profit from the trade overall.

External State Support

During the Cold War, what would likely have been considered crime or mere banditry became imbued with political significance as the United States and the Soviet Union provided financial and military resources to their respective proxies in places like Angola, Afghanistan, and Nicaragua. With the end of the Cold War, many developing nations accustomed to the largesse from their superpower patrons were attenuated and were once again vulnerable to small-scale acts of criminal violence and banditry. At the same time, the end of superpower subsidies to insurgents made them turn to criminality for resources, which was made easier with the new influx of readily accessible small arms and light weapons. The withdrawal of superpower sponsorship also degraded the ideological coherence of many movements. And conflicts that might have before been viewed through a Cold War "political" lens instead became seen as criminal conflicts, especially in places like West Africa and the Balkans, where at times violence bordered on anomie. To be sure, many insurgents rely on criminality for financing, and it is this fact that explains much of the apparent rise in criminal violence—with the dissolution of the Soviet Union, superpower financing of proxies was withdrawn, making states weaker and more susceptible to attack. Criminal and insurgent groups that previously relied on state financing were forced to either become criminals or fade away.

External state support can take any number of forms: training, safe haven and transit, intelligence, financing, direct military support, political support, and propaganda, and so on. As Seth Jones and Patrick Johnston have concluded, "insurgencies that receive outside support are substantially more likely to outlast counterinsurgency efforts and ultimately overthrow incumbent regimes or force concessions than those without a foreign patron."[75] Groups like Hezbollah, which receives hundreds of millions of dollars from Iran, have been able to transition from terrorist group to insurgent organization to full-on hybrid politico-military powerhouse. Several scholars have found that terrorist organizations with more allies, especially external states, tend to be more lethal.[76]

WHAT ARE OPERATIONAL CAPABILITIES?

"Insurgent groups are more likely to negotiate if they believe they have little chance of success on the battlefield," concludes Byman.[77] Insurgent groups' chances of success on the battlefield are directly linked to the ability of the insurgents to wage successful attacks on their adversaries. The operational capacity of an insurgent organization is comprised of the activities that allow the insurgents to sustain a series of successful attacks.[78] These operational tools include: weapons, sanctuary/safe haven, intelligence, training, and financing/funding. For those insurgents receiving outside assistance, I include the factors external weapons and direct military support as sub-elements of the weapons category. Sanctuary also takes into account the factor operational space, which is the time and space to plan, train for, and execute attacks.[79] As part of intelligence, I assess operational security (OPSEC) and where relevant, deception skills. For training, I consider any forms of technical expertise provided to the insurgents. Financing is fairly straightforward and examines all sources of insurgent funding, including both licit and illicit.

Weapons

Like money, weaponry is another category which seems fairly self-evident as a necessity to insurgents. Insurgency is a form of irregular warfare that matches the weak against the strong. Since terrorism is a primary component of most insurgencies, small arms and light weapons (SALW) are common. For the entrepreneurial insurgent, a wide range of ingredients can be used to fashion explosives, from the crude to the sophisticated. Weapons used by insurgents include: explosives, small arms, shoulder fired missiles, mortars, and in the former Soviet Union, Grad rocket launchers. African insurgencies have mostly featured small arms like AK-47s, while insurgencies in the Balkans, Caucasus, and Central Asia benefited from the availability of former Soviet stockpiles, including tanks and artillery. In Chechnya, insurgents used heavy-caliber machine guns and rocket-propelled grenades (RPGs) with great skill during an impressive military display against Russian COIN forces on numerous occasions.[80] A decade before the Chechen conflict, Afghan *mujahedin* used Stinger missiles supplied by the Central Intelligence Agency (CIA) to shoot down Soviet helicopters.

When insurgents are unable to obtain the weaponry necessary to challenge the COIN force, they often seek the assistance of an external sponsor. In Northern Ireland, the PIRA established a steady pipeline with Libya. Qaddafi supplied the PIRA with hundreds of small arms as well as over 2,500 kg of Semtex.[81] PIRA bomb makers crafted highly lethal explosive devices with the Libyan-supplied, Czech-made explosives. During the Cold War, the United States and the Soviet Union respectively supplied weapons to insurgents fighting proxy wars in places like Angola, El Salvador, and Afghanistan.

Before reversing its policy in 1987, the government of India supplied LTTE insurgents with weapons and munitions in their fight against the Sri Lankan government.[82] Belgrade bolstered the Bosnian Serbs during the Balkans wars while Russia offered heavy weapons and armor to insurgents in Moldova, Abkhazia, and Nagorno-Karabakh. States are not the only source of external weapons. In West Africa, the Caucasus, and South Asia, arms trafficker Viktor Bout supplied small arms and light weapons to insurgents fighting protracted conflicts throughout the late 1990s and early 2000s. Finally, diaspora communities can be an external supplier of weapons and other military-related resources through long established foreign networks.

Direct military support to insurgents can range from minimal to extensive. As Byman observes, "direct assistance is rare, but when it occurs it usually has a tremendous impact on the fighting."[83] Direct military support can consist of a state (or in the case of NATO, a collection of states) using its own army to assist insurgents in battle. In 1999, NATO's bombardment of the Serbs was the tipping point in the Kosovo conflict. Airstrikes lasted for 78 days and pulverized Slobodan Milosevic's Serb fighters, which paved the way for a KLA victory and independence for the Republic of Kosovo 10 years later. More recently, NATO airstrikes ousted longtime Libyan strongman Muammar Qaddafi from power after nearly four decades in power. As of May 2015, the situation in Libya was bordering on anarchy.

Intelligence

Intelligence, as it is defined in this research, is the information that insurgents need to identify a target, develop a plan to attack that target, and understand the ramifications that the attack will have for a range of actors, to include the host nation government and COIN force, the insurgents' supporters and wider constituency, and finally any powerful regional or international actors that may be involved in one way or another.[84] In Iraq and Afghanistan, insurgents frequently attack American soldiers with improvised explosive devices (IEDs). Ideally, the insurgents try to find out when an American patrol will be passing through the area, what kind of vehicle it will be (armored Humvee, unarmored Humvee, Mine-Resistant Ambush Protected tank, etc.) and approximately how many soldiers each vehicle can hold.

FARC developed a robust intelligence capability over time and uses money acquired through the drug trade to bankroll a network of informants, including some in the Colombian security forces.[85] In recent years, the Taliban and the Haqqani network have relied on timely and accurate intelligence from insurgents who have infiltrated the Afghan National Security Forces (ANSF) to conduct an assassination campaign against government and military officials in the Karzai-led government. These "spies in the castle," as J. Bowyer Bell has referred to them, play a critical role in hampering the COIN forces' ability to operate effectively against insurgents. External state sponsors are another source of intelligence for insurgents. In West Africa, Liberian Warlord Charles Taylor and the National Patriotic Front of Liberia (NPFL) supplied the RUF with intelligence during Sierra Leone's 10 year long insurgency.

Insurgent organizations can follow either a minimalist model or a maximalist model of intelligence. The PIRA was an example of the former, with a nonexistent formal intelligence structure, emphasis on planning the next attack, and reliance on the Catholic community for snippets of important information. On the contrary, Hezbollah adheres to the maximalist model of intelligence, retaining the full spectrum of capabilities, including robust signals intelligence (SIGINT) and human intelligence (HUMINT) capabilities.[86]

Differentiated from command and control or operational space by the necessity to prevent COIN forces from sabotaging a potential attack, operational security requires significant resources to maintain the integrity of a planned operation.[87] Insurgent groups overly concerned with operational security are typically fighting a COIN force with highly trained and capable intelligence operatives. Groups like the PIRA, Hezbollah, and Hamas build in overlapping redundancies while planning operations to mitigate COIN force penetration of an active plot. The more resources insurgents are forced to devote to operational security, the less time and energy they will have to maintain the cohesion of the group. In Northern Ireland, British COIN forces waged a high stakes game of spy versus spy against the PIRA in what many have referred to as "the Dirty War," meaning the war fought between British elements like MI5 and the Force Research Unit (FRU) and the PIRA's intelligence wing.[88]

Sanctuary

During the Vietnam War, Vietcong insurgents enjoyed sanctuary in several states adjacent to South Vietnam, including Cambodia and Laos. Vietcong bases over the border were used for training, arms stockpiling, operational planning and, a sanctuary for insurgents on the run and other seeking rest and recuperation.[89] In Afghanistan, the Taliban and the Haqqani network manipulate the border with Pakistan as a strategic advantage against both NATO and Afghan forces. As the United States well remembers, cross-border safe haven in Pakistan was a boon to the CIA-supported *mujahedin* in their fight against Soviet COIN forces.

In the 1970s and 1980s, PLO guerillas used Lebanon and Jordan as sanctuaries. Prior to the United States-led invasion of Afghanistan in 2001, Al-Qaida used Sudan and Afghanistan as home base at different points. "Sanctuary substantially increased al-Qaida's financial requirements, but that safe haven lowered overall needs of covertness, eased command and control, enabled extensive training and planning, and generally allowed terrorist groups to operate at a far lower marginal cost per attack," according to Rabasa et al.[90]

In their study on how insurgencies end, Connable and Libicki discuss the subject of sanctuary at length. One of their key findings is that *sanctuary is vital to insurgencies*.[91] Their detailed analysis of Al-Qaida in Iraq (AQI), Communist insurgents in Greece, and the Taliban insurgency in Afghanistan reinforce the importance of a space where insurgents can train, rest, and organize unmolested by counterinsurgents. Sanctuary has also been a major factor in insurgencies in Malaya, Thailand,

Mozambique, Guatemala, and Nicaragua, among others. Securing national borders to blunt an insurgency is a COIN force imperative, but the reality is that borders are difficult to seal. Still, it is not impossible. COIN forces in Turkey, Israel, India, Morocco, and France have all quelled insurgencies by closing down the border and eliminating external sanctuaries.[92]

Operational space is critical to insurgencies. This is the space used by insurgents to plan, train, rest, recuperate, resupply, and hide those members being actively sought by the security forces. An ideal type of operational space is an "ungoverned territory," which is more often an alternatively governed territory ruled by unsavory actors like warlords, criminal gangs, or militias. The dimensions of ungovernability include: the level of state penetration into the society, which entity holds a monopoly on the use of force, the degree of control over the borders, and the potential for external interference in the area.[93]

How conducive these areas are to insurgents depend on several variables such as the adequacy of infrastructure and operational access, sources of income, demographic and social characteristics, and invisibility, or the extent to which insurgents can blend in with the local population.[94]

Training

As it would be for any soldier or fighter, training is a highly valued component of an insurgent's repertoire. Training requires both individuals with the technical knowledge or knowhow to train others, as well as an area where insurgents can train far from the watchful eye of the government. Deserts, jungles, and mountainous terrain all serve as ideal training areas for insurgents. But even more important than carving out the space to train, to truly hone their skills handling weapons, constructing bombs, and conducting surveillance and reconnaissance, insurgents need the technical expertise of individuals with practical experience. The Internet or a beat up old version of *The Anarchist's Cookbook* can only take one so far.

Technical expertise is an advanced form of training. It extends beyond explicit knowledge and into the realm of tacit knowledge. As Dennis Gormley explains, tacit knowledge "can't be written down."[95] On the contrary, tacit knowledge can only be acquired "through an often lengthy process of apprenticeship" as it is "the product of a unique social and intellectual environment composed of highly skilled senior and junior colleagues, who pass this specialized knowledge around from one individual to another."[96] In his work on Islamist militancy, Michael Kenney resurrects the work of ancient Greek philosophers to elucidate the difference between explicit knowledge and technical expertise. Kenney's analysis of *techne* and *metis* is an important contribution to the literature on organizational learning in terrorist and insurgent groups. While *techne* is abstract technical knowledge codified in documents, *metis* is "intuitive, practical knowledge" that can only be institutionalized by "engaging in the activity itself, rather than by formal study."[97] Whether it is called technical expertise, tacit knowledge, or *techne*, a strong case has been made for the six fingered bomb maker.

WHAT ARE ORGANIZATIONAL CAPABILITIES?

In their theoretical analysis of leadership, Daniel Byman and Kenneth Pollack conclude that "international relations cannot be understood if the role of the individual is ignored."[98] The organizational capacity of an insurgent group is comprised of those activities that sustain the group's existence as a cohesive entity.[99] Leadership is the most important component of a group's organizational capacity. The leadership of an insurgency provides strategic direction to the movement, issuing directives and making the major decisions that affect every aspect of the organization. It requires leadership to provide vision, direction, guidance, coordination, and organizational coherence to other aspects of the insurgency, including the combatants ("foot soldiers"), political cadre, auxiliaries, and mass base.[100] Leadership touches upon all facets of the insurgency and is closely connected with command and control, ideology, recruitment, and public relations. Command and control will also include an analysis of the group's organizational structure and any organizational aid that was important to the group. In cases where outside actors provided political support or propaganda to an insurgent group, this factor will be considered under the category of public relations.

Leadership

Command and control is the mechanism by which insurgent groups plan, coordinate, and execute attacks.[101] A command and control network functions according to how the group is organized, or its organizational structure. To ensure that an attack will be carried out, insurgent leaders will often attempt to build a degree of redundancy into their network. However, the more people that are made aware of an operation, the greater chance there will be for the attack to be compromised as a result of a leak or penetration.[102] Technology and communications are impacting the command and control networks of insurgent groups by allowing individuals to stay in contact even when they are physically located in disparate places.

Like other organizations, how an insurgency is structured will have implications for how it conducts operations and how it is countered.

Moreover, organizational structure and design can impact a group's ability to both impart and import knowledge, the latter of which is critical to group survival. An insurgency can be vertical, or top-down, issuing orders from the top to be executed by those below. Vertical leadership has both advantages and disadvantages. On one hand, in a vertically structured organization, once a decision is made it is passed down and carried out with little friction. Subordinates understand their role and are keen to follow directions with a minimum amount of pushback. A major disadvantage, however, is that in a vertical organization, if a leader is lost (or in the case of an insurgency, eliminated through kill or capture), the organization will lack direction and guidance for a definite period of time. Even if a capable understudy steps in to fill the void, a period of transition will ensue, and some degree of resulting confusion is inevitable. Still, this is not always the case, as FARC has exhibited relatively smooth succession.

Horizontal organizations, sometimes known as "flat," "networked," or "matrix" organizations are becoming increasingly common in the contemporary environment of information flows and technological innovation. In a horizontal organization, leadership is seen as a total system rather than the domain of a single people or small cadre of individuals. Like vertical organizations, horizontal organizations have both advantages and disadvantages. In a horizontal organization, more people have access and authority to decisions, which makes the vetting process more thorough, but can also prolong both reaching and implementing a decision. In an insurgency, horizontal networks are less prone to decapitation strikes, where the elimination of a charismatic leader of a group can be a crushing blow.[103] But what effect does the structure of an insurgency have on the group's decision to negotiate or continue fighting? Are vertically structured groups more likely than horizontally structured groups to make one decision or another? Once a decision is reached, which structure will be more amenable to implementing this decision? Is splintering a likely second order consequence?

Ideology

Ideology has been, and will continue to be, a way for insurgencies to gain recruits and amass popular support. Ideologies are crucial for insurgent groups because they explain the struggle to its followers and articulate a platform to resolve grievances, both perceived and real. As the U.S. Army and Marine Corps Field Manual 3–24 (FM 3-24) notes, "The most powerful ideologies tap latent, emotional concerns of the populace," and can be based on religion, nationalist, ethnic, tribal, or cultural aspirations, a desire for justice or vengeance, or liberation from occupation.[104]

Writing over 50 years ago, Eric Hobsbawm alluded to the absence of a "common movement" as one of the major shortcomings of rebel groups.[105] What he meant was that these groups lacked an innovative, shared, explicit ideology to motivate and mobilize the group's followers.[106] Thomas Marks sees a close linkage between leadership and ideology, which then connect to goals, noting, "If the ideological approach of the leadership is able to hold sway, insurgency will result. The movement will go on to pursue *political* goals, normally the effort to remake the system, either defensively (e.g., separatism) or offensively (e.g., revolutionary war, the purposive effort 'to make a revolution')."[107] One way of conceptualizing ideology is analyzing whether the group is ideologically flexible, rigidly dogmatic, or somewhere in between.

Popular support for an insurgency has been the focus of scholars and practitioners of both insurgency and counterinsurgency alike. Indeed, Mao realized the importance of maintaining the goodwill of the population, not from an altruistic perspective but from a pragmatic standpoint. Sir Gerald Templer of the British military is credited with coining the term *hearts and minds*, during his tenure in command of the Malayan Emergency. Even today, the American military in Afghanistan is keen to avoid civilian casualties for fear of alienating the population and pushing Afghan civilians closer to the Taliban and Al-Qaida.

Once an insurgency is under way, the host nation government and COIN force can choose to respond to threats in any number of ways. Often times, the first reaction is a move to crush the insurgency before it grows into a more formidable threat. However, the use of overwhelming force can sometimes backfire, leading the insurgency to metastasize. Scholars have noted that repression, especially the disproportionate use of force in response to an insurgency, can have the unintended effect of increasing support for an insurgency.[108] Argo contends that violence has a polarizing effect on the population and reprisals can easily elevate a low-level conflict into a more aggressive insurgency.[109] Moreover, when the COIN force is perceived as an occupying power, insurgent resistance is fierce and increases the likelihood of suicide attacks.[110]

Accompanying components of repression include humiliation, intolerable frustration, alienation, and hatred.[111] Daily reminders of an individual's status as a second-class citizen in his or her own homeland can push one to support or join an insurgent organization.[112] A dearth of economic opportunities, a repressive political culture, and a nonexistent civil society also qualify as elements related to fertile ground for insurgency.[113] In some cases, as we have seen in Western Europe, prison becomes an incubator for radicalism and extremism, transforming common criminals into committed ideologues intent on perpetrating acts of violence not for profit, but because of politics. Finally, a growing body of research suggests that insurgents can generate and maintain support as the desire for resistance within a community gains acceptance as the support of a public good. Fair and Shepherd argue that insurgents provide resistance and that, by extension, anyone who also wants resistance benefits from that provision and seeks to continue some level of support, whether active or passive.[114]

Human Resources and Recruitment

Popular support is also critical to consider when considering the translation of passive support into more active forms, including recruitment into an organization. No insurgent organization can sustain itself without replenishing the ranks of its captured or killed. While scores of Islamic State in Iraq and Syria (ISIS) fighters are killed each day, an untold number of new recruits regularly travel to the Middle East from around the world to join the group. Like social movements, insurgent groups must attract members outside of their hardcore.[115] Pinpointing precisely why an individual decides to join an insurgent group can be difficult, but a host of factors have been identified in the literature that suggest reasons why certain people choose to rebel against the state. Furthermore, it is clear that insurgent organizations seek to actively recruit new members into their ranks and have several platforms for achieving this objective. As Todd Helmus notes, "group socialization processes are inherently active in organizational recruitment and indoctrination efforts."[116]

Recruitment efforts can vary from one-on-one meetings, where motivation and qualifications are assessed and potential recruits selected, to more informal gatherings which can take place at private homes or religious summer camps.[117] Moreover, recruitment can take the form of a formalized process, as in targeting Saudi recruits for Iraq, Jemmah Islamiyah efforts in Southeast Asia, LTTE campaigns in Tamil schools, and PKK outreach at cultural centers.[118] Other recruitment efforts are less formal and include the personal indoctrination of friends, which is a common tactic of groups like the Algerian Armed Islamic Group (GIA) and the Salafist Group for Preaching and Combat (GSPC).[119] Clan or tribal connections are another common form of recruitment into insurgent groups and many groups use social services to attract new members into their ranks.[120]

Low levels of popular support do not necessarily doom an insurgency to failure. On the contrary, groups can continue to wage a successful insurgency even with just a modicum of support, although the minority must be considered an "active minority" for the insurgents to sustain momentum. In many cases, earnest recruitment by the insurgents is unnecessary. Brutal, coercion-driven strategies can help swell insurgent ranks, negating the need for the insurgents to actively recruit. In the early 1970s in Northern Ireland, widespread reports of the British using torture against PIRA prisoners was an effective insurgent recruiting tool in and of itself.[121]

Media, Public Relations, Propaganda, and Publicity

In the battle for hearts and minds, insurgents are aware that media and public relations efforts are important tools in winning the battle of perception. Information operations (IO) have become central to irregular warfare. Counterinsurgents have public affairs officers, strategic communication specialists, and entire units devoted to psychological operations (PSYOP). In the twenty-first century, social media, the Internet, and communication technology are shaping the battlefield in ways previously not possible. Publicity allows insurgents to promote their ideology, galvanize supporters, and disseminate their message to a wide audience. The PIRA had its own newspaper, *An Phoblacht*, which it used to reach not only Republicans in Northern Ireland, but also supporters comprised of the Irish diaspora spread throughout parts of North America, Europe, and Australia. In general, insurgents target three primary audiences through their public relations campaigns: their own members and constituents, supporters outside the group, and enemy forces.

Political support is not limited to the insurgency itself. External sponsors can provide insurgents with a range of political support. This support can be diverse and includes: access to a state's diplomatic apparatus, vocal support for recognition in the international arena, persuading NGOs and charities to provide support to the group directly, and even denying support to the government opposing the insurgents.[122] In both Kosovo and Sudan, American backing of insurgent groups not only tipped the scales militarily, but also went a long way to helping these nations acquire legitimacy at the United Nations. In Libya, NATO support to the rebels has been an important part of the post-Gadhafi era, although the outcome in that country is very much uncertain, especially as Western attention has been focused on countering the threat of ISIS. Propaganda, though often considered a pejorative term and associated with *deception* and *falsehood*, can be an important tool in influencing a target population. In an era of social media, the Internet, and satellite television, an effective propaganda campaign is an extremely valuable weapon at the disposal of both the insurgents and the counterinsurgents.

COUNTERING THE FINANCING OF TERRORISM, INSURGENCY, AND IRREGULAR WARFARE

When it comes to countering the financing of terrorism, insurgency and irregular warfare, rather than break the evolution of this problem set into several distinct time periods, it is perhaps best to think in terms of the before and after—pre- and post-9/11. After the attacks of September 11, 2001, the U.S. government sought to undertake tactical actions aimed at disrupting individual nodes in the terrorist financial network as well as to implement a range of strategic initiatives with the ultimate goal of transforming the environment in which these militants operated.[123] To be sure, there has been much progress to date, especially with respect to stymieing Al-Qaida's efforts to raise, store, transfer, and spend money. However, new and more odious threats loom on the horizon, as demonstrated by the rapid rise of ISIS in the summer of 2014, the continuing rampage of Boko Haram throughout Nigeria, and the revival of Al-Qaida in the Arabian Peninsula (AQAP) in Yemen. Continued efforts to counter the financing of terrorism, insurgency and irregular warfare are the *sine qua non* of a comprehensive strategy to meet the growing challenge of transnational terrorism and the threat posed by Salafist jihadists and other violent non-state actors.

Pre-9/11 Efforts

One of the first efforts to combat the financing of terrorism, even though it was initially considered legislation to deal with money laundering, came in the form of the 1970 Bank Secrecy Act (BSA), also known as the Currency and Foreign Transactions Reporting Act. The BSA required banks to maintain an audit trail of large transactions and to provide law enforcement authorities with access to sensitive information.[124] In 1977, the International Emergency Economic Powers Act (IEEPA) presented the president with the ability to block U.S. imports from and exports to any entity designated under this law, with assistance from the Office of Foreign Assets Control (OFAC). Still, it was not until 1985 that financial institutions were required to submit suspicious activity requests (SARs) at the impetus of the Office of the Comptroller of the Currency. The next year, in 1986, money laundering was designated as a federal crime under the Money Laundering Control Act. In 1989, the Financial Action Task Force was established at the G7 Summit in Paris as a response to growing concern over instances of money laundering in the international financial system.[125]

Following the collapse of the Soviet Union in the early 1990s, the United States ascended to its role as the world's lone superpower, although this did nothing to insulate Washington from the threat posed by global terrorism. If anything, as the world's sole hegemon, the United States became an even more attractive target of a range of non-state actors, including Al-Qaida (even though it was the United States that helped the Afghan *mujahedin* drive out the Soviets in the 1980s). Nevertheless, the lion's share of attention focused on anti-money laundering rather than combating the financing of terrorism. Indeed, the 1992 Annunzio-Wylie Act strengthened the sanctions for BSA violations and established a Bank Secrecy Act Advisory Group. Three years later, in 1995, the financial intelligence units (FIUs) of 20 separate countries established the Egmont Group, an organization designed to foster cooperation among states in the areas of information exchange, training and the sharing of expertise in the fight against money laundering and the financing of terrorism.

Following the 1998 Al-Qaida attacks on the U.S. embassies in Kenya and Tanzania former terrorism czar Richard Clarke established a National Security Council (NSC)-led interagency group to focus on the financing of terrorism.[126] In 1999, French-led efforts at the United Nations resulted in the adoption of the UN Convention on the Suppression of Terrorist Financing. Despite the growing threat from international terrorism, know-your-customer (KYC) requirements proposed by Treasury and federal regulators met resistance from both the banking industry and influential elements of the U.S. Congress. Even as the United States continued to struggle with making progress against CFT, the international community forged ahead. In 2000, the UN Convention against Transnational Organized Crime was adopted, as was UNSCR 1333 which sought to contain the Taliban in Afghanistan while the Financial Action Task Force produced "Name & Shame" list of Non-Cooperative Countries or Territories (NCCTs). In March 2000, Treasury was nominated as the new home for the Financial Assets Tracking Center although according to Clunan, this center never "fully functioned" at Treasury (it was taken over by the CIA in late 2002 and renamed the Foreign Terrorist Asset Tracking Group, or FTATG).[127]

Post-9/11 Efforts

Following the Al-Qaida attacks of September 11, 2001, the Bush administration signed Executive Order 13224, which was specifically designed to "starve the terrorists of funding" by blocking property and prohibiting transactions with persons who commit, threat to commit, or support terrorism.[128] For good measure, the United Nations Security Council unanimously adopted Resolution 1373, which called on all UN member states to criminalize the use or collection of funds intended, or known to be intended, for terrorism, in addition to freezing funds and assets; prohibiting aid or provision to terrorists; refraining from providing any support; and denying safe haven to those who finance, plan, support, or commit terrorist acts.[129] The USA PATRIOT Act expanded the ability of law enforcement and the intelligence community to access and share financial information regarding terrorist investigations.[130] Shortly after 9/11, the FBI established an interagency Financial Review Group which became known as the Terrorist Financing Operations Section (TFOS), while the U.S. Customs Service established Operation Green Quest and the Department of Justice allocated more resources to combating the financing of terrorism as well.

In October 2001, the Financial Action Task Force expanded its purview beyond money laundering to include the financing of terrorism and offered nine special recommendations to deal with issues including, but not limited to: alternative remittances, wire transfers, NPOs, cash couriers and the freezing and confiscating of terrorist assets.[131] Other post 9/11 developments include the provision of technical assistance toward compliance by the International Monetary Fund (IMF) and World Bank, as well as greater involvement in CFT by the Egmont Group. Accordingly, most international cooperation has been kinetic, focused on the capturing and eliminating of terrorist financiers, rather than in special designations and bolstering the implementation of the CFT regime.[132] While helpful, focusing solely on kinetic efforts at the expense of a more comprehensive approach is myopic and only serves to fuel the debate between those who favor the "freeze and seize approach" and those who find greater utility in "following the money" to develop a more robust intelligence picture of individual terrorist and insurgent networks.

While there was a definite need to devote more resources to CFT following the 9/11 attacks, inevitably, bureaucratic battles soon arose over jurisdiction. The creation of new agencies, like the Department of Homeland Security (DHS), contributed to the stovepiping of information and the protection of "rice bowls" within different departments of government, precisely the kind of issues that the bureaucratic reorganization was intended to ameliorate. Still, despite occasional infighting, there has been considerable progress achieved on elevating the importance of combating the financing of terrorism. Since 2003–2004, there has been a marked increase in the appreciation for financial intelligence (FININT).[133] Put another way, in a post 9/11 world, the Treasury Department, which created the Office of Terrorism and Financial Intelligence (TFI) and the Office of Intelligence and Analysis, now has a seat at the table with "the big boys of national security"—the CIA, the NSA, the FBI and the Defense and State departments.[134]

CHAPTER 2

The Provisional Irish Republican Army (PIRA): "The Troubles" in Northern Ireland

BACKGROUND

The Provisional Irish Republican Army emerged from the struggles of the civil rights movement in Northern Ireland in the late 1960s.[1] Original in many ways, the group was also the continuation of a militant Irish Republican movement that traced its legacy back to the 1790s, when Theobald Wolfe Tone and the United Irishmen formed a "brotherhood of affection, a communion of rites and union of power among Irishmen of every religious persuasion."[2] The Provisionals, or "Provos" as they were referred to, waged a 30-year long insurgency against the security forces of Northern Ireland, while also clashing directly with Protestant paramilitaries during spasms of sectarian conflict. To grow the organization over time, the PIRA relied on both the gray and dark economy.

Funds were used for a variety of purposes including the purchase of sophisticated weaponry, operations and logistics, and to develop the group's political wing, Sinn Fein. James Adams concludes that the Provos became involved in organized crime to provide the estimated $7 million per year they needed to pay full-time insurgents and support a growing political base.[3] In contrast to other parts of the PIRA, the "Finance Department" consisted of very few individuals. Financial operations, specifically the management and use of funds, were entrusted to a small cadre within the organization.[4] To disrupt the PIRA's funding stream, the British government relied on an extensive counterintelligence network while also targeting the group's leadership for kill, capture, and imprisonment. The cooperation of authorities in the Republic of Ireland (ROI) and the United States was also essential in hampering the group's financial network.

HOW THE PIRA FUNDED ITS ACTIVITIES

The Provisional Irish Republican Army, like other insurgent groups, relied on a combination of gray and dark activities to meet the financial requirements necessary to manage a successful insurgent organization. While finance does not necessarily inhibit an insurgent group from waging war against the state, it does limit "the extent and sophistication of a terrorist organization's activities."[5]

For the PIRA, funding was such a critical resource because of the group's wide range of activities and responsibilities. From the start, insurgent leaders understood that fighting an adversary as formidable and well-resourced as the British military required substantive resources for the insurgency to have even a remote chance of success. This, in turn, necessitated a vast array of weaponry and the maintenance of a complex organizational infrastructure—both expensive to acquire and sustain. PIRA operating costs resulted from a number of critical group functions, including: paying the salaries of its members; acquiring weapons and munitions; planning and preparation for operations; sustaining the families of PIRA prisoners and members killed in action; and supporting the growth and maturation of its political wing, Sinn Fein.

What is known of PIRA fund-raising is that it was organized, task specialized and person-centered with funds earmarked to sustain the group's operational and organizational capabilities. As a rule, PIRA funding activities did not make its members personally wealthy and fund-raising efforts relied on influential networks in both the gray and dark worlds. Moreover, PIRA funding operations were opportunistic, adaptive, entrepreneurial, and sensitive to an array of both internal and external forces.[6]

Gray Economy

For the Provos, the gray economy consisted of diaspora support, charities, various types of fraud, money earned from legal businesses, and money laundering. From the late-1960s until the mid-1980s, financial support from the United States flowed largely unabated, with the Irish-American diaspora and numerous charities, chief among them the Irish Northern Aid Committee (NORAID), playing an indispensable role.[7] The FBI and British intelligence estimated that NORAID declared only approximately one-quarter to one-fifth of the funds it raised. Undeclared funds were siphoned off to purchase arms, or sent to Dublin and Belfast covertly. Intelligence and law enforcement agencies always regarded NORAID and the PIRA as symbiotic organizations.[8]

Diaspora Support

Diaspora communities can be an external supplier of weapons and other military-related resources through long established foreign networks. The PIRA had its own newspaper, *An Phoblacht*, which it used to reach not only Republicans in Northern Ireland, but also supporters comprising of the Irish diaspora spread throughout parts of North America, Europe, and Australia. "The enormous Irish-American population has always felt a strong sentimental attachment to 'the old country' and this has been translated into a steady stream of cash and guns to the IRA, 'critical enablers of the group's longevity.' "[9]

Both the United States and the Republic of Ireland were popular destinations for insurgents, but the United States in particular, served as a safe haven for Republican terrorists, especially those on the run. According to Daniel Byman, "The diaspora [also] acted as a safe haven for IRA fugitives. The Irish Northern Aid Committee (NORAID) helped IRA operatives find new identities and jobs in the United States, enabling them to escape justice in Northern Ireland."[10] Some PIRA insurgents fled to America and assumed a new life, where they blended in with the other Irish immigrants in working-class populations through New York City— including Queens, Manhattan, and the Bronx, where many worked as bartenders or in the construction industry. Insurgents would spend anywhere from days to years hiding outside of Northern Ireland, sneaking back into the country to execute attacks or deliver weapons before disappearing once again. One of the main efforts of the diaspora was work done through NORAID.

Charities

Besides serving as a physical safe haven for fugitives, the United States was also a place where PIRA sympathizers and affiliates were given free rein to fund-raise. "The IRA's ability to enjoy a haven in the United States and to raise money was bolstered by U.S. laws governing the rights of those engaged in political activity, even if such activity involved violence," notes Byman.[11] NORAID was founded in the Bronx in 1970 (based at 273 East 194th Street) by Michael Flannery and over the course of the conflict managed to raise between $3 and $5 million for "the cause," by soliciting donations from the Irish diaspora and Irish-American activists in major cities throughout the country, including New York, Chicago, Boston, and Albany.[12] NORAID attempted to erect a façade of plausible deniability, consistently suggesting that there was no link whatsoever to the PIRA's military activities. On the contrary, the organization claimed that it was merely a charity established to provide financial assistance to *the families* of PIRA members who were "suffering hardship as a result of sectarian strife."[13]

Since the primary responsibility of NORAID was to raise funds for the Provisionals, it became the main vehicle through which American donations flowed.[14] The organization benefited greatly from a mature infrastructure of previously established groups, like the Ancient Order of Hibernians, myriad unions (police, "Longshoremen," etc.), and a network of Irish pubs throughout the Northeast United States.[15] NORAID enjoyed spikes in fund-raising following acts of high-profile British violence like Bloody Sunday, an incident that was perceived as the group's first big publicity break. Much of NORAID's support came from the conservative, anti-Communist trade union movement in the United States.[16] Besides being a major recruiting boon for the PIRA, the donations offered to NORAID following Bloody Sunday foreshadowed the strength of the financial link with the Irish-American diaspora.[17] The hunger strikes and death of Bobby Sands and nine other men in 1981 also provided a resurgence of NORAID fund-raising efforts.

During the height of the conflict, counterterrorism efforts cost the British government an estimated £4 million ($6 million) a day.[18] But unlike a small NGO, the United Kingdom could sustain these expenses. External support to the insurgency could not. Like other terrorist support systems, NORAID's bureaucracy grew cumbersome. A substantial portion of funds never made it to Northern Ireland and the PIRA, and were instead diverted to pay for salaries and propaganda in the United States.[19]

Another budgeting concern for the PIRA leadership was the sustenance of the families of insurgents who were killed or in prison, men (and their families) who were "on the run," and PIRA members who had served extended jail terms and as a result, were highly unlikely to secure employment in the licit sectors of the economy. While the families of prisoners received financial support on a weekly or monthly basis, for various reasons it is unknown exactly how much money was reserved for these expenses.

While the official line in pubs and fund-raising dinners was that the money would go toward sustaining the families of PIRA prisoners, many of those donating were well aware that a portion of the money, if not most of it, would be diverted to purchasing arms and explosives to continue the "armed struggle." Nevertheless, longtime IRA supporters George Harrison and Martin Flannery (the former an IRA veteran who fought the "Black and Tans" in the 1920s), always denied that the money went for guns. They admit that money was collected for guns, but this was kept separate from the money used to support the families of those most directly affected by "the Troubles."[20] Official public statements and facts on the ground rarely converged.

Fraud

The PIRA engaged liberally in tax "fiddles" involving the use of false tax exemption certificates (on building sites throughout Northern Ireland) as one of several fraud-related money making enterprises.[21] The Northern Ireland Housing Executive was a common target of fraud by terrorists, who also sought to devise complex scams to deceive European Community regulations, including mortgage frauds and false accounting.[22]

The South Armagh contingent of the PIRA raised important funds for the group through both agricultural and animal subsidy fraud, aided during the 1980s, relying on Slab Murphy's farm, which straddled the Northern Ireland–Republic of Ireland border.[23] These frauds involved false claims for different rates of agricultural subsidies on different sides of the border and involved goods such as butter, beef, pork, lamb, and cattle. These goods were exported from the Republic to Northern Ireland, thus earning an export subsidy before being smuggled back across the border and exported again at a later date. Other forms of fraud perpetrated by the PIRA include social welfare fraud and petrol fraud, the latter of which took advantage of different rates of excise duties on either side of the border for fuel oil (petrol and diesel).[24]

Legal Businesses

The PIRA counted pubs, private security firms, taxicab services, guesthouses, courier services, social clubs, cars and machinery, construction firms, and restaurants among its licit activities through which to both earn and launder money.[25] Amongst its businesses, the PIRA counted pubs in Boston, Finglas, Co. Dublin, Coolock, Dublin city center, Letterkenny, Co. Donegal, and Cork, with other small pubs throughout the Republic. Other businesses included video shops, a haulage company, and quasi-legal drinking clubs called *shebeens*, which could be outfitted with illegally installed slot machines.[26] The PIRA established the Andersonstown Cooperative Industrial and Provident Society, which then purchased legal businesses, including a butcher's shop, a supermarket, and a construction business.[27] As Keith Maguire remarked, "By the late 1980s, terrorist groups had become businessmen with terrorist interests."[28]

From the point of view of the PIRA's leadership, the move into legal businesses was necessary. It meant that dirty money could be made clean, and this clean money could be used for legitimate purposes, like financing the group's growing political wing, Sinn Fein. However, when terrorists move into the licit, private sector, they expose themselves as vulnerable to those agencies looking to combat them. Adams has described this phenomenon thusly, remarking, "Terrorists are extremely good at using their muscle to beg, to steal or to borrow but do not operate as well in a semi-legitimate way (with the exception of the protection companies). When they have to file accounts and turn in a regular profit, they are less effective."[29] The turning point, however, in the PIRA's reliance on legal businesses was when the group determined that to defeat the British, it would have to fight "the long war." As such, this drove the need for sustainable funding, which in turn meant figuring out how to make the proceeds of the organization's numerous ventures into legitimate funds through investment in businesses and companies.[30]

Money Laundering

The PIRA laundered money in a number of ways. One method was to work with failing business owners to help resuscitate their companies. A PIRA member would supply the business owner with cash and bank drafts (this money could come from "short-term loans" from PIRA associated, armed robberies, etc.). Successful ventures were those that provided a return on investment, especially those that happened quickly and without strings attached. Of note, the PIRA was at times willing to engage with individuals outside of its established networks, which made the organization vulnerable. Accountants used by the insurgents were sometimes able to secure fraudulent bank references from unscrupulous bank managers (in exchange for cash or out of ideological affinity, or both) that would allow them to buy property and businesses.[31] An important point to note, as highlighted by Horgan and Taylor, is the distinction between running a successful business and executing a successful money laundering scheme, which are not mutually exclusive. Indeed, even when a business is sold at a loss, the loss must be framed in the context of already illegally obtained money.[32] A very small cadre of individuals was tasked with money laundering, with operations coordinated by members or associates skilled in banking and accounting.[33]

Dark Economy

The scale and scope of the PIRA's internal funding capabilities is complex. To generate the income necessary to operate the organization on a day-to-day basis, the group engaged in a wide array of illegal activities, including—KFR, armed robbery, smuggling, extortion and "riding shotgun"[34] and external state support. Less lucrative, but still valuable activities included film piracy (including pornography) and automobile theft.

Kidnapping for Ransom (KFR)

Kidnapping for ransom is one of the most insidious forms of organized crime. It contributes directly to instability in a country and presents a challenge to the legitimacy of the state and its security forces. Other corrosive effects include inducing a climate of fear among both domestic and multinational corporations, which in turn affects the economy. KFR targets often include wealthy businessmen or executives of successful companies.

In October 1979, the PIRA kidnapped Ben Dunne, the wealthy scion of a family that owned a chain of retail stores throughout Ireland. The operation is thought to have netted the PIRA £750,000.[35] Two months later, in December 1979, the PIRA kidnapped Margaret Fennelley, the wife of a bank manager. Two more daughters of bank managers in Dundalk and Ardee (Co. Louth), respectively, were kidnapped and ransomed for £50,000 each.[36] Through it failed to net a ransom, one of the most "impressive," if not bizarre "kidnappings" pulled off by the PIRA was the February 1981 kidnapping of a thoroughbred horse named Shergar. Other kidnappings executed by the insurgents included the following:

- Canadian businessman and multimillionaire Galen Weston
- Alma Manima (a scheme which allegedly resulted in a £60,000 payday)
- Associated British Foods executive Don Tidey
- Jennifer Guinness, the daughter of merchant banker

Kidnappings were not always necessarily for ransom. Sometimes, as was the case with the kidnapping of Caroline Moorland, the intent is intimidation or revenge against perceived informers. Moreover, kidnappings often had unintended consequences. The kidnapping of Don Tidey resulted in the death of an Irish soldier and *Garda, or Irish police,* who were killed in a firefight with the PIRA.[37] Events like that led to a loss of popular support for the insurgency, which in effect led the PIRA to reconsider KFR as a viable form of fund-raising.

Armed Robbery and Theft

Though not all armed robberies in Northern Ireland during "The Troubles" could be traced back to the Provos, many that were among the most valuable and well organized can be attributed to the group. Indeed, certain active service units (ASUs) specialized specifically in armed robbery.[38] In addition to stealing cars and antiques, the PIRA focused on banks, post offices, and building societies, as robbery remained "one of the PIRA's main 'outwardly' sources of funding, if not the single main source" during various periods of the group's existence.[39] Armed robberies provided a consistent flow of money to the insurgents, especially in the 1980s. In 1984 in Northern Ireland there were 622 armed robberies totaling $1.2 million; the previous year, 359 robberies netted an estimated $6 million.[40]

As a method of fund-raising, armed robbery and theft fell out of favor for several reasons. First, as the success and popularity of Sinn Fein increased, there was a need not only for more funds (which meant expanding *beyond* just armed robbery), but moreover, armed robberies "created a bad name" for the PIRA.[41] In June 1996, a *Garda* named Jerry McCabe was shot and killed by an insurgent unit, provoking backlash against the PIRA during a critical period in the conflict's final phase.

Smuggling, Trafficking, and Counterfeiting[42]

To diversify its criminal portfolio, the PIRA engaged in the smuggling and trafficking of goods, both licit and illicit. This included cross-border smuggling and trafficking, the most notorious of which involved pigs, cattle, livestock grain, and animal antibiotics. At one point in the 1980s, customs officials identified 240 unauthorized border crossings (and these were only the ones they knew about). The border between Northern Ireland and the Republic offered the insurgents numerous opportunities to ferry smuggled goods back and forth while evading capture. South Armagh developed a reputation as "bandit country," where hijackings were common, thieves and traffickers dominated, and locals refused to speak with the authorities.

Through some of its smuggling activities, the PIRA was able to take advantage of the sales tax (VAT) on luxury goods and alcohol. In addition to the aforementioned activities, the PIRA also dealt in counterfeit goods, ranging from videos (including pornography) to CDs, computer games, contraband cigarette lighters, and brand-name jeans.[43] According to Dingley, the PIRA's counterfeiting and smuggling operations grew so expansive that the group acquired its own factories in Eastern Europe and Turkey, where counterfeit goods could be produced before being shipped back to Northern Ireland and sold for a profit.[44] Licit and illicit goods were smuggled along transportation and distribution networks that doubled as arms smuggling routes. The PIRA's smuggling operations extended from Northern Ireland all the way to China.[45]

Extortion and Protection

In what has been dubbed by James Adams as the PIRA's "Capone discovery," the leadership learned that the organization could raise significant amounts of money from coercion. The group would demand protection money from publicans, local businessmen, shopkeepers, and so on. The maturation of this crime pointed to the later establishment of security companies; by hiring the right company, business owners could almost certainly avoid extortion. This allowed the PIRA to "provide a legitimate veneer for what remains a simple racket."[46]

Another popular tactic was strong-arming business owners to add "ghost" employees to their payrolls. Extorting building sites was particularly easy if the builders were small local businesses because this often meant that the owners not only worked, but also lived in the area. Extortions of small business became so frequent and commonplace that the Inland Revenue eventually allowed businesses to claim the extortion money they paid against their tax burden.[47]

This reliance on extortion demonstrates the complex nature of insurgent groups. On one hand, the PIRA was widely revered as a true protector of Catholic neighborhoods, but it could also be predatory in nature, strong-arming the very population it was sworn to protect. Furthermore, there was follow through taken after a series of verbal threats. In August 1985, PIRA insurgents shot and killed Seamus McEvoy after he refused to pay £8,000 in protection money.[48]

External State Support

An important component for the insurgents' external state support was the relationship the PIRA developed with Muammar Qaddafi's regime in Libya, an ardent opponent of the British. Contact was formalized between the Provos and the Libyans in August 1972, which immediately served as a boon to the PIRA's finances.[49] Accordingly, the PIRA secured approximately $3.5 million from Qaddafi which could be used to keep the organization afloat in its nascent stages. This relationship was temporarily severed in the mid-1970s due to disagreements between senior PIRA leaders and high-ranking members of Libyan intelligence, but was later reestablished following the death of 10 Republican prisoners on hunger strike in 1981. Between contributions from abroad and the PIRA's internal activities, revenue for the group in the mid-1980s is thought to have totaled somewhere around £7 million per year.[50]

WHAT THE PIRA ACHIEVED WITH THESE FUNDS

With all of the money produced from the PIRA's portfolio of rackets, the group was able to greatly enhance its ability to conduct operations against both the Loyalists and British troops, both in Northern Ireland and abroad. The Provos consistently had access to first-rate weaponry, in turn allowing the group to escalate its campaign of terror at different intervals over the course of the conflict. On the organizational side, the group's endowment made remaining a cohesive unit easier, thus promoting longevity. By subsidizing their full-time members and the families of those members, PIRA insurgents were able to specialize in designated skills, from bomb-making to sniping to counterintelligence.

To be sure, when a group has to exert maximum energy on obtaining funds, there is less of an opportunity to plan for and execute attacks. Furthermore, a group constantly and solely focused on earning money, similar to the way an organized criminal organization would operate, would have insufficient time to build a political wing, as the PIRA did over time with Sinn Fein. By expanding its moneymaking ventures across such broad swaths of the gray and dark economies, the PIRA diversified its revenue base, thus ensuring consistent access to much-needed funds.

There is little doubt that without such a robust financing network, the PIRA would never has been able to expand its operations beyond Northern Ireland and transform the group into the potent fighting force that it ultimately became. In sum, financing played a significant role in the success that the PIRA enjoyed against British COIN forces and allowed the group to remain relevant for nearly 30 years, before transitioning its efforts into the political arena.

Operational Capabilities

If leadership provides the brains of an insurgency, then its operation tools, or resources, serve as the lifeblood. Put simply, operational tools are used to defend territory, plan and execute attacks, deter adversaries, and destroy enemies. Without weapons, money, intelligence, training, and sanctuary, insurgents are only capable of waging a limited struggle. Because insurgents are most often, if not always, militarily inferior to the COIN force or host-nation government (this is what makes the conflict *asymmetric*), operational tools are critical to help sustain the insurgency and afford the insurgents with a slightly more level playing field. For the PIRA, this was certainly the case as it fought Protestant paramilitary groups, Northern Ireland security forces, and the British Army.

Operational tools are indispensable to insurgents. At the same time, not all resources are created equal. Some are critical, others are valuable but not essential, and still others are only of minor import. The PIRA's most valuable operational tools were sanctuary, training, and funding. To counter these capabilities, the COIN forces relied upon subversion, intelligence, and infiltration.

Weapons

Obtaining the material resources for guerilla war is expensive, especially when, like the PIRA, the group has a desire to acquire high-tech weaponry including surface-to-air missiles (SAMs) and SAM launchers, Russian-made (RPG) launchers, machine guns, assault and sniper rifles, and heavy weaponry like the Barrett Light-50 heavy machine gun.[51] Due to the largesse of weaponry bestowed upon the group by Qaddafi, which is covered in detail later in this chapter, in the 1980s the PIRA had less of a need to devote a substantial portion of its operating budget to acquiring weaponry. Furthermore, the explosives used by the group were almost exclusively being made by the PIRA themselves.[52] PIRA bomb makers, or engineers as they were called within the group, were universally acknowledged to be among the most skilled in the world at their craft. That most of the ingredients needed to construct homemade mortar equipment and homemade bombs could be obtained at a relatively low cost merely allowed the group to spend more of its budget on cutting-edge electronics, like radio-controlled detonation devices, to pair with its bombs.[53]

Within the group, innovation was prized. Insurgents designed new explosive devices using a clever array of, at first, remote manual detonators and later, automatic detonators to make their bombs more precise and targeted.[54] The group also developed its own take on already-existing weapons, including the improvised projected grenade (IPG) and the projected recoilless improvised grenade (PRIG).[55] By developing precision-guided weapons, the PIRA sought to maximize COIN force casualties while reducing harm to civilians, thus helping the group to enjoy what it deemed as acceptable levels of popular support in Northern Ireland.

The PIRA maintained numerous weapons caches in both Northern Ireland and the ROI. As part of the group's "long war doctrine," which committed members to a lifetime of conflict, the insurgents stockpiled weapons, hoarded explosives, and relentlessly searched for ways to acquire the most modern and lethal technology. Acquiring and amassing weapons remained a top priority of the PIRA until the very end. Invariably throughout the conflict, British COIN forces and ROI police (*Gardaí*) intercepted large weapons shipments and successfully executed several high-profile arms recovery operations, yielding substantial amounts of weaponry. Despite setbacks, however, the PIRA always remained active. The insurgents maintained at least five bomb-making factories in the Republic at all times. Most of these facilities were extremely secure and in some cases were constructed as fortified bunkers.[56] It was also not uncommon for the PIRA to use the home of widows and single mothers to hide their weapons. This particular demographic drew less attention from the police and was able to earn some extra money by providing the PIRA with a critical service, while also contributing to the insurgents' cause.

Intelligence

As the organization evolved and matured, the insurgents became more specialized. Select insurgents were schooled in bomb-making while others were groomed as snipers, logisticians, or intelligence experts.[57] Intelligence, along with the following departments—Quartermaster, Security, Operations, Foreign Operations, Finance, Training, Engineering, Education, and Publicity—was one of the GHQ's designated priorities.[58] The focus on intelligence became more intense following the switch to a cellular structure in late 1970s, where the intent was to treat intelligence at the local level as a specialized function.[59]

Developing and maintaining an extensive network of sources was one of the PIRA's top priorities. Members specializing in intelligence were tasked with a range of activities, from collection, collation, storage, and dissemination to surveillance and reconnaissance. Since operational security was the *sine qua non* of successful operations, the PIRA needed to ensure that those conducting attacks remained safe, but also that collateral damage (especially civilian casualties) remained low. Intelligence was also critical to monitoring the movements of high-value targets, including high-ranking members of the security forces and paramilitary groups. The PIRA actively sought intelligence to help facilitate targeting priorities and much of this intelligence came from the local community.

Sanctuary, Safe Haven, and Operational Space

In an insurgency, establishing a sanctuary is integral to success. For the majority of its terror campaign, the PIRA took advantage of safe havens around Northern Ireland, as well as sanctuaries in both the Republic of Ireland and the United States, although each country was used for different purposes at different times. The United States was mostly a place for insurgents to raise funds, evade capture, and coalesce political support; the ROI served as a "rear base" from which insurgents could hold important meetings, plan attacks, conduct weapons training, and amass their arsenal. During the 1980s, many PIRA fighters spent time in Libyan training camps at the invitation of Libyan leader Colonel Muammar Qaddafi.

From safe houses located south of the border, PIRA insurgents could hide out after conducting an attack in the North. Safe houses provided insurgents with a place to lay low and a change of clothes to discard any evidence from an attack, including blood and gunpowder residue. The most important function of safe havens south of the border, however, was the ability of the PIRA's most senior members to gather in one location without being detected or arrested by the authorities. Clandestine movements need to avoid detection, and depending on group cohesion and organizational structure, the loss of an insurgent group's top leadership can deliver a potentially fatal blow to the organization. The General Army Convention (GAC), a meeting of the PIRA's senior leadership, was held at various locations throughout the ROI. This allowed the group to debate high-level decisions regarding the organization, including its military strategy, the role of politics, leadership composition, and the future direction of the organization.

Long an under-researched aspect of insurgent organizations, the amount of money needed to successfully execute lethal operations against COIN forces "extends far beyond the purchase of a gun and bullets which culminate in an attack."[60] The planning and preparation for operations included, but were not limited to: transport costs, the maintenance of weapons storage sites, the support of safe houses, vehicles used to transport arms, and the purchase of radio equipment. Transport costs included the price of petrol used in transporting the operatives to and from the scene of the attack or the purchase of train, bus, or airplane tickets for international operations.

Payments were made to those individuals who allowed their homes or property to be used as weapons storage sites as well as to those whose homes were used to hide prisoners, many times for extended periods, in order to avoid detection by security forces following a PIRA operation. While these may seem like banal details, they are essential to executing a successful attack. Besides a reputation for brutality, PIRA insurgents were meticulous planners. Finally, the PIRA purchased between six and eight cars to transport arms from storage sites to border areas, as well as radio equipment for monitoring the movement of security forces prior to and following an attack.[61]

Training

Considered one of the most lethal insurgent groups of the modern era, it is essential to examine the tactics, techniques, and procedures that proved so critical to the success of the PIRA. The PIRA believed that if it ever had a chance to defeat the British militarily, its own fighters would have to hold themselves to the same rigorous training standards endured by elite units like the British Special Air Service (SAS). By placing an emphasis on training, the leadership was able to identify highly capable recruits who took pride in honing their craft, whether it was bomb-making, sniping, or reconnaissance.

A shared culture and history, geographical proximity, and a lingering resentment of the British made the ROI the most logical safe haven for PIRA members and new recruits who were instructed in small arms handling, target practice, demolition techniques, and general field craft.[62] The long border was hard to defend and in some cases PIRA members owned property that straddled both sides of the border. Northern Command included not just the six counties of Northern Ireland, but also the five border counties of Louth, Cavan, Monaghan, Donegal, and Leitrim.[63]

Besides geography, the Republic was a model sanctuary because it had a relatively sympathetic population, limited internal security force activities, and vast rural areas where the insurgents could disguise their activities from the authorities.[64]

To allow for diversification without diluting an acquired specialization, "units used rotation or 'apprenticeship' processes to spread specific types of knowledge or expertise."[65] Specialization afforded the insurgents a degree of tactical and operational flexibility. Attacks were tailored to the abilities of different units in different areas of operation. Units operating in more rural areas like South Armagh typically experienced a slower learning curve and were given the opportunity to immerse themselves into a specialization slowly and with the deliberate oversight of battle-tested mentors. In contrast, units that operated in Belfast and other urban areas known for a high operations tempo were thrown "in at the deep end quickly," which led to more mistakes and a greater chance that something could go awry with an operation.[66]

Certain cells within the explosive unit were tasked with institutionalizing the production of the bombs' electronic components.[67] This effort was a defensive countermeasure, aimed at ensuring that PIRA bombs would not be prematurely detonated by the security forces or explode inadvertently, killing PIRA members or innocent bystanders. To avoid complacency, the PIRA trained not only its own members, but also traveled abroad to develop a network with other terrorist and insurgent groups that would allow it to hone its skills and learn new techniques and guerilla tactics. The Provos exchanged training tips and tactics with myriad terrorist groups including FARC, the PLO, the Popular Front for the Liberation of Palestine (PFLP), and Fatah.[68] In July 1973, PIRA insurgents attended a meeting in Libya with members from the German Baader-Mainhof gang, the Japanese United Revolutionary Army, the Liberation Front of Iran, the Turkish People's Liberation Army, and the Uruguayan Tupamaros.[69]

Organizational Capabilities

The leadership of the PIRA was responsible for taking the group's vast resources, as described above, and translating them into effective action. This had to be accomplished while maintaining group cohesion, a difficult task considering COIN force infiltration of the PIRA. The organization sought to achieve this through five main components—command and control (to include organizational structure), group composition, ideology, popular support, and public relations/propaganda. Each of these elements played a crucial role in determining the insurgency's trajectory, as each individual component affected the organization's strategic decision-making. Moreover, during the course of the 30-year conflict, each element changed considerably, altering the PIRA's path along the way from violence to power sharing.

Leadership

As Sinn Fein became more prominent—both within Ulster politics and in relation to the PIRA overall—the financial resources needed to cover the group's ever evolving infrastructure inevitably grew too. In addition to the organization's headquarters in West Belfast, Sinn Fein established offices throughout the Republic of Ireland, held many public meetings and gatherings in hotels and pubs, and incurred substantial costs to remain competitive in local elections.[70] Adams noted that British officials estimated that the expenses to operate Sinn Fein were three times what it cost to operate the PIRA as a militant group alone. When asked where Sinn Fein got the funds to run electoral campaigns, Gerry Adams sardonically replied, "We run cake fairs and things."[71]

For a group like the PIRA, with a constantly evolving political wing in Sinn Fein, financing was even more important than for pure militant groups. "Finance is one of the most important long-term, fundamental, limiting factors for the development of a terrorist group and its political wing," notes Horgan.[72] Finance became seamlessly integrated into Sinn Fein more broadly, as its "advice centers" doubled as centers of illegal economic distribution, record-keeping, and personnel who could be tasked to partake in a range of economic rackets.[73] When the decision was made to turn away from armed robbery as a financing mechanism, the leadership began to emphasize local donations from collections throughout Ireland (both north and south), especially from the Gaelic Athletic Association and Republican Clubs.[74]

Ideology

The PIRA was born of an ideological split in 1969, with staunch Marxists led by Cathal Goulding forming the Official IRA and Sean MacStiofain leading what would become the PIRA. At the core of the dispute was the Provisionals' commitment to violence as both a means of protection and of achieving political goals. For the new guard, older members' ideological fervor obfuscated the IRA's traditional focus on militarism.[75] A young Gerry Adams had no illusions about the utility of militarism. "There are those who tell us that the British Government will not be moved by armed struggle... [Yet] the history of Ireland and of colonial involvement throughout the world tells us that they will not be moved by anything else."[76]

The PIRA is typically referred to as an ethno-nationalist group. However, this description hardly does justice to explaining the intricacies of the group's ideology. Combined with a strict adherence to armed resistance against what it viewed as oppressive British imperialist policies, the PIRA's political thought could most aptly be described as an amalgamation of "socialist politics and violent aggression."[77] Over the course of its lifespan, the organization espoused affinity for groups in Cuba, South Africa, Palestine, Vietnam, Nicaragua, and El Salvador. Many Irish Republicans were convinced that the British presence in Northern Ireland was motivated by economic gain, not cultural affinity, and certainly not for providing governance beyond Loyalist communities (even though Catholics were eligible for, and many did receive, welfare benefits from the British state).

What the conflict was *not* about was religion. "There is not one IRA statement that would cite the Bible or Catholic doctrine in support of, or as justification for, any of its actions."[78] On many issues, the leadership of the Roman Catholic Church in Ireland and the PIRA's leadership were at odds.

The conflict in Northern Ireland involved an ethnic dimension, but at its core, the insurgency was, like all insurgencies, about politics. Though the differences were more substantive, on the face of things Catholic simply meant Nationalist, or Republican; Protestant was interchangeable with Unionist, or Loyalist. Throughout its lifespan, the PIRA, or at least the most influential among its leadership, came to recognize that violence was no longer an effective means of realizing its political aspirations. Violence did advance short-term objectives, especially when paired with "armed propaganda."[79] But longer-term goals, including the PIRA's stated aim to remove any semblance of a British presence from the North, came to be seen as political problems with political solutions.

Human Resources and Recruitment

Upon being sworn into the group, newly-minted PIRA members pledged an oath to uphold the values of the *Óglaigh na hÉireann* and were anointed as "Volunteers of the Provisional Irish Republican Army."[80] And just as in a volunteer army, volunteers chose to enter service, but did not work for free and were given regular pay. Sometimes referred to as the human resources dimension of insurgency, fighters still need to be remunerated for their services. This compensation took the form of cash payments, so insurgents could take care of the needs of their families and maintain a reserve of money for ordinary activities like food and shelter, when it was not provided directly by the group. Some members held down regular jobs in addition to their PIRA activity while others were considered too valuable and central to the organization to focus their energy anywhere other than on the organization itself. These individuals were considered "full-time staff," and were likely known to the security services. More often than not, this meant they needed to take care to conceal their activities and movements and lead an extremely clandestine existence.[81]

Although the figures are still a matter of debate, reports indicate that up until 1994, ASU members received £30–£40 per week, depending on their actual role in the organization as well as the geographical location from which they operated (think of it in terms of destination-based per diem). Taking into account the PIRA's 400–500 estimated members, weekly pay-outs totaled £12,000 or more.[82] Conventional wisdom holds that when individuals receive a regular salary, they are less likely to supplement their incomes by engaging in illegal criminal activities, which bring unwanted attention on the group and expose members to arrest, prosecution, and the possibility of being "flipped," or turned into an informer, or "tout," against the group.[83]

The PIRA was keenly aware of the importance of community support in executing a successful guerilla strategy. In the *Handbook for Volunteers of the Irish Republican Army,* or the Green Book as it sometimes referred to, the PIRA laid out clear guidelines for collaboration with the local population.[84] According to Cronin, "terrorist groups generally cannot survive without either active or passive support from surrounding populations."[85] The PIRA collected "donations," from the Catholics in Northern Ireland who viewed its existence as crucial to their own survival and would therefore do anything necessary to ensure its continuation.[86]

Media, PR, Propaganda, and Publicity

The use of public relations and propaganda in modern day insurgency is considered "a given." With the ubiquity of social media and the low cost of communication technology, news that the Taliban use the social media site Twitter to report attacks (many of them fictitious or prone to hyperbole) is met with a yawn. When the PIRA was beginning its campaign of terror against the British state in the early 1970s, media was considered a fairly unique innovation. The PIRA developed its own newspaper, Dublin-based *An Phoblacht*, the first edition of which appeared in early 1970.[87] In June 1970 the Provos resurrected *The Republican News*, which would become the most widely read newspaper in the North. The PIRA used its newspapers for three main reasons.

The PIRA used its newspapers to justify its actions on both moral and political grounds. When PIRA operations went awry and innocent bystanders were killed or injured, the Provos tried to explain the problem away through propaganda, always directing blame toward the British. Second, *An Phoblacht* and *Republican News* were used to provide an outlet for Sinn Fein, once the organization began to contest elections. The media element of the conflict became a more important feature of Republican strategy as Sinn Fein took on greater importance and elevated itself beyond its former status as "the IRA's poor second cousin."[88] A key figure in the PIRA's media activities was Danny Morrison, a former editor of a magazine for the Belfast College of Business Studies, who take over as the editor of *Republican News* in 1975. With Morrison at its head, *Republican News* became "more impressively edited and more professional."[89] Third, both PIRA periodicals were used to explain the group's strategy, especially as it changed, to numerous audiences including: the PIRA's own members, its wider community of supporters, the Irish-American diaspora, British government officials, and anyone else willing to listen.

HOW THE PIRA FINANCING WAS COUNTERED

Efforts to counter terrorists' finances can be divided into kinetic and non-kinetic activities. The former include raids, arrests, operations, as well as the creation of the task forces necessary to conduct these activities. Non-kinetic activities include the passing of legislation, intelligence sharing, and multiagency cooperation. The British played up the lie that NORAID was the primary source of PIRA funding during the conflict. By doing so, this placed additional pressure on the United States to crack down on the group, which many politicians were reluctant to do since the PIRA never attacked the United States and the Irish lobby remained a powerful force in American domestic politics.[90] Over time, British propaganda grew more successful, as Washington rarely criticized official British policy.[91] In 1977, the British convinced four well-known Irish-American politicians to publicly condemn support for the PIRA.[92]

Although Irish militants had enjoyed sanctuary in the United States since the time of America's Civil War, the situation began to change in the late 1970s and early 1980s, as British Prime Minister Margaret Thatcher pressured U.S. President Ronald Reagan to clamp down on PIRA fund-raising and political activity throughout the United States.[93] Prior to Thatcher's persistence, the PIRA enjoyed unfettered access to politicians, influential business leaders, and other powerbrokers who sympathized with its cause. The other major change over the conflict's duration was the priorities and competence of the Irish and British security forces. In the early 1970s, following British policies like internment, the Irish police were not likely to interfere with the insurgents. "As sympathy for their cause in the Republic exploded, IRA fugitives could now find sanctuary across the Border, safe in the knowledge that the *Gardaí* would not throw them behind bars," recalls Moloney.[94] But over time, the PIRA's brutality earned its members no favor among the *Gardaí*, whose colleagues (Catholics, just like PIRA insurgents) had been injured or killed while attempting to apprehend insurgents operating or hiding in the ROI. After years of dealing with PIRA militants using the country as a safe haven, the *Gardaí* eventually grew to become a quite effective security force. The Irish police even collaborated with British authorities to disrupt ongoing PIRA plots, planned operations, and future activities.

Kinetic Activities

A turning point in the countering of PIRA fund-raising came following the assassination of Lord Mountbatten by the PIRA in 1979. After his death, the FBI changed their neutralist policy and, moving forward, agreed to cooperate with British intelligence to act on information provided Provo activity.[95] Several years later, following the bombing of the Grand Hotel in Brighton in 1984, the security forces increased efforts to gather intelligence on the PIRA by commissioning the Terrorist Intelligence Gathering Evaluation and Review committee (TIGER).[96]

In 1985, the British government commissioned a review of threat finance, designated as the House of Commons Select Committee Report. This report followed a review from the previous year by Sir Derek Hodgson, who was looking into the recovery of profits from crime. For the first decade of the conflict, Inland Revenue was the organization primarily tasked with investigating fraud before it became apparent that these types of investigations required a multiagency approach to be successful.[97] Inland Revenue was not without its successes—over a five year period in the mid-1980s, nearly 100 people were convicted of fraud in excess of 13 million pounds—but its experience with terrorist fraud was primarily on frauds on building sites involving tax-exemption certificates. To effectively counter insurgent financing the British needed to create a specialized unit.

The C13 Anti-Racketeering Squad was first established in 1982 by the Royal Ulster Constabulary (RUC), although the initial force was comprised of merely 20 officers. The unit was given more prominence when Hugh Annesley became Chief Constable of the RUC and Tom King became Secretary of State for Northern Ireland. The C13 sought to turn those who were convicted of racketeering against their respective organizations, thus trading a reduced sentence or freedom from prosecution in return for intelligence on the insurgents. The Special Branch and the Anti-Terrorist Branch already dealt with aspects of the fight against terrorism, but C13 was the first unit created to specifically track the funding of terrorist groups.[98] By 1992, this outfit forced the closure of 54 republican drinking clubs and by the end of 1993, more than 400 people had been prosecuted for offenses totaling over 50 million pounds.

Resources increased as threat finance was recognized as a critical piece of the insurgency and the counterinsurgents were successful in arresting and prosecuting both Republican and Loyalist terrorists. There have been previous successful operations against the PIRA, including an FBI sting operation dubbed "Operation Bushmill," which targeted an arms trafficking ring operating from North Carolina as well as Operation Hit and Win, but operations conducted by the RUC in the early 1990s were equally impressive.[99] Operation Whiplash was launched in 1990 by the RUC and aimed at racketeering targets in Belfast. Two years later the RUC carried out Operation Christo, an operation that attacked PIRA financing activities in the border area.[100]

Non-kinetic Activities

Kinetic activities further enable non-kinetic activities and vice versa. In February 1985, the government in Dublin passed special legislation that seized over $3 million held in a Bank of Ireland bank account. The money was originally deposited by Associated British Foods after being transferred from a Swiss bank account to an account in New York City, opened by a man using a false passport. Once withdrawn from the account in New York, the money was deposited in the Navan branch of the Bank of Ireland in the Irish Republic. This all originated from a series of PIRA kidnappings and bombings.[101]

The Prevention of Terrorism Act (Temporary Provisions Act) of 1989 was enacted by the government of Northern Ireland to counter terrorist abuse of security companies by tightening the regulatory framework.[102] The act also gave the government the power to license security companies and check employee history for membership or involvement with terrorist groups, which was popular with both private security industry employers and the unions. Licenses could be denied to or revoked from security companies that employed known terrorists.[103]

The other major task force established to counter threat finance in Northern Ireland was the Terrorist Finance Unit (TFU), which was housed within the Northern Ireland Office and comprised of financial and research experts intended to complement the RUC's Anti-Racketeering Squad. The TFU was able to overcome jurisdiction restraints placed on the RUC in areas of VAT, Income Tax, and Social Security Fraud. The TFU was a coordinating interagency model of policing, as it collaborated with personnel from other agencies, including policemen, customs officers, accountants, and Inland Revenue investigators.[104] According to Norman, "the predominantly reactive orientation of fraud and financial investigations has been displaced by a political will to target proactively this form of offending in gathering information and intelligence using the wide-ranging powers of the Authorised Investigators."[105] In addition to the TFU, the United Kingdom also set up the Joint Action Group on Organized Crime of the Metropolitan Police. This was a complex coordinating structure established in November 1992, shortly after the creation of the U.K.'s National Criminal Intelligence Service. In all, 25 agencies agreed to collaborate to counter organized crime as part of the Joint Action Group.

CONCLUSION

In 1998, the insurgency in Northern Ireland officially came to an end with the signing of the Good Friday Agreement. This historical agreement was the culmination of 30 years of conflict in Northern Ireland. Thirteen years after the signing of this historic peace deal, all parties to the conflict have remained focused on politics, as a lasting peace has settled in throughout the country, pockmarked with only episodic acts of violence practiced by fringe groups and criminals.[106] The Provisional Irish Republican Army laid down its arms and stepped aside for Sinn Fein, completing a process that had begun years earlier.

By the late 1980s and early 1990s, the operational tools most important to PIRA success on the battlefield had all been blunted to one degree or another. Both the American and Irish governments cracked down on allowing PIRA insurgents to use their countries as a safe haven. Insurgent freedom of movement in the United States and the Republic of Ireland were severely constrained. With a restricted sanctuary, the group could no longer train its members the way it had before, which contributed to shoddy operational execution. Finally, by the latter stages of the conflict, Irish-America had been persuaded to cease funding the hard-line elements of the group bent on continued violence. Manpower and resources were now almost completely shifted to Sinn Fein, and those who wanted to be seen as supporting the "good fight" would follow suit.

CHAPTER 3

The Liberation Tigers of Tamil Eelam (LTTE): A Diversified Funding Portfolio

BACKGROUND

British Ceylon gained independence in 1948 and has been known as Sri Lanka since 1972. Sri Lanka has a population of 20 million people, the majority of whom are ethnic Sinhalese (74 percent). Another 18 percent of the population is Sri Lankan Tamil (6 percent of whom are Upcountry or "Estate Tamils") who are primarily Hindu, while another 7 percent are Tamil Muslims. The remaining population, less than 1 percent, is comprised of small numbers of Sinhala Christians, Anglo-Sri Lankans, and descendants of European settlers.[1] The conflict between Sinhalese Buddhists and Tamil Hindus initially stemmed from differences in tradition, heritage, language, religion, and color and the fact that Sri Lankan Tamils were highly educated and thus represented disproportionately in commerce, professional opportunities, and government service. Due largely to their superior numbers, the Sinhalese were politically more powerful than the Tamils and beginning in the 1950s, began to discriminate against Tamils in areas including education, religion, and language. K. M. de Silva, a Sri Lankan historian, observes, "the Sinhala have sometimes thought of themselves as a chosen people with a providential mission, who are for that reason entitled to cultural, linguistic, and political supremacy in Sri Lanka."[2] This discrimination was accompanied by a rise in Sinhala nationalism, which grew stronger even as Tamil leverage was further reduced. Four main factors can be traced to the rise of Sinhala Buddhist nationalism in Sri Lanka following independence in 1948: a backlash against British colonialism, the material conditions associated with nationalism (these included communication, transportation, industrial production, mass markets and mass politics, general systems of public educations, and a Weberian bureaucratic component with administrative structures designed to support standardized mass society),[3] perceptions of an antiquated and inequitable distribution of resources and positions (especially in the government), and a desire to exercise majoritarian rule with all the benefits this type of government afforded.[4]

The Tamil insurgency began in earnest when violence erupted in northern Sri Lanka in the early 1970s. Several Jaffna politicians were targeted for assassination and in 1974 a common criminal by the name of Chetti Thanabalasingam founded the Tamil New Tigers (TNT).[5] To counter intimidation of the Tamil minority in a highly polarized society, the Tamil United Liberation Front (TULF) emerged in 1976 amidst calls for a separate Tamil state. Two years later, a small group of hardcore Tamils broke off from TULF to form a separate Tamil organization—the LTTE were born.[6]

HOW LTTE FUNDED ITS ACTIVITIES

Finance sustains an insurgent group and offers a sense of hope, even when insurgents may not be winning on the battlefield. The LTTE had a limited capacity to raise funds internally in Sri Lanka, so the diaspora movement took on added significance. Different people surely donated for different reasons—shared ethnicity, religious fervor, genuine sympathy, coercion. Some donated very small amounts, while others donated hundreds of thousands of dollars. The LTTE collected donations from co-ethnics in Canada, France, Australia, Norway, the United Kingdom, and Switzerland, reflecting both the high concentration of Tamils in those countries as well as the lack of specific legislation outlawing the group from fund-raising.[7] In all, Peter Chalk estimates that an astonishing 80 to 90 percent of the LTTE's "war chest" originated abroad.[8]

Gray Economy

The gray economy enabled the Tigers to engage in a range of kinetic and non-kinetic activities. Money donated from abroad or earned through legally-owned Tamil businesses was used for more than just purchasing arms. Through its vast financial architecture, the LTTE was able to pay for the exorbitant legal fees of the group and its members. One example is especially revealing. According to Chalk, following the 1995 arrest of the LTTE's representative to Canada, Manicavasagam Suresh, the group organized demonstrations and a mass mail-out campaign that portrayed Suresh as a victim and accused the authorities of persecuting the Canadian Tamil population. Moreover, the group hired two highly paid lawyers to defend Suresh, including New York-based Viswanathan

Ruthirakumaran (who happened to be the head of LTTE operations in the United States).[9] When the group was designated as a terrorist organization by the United States in the late 1990s, Ruthirakumaran hired a leading U.S. law firm headed by Ramsey Clark, the former Attorney General during the Johnson administration.

Diaspora Support

Each year the LTTE generated between $24 and $36 million in revenue. According to Chalk's estimates, the group reaped $800,000 a month from Canada, $500,000 a month from Scandinavia, just shy of $400,000 a month from the United Kingdom, $250,000 from Australia, and another $200,000 from the United States.[10] Following the ethnic riots of 1983, thousands of Tamil refugees fled overseas to India, Australia, Canada, and the United Kingdom.[11] This sowed the seeds for the Tamil diaspora and the transnational nature of the LTTE's insurgency. The global diaspora was a major part of the organization's fund-raising and propaganda network. But the Tamil Nadu sanctuary was the heartbeat of the LTTE's military infrastructure. Insurgents connected with insurgents, but also formed bonds with elements of the Tamil Nadu political class, including with political groups such as the Dravida Munnetra Kazhagam, the Kamaraj Congress, and the Pure Tamil Movement.[12] These political ties would prove extremely valuable over the course of the insurgency.

Charities

Organizations like the Tamil Relief Organization (TRO) remained closely linked with the Tigers and were described as a veritable humanitarian arm of the LTTE.[13] This link grew stronger following the 2005 tsunami.[14] The LTTE essentially controlled where and how NGOs operated, and then used its provision of services to enact support and even recruit. Moreover, the group used a steering committee to direct aid from Colombo, in effect claiming goodwill for services provided by the state. While the LTTE did rely on charities to provide financing, the group also co-opted charitable organizations and NGOs to supply its members with a veneer of legitimacy in areas where these nonprofits operated. As they solidified control over the northern and eastern Tamil-dominated provinces of Sri Lanka, the LTTE needed to use its resources to provide for its constituents. As the conflict wore on and the Sri Lankan government became more adept at countering the group's funding streams, it increasingly turned to more predatory measures like extortion and coercion. In December 2009, three individuals in Australia with links to the LTTE pleaded guilty to the collection and transfer of over $1 million to a proscribed terrorist organization.[15]

Fraud

Although drug trafficking and human smuggling are two of the more well-known organized criminal activities perpetrated by the LTTE, the group also relied on various types of fraud (credit card, social security, immigration, bank, casino, etc.) to bankroll its operations.[16] Indeed, in 1999, the Royal Canadian Mounted Police reported that Tamil street gangs operating in Toronto were sending the proceeds from bank and casino fraud back to the organization's leaders in Sri Lanka. In addition to perpetrating criminal activities in Canada, the LTTE also became proficient at credit card fraud in Great Britain and social security fraud in France.[17]

Legal Businesses

While the LTTE did raise money through a range of organized criminal activities, much of the money donated by the Tamil diaspora was used for the creation of legitimate Tamil businesses. Beginning in 1983, the LTTE opened up restaurants in Tamil Nadu and Paris, France and eventually branched out to London, Toronto, and Cambodia.[18] The Tigers' brain trust also thought it wise to invest in stock and money markets. The group also maintained an impressive real estate portfolio. This entrepreneurial spirit extends to the sale of newspapers, videos, and Asian spices. Members and activists invested in travel agencies, grocery stores, printing presses, money exchange and transfer agencies and import-export firms.[19] The group diversified its asset base from agriculture to finance, invested in a number of farms, started finance companies, and constantly sought out other high-profit venues.[20] When donations were supplied to the LTTE the group used them as seed money to start and grow businesses, from telephone services to community radio stations. Tamils have historically been linked to commodity buying and selling, especially gold, so the LTTE aggressively entered this market too.

Money Laundering

Funds generated from legal businesses would be diverted to the group's war aims and ill-gotten gains from an array of smuggling activities were laundered through Tamil-owned legal businesses and money exchange and transfer agencies (similar to *hawalas*) to evade detection by authorities. The LTTE became involved in the film industry, first through trading and investing, but later by founding video and CD shops, which generated sizeable revenue.[21] Because the LTTE earned so much money through drug trafficking, it was essential that the group developed a proficiency in money laundering in order to make those profits usable. Indeed, money raised through the sizeable Tamil community in Canada was allegedly laundered through German and Singaporean banks which helped fund the purchase of explosives in Ukraine which were then used to blow up the central bank in Sri Lanka.[22] The LTTE was also suspected of maintaining a limited money laundering infrastructure in Indonesia.[23]

Dark Economy

LTTE members engaged in almost every form of organized crime possible, from drug trafficking to extortion and arms smuggling. The LTTE's vast criminal enterprise, detailed at length throughout this section, also enabled weapons procurement by putting the group's members in touch with a wide range of nefarious individuals, including arms dealers, weapons brokers, and intermediaries. According to Peter Chalk, the Tigers acquired U.S. Stinger-class missiles from the PKK in 1996 and used these weapons to shoot down a Sri Lankan civilian *Lionair* jet in 1998.[24] Several years earlier, in April 1995, the LTTE shot down two Avro transport aircraft of the Sri Lankan Air Force, killing everyone on board. This was the first known use of missiles by the insurgents and observers argue that the introduction of missiles changed the dynamics of the conflict from that point forward.[25]

Kidnapping for Ransom (KFR)

Although not as prolific as some groups in South Asia, such as the ASG, the LTTE did indeed help realize their financial objectives through kidnapping for ransom.[26] Since the Tigers were acutely aware of not alienating potential supporters, kidnapping was not a tactic that was employed frequently, although it did happen from time to time when the group needed to raise funds quickly, as occurred in March 2006 when the LTTE kidnapped three teenagers.[27] For the most part, the LTTE's portfolio of other criminal activities was so lucrative that the group felt little need to risk alienating potential supporters by engaging in this lurid practice. During the last phase of its struggle, desperate to replenish the ranks of a rapidly depleting military force, the LTTE occasionally resorted to kidnapping teens and young children to help it fight against the Sri Lankan security forces.

Armed Robbery and Theft

Beginning in the mid-1980s, Tamil groups embarked on a bank robbing spree in Jaffna. Out of ignorance, the LTTE argued that it was stealing from the "public" and not the Tamil people.[28] Armed robbery of banks was employed by the Tigers early in their tenure, but faded in popularity as a fund-raising tactic through the years. Also in the early stages of the insurgency, Tamil militants pillaged and plundered the residences of non-ethnic Tamils living in Sri Lanka. Over time, as the organization developed its maritime capabilities, it was able to take advantage of robbing ships and vessels on the high seas. To be sure, piracy was a lucrative form of robbery for the LTTE.[29] In some cases, Tamil militants have received funding to *prevent* theft and armed robbery—like the PIRA and other groups, LTTE members were paid to "ride shotgun" and provide the "muscle" for international drug shipments.[30]

Smuggling, Trafficking, and Counterfeiting

Involvement in the drug trade first became apparent as early as 1984 when Swiss police reported that Tamils were responsible for trafficking approximately 20 percent of the heroin coming into the country.[31] The "Tamil connection" in Switzerland, as it came to be known, was eventually dismantled by the police, although the drug market in Sri Lanka itself expanded, with an estimated 100,000 users by the end of the 1990s.[32] Italian police also broke up several Tamil heroin rings throughout the 1980s. Sri Lanka's geographic proximity to the Golden Triangle of Laos, Myanmar, and Thailand, combined with the LTTE's advanced maritime capabilities made heroin trafficking an obvious racket for the group to pursue.[33] The Tigers' reach also extended into Pakistan, where they linked up with notorious Indian crime boss Dawood Ibrahim and his "D-Company" gang. They used the port city of Karachi to solidify a foothold in South Asia and diversify smuggling activities to include humans, in addition to heroin.[34] The Sri Lankan government reported that the LTTE's human trafficking business netted the group approximately $340 million by smuggling 17,000 people to 11 different countries.[35]

The smuggling and trafficking of humans provided the LTTE with the funds necessary to continue its operations.[36] LTTE insurgents became experts in the illicit movement of people, arms, and equipment, all of which requires specialized skills and access, including access to (or the ability to produce) fraudulent international documents, including visas, passports, end-user certificates, business regulations, shipping licenses, and so on.[37] In Europe and Australia, LTTE members perfected the counterfeiting of currencies.

Extortion and Protection

Extortion often involved coercion, with direct threats of implied violence to those who failed to "donate" to the Tigers' war chest.[38] Other times, extortion was accompanied by intimidation, blackmail, beatings, and threats against family members, both in Sri Lanka and abroad. Finally, the insurgents levied "taxes" on a network of Hindu temples in the United Kingdom and Canada.[39] The LTTE also made money through extortion in Germany. In Sri Lanka, traffickers of illicit commodities brought drugs and other contraband into the country through LTTE-controlled territory.[40] This allowed the group to extort the traffickers by demanding they pay a "tax" or "donation" for moving ahead unmolested. LTTE protection rackets in the émigré communities of Toronto raised an estimated $1million a month.[41]

External State Support

In any insurgency, diversifying the source of a group's weapons is critical, as the LTTE learned in 1987 when the Indians withdrew their sponsorship. Per the terms of the Indo-Sri Lankan Peace Accord, the Indian government agreed to cease its support for the Tigers by cutting off the arms pipeline. The importance of diversification was even more apparent following the downfall of one of the LTTE's main rivals, the People's Liberation Organization of Tamil Eelam (PLOTE). PLOTE was crippled when a shipment of weapons destined for the group was intercepted in Madras (now Chennai) and the group's leaders forfeited a $300,000 down payment already paid to the Palestinian group al-Fatah.[42] Keen not to suffer a similar fate, the LTTE developed contacts abroad, and soon engaged in procurement activities in Northeastern and Southeastern Asia (especially China, North Korea, Cambodia, Thailand, Hong Kong, Vietnam, and Myanmar), Southwest Asia (Afghanistan and Pakistan), former Soviet Republics (primarily Ukraine), Southeast Europe and the Balkans (Greece, Bulgaria, Cyprus), the Middle East (Turkey, Lebanon), and Africa (Nigeria, Zimbabwe, and South Africa).[43]

The South African connection proved particularly fruitful for the Tigers. Situated between the active arms markets of Mozambique and Angola, weapons dealers in South Africa provided the LTTE with consistent access to a steady supply of small arms.[44] Furthermore, South Africa maintained a fairly robust communications and transportation infrastructure, which made it an attractive location for illicit activity.[45] For most of the 1990s, the Tigers used Myanmar as a logistical hub but later moved the bulk of their operations to Bangkok. Thailand's geography, established international business presence, and easily corrupted security officials made it an ideal choice for the LTTE's logistical hub.[46]

From the post–Cold War arms bazaars in Beirut and Peshawar, and especially those in Cambodia, Myanmar, and Afghanistan, the insurgents acquired rapid-fire pistols, assault rifles, rocket-propelled grenades, and surface-to-air missiles. Ammunition needs were met through intermediaries in Bulgaria, the Czech Republic, and North Korea, which supplied mortar, artillery, and 12.7 mm machine gun rounds.[47] Occasionally, as it did in Mullaithiu in 1996, the LTTE would raid Sri Lankan military bases and steal whatever weapons were available. The Mullaithiu raid proved extremely bountiful, as the insurgents acquired multi-barrel rocket launchers (MBRLs), T69-1 RPG launchers, artillery batteries (122 mm, 130 mm, 152 mm), various mortars (120 mm, 106 mm, 81 mm, and 60 mm) and an array of anti-armor and anti-aircraft systems, to include W-85 anti-aircraft guns.[48] Finally, the group rounded out its arsenal through the procurement of explosives from suppliers in the Ukraine and Croatia.[49]

WHAT LTTE ACHIEVED WITH THESE FUNDS

The LTTE's efforts to procure weapons and establish a global arms network brought it in contact with several other insurgent and terrorist groups. In addition to Khalistan-oriented Sikh insurgents, Kashmiri *muja-hedin*, and Middle Eastern militants, the Tigers forged links with over 20 separate Tamil Nadu separatist groups.[50] While many of these relationships were temporary and tactical, more an example of strategic cooperation than a long-standing relationship, others proved durable and resulted in considerable tacit knowledge transfer. Jemaah Islamiyah (JI) insurgents were trained by LTTE Sea Tiger officers in seaborne suicide tactics in Indonesia.[51] Technological exchange occurred with Indian insurgent groups such as the United Liberation Front of Assam (ULFA) and the Communist Party of India (Marxist-Leninist) People's War, also known as the Andhra Peoples War Group, or PWG.[52] When PWG member Marepalli Basavaraju was apprehended by the Indian government he admitted that his group had received explosives training from an LTTE expert in land mine technology.[53]

The LTTE have allegedly served as an intermediary between insurgent groups and have transported arms to the ASG on behalf of Harakat-al Muhahideen, a Pakistani militant group linked to Al-Qaida.[54] Though the group became wary of associating with Al-Qaida or Al-Qaida affiliated groups following the attacks of September 11th, the LTTE continued to train divisional commanders of the Communist Party of Nepal-Maoist (CPN-M).[55] Other insurgent groups known to commiserate with the LTTE at various times during its existence include the FARC, the African National Congress (ANC) in South Africa, the South West African People's Organization (SWAPO) in Namibia, the Eritrean People's Liberation Front (EPLF), MILF, the Tigrayan People's Liberation Front (TPLF) in Ethiopia, Hezb-i-Islami Gulbuddin (HIG) in Afghanistan, the Japanese Red Army (JRA), and the PFLP.[56]

Linkages with a smorgasbord of insurgent groups allowed the LTTE to circumvent existing international arms control conventions and add to an already potent arsenal. The LTTE's relationship with the Khmer Rouge in Cambodia was integral to its ability to obtain weapons. These deals took place across the Cambodian border in Trang, Thailand, where the weapons would be purchased and then moved along the Andaman sea coast, where they were shipped across the Bay of Bengal to LTTE insurgents in Sri Lanka.[57]

Operational Capabilities

LTTE's operational tools included weapons, sanctuary, and funding, pitted squarely against a Sri Lankan COIN force that waged a take-no-prisoner war to exterminate Prabhakaran and the LTTE. But perhaps the most impressive was the LTTE's world-class maritime capabilities. Flush with cash, Prabhakaran understood that if his group were to have a legitimate chance to defeat the Sri Lankan military, the Tigers had to develop an effective maritime capability. In 1984, Prabhakaran created the Sea Tigers, which consisted of two groups. The first group concentrated on tactical actions while the second group was responsible for the LTTE's expanding fleet of merchant ships, known as the Sea Pigeons, which ferried both licit and illicit goods. Within this division were thirteen sections, including the Sea Battle "Regiments," Underwater Demolition Teams, Sea Tiger Strike Groups, and a Radar and Telecommunications Unit. A Marine Engineering and Boat Building Section, a Maritime School and Academy, a Recruiting Section, and sections to support ordnance, personnel, and logistics were all part of the Sea Tigers' shore infrastructure.[58]

Weapons

The LTTE's weapons procurement network has been called the "most secretive" of the group's international operations.[59] The earliest identified network was run by Sothilingam Shanthakumar, a smuggler from the Valvettithurai, a fishing port that serves as the base for a distinct caste of Tamil fishermen.[60] Until 1987, the LTTE relied almost exclusively on the Indian intelligence services, especially the Research and Analysis Wing (RAW) to provide arms and explosives.[61] From 1987 onward, following the Indo-Sri Lankan Peace Accord, the LTTE sought to diversify its source of weapons and made the establishment of a global procurement network one of its top priorities. The Tamil Tigers also used explosives to establish themselves as one of the most feared insurgent groups in the world, known for their extensive use of suicide bombing. Finally, the group developed legitimate air and sea capabilities to complement its ground forces, thus rounding the organization into a comprehensive military threat.

The LTTE's procurement network was led by Tharmalingam Shanmugam, alias Kumaran Pathmanathan and known in shorthand simply as "KP." He was so closely associated with the Tigers' arms network that their global weapons operations were referred to as the "KP Department."[62] The "KP Department" prioritized the acquisition of explosives, but unlike the PIRA, the LTTE was not adept at producing these indigenously. In August 1994, the "KP Department" arranged for the shipment of between 50–60 tons of RDX and TNT explosive acquired through the Rubezone Chemicals plant and sent from the Port of Nikolayev in Ukraine to Sri Lanka. The deal was brokered through an LTTE front company known as Carlton Trading, which was based in Dhaka, Bangladesh, and facilitated through the use of false end-user certificates.[63] Other front companies were set up in Chittagong, Yangon, and Kuala Lumpur.[64] The LTTE's weapons inventory, in addition to the arms and equipment listed above, also included a T-55 tank, Russian-made Strela-3 man-portable air defense systems (MANPADS), six Czech built Zlin Z-143 single-engine aircraft, 50 to 100 frogman kits and five to 10 underwater scooters, a fleet of 500 to 1,000 fiberglass boats, between six and 10 Mirage-class boats, and four partially completed submersibles.[65] The insurgents used Global Positioning System (GPS) to more accurately deploy their missile projectiles well before the COIN force acquired this same capability.[66]

Intelligence

Although the insurgents had utilized guerilla tactics to devastating effect against the COIN force, the LTTE realized that to stave off defeat, it had to counter Colombo's moves by enhancing its capabilities and upgrading its infrastructure. As part of its efforts to innovate in the area of weapons technology intended to blunt COIN force countermeasures, the LTTE diverted resources to its two operational wings that functioned as suicide strike teams, the Black Tigers and the Sea Tigers.

The LTTE developed the capability to assassinate Sri Lankan government officials, foreign officials, and high-ranking members of the COIN force military services. When the LTTE wanted to renege on a peace agreement, the group commonly used assassination of a top Sri Lankan official to convey this message clearly.

Prabhakaran's ironclad grip over the organization started to fray beginning in the early 1990s, when he ordered the execution of long-time confidant and high-ranking LTTE member Mahattaya. Prabhakaran accused his erstwhile colleague of plotting with the Indian army's RAW to kill the top leadership of the group, including Prabhakaran himself.[67] A second and even more devastating schism occurred with the defection of one of the LTTE's top commanders, Vinayagamoorthy Muralitharan ("Karuna") in early 2004. The falling out between Prabhakaran and Karuna effectively split the LTTE in two; the former retained control of the northern faction while the latter came to exert control of the Tigers' eastern faction. When the split led to open conflict between the two

Table 3.1

Liberation Tigers of Tamil Eelam Technological Innovations[1]

Innovation	Purpose	Intended Mitigation of Government Countermeasures
Wax-coated wiring in explosive devices	Prevent emission of explosive vapors	Defeat detection by sniffer dogs
Airtight casing for explosive devices	Prevent emission of explosive vapors	Defeat detection by sniffer dogs
LED indicator lamps in bomb circuits	Verify "live" circuitry	
Secondary, tertiary detonation triggers in explosive devices	Provision of internal fail-safe mechanism	
"Explosive bra cup" design for suicide vest	Conceal explosive slabs	Defeat physical hand searches
Elongated fuel tank in vehicle bombs	Conceal explosive devices	Defeat detection by "dipper" probes
Chassis molded, mint-laced explosive devices	Conceal explosive charge and prevent emission of explosive vapors	Defeat causal visual inspections and detection by sniffer dogs
Hollowed out, shallow superstructure for suicide boats	Increase speed and reduce surface detection	Minimize radar cross-section
Penetration rods affixed to suicide boat prows	Amplify explosive force	Defeat hardened SLN superstructures
Mini submarines for diver operatives	Covert de-bussing inside harbors	Defeat port harbor patrols
Prepaid SIM cards, single satellite signals for communication devices	Avail secure communication	Defeat government communication intercepts
Discursive writing, Slidex chart for coding communications	Avail secure communication	Defeat government counterintelligence

[1]Brian Jackson, *Breaching the Fortress Wall: Understanding Terrorist Efforts to Overcome Defensive Technologies*, Santa Monica, Calif.: RAND Corporation, 2007, p.80.

Table 3.2

Major LTTE Assassinations

Name	Title	Date
General Ranjan Wileratne	Minister of Defense	March 1991
Denzil Kobbekaduwa	Army general	August 1992
Wijaya Wimlaratna	Army general	August 1992
Lakshman Wijeratna	Army general	August 1992
Clancy Fernando	Navy commander	November 1992
Lalith Athulathmudali	Former national security minister	April 1993

groups, the Sri Lankan government's special task force supplied Karuna's fighters with arms and sanctuary in return for intelligence about the LTTE's northern units.[68] Karuna subsequently handed over the LTTE playbook, which the COIN forces used to plan their final offensive.

The most important of the seven commands is the military wing, which was structured very close to the organization of a conventional professional army. Within the military wing were the Sea Tigers (navy), Black Tigers (suicide commando unit), and an elite intelligence outfit.[69] A rudimentary air capability existed for a short time as well. Beneath the military wing was the political wing, led by Tamil Chelvam and Anton Balasingham. The Sea Tigers were divided into two separate wings, one for amphibious operations and another for merchant marine type duties. This branch of the Tigers maintained an extensive organizational structure, including a substantial female naval unit. The Sea Tigers had their own naval intelligence cell and the group also worked closely with the Black Tigers. The Black Tigers were suicide commandos selected from the most elite LTTE recruits. This wing of the organization was "fully integrated" into the LTTE's land and sea operations.

Sanctuary, Safe Haven, and Operational Space

Sanctuary proved indispensable to the Tigers for four principal reasons. First, the Tamil diaspora provided the LTTE with virtually a global sanctuary. Second, the physical sanctuary maintained in Sri Lanka's Northeast, particularly Jaffna, allowed the insurgents to train without fear of COIN force infiltration. For years, a sympathetic Tamil population and government in Tamil Nadu, India (located a mere 28 kilometers across the Palk Strait and home to 60 million ethnic Tamils) acquiesced to the LTTE's need for a physical foreign safe haven. The Tamil Nadu sanctuary was facilitated by the relationship between Prabhakaran and

P. Nedumaran, a senior politician in India. Tamil Nadu demonstrates that for sanctuary to be valuable, it need not be geographically contiguous. Third, sanctuary became a de facto headquarters for the LTTE and a place where the group established a system of governance to rival that of the Sri Lankan state. It also prolonged the duration of the conflict because it allowed insurgents to evade arrest and offered the Tigers a secure area to rest, recuperate, replenish, and rearm.

For those insurgents who needed a hiatus from fighting in Sri Lanka, Tamil Nadu was an ideal destination, especially for fighters whose absence from the conflict would only be temporary. As early as the 1970s, Tamil militants, including Prabakaran, evaded arrest for crimes by fleeing to Tamil Nadu.[70] The LTTE purchased safe houses and communication centers in Tamil Nadu where militants on the lam and attempting to evade capture could hide, without removing themselves too acutely from the battlefield. Besides safe houses, the insurgents used factories to manufacture uniforms and weapons.[71] There were even hospitals run by the insurgents that were used to treat wounded fighters. As they solidified control over the northern and eastern Tamil-dominated provinces of Sri Lanka, the LTTE used these areas to build an extensive network of bases and defensive fortifications.[72] The group's unofficial headquarters was located in the town of Kilinochchi in Northern Province, located approximately 100 km southeast of Jaffna. By establishing a de facto shadow government in the north and east of the country, the LTTE gained legitimacy at the expense of the Sri Lankan state.

In the early years of the Tamil insurgency, Indian Prime Minister Indira Gandhi lacked the political clout to convince Tamil Nadu's chief minister, M. G. Ramachandran, to close down the LTTE training camps that operated free from scrutiny. Ramachandran possessed no great affinity for the insurgents, but he needed to be seen as sympathetic toward a group that could claim widespread popular support in the community and had already been embraced by Ramachandran's political rival, Muthuvel Karunanidhi.[73] Blowback from Indira Gandhi's tacit support of the movement would come full circle over a decade later, when a Black Tiger attack killed her son Rajiv Gandhi, then prime minister. In 1995, feeling pressure, the LTTE established a permanent base in Twante, an island located off of the coast of Myanmar.[74] The Sri Lankan government pressured Myanmar's military junta to dismantle the Tigers' base, so in January 1996 the LTTE vacated Twante and developed a base on an island located off of Phuket, Thailand.

Training

By mid-1987, approximately 20,000 Tamil militants had been trained in India, which included camps in Tamil Nadu, as well as specialized training which occurred in New Delhi, Bombay, and Vishakhapatnam.[75] In addition to these locations the Tigers received training in Uttar Pradesh and Karnataka and established camps in Salem and Madurai.[76] For the majority of the conflict, the most promising insurgents were sent for training outside of Sri Lanka's borders, while the rest were trained in camps located in the forested areas of the north.[77]

The average training cycle for an LTTE recruit lasted approximately four months. Those insurgents who displayed skill or advanced military acumen were handpicked to attend specialized training courses to prepare for task-specific roles in the group's intelligence, communication, explosives, or naval components.[78] In 1994, the LTTE implemented a training school designed specifically for "officers," which included a rigorous curriculum that incorporated lessons learned from previous battles against the COIN forces. In the realm of intelligence, the LTTE trained specialized members for each phase of the intelligence cycle, including a cadre of insurgents whose only job was the collection and analysis of long-term intelligence on both potential and real targets.[79]

Tamil Nadu was critical to the LTTE's longevity and the group even managed to train and operate there while fighting the Indian Peace Keeping Force (IPKF) in the late 1980s, primarily due to a combination of popular support among the locals, government apathy, and "cynical bureaucratic ploys of the intelligence agencies."[80] The LTTE's tentacles extended deep into Tamil Nadu. They constructed a dense network in the Thanjavur district between Nagapattinam and Adiramapattinam, Vedaranyam, and Point Calimere. The local administration was co-opted or subverted, among them police and politicians. Fishermen, farmers, and smugglers served as the manpower for an ever-growing sanctuary.

A highly sympathetic population was a contributing factor to the LTTE's ability to achieve so much success in using Tamil Nadu and other Indian areas as sanctuary, although the Jaffna peninsula in Sri Lanka proper was unmatched in value. The Tigers so thoroughly controlled the Northeast of the country at various points throughout the conflict that they were able to build mock ups of the actual venues they planned to attack. These real-life models were constructed by the map and models department within the group.[81] Some of the more devastating attacks ever conducted by the group—international airport, World Trade Center, Central Bank—resulted from this type of training.[82]

Organizational Capabilities

Since the ultimate prize for insurgents is control of the state, constructing a shadow government is a necessary prerequisite. The LTTE's sanctuary afforded the Tigers with the opportunity to build a parallel system of government in the areas under their control. In many parts of the north and east, this included courts of law, municipal administration, a police force, a customs service, a tax and legislation code, a banking system, and a television and radio network.[83] During long stretches of the conflict, traveling from government-controlled areas to Tiger redoubts required passing through well-guarded border control posts that include identification checks, goods inspection, and the collection of customs fees.[84]

LTTE political liaisons met with Tamil Nadu politicians in Chennai, the capital, but eleven other districts served as part of an extensive military infrastructure, each connected by a high-tech wireless network. The districts were the center of the LTTE's war supplies and are listed in no specific order with the military specialty in parentheses: Dharmapuri (procurement of explosives), Coimbatore (arms and ammunition manufacturing), Salem (explosives manufacturing), Periya (Erode) (military clothing manufacturing), Vedaraniym (coastal area from where supplies were dispatched), Madurai (transit area), Thanjavur (communications center), Nagapattinam (landing area for supplies from ships), Rameswaram (refugee reception and recruitment), Tiruchirapalli (treatment of wounded insurgents), and Tuticorin (trade in gold, silver, narcotics, and other goods).[85]

Leadership

Velupillai Prabhakaran was born in the northern coastal town of Valvettithurai on the Jaffna Peninsula in 1954 and grew up amidst poverty, violence, and oppression, during a time when Sri Lankan Tamils struggled for equal status with the Sinhalese. He was born into the Karaiyar caste, a relatively low-ranking rung of Sri Lankan society. The most common profession for men from Prabhakaran's village was to become a maritime smuggler. From the little that is known about the LTTE's reclusive leader, he was married to Mathivathani Erambu and had two children, a daughter Dwaraka and a son Charles Anthony, named after one of the Tigers' most famous fighters, Charles Lucas Anthony, who was killed in the early 1980s. Physically, he was short and portly, which sometimes masked the steely determination hidden beneath an otherwise unassuming veneer of calm and quiet focus.

Within the LTTE, Prabhakaran remained a Tamil nationalist first and foremost. Similar to other well-known insurgent commanders, he was known to live a monastic lifestyle and mostly eschewed material comforts. Gordon Weiss characterizes Prabhakaran, and similar insurgent leaders, by describing them in the following manner: "unlike ordinary mortals, they turn their backs on the ordinary relationships, quotidian fears and communal safety nets that nurture and restrain others."[86]

Two interesting aspects of Prabhakaran's leadership were the cult of personality that formed around the leader and his constant paranoia throughout his tenure as LTTE leader. Most accounts of Prabhakaran make reference to his status as a hero who was afforded a godlike worship by LTTE cadres and elements of the Tamil population. Followers swore an oath of loyalty to Prabhakaran himself, and referred to him strictly as "Leader," because his actual name was known to inspire so much awe.[87] In speeches, his language was both inspirational and visionary, and often evoked the nationalistic pride held by many of his followers. As related by Post, a Jaffna psychiatrist described the impact of Prabhakaran's leadership, noting that many LTTE members "regard Prabhakaran as higher than their own god," and many would make pilgrimages to his former home as something akin to a spiritual ritual.[88] Pictures of Prabhakaran adorned homes and businesses throughout rebel-held areas, yet "According to scores of accounts from defectors and others who escaped Tiger tyranny, many of his [Prabhakaran] own lieutenants were murdered; Tamils who criticized him, even mildly or in jest, were banished to dungeons, starved, and hauled out periodically for battering by their guards."[89]

Ideology

The Tamil Tigers are often classified as an ethno-nationalist terrorist group.[90] Translated loosely, this means the LTTE was comprised of ethnic Tamils and sought freedom for a clearly defined national territory (Eelam). Still, because the Tigers' core group was initially comprised of students living abroad, there was also the requisite Marxist influence of stereotypical "coffee house revolutionaries."[91] Among Tamil insurgent groups, the Tamil Tigers were not unique in their taste for left wing politics. Both the PLOTE and the Tamil Eelam Liberation Organization were Marxist groups, and the Janatha Vimukthi Peramuna (JVP) were Maoists.[92]

Insurgent political thought, however nascent, requires a modicum of organization. So when violence broke out in 1983, the ideologically-inclined Tamil groups were best placed to protect Tamil neighborhoods. With this protection came a platform, which the various groups used to spread their ideologies. After the 1983 riots, non-Marxist groups were engulfed by the Marxist groups through both persuasion and coercion.[93] Though at first the LTTE adopted Marxism as an ideology of convenience, the intensity of the group's radical leftist beliefs grew more fervent over time.[94] Balasingham, the LTTE's aforementioned theoretician, explained the LTTE's ideology as follows: "our total strategy integrates both the national struggle and class struggle, interlinks both nationalism and socialism into a revolutionary project aimed at liberating our people both from national oppression and from the exploitation of man by man."[95]

The LTTE fought for a united Tamil Eelam homeland in Northeast Sri Lanka. Like the PIRA, independence was considered the ultimate goal and objective of the organization. Some members figured that if Marxism could shepherd the process toward this end, then so be it. Most foot soldiers fought for justice and the opportunity to redress grievances, while the leadership spoke of leaving behind the chains imposed by the twin evils of capitalism and imperialism.[96]

Under the leadership of R. N. Dixit, the Indian High Commission in Colombo devoted significant resources to determine which groups were "really Marxist" and which groups were frauds. But Dixit failed to understand the motivation of the insurgents, Marxist or otherwise. That the insurgents *considered* themselves Marxist, used Marxist models in their strategic analysis and decision-making, tactically employed classic Marxist clandestine techniques and couched their language in Marxist phraseology was most important.[97]

Human Resources and Recruitment

Both insurgent theorists and social movement scholars highlight the importance of the links between grievances and the provision of popular support. The "Sinhala Only" Act of 1956 was the opening salvo in the area of language, making Sinhalese the sole official language of the country. Affirmative action policies were then instituted in the country's universities, making it more difficult for Tamils to receive a quality education. At a certain point in the conflict, revenge and the themes of repression and occupation became the overarching concerns of the Tamils. Sinhala nationalism was on the rise and exploded with the anti-Tamil pogroms of July 1983. The "Black July" riots of 1983 resulted in the deaths of between 1,000 and 3,000 Tamils with thousands more wounded and raped. Countless others had their homes and shops burned to the ground.[98] In some areas, civilians were pulled from their homes by Sinhala mobs who carried voter registration lists to determine which families were Tamil.[99] "Black July" was a watershed event in the conflict and one which caused the Tamil population to throw its support behind those who were willing and able to protect those that remained (hundreds of thousands of Tamils fled abroad, while an additional 100,000 settled in refugee camps) and transformed Tamil militancy into "an engine of popular resentment."[100]

By the 1990s, the LTTE relied more on violent and coercive methods to generate and maintain popular support than it had at any point previously in the conflict. The group employed what Jannie Lilja terms *territorial entrapment* and *social entrapment* to induce cooperation and attitudinal support from its constituency.[101] Social and cultural obligations to support the Tigers were reinforced by a mixture of propaganda speeches and restrictions on the movement of Tamils. The recruitment patterns of fighters into the organization mirrored the evolution of the popular support of the Tamil population. The LTTE's command and control was vertically structured, with the Central Governing Committee at the top of the organization. The hierarchical structure of the group included a bell-shaped middle stratum of leaders built into the organization to provide the LTTE with a measure of redundancy and defend against the Sri Lankan Armed Forces' (SLAF) strategy of targeting Prabhakaran with a decapitation strike.[102]

The LTTE's entire movement counted approximately 15,000 cadres, to which an additional 3,000 to 4,000 personnel served with the Sea Tigers.[103] The organizational structure was "two-tiered," geographically structured, and composed of seven regular commands each led by a district commander. Prabhakaran oversaw the seven district commanders and chaired the Central Governing Committee, charged with oversight for the military and political tiers of the organization. Insurgents within the seven commands were members of either a political wing or a combat group and further divided into specialized subdivisions.[104] The LTTE operated as a meritocracy—it promoted insurgents and afforded them more responsibility with performance, rather than seniority. Upon promotion, the fighter received increased command responsibilities.[105]

Media, PR, Propaganda, and Publicity

Among insurgent groups, the LTTE was one of the first groups to realize the importance of a robust public relations and propaganda machine in winning the battle for hearts and minds and operated a transnational network with offices located in the United Kingdom, France, Germany, Switzerland, Canada, and Australia.[106] In Toronto, the group operated four 24-hour radio stations, 10 weekly newspapers and Tamil language television programs.[107] But of all its overseas bases, none was more integral to success than the LTTE's British headquarters. The LTTE International Secretariat has operated continuously in London since 1984.[108]

The bulk of the group's efforts directed its message to various segments of the Tamil diaspora (those that would contribute money to the group) and politicians and human-rights activists who might be able to influence the situation from a diplomatic or political perspective. The primary messages put forth by the LTTE were the following: Tamils are the innocent victims of a Sinhalese orchestrated campaign of genocide and annihilation; Sri Lankan Tamils (who account for a mere 12.5 percent of the population) have been subjected to severe discrimination and both overwhelming and disproportionate military oppression; and due to the long history of discrimination and oppression, Tamils and Sinhalese can never coexist peacefully in a single state.[109]

To get its message out, the LTTE distributed graphic videos, pamphlets, calendars, and other publications that demonstrated the Sri Lankan government's deadly military strikes, with resulting collateral damage and the slaughter of civilians. Sympathy for the plight of the Tamils helped generate a more pliable diaspora community, which responded in kind by donating money to the LTTE and offering its members sanctuary abroad. The LTTE's public relations machine became so effective that attempts by the government in Colombo to counteract its propaganda activities fell short.[110] LTTE publications included journals and newspapers, and in North America alone, there were over 40 Sri Lankan Tamil newspapers, more than three-quarters of which were managed by the LTTE or associated front groups. To put this in perspective, "the LTTE propaganda and fund-raising network is superior to other extant networks such as Hamas, Hezbollah, Kashmiris, or the Basques," judges Rohan Gunaratna.[111]

In 2002, the Sri Lankan government allowed the Tigers to broadcast their previously banned "Voices of Tigers" FM radio station throughout northern Sri Lanka.[112] The LTTE also established an online presence, creating a "virtual Tamil nation," that provided a treasure trove of information related to the LTTE, its origins, Prabhakaran, and atrocities committed by the SLAF.[113]

HOW LTTE FINANCING WAS COUNTERED

Throughout the course of the insurgency, the LTTE consistently expanded and diversified its sources of income. In the early to mid-1980s, drug trafficking was a consistent revenue stream, but this changed over time. As the conflict wore on it became more and more difficult for the LTTE to sustain its fund-raising network. Donations that were once offered freely later had to be coerced. Once Western nations like the United States and the United Kingdom began to crack down on LTTE activities within their respective countries, the group increasingly devoted more time and energy to organized crime as a method of financing its activities, including human smuggling. After the LTTE was proscribed as a terrorist organization in countries where it once raised funds freely, this shift opened the LTTE up to arrest and prosecution. In 2005, Canada outlawed LTTE fund-raising networks. This proved a devastating blow to the insurgents, who lost an estimated $12 million from the Canadian connection.[114] The loss of revenue from Canada was a major factor in the LTTE's final defeat, especially because it occurred at the same time as the Sri Lankan COIN force was receiving $1 billion annually in military and financial aid from Beijing, as the Chinese sought to expand development rights for port facilities in South Asia.[115]

Kinetic Activities

For the majority of the conflict, the approach of the Sri Lankan government was almost purely kinetic, albeit somewhat cumbersome and counterproductive at various points. On balance, the leadership in Colombo lacked an appreciation for the importance of countering the LTTE's financial architecture. Instead, the government sought to counter the insurgency through an authoritarian approach.

In early March 2004, Vinayagamoorthy Muralitharan, known as "Colonel Karuna," defected from the LTTE. Karuna took his autonomous, geographically concentrated Eastern Province army with him. The Eastern faction became Tamil Makkal Viduthalai Pulikal (TMVP) and subsequently joined the counterinsurgents in their fight against the LTTE, now mostly a Northern Province organization. Karuna's defection struck a blow to the LTTE's command and control.[116] The split sapped the morale of the LTTE and limited its operational effectiveness. Once the Eastern faction split from the Tigers, the LTTE's ability to conduct conventional operations was severely curtailed. Sri Lankan COIN forces benefited tremendously from TMVP intelligence and manpower in the Eastern Province.[117] Karuna led his fighters against LTTE insurgents in the coastal areas of Batticaloa-Ampara in the east. Throughout 2006, the TMVP killed 82 LTTE insurgents while the Tigers only managed to kill 27 TMVP fighters.[118]

Even for a group with traditionally high levels of fratricide like the LTTE, few could have predicted Karuna's split and even fewer could have predicted the impact it would have on the Tamil Tigers. A purely kinetic analysis of Karuna's defection reveals that once his force of 500–600 fighters switched sides, the LTTE began to operate as more of a conventional military, rather than as an insurgent force.[119] This strategic miscalculation played directly into the hands of the Sri Lankan COIN forces, which had spent much of the past decade upgrading its conventional forces with the help of China.

With the breakdown of the Norwegian-led peace process in 2006, and "Colonel Karuna" now siding with the Sri Lankan government, the COIN forces and the LTTE went back to war in late July. After the insurgents cut off water to the paddy fields surrounding Mavil Aru, COIN force jets attacked LTTE camps in the area. Bitter fighting ensued and continued to ebb and flow over the next two years. In March 2007, the LTTE's Air Tigers struck a COIN force airbase in Katunayake. This was the first recorded insurgent air strike without the assistance of an external state supporter in history.

"Colonel Karuna's" defection provided the Sri Lankan government and military with a treasure trove of intelligence while serving the dual purpose of attenuating the strength of the group. With Karuna and his troops no longer defending the East, but instead helping to overtake it, the COIN forces captured Sampur, Vakarai, and other parts of the Eastern province. Between 2008 and 2009, the COIN forces launched an offensive in the northern part of the island and won the Battle of Kilinochchi in the Eastern theatre, effectively tightening the noose on the LTTE's top leadership.[120] The Tigers' demise was cemented on May 18, 2009 when Prabhakaran was killed in fighting near Nandikadal Lagoon in northeastern Sri Lanka.

Non-kinetic Activities

It took overseas governments many years before any of them decided to take earnest action against the LTTE. In countries including Canada and the United Kingdom, there was serious resistance to proscribing the group as a terrorist organization until the very end. The result was that the LTTE had a free rein to organize fund-raising activities and tap the diaspora for voluntary (and involuntary) contributions. Once the Canadian and British governments did proscribe the group, this allowed them to start to drafting legislation and implementing procedures to counter the group's finances.[121] Even after being proscribed, the LTTE continued to raise money through charities and front companies. What made it difficult for both Canadians and British effort to adequately use the legislative means at their disposal was that the Tigers owned a number of legitimate businesses in Canada and Europe. These were businesses like jewelry stores, pawn shops and telephone outlets that were initially set up with LTTE seed money and a percentage of the profits were given back to LTTE through various third parties.

For its part, the leadership of the Sri Lankan state embarked upon a major diplomatic offensive to persuade the international community to side with the government in Colombo. These efforts were aided by the events of 9/11, which led many nations to look at the world in more dichotomous terms. By and large, the LTTE was now considered a global terrorist threat with alleged links to Al-Qaida, whether or not these links were real or imagined, the mere allegation, gave this message some resonance. Sri Lanka trained its diplomatic corps to serve as liaisons with foreign governments in an information offensive designed to highlight the dangers of the LTTE. For the most part, this offensive focused on countries where the Tamil diaspora maintained a presence, including Australia, Norway, France, the United Kingdom, Canada, and to a lesser extent the United States.[122] The challenge for these countries was that their own domestic constituencies were influential and there were many politicians that depended on Tamil votes. Not to be outdone, the LTTE maintained its own political council whose main job was to portray the LTTE as a legitimate organization protecting Tamil human rights.

CONCLUSION

The insurgents raised enough money to amass an extensive arsenal, which provided the group with the flexibility to fight as guerillas, or if it chose, to battle SLAF COIN forces in more conventional warfare. Most insurgent groups engage in asymmetric conflict because it is their only option. But the LTTE was one of the most dynamic groups in history, partly due to its ability to fight in a number of ways. An evaluation of the LTTE's military capabilities by Jane's supports this assessment:

At its peak, prior to the 2008–2009 SLA offensive, the LTTE had successfully developed and implemented an impressive range of conventional and non-conventional tactics, and was able to routinely strike at a wide range of different targets. The group earned a reputation for its mastery of conventional, land-based warfighting, regularly deploying its battle-hardened cadres against heavily fortified military targets. Such operations frequently showcased the LTTE's ability to coordinate direct and indirect fire, and on occasion LTTE ground forces even mounted combined arms operations together with the group's naval and air wings. Unusually for a sub-state group, the LTTE was able to supplement its mastery of maneuvre warfare with an effective use of positional warfare.[123]

The 2002 cease-fire solidified the northeast as a Tamil home base by granting the LTTE autonomy and freedom of movement. The Tigers recognized that the population was a contest between the insurgents and the COIN forces. But because the LTTE lacked the resources of the NGO community, the Tigers' political wing worked closely with civil society organizations. After the United States declared the LTTE a foreign terrorist organization (FTO) in 1997 and a Specially Designated Global Terrorist group in November 2001, became much more difficult for the Tigers to raise funds through NGOs and related charities.[124]

CHAPTER 4

Hezbollah: Financing the Party of God

BACKGROUND

Literally translated as "the Party of God," Hezbollah[1] was formed in the midst of an internecine civil war that would wreak havoc in Lebanon for 15 years, ending only in 1990.[2] The group emerged from the extremely complex patchwork of ethnic and religious groups in Lebanon and draws its support almost exclusively from the Shia communities in the country's capital city, Beirut, and its surrounding environs, southern Lebanon, the Bekaa Valley, and the Hirmil Region.[3] Similar to other insurgent movements throughout the Middle East, Hezbollah receives support and is influenced by powerful actors in the region, including Syria and Iran, the latter of which was the "principal moving force" behind the group's creation.[4] Attacks abroad are orchestrated and conducted by the group's international terrorist wing, known synonymously as the Islamic Jihad Organization (IJO) or the External Security Organization (ESO).

HOW HEZBOLLAH FUNDED ITS ACTIVITIES

Hezbollah's funding stream derives from a combination of state sponsorship, an array of organized criminal activities, donations made from the Lebanese diaspora and other sympathizers abroad, as well as legitimate businesses. Unlike other groups that need to spend precious time and energy figuring out how to finance their day-to-day operations, Hezbollah enjoys the benefits of foreign patronage, which allow its members to focus on fund-raising in other arenas, including expatriate remittances, front companies located both within Lebanon and abroad (primarily in Africa, Latin America, and Asia) and various forms of crime ranging from cigarette smuggling to film piracy to credit card fraud.

Indeed, sustaining the organization's ever-growing legitimate portfolio makes its criminal activities that much more critical. The group has also been accused of dealing in more pernicious forms of crime, like the trade in conflict diamonds and narcotics smuggling. In 2011, an investigation into the Lebanese Canadian Bank revealed that Hezbollah maintained extensive ties to the South American cocaine trade.

Gray Economy

Conventional wisdom among regular observers of terrorism points to Al-Qaida as the first terrorist organization with a true transnational capability. In reality, Hezbollah is the most globally capable organization in terms of both fund-raising and operational capacity, having success- fully executed attacks in Argentina, France, and Saudi Arabia. Part of Hezbollah's success in raising funds through the gray economy is directly tied to its global reach. Wherever an opportunity presents itself—from Latin America to West Africa to Southeast Asia—Hezbollah has the ability to capitalize. A transnational diaspora, robust charitable organizations, and a range of legal businesses to launder money are a perfect comple- ment to Hezbollah's dark economic activities.

Diaspora Support

A worldwide Lebanese diaspora has allowed Hezbollah to extend its network to nearly every continent, with the most prominent diaspora communities located in West Africa and Latin America. After 9/11, the tri-border region where Paraguay, Brazil, and Argentina meet was identi- fied as an "ungoverned space" where terrorists lived, trained, plotted, and raised money. The tri-border region, or "Triple Frontier," is frequently cited as one of the most lawless places on the planet.[5] Lesser known areas where Hezbollah has established a presence include Uganda, South Africa, and several Southeast Asian countries including Malaysia, Thai- land, and Singapore.[6] Investigations of the group's high-profile attacks against Israeli and Jewish targets in Argentina in 1994 and 1996 revealed "official Iranian involvement," to include training and logistical support.[7] In the case of the attacks in Argentina, Imad Mughniyeh and Iranian Intel- ligence Minister Ali Fallahian were implicated for their role in helping to coordinate and execute the bombings.[8]

The Lebanese diaspora living in Africa is known to contribute signifi- cant funding to Hezbollah's agenda. This became evident when in December 2003, a Beirut-bound *Union Transport Africaines* flight crashed in Benin, West Africa while attempting to takeoff. Press reports from the Arab world at the time indicated that a Hezbollah "foreign relations offi- cial" and two of his aides were among those killed in the crash. The dead officials were carrying approximately USD $2 million in donations obtained from Lebanese nationals in West African countries, including Guinea, Sierra Leone, Liberia, and Benin, among others.[9] The Israelis have reported that Hezbollah raises hundreds of thousands of U.S. dollars annually in Africa, soliciting donations from wealthy sympathizers from Senegal to South Africa.[10] An estimated 120,000 Lebanese émigrés live throughout the region, many of whom are involved in import-export businesses.[11]

Charities

The Martyrs Foundation is a Hezbollah charity that provides both financial and operational support to the group, including direct support to operations during the July–August 2006 conflict with Israel as well as direction and financing for terror cells in Gaza related to both Hezbollah and Palestinian Islamic Jihad (PIJ).[12] Money from the tri-border area in South America has been traced directly to the foundation, including shortly after the 9/11 attacks, when Paraguayan antiterrorism authorities discovered hundreds of receipts in Assad Barakat's Casa Apollo electronics shop linked to Hezbollah's Martyrs Foundation.[13] According to Levitt, the Martyrs Foundation is "a massive entity that openly concedes to supplying charitable funds to the families of Hezbollah suicide bombers."[14] But the charity is more than just a funding stream. Indeed, the Martyrs Foundation, in addition to other Hezbollah charities like the Mahdi Scouts and the Shia schools, are an extension of Hezbollah into the community.[15] The Martyrs Foundation operates in different countries under different auspices. In Germany, the organization was known as the al-Shahid Social Relief Institution and in the United States its satellite was called the Goodwill Charitable Organization, based in Dearborn, Michigan and responsible for funneling contributions from members and supporters directly to Hezbollah leaders in Lebanon.[16]

Fraud

Hezbollah's connections abroad provide the group with a broad array of ways to make money through various frauds, schemes, and scams. The Greater Detroit metropolitan area and Dearborn, MI are areas home to large Arab and Arab-American populations. Within these populations, Hezbollah has sought and received both active and passive support from sympathizers and operatives. The group's members have been implicated in everything from mortgage fraud to food stamp fraud (to include the misuse of grocery coupons) to credit card fraud, which has proved a lucrative endeavor. Hezbollah has also engaged in telecommunications fraud, which involved selling long distance telephone access through services obtained fraudulently, and by cloning the identification of mobile phone subscribers.[17]

The credit card fraud worked in the following way. First, front companies would process transactions made on credit cards that they knew would never be settled. Second, these front companies would be paid by the banks and credit card companies. Next, the members of the conspiracy would declare bankruptcy to the creditors, who in turn could not collect on the debt incurred. Finally, in order to hide assets from bankruptcy court, members of the group "sold" their homes to their wives or adult children.[18]

Hezbollah's fraud network included operatives in Michigan, California, Florida, Georgia, Illinois, Kentucky, Missouri, New York, North Carolina, and West Virginia. Globally, frauds were successfully perpetrated in the United States, Canada, Lebanon, Brazil, Paraguay, and China, to name just a few countries. Not only is the group's transnational reach impressive but the talent on its payroll is too. Without question, Hezbollah has been able to call on highly skilled criminals, including computer hackers who were alleged to have breached the networks of over 138 different financial institutions, from New Zealand to Switzerland.[19]

Legal Businesses

Just like most groups that earn significant amounts of money through a variety of illicit and quasi-illicit means, Hezbollah maintains a portfolio of businesses that it uses to launder money, disguise criminal activities, and evade authorities and law enforcement officials. Like most of Hezbollah's enterprises, these businesses span the globe. It is not entirely clear how closely Iran is involved, but according to Levitt, "The IRGC is known to operate front companies and employ agents in Dubai, a critical transshipment point for goods—both legitimate and illicit—from around the world to Iran."[20] Furthermore, Hezbollah maintains several front companies throughout sub-Saharan Africa, in countries including Angola and the Democratic Republic of Congo (DRC). In addition, the U.S. Treasury Department has targeted businesses in The Gambia, Sierra Leone, the British Virgin Islands, and Lebanon.[21]

In the United States, front companies included Sigma Distribution, Inc. and Byblous Distribution Investment, Inc., the latter of which was a perfume distribution company. Other front companies included Arosfram, a food import company, and Tajco Company, LLC, a property developer in Lebanon. Still, perhaps one of Hezbollah's most valuable assets is Jihad al-Binaa (JAB), (translated as "Construction Jihad"), widely recognized as the group's reconstruction and humanitarian assistance wing. As Kilcullen recounts, within days of the cease-fire that ended the July 2006 33-day war with Israel, JAB deployed teams to assess the destruction of Beirut's suburbs. JAB helped Hezbollah garner crucial political capital among its constituents following the war, as the group leveraged its nonmilitary capabilities to help balance the military losses it incurred.[22]

Money Laundering

The Lebanese Canadian Bank (LCB) has been accused of helping the Shiite terrorist group launder its profits from cocaine trafficking by mixing drug proceeds from money earned through the sale of used cars, purchased in the United States and resold in Africa.[23] In 2011, the Obama administration accused the LCB of laundering money in connection to a complex smuggling ring that involved narcotics shipped from Latin America through West Africa and to Europe. The ring also allegedly involved used automobiles purchased in the United States and sold in West Africa.[24] The U.S. Drug Enforcement Administration (DEA) insists that over $300 million was transferred to the United States for the purchase of used cars, which were then sold and the money sent through Hezbollah networks to the group's finance committee in Lebanon.[25] Hezbollah has also laundered money through hawala dealers, money service businesses like Western Union, and charities, in addition to smuggling bulk cash packages onto airplanes and hiding money in the tires of used cars shipped overseas. A DEA investigation found that the Lebanese Canadian Bank also did business with a Belgian diamond trader named Ibrahim Ahmad, whose clan (according to a UN report) has ties to Hezbollah and was involved in counterfeiting, money laundering, and diamond smuggling.[26]

Dark Economy

Lebanon's 15-year civil war helped expand Hezbollah's dark economy by relocating supporters and sympathizers to other parts of the world. And just around the time Lebanon's civil war was coming to a close, the horrific civil wars in Liberia and Sierra Leone made it easier for Hezbollah to exploit the natural resources of West Africa. As noted above, Lebanese traders and merchants have been active in the region stretching back decades. The Lebanese presence grew even more robust during Lebanon's own civil war, which raged over a 15-year period between 1975 and 1990. Lebanon's once robust economy was devastated by the civil war, as several generations of Shia left the northern Bekaa and the Hirmil Region to find work in West Africa, many becoming quite successful.[27]

Kidnapping for Ransom (KFR)

For Hezbollah, kidnapping has been less about collecting a ransom and more about terrorizing Israelis living abroad and acquiring persons that can be traded in future swaps for imprisoned terrorists. Kidnapping rings have been active throughout Africa, not just in the traditional Hezbollah stronghold of West Africa, but also in East Africa, in countries including Eritrea, Ethiopia, Kenya, Somalia, and Tanzania. As Levitt notes, "Hezbollah's interest in kidnapping Israelis appears to have been an Islamic Jihad Organization (IJO) innovation—a new take on an old tactic—executed as a means of collecting intelligence and securing the release of comrades incarcerated in Israel's and other countries' jails, completely different from the classic model of kidnapping for ransom."[28]

Kidnapping teams mostly operated within clan and family networks to maintain operational security and throughout the mid- to late-1980s, Hezbollah targeted Russian diplomats, Israeli soldiers, American intelligence officials, and French citizens. The CIA station chief in Beirut was kidnapped, tortured, and subsequently executed in 1984. In return for kidnapped French citizens, France agreed to release the Lebanese terrorist Anis Naqqash and four of his accomplices, and agreed to the unfreezing of financial assets and military hardware for Iran.[29] Two years later, in 1986, two Israeli soldiers were abducted from the occupation zone. In 1988, Hezbollah abducted Lt. Col. William Higgins, head of the 76-man Observer Group Lebanon (OGL). In exchange for his release, the terrorists demanded the withdrawal of Israeli forces from south Lebanon; the closure of all American diplomatic missions in the Middle East; release of all Lebanese detainees held in Khiam prison and all Palestinian prisoners in Israeli jails; and finally, the rather abstract (and unrealistic) demand of "the end of US influence in Lebanon."[30]

In late 2000, Hezbollah began targeting Israeli soldiers in the disputed Sheba Farms region, snatching three soldiers during a cross-border raid in October of that year. (The three soldiers—Benny Avraham, Adi Avitan, and Omar Sawaid—were executed by Hezbollah).[31] That same year, in October, Hezbollah arranged an elaborate kidnapping of Elhanan Tannenbaum, an Israeli reservist colonel, during an alleged drug deal in Dubai.[32] In 2003, Hezbollah operatives planned to kidnap a former Israel Defense Forces (IDF) colonel and diamond trader in Cameroon. Finally, the most recent Hezbollah kidnapping in July 2006 of two Israeli soldiers on patrol, Sergeant Ehud Goldwasser and the patrol's commander, Eldad Regev.[33]

Armed Robbery and Theft

While Hezbollah is not necessarily known for armed robbery, it does deal in stolen money and goods, pilfered from a cross-section of sources.

Among the stolen goods that Hezbollah traffics are inane items like socks and toilet paper, but also cutting edge technology and electronic gadgetry that the group makes thousands of dollars from, like the newest cell phones, laptops, and game consoles, including Sony PlayStation systems. In some cases, "blood money," as it has been called, is stolen currency purchased by the group for 65 cents on the dollar. The money is stolen abroad and then smuggled from Iran through Turkey and Syria into Lebanon, with some of this money emanating in Iraq.[34] Similar to archetypal mafia organizations, Hezbollah is able to make a profit off of a dizzying array of seemingly benign goods, including baby formula.

Smuggling, Trafficking, and Counterfeiting

Among the goods that Hezbollah has been known to counterfeit, including fake Nike sneakers, unlicensed T-shirts, knockoff sports jerseys, DVDs, zigzag rolling papers from Indonesia (commonly used to roll marijuana), perhaps the most lucrative has been Viagra from China. From a more sinister perspective, the group has also been known to make, sell, and use counterfeit passports and national identity cards, as well as counterfeit currency (with the help of Iran).[35] Considering all of Hezbollah's counterfeiting, smuggling, and trafficking operations, among the most lucrative scams the group executed was a cigarette smuggling ring based in Charlotte, North Carolina. Cartons of cigarettes purchased in North Carolina for USD $14 could be sold in Michigan for twice as much. In all, it is believed that Hezbollah earned tens of thousands of dollars by transporting and selling untaxed cigarettes throughout the United States.[36]

In February 2003 alone, it is alleged that Hezbollah raised nearly US $2 million through the illegal diamond trade.[37] Many of these diamonds were mined in Sierra Leone and then transported through Liberia and Guinea.[38] Next, they were sent abroad to the world market, to cities including Antwerp, Dubai, London, Tel Aviv, New York City, and Mumbai. Antwerp is the center of the global diamond trade and authorities there estimate that less than a third of US$600 million worth of diamonds exported annually from Congo are done so legally. According to a Belgian intelligence report dating back to 2000, individual Lebanese merchants and entire companies have been linked to Hezbollah, among them Imad Abdul Reda Bakri, Ali Ahmad Ahmad, Afrostars Diamonds BVBA, Triple Diamonds NV, and Ezzideen Diamonds BVBA.[39]

Hezbollah has been particularly active in the war-torn DRC over the years, where its members have exploited the country's vast natural resources, which include diamonds but also gold, uranium, and tanzanite.[40] Perhaps even more troubling, Al-Qaida reportedly used the same model and contacts as Hezbollah when operating throughout West

Africa.[41] Hezbollah members and Israeli diamond buyers have even placed business above politics or personal animosity in an effort to collaborate in moving diamonds onto the global market from Sierra Leone, the DRC, and Angola. The expression that came to characterize this working relationship was, "here we do business, there they do war."[42]

These same networks used by Hezbollah to transport diamonds and licit goods can also be used to transport narcotics. In recent years, West Africa has emerged as a critical hub in the global cocaine trade, with South American cocaine transiting through the region before being shipped abroad to Western Europe and parts of Asia, including Russia. Lebanese networks, and specifically Hezbollah, are one of the main players involved in the import and smuggling of cocaine from West Africa across the Sahel and on to Europe.[43]

High levels of corruption, a lack of the rule of law, and police forces overwhelmed by general security issues, to say nothing of counternarcotics, make West Africa the ideal "soft target" for drug traffickers. This is especially true of criminals who are seeking to use the region as an area to forge new criminal relationships and illicit partnerships.[44] It is unknown whether or not the rise in drug trafficking through the West African conduit is driven by Hezbollah, or whether its members are merely opportunists, taking advantage of a longstanding financial and logistical network already in place (to include logistical networks used to smuggle arms).

Known Hezbollah supporters and brothers, Ali Farhat and Hassan Farhat, were accused of trafficking in cocaine, heroin, and marijuana, in collaboration with a Nigerian drug dealer in possession of a Canadian immigration document.[45] More broadly, Hezbollah has also dealt methamphetamine and in the last several years has been receptive to a burgeoning relationship with Mexican drug cartels. Hezbollah operatives have been accused of trafficking in arms, drugs, and women. Indeed, Hezbollah operatives have been tied to Poland, Hungary, Moldova, the Balkans, and Romania.[46] Another Hezbollah hangout and criminal hotbed is Margarita Island, located off the coast of Venezuela.

Extortion and Protection

Hezbollah's foray into extortion and protection grew out of a copycat mechanism after watching the success of its erstwhile rival, Amal, a group which collected nearly USD $2 million from Lebanese expatriates across Nigeria, Liberia, and Cote D'Ivoire. These individuals paid, because they warned that if they eschewed such payments, their families in Lebanon would be targeted.[47] In an attempt to emulate the success of Amal, Hezbollah also began conducting Mafia-style shakedowns and threatening the welfare of relatives living back in Lebanon if "donations" were not paid.

Other than necessity, it remains unclear why a group so concerned about its image as a protector, would turn to such parasitical means of obtaining money. When Hezbollah's threats have gone unheeded, the group has employed thugs to attack commercial businesses and employ "Chicago-style racketeering" methods to collect cash. Living among the mostly middle-class Lebanese traders in West Africa is a small number of multimillionaires who have made their money from import-export, manufacturing, and agro-industrial companies. According to the European Union, although only a small portion of Lebanese in West Africa are sympathetic to Hezbollah's goals, many business owners pay the extortion money as a way of keeping the group "off their backs."[48]

External State Support

From Iran alone, Hezbollah is estimated to receive between $200 million and $350 million annually.[49] This money is transferred to the terrorist group in deliveries of cash, in the form of weapons, and through private charities linked to Iran's leadership.[50] Even as its own economy suffers under increasing sanctions, Iran continues to fund Hezbollah because the simple fact is that Iran needs Hezbollah. The showdown over Iran's nuclear program has led to an escalating "shadow war" between Iran on one side and Israel and the United States on the other.[51] This war has the plotlines and characters of a great spy novel. Iran accuses the Tel Aviv-Washington alliance (with the tacit blessing of Riyadh) of assassinating its nuclear scientists, launching sophisticated cyber attacks aimed at crippling its ability to enrich uranium, and funding anti-Iranian terrorist groups like Jundallah.[52] Besides targeting Israeli diplomats and embassies abroad, Iranian nationals and Hezbollah members were implicated in a foiled assassination plot that involved hiring Mexican gang members to kill the Saudi ambassador to Washington.[53] From a conventional military standpoint, Iran is limited in what it can do to strike back at its adversaries, so many observers believe this will lead Tehran to continue funding Hezbollah to provide it with the operational ability to strike on Iran's behalf.[54]

There is no doubt that Iran has played a major role in Hezbollah's rise from a disorganized militia to a powerful politico-military force in Lebanon, although Tehran's influence has waxed considerably since the death of Khomeini. Khamenei lacks the same currency with Hezbollah's leadership and "although in theory Khameini has the final say, his role appears to be more subtle," never overruling a single decision made by the Consultative Council.[55] His influence via Hezbollah is *de jure* rather than *de facto* and as his approval has been reduced to little more than a rubber stamp.

The relationship between Iran and Hezbollah is based on a shared ideology and a financial backing that provides Hezbollah with both money and weapons to ensure that Israel must account for the threat on its border. But despite Iranian largesse, Hezbollah does not take orders from Tehran nor does it operate at the behest of the Iranian government, the *Pasdaran*, or the Supreme Leader.[56] Most experts agree that Iran had no operational involvement with the planning and execution of Hezbollah's 2006 conflict with Israel.[57] Still, after observing the popularity that the battle generated for Hezbollah throughout the region, the Iranians were quick to take credit. More recently, Israel's Prime Minister Benjamin Netanyahu has accused Iran of using Hezbollah to strike at Israeli targets abroad, including the July 2012 suicide bombing of a Bulgarian bus that killed five Israeli tourists.[58] Other attacks have been thwarted in locales as diverse as Cyprus, Kenya, India, Thailand, and Georgia.

Unfolding events in Syria will undoubtedly affect Hezbollah. Syria has served as the main conduit for Iranian arms passing into Hezbollah-controlled Lebanese territory. Moreover, Syria has worked tirelessly behind the scenes to manipulate Lebanese internal political dynamics from 1992 until 2005, when Syria was forced minimize its presence in Lebanon following the assassination of Lebanese Prime Minister Rafiq Hariri in February 2005.[59] Up until the 2005 Cedar Revolution in Lebanon, Syria relied on Hezbollah and to a lesser extent the Lebanese government to further its regional policy objectives, especially as these related to countering Israeli hegemony in the Middle East.[60]

WHAT HEZBOLLAH ACHIEVED WITH THESE FUNDS

Through its reliance on the gray and dark economies, Hezbollah has grown both its operational and organizational capabilities. On the operational side, such a vast war chest has allowed Hezbollah to purchase the newest arms, munitions, and technologies; operate a sophisticated intelligence network; train its recruits; and control precious territory. The group's organizational capabilities have been bolstered by its bank account as well. Leadership, ideology, human resources (to include recruitment), and media have all received a boost from a steady flow of funding.

Hezbollah is unique because it is such a richly resourced organization. This embarrassment of riches has allowed Hezbollah to create an extensive social services network throughout Lebanon, build a sophisticated political party complete with its own media wing, and maintain an arsenal of high-tech weaponry that affords it the ability to conduct terrorist attacks abroad or stand its own against Israel, the most feared military force in the region.

Operational Capabilities

Throughout much of its existence, Hezbollah has enjoyed state support not only from one regional power, but from two. In the history of insurgencies, this arrangement is rare, and it is one of the main reasons why the group has established itself as a major force in Lebanon. Syria and Iran have provided Hezbollah with a wide range of resources, including sanctuary, intelligence, training, organizational aid, financing, and weapons. The Lebanese diaspora communities in Latin America, West Africa, and Southeast Asia have also given Hezbollah financial support and a transnational intelligence gathering capability. These communities abroad have been linked to organized crime, with funds sent from Ciudad del Este, Abidjan, and Bangkok back to Beirut.

Weapons

In Lebanon, Hezbollah relied on resourcefulness and Iranian sponsorship to keep its arsenal current. Besides making Hezbollah more lethal, weapons and matériel were a resource that helped sustain the group since the early 1980s, contributed to its victory over intra-Lebanese rivals, made the group a more versatile threat, and had a major psychological impact on Israel. In his assessment of Hezbollah's performance in the July 2006 battle with Israel, Andrew Exum writes, "Hezbollah trained on, maintained, and used all of its weapons systems in a skilled and disciplined manner."[61] Hezbollah's stockpile of Russian made, wire-guided and laser-guided antitank missiles even managed to destroy Israel's most modern tank, the Merkava.[62]

More than 500 Hezbollah arms caches are thought to exist in southern Lebanon alone.[63] Without the largesse of weapons and matériel shipped into Beirut from Damascus and Tehran, Hezbollah might not have "prevailed" in its quest to achieve ascendancy *within* Lebanon itself. The group boasts a diverse armory that allows it to function as a guerilla group or a small-scale conventional army. Besides small arms proficiency, Hezbollah is comfortable with explosives—both smaller, improvised explosive devices or large truck bombs. In southern Lebanon, insurgents would detonate homemade claymore mines containing nails and antipersonnel ball bearings to great effect, a tactic that was adopted by Shia insurgents in Iraq.[64] In addition to what looks like a typical weapon inventory for insurgents, Hezbollah has obtained plenty of "toys," such as global positioning systems, advanced aircraft analysis and design software, stun guns, nitrogen cutters, naval equipment, ultrasonic dog repelling equipment, and laser range finders.[65]

While most insurgent groups learn how to use guerilla techniques, not many evolve into forces fully capable of fighting as a conventional military able to master so many different kinds of weapons. In its July 2006 battle with Israel, Hezbollah skillfully employed a bevy of weapons systems, including: small arms (AK-47s, M-16s, and M-4 carbine rifles), short range (0–25 km) surface-to-surface rockets (122 millimeter katyusha), mid-range (>25 km) surface-to-surface rockets ("extended-range katyushas, Fajr-3, Uragan, Fajr-5, Khaibar-1, and Zelzal-2), shore-to-ship missiles (C-701, C-802 Noor), unmanned aerial vehicles (Mirsad-1), and antitank missiles (RPG-29, AT-13 Metsis-M, AT-4 Spigot, AT-3 Sagger, TOW, AT-5 Spandrel, AT-14 Kornet-E).[66] Most of these weapons were made in Russia, Syria, and China. Mimicking Israel's worst kept secret regarding its nuclear weapons, Hezbollah currently maintains a policy of "strategic ambiguity" about its antiaircraft capabilities, declining to confirm or deny the possession of advanced Scud missiles in its replenished arsenal.[67]

Intelligence

In Hezbollah's ongoing conflict with Israel, its intelligence network proved to be one of its most valuable assets, especially as the organization evolved over time. In southern Lebanon, the group developed an informal intelligence gathering network that complemented its official intelligence apparatus, modeled after the Iranian Ministry of Intelligence and Security (MOIS). Hezbollah's intelligence network was critical to its success against Israel in four main ways: operations security (OPSEC), infiltration and subversion, surveillance and reconnaissance, and psychological operations (PSYOP).

Through meticulous intelligence gathering and a sophisticated PSYOP campaign, Hezbollah waged a war of attrition using "persuasion, communication, and the shaping of perception," in addition to a range of guerilla tactics aimed at wearing down the Israelis.[68] In a direct attempt to attenuate Israel Defense Forces (IDF) morale and influence both Israeli government policymakers and the Israeli public, al-Manar ran a series titled "Who Is Next?" in reference to the daily segments showing soldiers being killed, while some footage revealed IDF troops retreating from Hezbollah attacks.[69] Hezbollah encouraged beleaguered South Lebanese Army (SLA) fighters to abandon their units and used them as "a source of invaluable military, political, and psychological information" in its effort to persuade Israel to withdraw.[70] By the late 1990s, SLA field intelligence operatives were selling maps to Hezbollah insurgents that detailed

IDF positions and routes to navigate minefields, in addition to information about SLA operations.[71]

The bulk of Hezbollah's intelligence responsibilities were directed by Imad Mughniyeh, who served as a bodyguard to Fadlallah and spent his early years with a specialized unit known as Fatah Force 17. Mugniyeh was a major player in Hezbollah's Special Security Apparatus (SSA). The SSA was comprised of the central security apparatus, the preventative security apparatus, and an overseas security apparatus. Mughniyeh relied on subversion to attack the Israelis from within, sowing seeds of doubt throughout the ranks of the SLA, crippling its ability to operate effectively within Lebanon.

As an insurgent force, Hezbollah dedicated its intelligence manpower to surveillance and reconnaissance, constantly watching IDF troops and movements, while simultaneously trying to avoid the ubiquitous eye of Israeli unmanned aerial vehicles (UAVs) and other high-tech equipment like ground surveillance radar, infrared sensors, and motion detectors. Hezbollah also sent militants to conduct auxiliary reconnaissance missions inside Israel in preparation for potential attacks.[72] Hezbollah is widely known to have developed a robust knowledge of critical infrastructure targets inside Israel, including a network of gas and electricity installations throughout the country.[73]

Operations security is an internal security mechanism that requires a high level of intelligence capabilities to function effectively. The goal is to obfuscate the identities of the individuals and plans for a single or a series of attacks. Iran's MOIS worked with Hezbollah's SSA on the most important aspects of operational security. Among these were assisting insurgents with concealing their identity while traveling abroad, procuring a host of critical resources (weapons, fake identity papers, money), and connecting insurgents with various "fixers" who acted as local liaisons.[74]

If COIN force intelligence can infiltrate or "flip" members of the insurgents' inner circle, it can strike a mighty blow at the resolve of the insurgents. To prevent this, Hezbollah has worked to form an "iron-clad security matrix," whose foundation is an encyclopedic collection of materials on all past, present, and new members of the group's internal security branch.[75] Rules are enforced by the ruthless Engagement and Coordination Unit, led at one time by Wafic Safa, a participant in the negotiations surrounding several prisoner exchanges with Israel.[76]

Hezbollah's intelligence capabilities matured as the insurgency progressed, despite Israel's earnest attempts to defeat the insurgents through military force. Hezbollah's ability to innovate on the battlefield is a direct byproduct of its vast and sophisticated intelligence-gathering network.[77] With Syrian and Iranian assistance, Hezbollah has transformed itself from a poorly-organized militia into a functioning army with the ability to attack with an array of weapons, from plastic explosives to antitank missiles. Counterintelligence became one of the organization's strongpoints, as members of its internal security forces grew into experts at identifying and removing infiltrators and ensuring secrecy within the group. In a nod to Israel's SIGINT capabilities, the insurgents eschewed even encrypted phone calls.[78] Focusing on subversion and infiltration, the group has at times even utilized Israeli uniforms and ammunition.[79]

Sanctuary, Safe Haven, and Operational Space

On July 18, 2012, a bus bombing in Bulgaria killed seven people, including five Israeli tourists. Hezbollah has been implicated in the attack in Burgas, a Black Sea resort town. The attack in Bulgaria is reflective of a wider trend—Hezbollah attacks outside of the Middle East, with other attempts occurring in Cyprus, Greece, and Thailand.[80] Perhaps even more troubling, the al-Quds Force, which is an elite unit within Iran's Revolutionary Guard Corps, has been working closely with Hezbollah even as it has planned its own attacks on diplomatic personnel in both India and the United States. Still, Hezbollah's transnational activities are nothing new. Indeed, the group has maintained a vast overseas network of operatives and associates, spanning the globe from South America to West Africa.

Following the deadly truck bombings in Argentina in 1992 and 1994, respectively, the tri-border area in South America where Paraguay, Argentina, and Brazil converge received far greater scrutiny.[81] This veritable "no-man's land" was long known as a place where Hezbollah operatives conducted business.[82] Following the attacks in Argentina, many Hezbollah members left South America and resettled in West Africa.[83] This region of Africa, long an ungoverned chunk of territory in its own right, is home to hundreds of thousands of Lebanese Shia Muslims, who provided Hezbollah members with a natural constituency and even some familial connections.[84]

In addition to the long established connections and networks of Lebanese traders in the region, West Africa is an ideal place for terrorists, insurgents, and criminals to engage in illicit activities without too much concern for law enforcement. The countries of West Africa are characterized by weak governments, little oversight, high levels of corruption, and porous borders. Formerly Liberia and currently Guinea-Bissau have been run as criminal states.

Since the mid-1980s, Hezbollah has enjoyed a diverse funding stream that includes both state-sponsored largesse and organized criminal activities. This diversity of funding is one of the main reasons why the group has established itself as a major force in Lebanon and a regional player across the wider Middle East. Syria and Iran have provided Hezbollah with a wide range of resources, including sanctuary, intelligence, training, organizational aid, financing, and weapons. The Lebanese diaspora communities throughout West Africa have also given Hezbollah financial support and a transnational intelligence gathering capability.

Since the implosion of the Syrian state and as a result of the austere economic sanctions levied against Iran for its continuing nuclear program, Hezbollah has been forced to look abroad for funding, particularly to the group's extensive network in West Africa. "The Party of God" maintains a significant presence in several West African nations, including Cote D'Ivoire, Senegal, Benin, Liberia, Sierra Leone, Guinea, and the Democratic Republic of Congo (DRC). Within these communities, Hezbollah members engage in an array of criminal activities, ranging from narcotics trafficking to gem smuggling to fund-raising to fraud and extortion.

Training

When it emerged in the early 1980s, Hezbollah was nothing more than an inchoate collection of Shia militants that had broken off from similar organization like Amal and the al-Da'wa party.[85] To help the organization develop, guidance was provided by the al-Quds (Jerusalem) Force of the Iranian Revolutionary Guards Corps (IRGC).[86] A group of 1500 Guards were dispatched to Lebanon to provide matériel support and train Shia militias in areas of recruitment, ideological inculcation, and military training.[87] These lessons also included how to conduct effective reconnaissance, gather intelligence, and suicide bombing tactics.[88] The training provided to Hezbollah by the IRGC not only drastically improved Hezbollah's operational capacity, but it also allowed Hezbollah to reach a level of expertise where its members could then train other terrorist groups, to include Hamas and the PIJ.

The IRGC contingent sent to train Hezbollah's aspiring insurgents trained the militants in a range of guerilla tactics and also taught some members how to properly utilize sophisticated weapons systems, including the BGM-71 TOW missile.[89] In the Bekaa region, 20 Iranian training officers of the IRGC, each a specialist in a different aspect of guerilla warfare, bestowed upon the Hezbollah members their knowledge of infiltration techniques, explosives, hit-and-run ambush style tactics, and range of counterintelligence methods.[90]

The main point about the training provided by the IRGC is that "Hezbollah members did not need to develop their own learning process; lessons were simply handed to them."[91] This meant that Hezbollah's learning curve would not be as steep as it was for other insurgent groups and in effect, the insurgents would not be forced to struggle through difficult setbacks before reaching a high level of efficiency.[92]

Part of the reason why the IRGC's training worked so effectively was because the Iranian trainers and the Hezbollah fighters would assess each mission after it was conducted. Studying after action reports is critical in warfare because when possible, it allows combat units to figure out what went wrong and what went right and then take the steps necessary to fix their mistakes. "Some of the more battle-hardened and seasoned fighters assessed each mission with their Iranian advisers to bolster the degree of surprise and effectiveness in preparation" for the next attack, according to Magnus Ranstorp.[93] The Iranian-led training camps throughout Lebanon became a "matrix of crucial guidance" and centers of learning that taught tactical agility and innovation.[94]

Organizational Capabilities

During its entire existence, Hezbollah has only been led by two individuals—Abbas al Musawi (assassinated by Israel in February 1992) and Hassan Nasrallah. To be fair, Iran retains a generous amount of influence with the Hezbollah leadership and the Islamic Republic's Supreme Leader Ali Khamenei is still revered as Hezbollah's "official" *marji al-taqlid*, or source of emulation. Other highly respected and learned Shia religious scholars including Iraq's Ayatollah Ali al-Sistani and Lebanon's Ayatollah Muhammad Hussein Fadlallah also hold sway within the inner circles of Hezbollah. Yet, even as current Hezbollah Secretary-General Hassan Nasrallah settles into his role as an "international celebrity," and thus muscles his way into gaining more autonomy from Tehran, the Iranian leadership continues to be a major part of the story of Hezbollah.[95]

Leadership

Unraveling the web of influence in Lebanese Hezbollah is not a straightforward process. Due to the extent of Iranian influence, it is difficult to identify whether it is Iranian mullahs who wield the most power, organic Lebanese Hezbollah party members, or revered Shia clerics from Iraq whose directives guide the course of the organization. Moreover, the legitimacy of different individuals has ebbed and flowed over the group's 30-year existence. The grassroots appeal of Hezbollah in Lebanese society has paved the way for "disproportionate weight in the party's decision-making process to members of the leadership who hold hard-line views on both social and political matters."[96] While certain leaders hold more austere views than others, Muhammad Ra'id, the head of Hezbollah's Political Council and a member of the group's Decision-Making Council, believes that Hezbollah members are best classified along a non-ideological continuum ranging from "flexibility and realism" to "less flexibility and less realism."[97]

Sayeed Hassan Nasrallah was elected secretary-general of Hezbollah in 1992 and has since become not only the most recognizable face of the group, but among the most influential and prominent Islamic leaders in the entire Middle East. As secretary-general, Nasrallah has been described as "an extraordinarily shrewd leader" who has sacrificed greatly for Hezbollah, to include losing his oldest son in a battle with the IDF.[98] Other caricatures of Nasrallah depict him as an "ingenious marketer" who "makes smart decisions" and holds an "almost erotic appeal" for his many followers throughout the region.[99] Nasrallah is credited with guiding Hezbollah's ideological shift over the years, which has been marked by "flexibility and adaptability," effectively allowing the group to "expand its base of support and sink deeper roots into Lebanese society."[100] Hezbollah expert Magnus Ranstorp has closely followed Nasrallah's ideological evolution during his tenure as secretary-general and believes that Hezbollah's "Lebanonization process" has been a major factor in the pragmatism characterizing this transformation.[101] Among the major changes that Hezbollah has undergone while under Nasrallah's tutelage are a tighter relationship with the Asad regime in Syria and occasional cooperation with erstwhile rival Amal. But even though Nasrallah has softened many of his "hard-line views," his reign has also overseen an increase in "resistance" activities directed against Israel.[102]

From his earliest days, Nasrallah has been a consistent advocate of attacking Israel. This resistance has included capturing Israeli soldiers, launching so-called "martyrdom operations," continuing to pursue conflict in the Sheba Farms area of the Golan Heights, and most recently, the July 2006 war against Israel that brought death and destruction to both sides. His undying enmity toward Israel has not softened since one of his earliest public interviews in which he declared that "Our strategy is to build a future for ourselves through confrontation with the Zionist enemy."[103] Despite Nasrallah's hard-line vis-à-vis Israel, this has not precluded him from adopting a softer stance in regard to Hezbollah's participation in the Lebanese political system. Frederic Wehrey observes, "[a]lthough previously supportive of a more militant, non-participatory role for Hezbollah in the late 1980s, Nasrallah came to accept the realities of the Lebanese political system."[104]

Hezbollah's secretary-general has repeatedly stressed that while the group would respond to Lebanon's domestic concerns with pragmatism and flexibility, its resistance activities "would constitute Hezbollah's non-negotiable priority, potentially in perpetuity."[105] And while Nasrallah's open defiance has indeed earned him the status of an "international celebrity," it has also invited a steady stream of criticism from prominent Lebanese voices. Following the July 2006 war against Israel, Gibran Tueni, the publisher of Lebanon's leading newspaper asked: "Who authorized Nasrallah to represent all the Lebanese, to make decisions for them and to embroil them in something they do not want to be embroiled in? Did Nasrallah appoint himself secretary general of the whole Arab world?"[106] But although opinion throughout Lebanon and the Arab world may remain divided on the appeal of Hezbollah's secretary-general, he undeniably remains a symbol of strength, defiance, and resistance to the West, as evidenced by the posters seen throughout the region that bear his image along with other populist leaders like Venezuela's Hugo Chavez and Iran's Mahmoud Ahmadenijad.[107]

Ideology

From the beginning, Hezbollah militants and their Iranian handlers adhered to an ideological worldview stemming from the shared experience of clerical training and religious study in the Shia seminaries of Najaf, Iraq. This ideological fervor encompassed three uncompromising elements, including a belief in Shia Islam, the supreme rule of the *wilayat al-faqih,* and a duty to practice *jihad,* or struggle in the name of Allah.[108] The main point here is that from day one, Hezbollah militants were dogmatic in their devotion to the austere version of Shia Islam being exported by Ayatollah Khomeini and his inner circle. Nevertheless, IRGC units provided the nascent movement with ideological guidance to reinforce these beliefs and urged Hezbollah's core membership to adhere to strict Islamic behavior while adopting an "anti-Zionist" platform that still defines the group to this day.[109] This "ideological indoctrination" was a deliberate campaign aimed at recruiting and training radical Shia throughout the Bekaa Valley.[110]

Hezbollah's ideology has been described as "a fiery mix of revolutionary Khomeinism, Shia nationalism, celebration of martyrdom, and militant anti-Zionism, occasionally accompanied by crude, neofascist anti-Semitism."[111] Its ideological approach is epitomized by Nasrallah, whose ability to preach in various terms—religious, nationalist, Arab, anti-Israeli—is an effective means to rally supporters to Hezbollah's cause.[112] As Norton observes, "ideological currents have shifted dramatically in the last two decades in favor of Hezbollah, which offers an ideological vision that many Shia now find persuasive."[113]

Not only does the group look to the teachings of the late Ayatollah Ruholla Khomeini for inspiration, but many scholars believe that Hezbollah is actually more faithful to the legacy of the Islamic Revolution than are most ordinary Iranians themselves. But not all experts agree on Iran's role in shaping Hezbollah's ideology. For example, As'ad Abu Khalil argues that it is "inaccurate" to describe Hezbollah as an Iranian creation and that the group's ideological platform is the product of the "Islamization" of Marxist-Leninist doctrine and theory.[114] Still, even a cursory glance at Hezbollah's founding charter as captured in its 1985 open letter addressed to the "Downtrodden in Lebanon and in the World," reveals language heavily colored by the Iranian revolution.[115] Indeed, Hezbollah's ideological links to Iran have helped shape the group's stance on the nature of conflict, the ideal character of the nation-state, how to relate to other Muslims, and finally, its overall approach to dealing with the West.[116]

Hezbollah's outlook can be considered binary. This ideological partition divides the world between the exploited and the exploiters, or the oppressed (*mustad'afin*) and the oppressors (*mustakbirin*).[117] This dichotomy attempts to convey the dualism and millenarianism of the Shia community which views itself as a perpetual underdog in its struggle to achieve equality and justice.[118] In Hezbollah's worldview, oppression takes many forms, including economic, cultural, political, and social and transcends both nationality and religion.[119] The central tenets of Hezbollah's charter include the obligations to struggle against secularism, injustice, and the oppression of the *ummah* by foreign imperialists, especially America and Israel.[120] In the words of Nasrallah's deputy Sheikh Na'im Qaseem, "even if hundreds of years should pass by, Israel's existence will continue to be an illegal existence."[121] According to Hezbollah's ideology, the mere existence of Israel is anathema.[122]

Human Resources and Recruitment

The Iranian Revolutionary Guards Corps dispatched to Lebanon was tasked with the difficult mission of creating something from nothing. The leadership in Tehran sought to cultivate a terrorist proxy that would remain faithful to the tenets of the Islamic Revolution while also serving as a strike force capable of carrying out Iran's dirty work yet affording the mullahs, who were often several steps removed, the luxury of plausible deniability. Israel's invasion of Lebanon in 1982 may have provided the impetus for Shia fighters to band together, but benefits helped too. IRGC members organized a comprehensive recruiting drive, which included a monthly stipend and other financial incentives such as subsidized education and no cost medical treatment for fighters and their families.[123]

Imad Mughniyeh functioned as the go-between among various factions of the organization and its associates. One of his main areas of effort was recruiting Lebanese expatriates abroad and preparing them for terrorist operations inside of Israel.[124] Highly prized recruits included anyone with foreign language skills, a "Western looking appearance," or a European passport, which would make international travel much less onerous. Much like Al-Qaida does today, Mugniyeh attempted to recruit foreign nationals who had converted Islam and could be thoroughly vetted and indoctrinated by the group. These individuals would be used for myriad purposes, from suicide attacks to auxiliary reconnaissance. According to Ranstorp, Germany was one of Mugniyeh's favorite recruiting spots. For missions that involved infiltrating Israel, he sought to build a network of Israeli Arabs.[125]

Hezbollah is a prominent example of an insurgent group that enjoys a significant amount of popular support, both domestically and within the wider Arab and Islamic world. Hezbollah's main base of support is located in three general areas: Beirut and its surrounding environs; southern Lebanon; and the Bekaa Valley/Hirmil Region.[126] Support for Hezbollah in Lebanon is apparent by its role as a major political player in Lebanon, as the group continues to consolidate power.[127] Anecdotal evidence from newspapers and journal articles suggests that Hezbollah is perhaps more popular than ever before.

In an effort to quantify this support, Simon Haddad of Notre Dame University in Jounieh, Lebanon has conducted comprehensive survey research to unearth the reasons for the group's "rock 'n roll" like status. Haddad's study concludes that the Party of God is so beloved in the Shia community for its adherence to religious piety and the social aspects of Islam. Furthermore, the majority of respondents polled held positive views toward the growth of the organization and its use of force, while backing Hezbollah's refusal to disarm in accordance with United Nations Security Council Resolution 1559.[128]

According to a World Public Opinion.org poll conducted in August 2006, support for Hezbollah was measured as the following: 96 percent of Shias, 87 percent of Sunnis, 80 percent of Christians, and 80 percent of Druze.[129] Hezbollah's popularity should come as little surprise. In contrast to other political parties and even the Lebanese state, Hezbollah provides a wide range of social services at little or no cost to the community. Hezbollah offers a "vast network of womb-to-tomb services" including hospitals, schools, orphanages, and credit programs.[130] In the absence of the state's ability to provide for all of its citizens, Hezbollah has filled the void and come to the rescue of the oft-neglected Shia community of southern Lebanon.[131] The Lebanese government has welcomed these efforts in recognition that they are required for domestic stability. Several scholars have found that when an insurgent group is the only provider of goods and services in an area, support for these organizations is higher than in areas where multiple entities supply services.[132]

These programs can be divided between large service providers and smaller, more specifically targeted outreach efforts.[133] Some of the larger services include JAB, or Construction Jihad, and the Islamic Health Committee (IHC), both opened in 1984. Three years later, in 1987, the Relief Committee of Imam Khomenei (RCIK) was opened in the Hrat Hreik section of the southern suburbs around Beirut.[134] The Relief Committee was responsible for the creation of an employment office as well as the formation of several technical trade institutes, including those open to women. These services, in addition to many others throughout Lebanon, receive funding from Iran. In the early years, Hezbollah reportedly received between five and ten million dollars a month, although Jaber suggests that it is possible that the figures are higher.[135] The funding has decreased over time, but financing from Iran is still considered a major resource for Hezbollah, which uses the money to maintain its ubiquitous social welfare infrastructure.

Media, PR, Propaganda, and Publicity

Hezbollah transmitted the first broadcast of its television station Al-Manar ("The Beacon") in 1991 and began regularly scheduled broadcasts a mere three years later. Al-Manar is also known as *Qanat Al-Moqawama*, or the Station of Resistance, and serves a critical function as the main dissemination point for Hezbollah news and propaganda. In addition to Al-Manar, Hezbollah maintains an extensive media operation that includes Al-Nur Radio, *Al-Intiqad Weekly Journal, Baqiatollah Islamic Magazine*, as well as a network of over 50 Web sites that operate in several languages, including English, French, German, and Arabic.[136] Al-Manar is not just a Lebanese phenomenon. Rather, its popularity has facilitated its growth into one of the leading news organizations of the Arab world. The station broadcasts worldwide via satellite and runs on an annual budget of roughly $15 million.[137]

Insurgency is armed politics, and a large part of politics is disseminating a favorable message to a target audience. Hezbollah's propaganda operations are sophisticated enough to allow for a two-pronged approach. The group targets both the "enemy audience" (Israel) and a "neutral audience." The main themes directed toward Israel are Hezbollah's unremitting resolve and determination to continue the fight; the notion that this conflict will be a long struggle; the futility of Israeli aggression; the quagmire of the conflict; the well-defined political aim of Hezbollah's cause; and finally, guilt-induced messages geared toward exploiting sympathetic Israelis, both citizens and soldiers alike.[138] To the neutrals, Hezbollah's propaganda reinforces the portrait of the Israelis as foreign occupiers intent on sullying Islam and occupying Muslim lands. Furthermore, Hezbollah attempts to convince neutral audiences that Hezbollah alone is the most legitimate entity in Lebanon and the only force capable of regaining Lebanon's sovereignty following decades of war and occupation.

Just as impressive as Hezbollah's television and video production is the group's extensive use of new media and information technologies, including its widespread presence on the Internet.[139] Nasrallah has his own personal Web site, complete with archives of his speeches and a photo gallery divided into various sections, including: military operations, Lebanese brigade, Islamic resistance, Al-Aqsa intifada attacks, Qana massacre, Mansoura massacre, and "other massacres." On Hezbollah-run Web sites, the term *Israel* is always placed in quotation marks and Israelis are frequently referred to as Nazis.

The content available on Hezbollah's Web sites is a reflection of the group's diverse agenda and includes: news and information, welfare and social services, religious indoctrination, personal information of Hezbollah leaders, anti-Israeli content, bulletin boards, and youth-oriented features.[140] Targeting youth is a bald attempt at recruitment. In 2010, to further its effort toward engaging the younger generation, Hezbollah developed an online video game application where players wage a war against Hezbollah's enemies, mainly the Israelis. Before the game begins, a player takes rounds of target practice against a lineup of well-known Israeli politicians.[141] The two primary Hezbollah-run Web sites are www.hizbollah.org and www.ghaliboun.net. When Israeli hackers interrupted service on these Web sites during the July 2006 war, Hezbollah's own hackers hijacked communication portals of companies, cable providers, and web-hosting servers in south Texas, suburban Virginia, as well as Delhi, Montreal, Brooklyn, and New Jersey.[142]

HOW HEZBOLLAH FINANCING WAS COUNTERED

Hezbollah's finances have been targeted by a number of countries, most prominently the United States and Israel. But going after Hezbollah's funding stream is not sufficient. To truly curtail Hezbollah's ability to operate, it is also necessary to target Iran, Syria, the Lebanese diaspora, and if necessary, segments of the Lebanese government and the Lebanese population (seeking to change the behavior of each entity). By targeting Iran directly, Hezbollah is being targeted by extension.

Still, Israel has relied in part, perhaps there has even been an overreliance, on kinetic force to disrupt Hezbollah operations. While seductive for their ability to solve short-term problems, kinetic actions like air strikes (especially in south Lebanon) merely play into Hezbollah's favor. After property is destroyed in Hezbollah territory, the group comes in with JAB and gets to play the role of "hero," thus further solidifying popular support for Nasrallah and his organization. Indeed, rather than targeted assassinations, Israel could also benefit from focusing on targeted sanctions against Hezbollah's patchwork of quasi-licit and illicit ventures.

Kinetic Activities

Operation Smokescreen was an FBI intelligence investigation (overseen by the Bureau's International Terrorism Operations Section) conducted in the mid-1990s that involved running sources and tapping phone lines. For the most part, the operation was a success, and resulted in criminal charges for 26 individuals accused of contraband cigarette trafficking, money laundering, racketeering, wire fraud, conspiracy, visa and marriage fraud, and material support to a terrorist group. Over 500 bank and credit card accounts were investigated as part of the financial analysis of the network.[143]

Operation Double Top was the direct result of the 1994 bombings of the Asociación Mutual Israelita Argentina (AMIA) bombings in Argentina. The operation brought together law enforcement and intelligence agencies from the United States and the tri-border countries, Argentina, Paraguay, and Brazil. To counter Hezbollah's financial activities in the region, Operation Double Top focused on disrupting commercial operations, burning containers, blocking bank accounts, stealing passports, and arresting Hezbollah members in the area.[144]

In October 1998, Philippine intelligence officials launched CoPlan Pink Poppy, aimed at identifying members of Al-Qaida's network in Southeast Asia. The operations came about as the result of a request by France that the Filipinos look into connections between Al-Qaida and Hezbollah.[145] Though the operation was terminated in 2000 due to a lack of funding, it was rejuvenated post-9/11 under the name Operation Kamikaze. The Operation centered around Hezbollah operative Pandu Yudhawinata, one of the group's key facilitators, especially with respect to growing its network throughout Southeast Asia, from Thailand to the Philippines.

Operation Bathwater was conducted to disrupt Hezbollah activities based in Michigan and grew out of information developed in January 1999 by U.S. Secret Service agents working with the Detroit Joint Terrorism Task Force (JTTF). Another operation focused on the financial element of Hezbollah's criminal enterprise in the United States, Bathwater uncovered the largest credit card fraud scheme in the country at the time.[146]

Non-kinetic Activities

In late 2004, the United States joined with Brazil, Paraguay, and Argentina to form the 3 + 1 Group on Tri-Border Area security, which focused on countering Hezbollah activity in the area, strengthening Paraguay's legal system, as well as the enforcement of immigration and customs laws.[147] Cooperation between the United States and the nations comprising the tri-border area has helped to diminish important funding streams to Hezbollah.[148] Targeted sanctions have also played an important role amongst the non-kinetic activities that countries have taken to counter Hezbollah financing. According to a report by the Congressional Research Service (CRS), the United States has used official terrorist designations and listings to impose financial and immigration sanctions on Hezbollah and its supporters, blocking assets under U.S. jurisdiction, prohibited American citizens from providing the group with financial or material support or engaging in financial transactions with Hezbollah and affiliated parties, and has prohibited entry into the United States and authorization of deportation for Hezbollah associated individuals.[149]

In addition to designating certain organizations as terrorist groups, individual members of those groups can be isolated for targeting. In June 2004, the U.S. Treasury Department designated Assad Ahmad Barakat, Hezbollah's treasurer in South America, as a "key terrorist financier" and someone "who has used every financial crime in the book, including his businesses, to generate funding" for Hezbollah.[150] More recently, in July 2013, the European Union designated Hezbollah as a terrorist organization, essentially blacklisting the group and freezing many of its assets throughout Europe, which in the past has served as a financial conduit for "the Party of God."[151] The move came after years of prodding by both the United States and Israel, as those countries realize the importance of collaboration in countering terrorists' finances. As Philippone notes, "success against Hezbollah's crime network will take significant interagency efforts and the ability of multiple organizations to share information and work together. Continuous legislative pressure will be needed to push law enforcement, intelligence and other government agencies to work together against a common enemy."[152]

CONCLUSION

Hezbollah is a unique insurgent group to analyze because of its truly hybrid nature. It is, without a doubt, part political party and part "army without a state." Why did Hezbollah choose the path toward "Lebanonization" in the first place and make a foray into politics if it never intended to make the full transition to political party? The short answer is, because it could. Hezbollah's decision to enter the Lebanese political system was not a default decision, but one that was debated at length within the group.[153] The rationale behind the decision was the following: by entering the political process, Hezbollah would become a legitimate actor in Lebanese politics. If the group was legitimate, then so was its continued resistance.[154]

At the time that Hezbollah made the decision, the group's political leverage over the Lebanese government, due in large part to Syrian backing, allowed it to stand for elections without having to jettison its weapons. Just two years removed from a decade and a half long civil war, the Lebanese Armed Forces (LAF) were in the process of being reconstructed. Hezbollah's operational tools, including its training, intelligence, *and* weapons, meant that it was the only Lebanese entity capable of defending the south of the country, which in 1992 was still occupied by the IDF (and would continue to be for another eight years). Moreover, unlike the nascent LAF, as a military force, Hezbollah was willing to take casualties defending Lebanon.

Still, joining the political process was not without its cost to the Party of God. In exchange for entrance into Lebanese politics, Hezbollah agreed to alter its objectives to achieve its domestic political goals. This included pursuing a more moderate political agenda, honoring the post-Taif confessional system, softening its rhetoric, and working with the majority government parties on a range of issues.[155] The most obvious concession Hezbollah made was to abandon its aspirations of remaking Lebanon into an Islamic republic ruled by *sharia* law. A further price to pay for achieving status as an opposition party within the government was the agreement not to use violence for domestic political purposes. Hezbollah's continued resistance against Israel in the zone of occupation was officially recognized as legitimate by the Lebanese government, a point insisted upon by Hezbollah's Syrian overlords.

CHAPTER 5

Hamas: Guns and Glory in Gaza

BACKGROUND

The Islamic Resistance Movement (*Harakat al-Muqawama al-Islamiyya*), or Hamas, emerged in 1987 as a Palestinian offshoot of the Muslim Brotherhood (*Ikhwan*). Hamas was initially welcomed by the Israelis as a counterbalance to Yasser Arafat's PLO,[1] a group that promoted an ideology of aggressive Palestinian nationalism, more worrisome to Tel Aviv throughout the 1970s and 1980s.[2] Perhaps most known for its reliance on suicide bombings, Hamas featured as a violent agitator in both the First Intifada (December 1987–September 1993) and Second Intifada (September 2000–February 2005) against Israel. In 2007, in what has been dubbed the "Battle of Gaza," Hamas clashed with Fatah in a conflict that saw hundreds of Palestinians killed. More recently, Israel has launched several major offensives against Hamas, including Operations Cast Lead during the Gaza War of 2008–2009, Operation Pillar of Defense in 2012, and in 2014 saw the sustained bombing of Gaza during Operation Protective Edge, aimed at destroying Hamas's network of tunnels below its territory.

Hamas relies on support from Iran, especially since the beginning of the Syrian civil war in 2011, which displaced key members of Hamas's leadership structure that had been headquartered in Damascus at the invitation of Bashar al-Assad, despite that country's own fraught history with the Muslim Brotherhood. Hamas raises funds through a variety of efforts, but most lucrative to the group are donations to charities linked to the organization as well as sponsorship from Tehran, which supplies Hamas with money, weapons, training, and equipment.

HOW HAMAS FUNDED ITS ACTIVITIES

By far, Hamas's most sophisticated avenue of raising funds is through the use of charities, while its most lucrative method of financing is external state sponsorship from Iran (this has changed over time, as the group's primary sponsor used to be Saudi Arabia). As Matt Levitt has recognized, Hamas charities and service organizations "provide cover for raising, laundering, and transferring funds, facilitate the group's propaganda and recruitment efforts, provide employment to its operatives, and serve as a logistical support network for its terrorist operations."[3] By 2015, Hamas's fund-raising network has achieved global reach, with the group establishing illicit funding schemes throughout the Middle East, Western Europe, North America, and beyond.

Gray Economy

Hamas's extensive network of charities is directly related to the concept of Da'wa, which is reflected in the group's efforts aimed at constructing an Islamic social welfare infrastructure.[4] While most of the group's financing emanates from the Gulf, the FBI believes that Hamas relies on the United States for a portion of its fund-raising base, in addition to constructing a logistical, propaganda, and military infrastructure in America. In order to avoid laws in the United States aimed at combating Hamas's financial support, the group's sympathizers routinely raised money for Hamas initiatives that made no mention of or has no association with the group's name.[5] Over the years, Hamas has utilized an array of front companies to conceal and launder money which is then used for planning and conducting attacks, as well as for myriad organizational requirements, which have only grown in importance since the group decided to reconsider its stance on participating in elections.

Diaspora Support

Because the Palestinians have lived a somewhat nomadic existence over the past half century, the diaspora is represented throughout the Middle East and Persian Gulf and further abroad from Western Europe to Latin America.[6] Like Hezbollah and Gamaa al-Islamiyah, Hamas has taken advantage of the Muslim diaspora in South America's semi-lawless tri-border area, a region known for money laundering, drug trafficking, and a host of other illicit and unsavory activities.[7] Closer to home, in Palestine and Lebanon, Palestinians in refugee camps support a range of Islamist groups, from Hamas and Islamic Jihad in Palestine to Hezbollah and Jamaa al-Islamiyya in Lebanon.[8] Historically, Palestinian expatriates and Muslim donors living abroad have provided Hamas with funding and support.

Members of Hamas's Political Bureau have received financial support from Palestinian and Muslim communities in both Britain and the United States.[9] In the late 1990s and early 2000s, an alleged Hamas conspirator named Jamal Akal was arrested and accused of receiving training in Gaza to conduct attacks in North America. Akal was instructed by Hamas leadership to rely on the Palestinian diaspora in Canada to help fund his attack, which would require purchasing a weapon and paying for his expenses while he monitored his targets before eventually attacking.[10] Still, the Palestinian diaspora scattered throughout the Middle East remains among the most potent and willing to assist the group, especially with financial support. In an online chat room in late 2001, Rantissi provided an account number for an account at the Arab Bank in Gaza to an individual claiming to be from Bahrain and interested in contributing to the Palestinian jihad.[11]

Charities

A panoply of charities either supports Hamas directly and explicitly or supports a wide range of radical Islamic charities that extend to include Hamas. Money funneled through charities supports a range of critical Hamas functions, including aid to the families of Hamas operatives that are imprisoned, wounded, or killed; the administrative expenses related to the charity offices' infrastructures; provision of social welfare services; and the other day-to-day minutiae that goes with running a complex politico-military organization.

Charities linked to Hamas have been implicated in terrorist attacks abroad, including in Europe. Charities connected to Hamas have been identified in countries including the United Kingdom, the United States, Germany, Denmark, Belgium, the Netherlands, and France, with lesser donations coming from charities in Asia and Africa.[12] In 1993, Hamas operative and Human Relief International employee Mohammad Sa'd Darwishy al-Shazy plotted terror attacks in Croatia against Jewish targets; Hamas militants have been linked to the Philippines for association with Al-Qaida front organizations operating in Manila. The group also has roots in Romania, especially on university campuses.[13]

Hamas does not discriminate between the amounts of donations it accepts. In addition to the millions flowing from wealthy donors and external state actors, Hamas collects donations at the grassroots level, often distributing collection boxes to commercial businesses and mosques. Between 1992 and 2001, the Holy Land Foundation for Relief and Development (HLFRD) collected $57 million and transferred over $6.8 million to Palestinian charities. Transfers to Hamas were around $900,000 in 1997 and as much as $2.4 million by 2000.[14] In 2001, The Holy Land Foundation allegedly funded Hamas activities to the tune of

$13 million, although the organization was shut down by U.S. officials shortly thereafter.[15] That same year, Yassin, founder of the Islamic Center, revealed that Hamas offered payments of between $2 and $3 million to the families of Palestinian suicide bombers.[16]

After the terrorist attacks of September 11, 2001, United States counterterrorism and law enforcement authorities adopted a hard-line with any organizations suspected of involvement with terrorism, whether or not those organizations or terrorist groups directly targeted the United States. Hamas-linked charities received increasing scrutiny. In 2002, a jury in Chicago found the HLFRD and Quranic Literacy Institute liable for the death of David Boim, who was shot by Hamas militants while waiting for a bus in Jerusalem in 1996.[17] In February 2006, the U.S. Treasury blocked the assets of an NGO in Ohio, KindHearts, which was accused of supporting Hamas financially.[18]

Fraud

Hamas, like Al-Qaida, Hezbollah and other militant Islamist groups, has engaged in fraud to raise money for its activities, although revenue raised through fraudulent schemes remains a fairly insignificant portion of its overall operating budget. At various points, Hamas raised money through credit card fraud, cigarette tax fraud, food stamp fraud, and the sale of fraudulent documents.[19] And fund-raising through fraud is not merely relegated to low-ranking members and hangers-on. Following his rather unceremonious exit from Jordan in the late 1990s, Khaled Meshall, a top Hamas commander, was charged with multiple offenses, including fraud.[20]

Hamas members also pursued a number of rackets and schemes to raise money in the United States that would then be sent back to the group's leadership in Gaza. In June 2005, two Dearborn-area men, Ahmad and Musa Jebril, were convicted of mortgage fraud charges after defrauding six banks for $250,000 and dozens of people of up to $400,000.[21] Following the conviction, the Jebrils and another associate were charged with attempting to bribe a member of the jury overseeing their trial.[22]

Legal Businesses

Similar to the charities and fraud-based money generating activities perpetrated by Hamas, the group's legal businesses and front companies are also global in nature. In the tri-border area of South America, Hamas is known to operate through multiple front companies designed to conceal its involvement in a host of illicit revenue generating activities and to launder the proceeds from various fraud schemes and tax evasion efforts.[23] In the United States, top executives of a Richardson, Texas-based Internet company named Infocom were indicted by a federal grand jury on December 18, 2002 for conspiracy to conceal financial transactions for Mousa Abu Marzook, a well-known Hamas commander.[24] Another well-known Hamas front company was the Sunuqrut Global Group,[25] a company owned by Mazen Sunuqrut, a Hamas activist, while still others included the Beit el-Mal Holding company, a public investment company in East Jerusalem; the Al Tadhoman Charitable Association, which owns part of the Yasfa dairy company and the Nablus Mall; the Al-Zakah Committee of Jenin, which runs a local hospital,[26] and the Al-Nubani furniture store, owned at one time by Ahmad Mohammad Abdallah al-Sharuf.[27]

Money Laundering

The extent of Hamas's network of charities, religious organizations, and front companies allows Hamas to launder money that is earned in both the gray and dark economies. Active conflict zones are ideal places for money laundering to occur through charities, because these kinds of organizations do not seem out of place in these areas and the flow of money is one directional. The Rammallah-al-Bireh zakat committee laundered and transferred funds raised in Jordan, Saudi Arabia, UAE, and Qatar through banks, hawalas, and businesses associated with Hamas.[28] When Saddam Hussein offered $25,000 to the families of Palestinian suicide bombers, the money was channeled from Baghdad through banks in Jordan and Ramallah.[29] As discussed above, the Sunuqrut Group was accused of laundering money on behalf of Hamas, as was the Al Ajouli money changing firm.[30] In the aftermath of 9/11, the Al-Aqsa Islamic Bank had its assets frozen after being accused of financing Hamas terrorism.[31] In the mid-2000s, there was serious concern that the Commercial Bank of Syria, state-owned and headquartered in Damascus, was laundering money on behalf of Hamas and several other radical militant groups.[32] More recently, in early 2012, Israel's Shin Bet conducted a probe that connected Chinese banks to the transference of money by Hamas prisoners.[33]

Dark Economy

While it is difficult to discern exactly what percentage of Hamas's funds come via the dark economy versus how much the group earns from the gray economy, in addition to receiving significant amounts of external state support over time, first from Saudi Arabia and more recently from Iran, it is well known that Hamas currently has a robust criminal enterprise that helps fund the organization. As with other criminal groups operating in Latin America's tri-border region, Hamas has insinuated itself into a comfortable position in the area, cemented ties and expanded its network of illicit activities and contacts. While its transnational criminal activities are not as impressive as that of Hezbollah, over the past decade Hamas militants have expanded its criminal portfolio to include a diverse range of income generating activities.

Kidnapping for Ransom (KFR)

While Hamas does engage in kidnapping as a tactic of asymmetric warfare and terrorism, the motive is typically the release of currently imprisoned Hamas members, rather than for financial profit. There is the Ahmed Abu Rish Brigades—a Gaza-based crew of former Fatah members with close ties to Hamas that have abducted foreigners in Gaza and announced ambitions to spread jihad beyond Israel—but overall KFR is not a primary method of Hamas fund-raising.[34] Still, no matter what the motive, kidnapping is still a crime, used by Hamas more as a tool of extortion and intimidation, instead of revenue generation. Indeed, on June 25, 2006, Israeli Sergeant Gilad Shalit, a member of the IDF was kidnapped by Hamas. Shalit was exchanged in October 2011 for 1,027 Palestinians in Israeli jails. The exchange, obviously disproportionate, was hailed as a strategic victory for Hamas by Khaled Meshall.[35] In June 2014, Hamas was accused in the kidnapping (and subsequent murder) of three Israeli teenagers in the West Bank. The incident was a primary factor in leading Israel to launch a 50-day siege of Gaza, partially aimed at destroying Hamas's intricate network of underground tunnels.[36]

Armed Robbery and Theft

Throughout its history, Hamas has been careful not to sully its image in the minds of the Palestinian people. Since Hamas consistently criticizes the Palestinian Authority (PA) as corrupt and guilty of theft, the organization has been very weary of being portrayed as predatory toward its own constituency. While in the United States and elsewhere some Hamas members have profited from the sale of stolen goods and merchandise, including infant formula that is stolen and resold and scams involving grocery coupons, armed robbery and theft in Gaza and the West Bank have been rare. That is, until as recently as March 2011, when Hamas was accused of forcibly removing approximately $250,000 shekels from a PA-backed fund's account.[37] More recently, especially following Israel's summer 2014 Operation Protective Edge, Hamas has been reeling. The group is desperately seeking funds to rebuild the infrastructure in Gaza, so continued disagreements with the PA could lead to similar incidents to the one that played out with the Palestine Investment Bank in 2011, when Hamas's police force demanded the money and threatened resistance would be met with force.

Smuggling, Trafficking, and Counterfeiting

Hamas has profited from the production, smuggling, and sale of tobacco products, including genuine and counterfeit cigarettes, as well as the sale of unlicensed t-shirts and other apparel.[38] In the tri-border area of Latin America, it is well-known that Hamas (perhaps emulating Hezbollah) has established partnerships with various drug trafficking organizations operating in the semi-lawless region.[39] The group has also been involved with drugs in the United States, at least on the margins—a pseudoephedrine smuggling scam in the Midwest involved bank accounts tied to Hamas.[40] Closer to home, Hamas's extensive network of tunnels in Gaza have long served as a primary conduit for weapons smuggling.[41] Another growing concern is the increasing lawlessness of Egypt's Sinai Peninsula, which borders the Gaza Strip. The Sinai remains an ungoverned territory, now used by jihadist organizations to smuggle weapons from looted arsenals in Libya.[42]

Extortion and Protection

Similar to Hamas's view on kidnapping for ransom, criminal activities like extortion and protection are often predatory, aimed at the very communities that are seeking protection. Hamas, unlike its on-again off-again rival Fatah, has largely been unscathed by accusations of extortion and racketeering,[43] although it still does collect *some* money from these practices.[44] In September 2012, an extortion ring responsible for the kidnapping of an Eritrean immigrant was uncovered by Israeli police and involved Hamas members, militants from the Sinai, and four Israelis.[45] Allegations from as recent as July 2014 allege that Hamas leaders, including Ismael Haniyeh, have benefited financially from a 20 percent tax imposed on all goods throughout Hamas-controlled tunnels in Gaza.[46]

External State Support

Prior to September 11th, 2001, Hamas received a significant amount of donations from Saudi Arabia although American pressure on the Saudis has helped to stem the flow of donations to the militant group, still, much of this has been made up from Tehran, now a major state sponsor even though Iran is a Shia nation and Hamas is a Sunni militant group.[47] Before Iran ascended as Hamas's primary sponsor, Saudi Arabia provided approximately 60 to 70 percent of the group's budget.[48] Both the Saudis and Iraqis under Saddam Hussein provided money to the families of Hamas suicide bombers—the former more than $100 million and the latter between $15 and $20 million.[49] The downside to isolating a group like Hamas is that it produces a vacuum which can be filled by countries like Iran. Hamas has gone on record to make it clear that it is open to receiving assistance "from anywhere so long as it comes without conditions that would compromise their principles."[50] During one trip to Iran in the mid-2000s, Ismail Haniyeh was provided with $36 million.[51]

For a long time, Syria was a major supporter (in many ways) but now this is changing drastically. The relationship has changed since the beginning of the Arab Spring. In February 2012 Hamas cut ties with Damascus, which caused tensions between Hamas and Iran.[52] Still, by distancing itself from Assad, Hamas gained the support of anti-Syrian regimes in Turkey and Qatar. When Morsi and the Brotherhood won elections in Egypt, Hamas was enthralled by the potential support now possible from Cairo. However, these hopes were dampened with the July 2013 coup by the Egyptian military and subsequent rule of General Sisi.

WHAT HAMAS ACHIEVED WITH THESE FUNDS

Since it burst on the scene in 1987, Hamas has evolved from an unknown offshoot of the Muslim Brotherhood into a politico-military force in Gaza and the West Bank. In 2002, the group's operating budget was estimated at around $30 million (40 percent from donors in Arab nations; 20 percent from Palestinians in the West Bank and Gaza; 10 percent from Iran; 10–15 percent from donors in the United States; and 15–20 percent from donors in other countries).[53] More recently, estimates place Hamas's per year financial support at $100 million, with speculation that approximately 80 percent of its revenue went to its social services empire while the remaining 20 percent was earmarked for Izz al-Din al-Qassam.[54] With this generous operating budget, Hamas has grown its organization into a lethal hybrid group capable of attacking Israel kinetically, while also boasting robust levels of popular support amongst Palestinians and Muslims throughout the Middle East. Hamas's war chest should also allow the group to weather the perturbations pulsing throughout the region four years after the advent of the Arab Spring, which is responsible for nascent alliances and a shifting balance of power. With greater resources to rely upon, Hamas is well positioned to follow the path of Hezbollah in Lebanon, cementing its status as a popular and organized political bulwark while also continuing to remain the vanguard of Palestinian militarism directed toward Israel.

Operational Capabilities

As Hamas has demonstrated through its lethal use of suicide bombing as an asymmetric tactic, the group is continuously seeking to innovate and devise deadlier methods of attacking its adversaries. And although the group is now synonymous with suicide attacks, according to Byman, "Hamas' military wing, once largely in the business of suicide bombings and cheap mortar attacks, morphed into a regular military force with thousands of troops under arms and more advanced weapons systems."[55] When Hamas demonstrates that it is able to deploy new technology efficiently, this helps the group internally and externally. Internally, the group wins favor among Palestinians for its competence compared with other groups. Externally, it is likely to attract further external assistance. From a public relations, financial, and logistical standpoint, Hamas leaders are wary of drawing the ire of the international community, or of alienating Palestinians, which is partially why the group confines its attacks to Israel, instead of striking out abroad.[56]

Weapons

As the First Intifada drew to a close in 1993, the situation for Hamas was dire—its military wing had a mere twenty machine guns in its arsenal.[57] It was around this time that the group adopted the use of suicide attacks, partially in response to a paucity of weaponry and designed to derail the Oslo talks. The popularity of suicide terrorism by Hamas was also motivated by the Hebron massacre of 1994 when Baruch Goldstein, an Israeli terrorist, shot and killed 28 Muslims at the Ibrahimi Mosque. In addition to the early to mid-1990s, the other main wave of Hamas suicide attacks took place during the Second Intifada, which lasted from September 2000 through December 2005. In March 2002, IDF officials claimed that Hamas tried to include cyanide in its suicide attacks.[58]

Suicide attacks have gained an appeal among Palestinian terrorist groups for three reasons, in particular. First, just as in Lebanon and Sri Lanka, a culture of martyrdom has been established, which glorifies suicide bombers as heroes. Second, suicide attackers only need to plan an infiltration of enemy territory, not an exfiltration. Third, suicide attacks eliminate the risks of capture and interrogation (although suicide attackers rarely have top-level information), evidenced by the fact that leading members of groups rarely, if ever, "martyr themselves" in this way.

Izzadhin al-Qassam, Hamas's military wing, has demonstrated an impressive level of proficiency in constructing bombs and IEDs, although both Kamal Ismail Hafez Kahisl and Muhi a-din Sharif, prominent Hamas members, were killed while preparing homemade explosives.[59] Electrical components and chemical supplies (ammonium nitrate, acetone, and nitrogen glycerin) needed to make a shrapnel-studded suicide vest cost approximately $150.[60] Some leading Hamas members, including Yihye Ayash, a Hamas bomb maker known as "the Engineer," have been responsible for constructing suicide vests at various points in the group's history.

In addition to shootings, grenade, and bomb attacks, Hamas militants are notorious for their use of Qassam rockets. During the 2012 conflagration between Hamas and Israel, the Israelis destroyed nearly all of Hamas's long-range rockets.[61] That Hamas was able to restock its supply to fight the Israelis again, two years later, indicates that Iranian support was generous during the interregnum. The sophistication of Hamas's rockets vary, with some of the more crude versions of the Qassam able to be built on a relatively modest budget (although you usually get what you pay for; inaccurate and malfunctioning). After Israel's assassination of Adnan al-Ghoul, the original architect of the Qassam rocket, Hamas sympathizers like Spanish engineer Marwan Ismail Dahman offered technical assistance to the group in order to redesign an enhanced rocket.[62]

Intelligence

Building a skilled and effective intelligence apparatus takes time and requires extensive resources. For Hamas, the sense of urgency is exacerbated by the range of adversaries arrayed against the group. The intelligence requirements for dealing with Israel are much different from the challenges associated with Fatah or Salafist groups in Gaza. Furthermore, Hamas's extensive reliance on suicide bombings requires intensive intelligence capabilities to plot and conduct these attacks successfully.[63] As with almost any group that relies heavily on suicide bombing, Hamas needs to remain acutely aware of public perception, particularly among its domestic constituency. While Hamas is not going to conduct surveys or polling, part of its intelligence apparatus is responsible for gauging the general mood of the Palestinian public, since Hamas must be responsive to its support base.

Hamas dedicates a portion of its budget to intelligence collection, specifically, to bribing officials in an attempt to penetrate the various intelligence agencies of the PA, the General and Preventive Intelligence services.[64] A Hamas special unit, named *Jehaz Aman*, is responsible for investigating both new recruits as well as any potential collaborators, thus mitigating either Palestinian or Israeli attempts to infiltrate or subvert the organization.[65] During the mid-1990s, when infighting between Hamas and Fatah approached a fever pitch, Hamas relied on its intelligence apparatus to identify and target suspected collaborators, which fed into a cycle of tit-for-tat revenge killings in Gaza.[66]

Hamas also directs some of its intelligence activities to monitoring the more recent rise of Salafist groups in Gaza, such as *Jund Ansar Allah,* a group that criticizes Hamas for its engagement in politics, agreeing to a cease-fire with Israel and its actions designed to prevent other militant factions from launching attacks against Israel from Gaza.[67] Like Al-Qaida and the Islamic State, many Salafist groups in Gaza are vehemently opposed to any form of elections and as these groups gain popularity, they threaten Hamas's ability to control Gaza as well as its legitimacy in the eyes of the most hard-line Islamists. The tentacles of the group's intelligence apparatus reach beyond the West Bank and Gaza. During their time in Jordan, Hamas operatives were accused of collecting intelligence on Jordanian officials.[68] In the United States, Hamas has engaged in low-level intelligence gathering, including preoperational surveillance of potential targets, which could be used for "off-the-shelf contingency planning."[69]

Sanctuary, Safe Haven, and Operational Space

As an organization, Hamas has led a peripatetic existence since its founding in the late 1980s. Hamas command has been headquartered abroad at various points throughout the organization's history, including in London, England, and Springfield, Virginia, alternatively, in the early 1990s.[70] In 1995, along with Islamic Jihad, Hamas relocated its operational headquarters to Damascus, while maintaining its political office in Amman during this time.[71] At other points, the group was offered sanctuary in Sudan by Hassan al-Turabi, the former Islamist political leader, who offered safe haven to Osama bin Laden and Al-Qaida.

Throughout the 1990s, many Hamas militants that operated from the West Bank and Gaza were jailed by the Israelis. As a result, the "external" leadership of the group sought refuge in places like Kuwait, Amman, Damascus, and the United States where they could "organize, recruit and raise money without Israel disrupting their efforts," according to Byman.[72] The Syrian sanctuary, in particular, provided Hamas with the operational space necessary to conduct training and planning. In early 2003, Hamas militants in Syria provided training to a pair of British Muslims of Pakistani origin who conducted a suicide attack at a popular bar frequented by Westerners in Tel Aviv.[73]

To be sure, much is in flux as a result of the Arab Spring and the ongoing civil war in Syria. Following the loss of its sanctuary in Damascus, Hamas also faces new pressure from the Egyptians. The new Sisi government in Egypt has tightened security along the Gaza border, shut down many of Hamas's tunnels (flooding some of them with sewage) and even harassed Gazan fisherman that stray into Egyptian waters. This loss of sanctuary has provided Hamas with a serious logistical challenge, especially considering how critical these tunnels have been for smuggling goods (including weapons) and infiltrating fighters into Israel.[74]

Training

Following the First Intifada, the Israelis deported 415 Hamas members to southern Lebanon, a curious move due to the proximity these members would be in with relation to Hezbollah. Overcoming the Sunni–Shia divide, Hezbollah trained the exiled Hamas members in a range of military tactics, a move that significantly strengthened Hamas's overall military capabilities when these militants returned to Gaza and the West Bank in 1993.[75] The Al-Aqsa Intifada, or the Second Intifada, commenced in September 2000 seemingly in response to then Israeli prime minister Ariel Sharon's visit to the Temple Mount.[76] During the next five years, training and technology exchange between Hezbollah and Palestinian groups would follow three general patterns, including direct person-to-person instruction (tacit knowledge transfer), physical technology exchanges, and even attempts by Hezbollah members to assume a modicum of operational control over the Al-Aqsa Martyrs Brigade, although this final point remains a matter of dispute in the literature.[77] While reports on whether or not Hezbollah attempted to seize operational control of specific Palestinian militant groups are contradictory, what is not up for debate is the value added to both Hezbollah and Palestinian militants as a result of Hezbollah fighters training the Palestinians in a host of guerilla warfare practices. Hezbollah not only receives training from Iran but in a case of "training the trainers" it teaches various Palestinian militant groups how to utilize the same techniques for which it once sought guidance.

An indirect benefit of the training provided to Hezbollah by the IRGC has been Hezbollah's ability and willingness to train Palestinian militant groups that also fall within Iran's sphere of influence. It is truly a "win all" situation because Iran furthers its interests by strengthening another enemy of Israel; the Palestinian groups become more adept at numerous terrorist techniques; and Hezbollah militants are able to practice their trade and hone their own skills without actually having to engage in conflict. Palestinian militants have trained at Hezbollah-run military training camps, which operate along three month cycles and include instructions on small arms, explosives, intelligence, and countersurveillance.[78] Hezbollah's support to Palestinian terrorist organizations extends beyond Hamas to include PIJ and the Al-Aqsa Martyrs Brigade and spans the gamut from the provision of logistical assistance to training in suicide tactics.[79]

Organizational Capabilities

While operational capabilities signal a terrorist's group's ability to plan and conduct attacks, organizational capabilities are more indicative of the group's level of cohesion. In turn, a group's cohesion can be a major factor contributing to longevity and the ability to achieve long-term objectives.

Once a group like Hamas decides that it wants to make the transition from a militant group to a hybrid entity that maintains an armed wing but also participates in the electoral process, this can be a significant strain on the group's operating budget. As such, once Hamas decided that politics would form part of its approach to seizing power, it was forced to dedicate more resources to the group's political leadership, ideological platform, human resources-type efforts, and media relations.

Leadership

In the early 1970s, Sheik Ahmed Yassin founded the al-Mujama al-Islamiya (the Islamic Center) which functioned as an umbrella organization for myriad religious outfits in Gaza. Almost 20 years later, Yassin founded Hamas, along with Abdel Aziz al-Rantissi and Mahmoud Zhahar. In the West Bank, Hamas's early leadership cadre consisted of Dr. Adnan Muswadda, Nagy Soubha, Sheikh Mohammad Fouad Abu Ziad, and Sheikh Jamil Hammami.[80] Yassin assumed the role of organizing new recruits in Gaza into operational cells, with no more than three cell members in a typical cell, while also occupying a chief role in the financing of Hamas terrorist attacks.[81] When Yassin and Rantissi were assassinated by the Israelis in 2004, Khaled Meshall, head of the organization's political bureau (the deputy head of the political bureau is Mousa Abu Marzouq), took on an even greater leadership role within Hamas. Meshall has a long history with Hamas, as he relocated to Jordan in 1990 and headed up the group's international fund-raising portfolio. He led what was known as *Kuwaidia*, or the Kuwaiti group, which played a prominent role within Hamas's political bureau. In 1997, the Israelis conducted a failed assassination attempt against him.

The Hamas organization lacks transparency in its structure, although it is well known that the group contains a *majlis-e-shura* (governing or consultative council) and a Politburo.[82] Hamas boasts political and military wings led by both internal and external officials.[83] Many of the group's leaders hold advanced degrees in technical and professional fields and furthermore, "their ability to influence the opinion of lower ranking Hamas members appears to be fairly high."[84] One of these leaders is Ismael Haniyeh, a senior political leader of Hamas who was elected prime minister of Gaza following the 2006 Palestinian legislative elections. His position has been contested since June 2007, during the height of the Hamas-Fatah internecine conflict.

Mohammed Deif is the commander of the Ezzedine al-Qassam Brigades since 2002. In reality, according to Levitt, "there is no meaningful distinction between the group's political, social and terrorist leadership."[85] When speaking of how much autonomy Hamas cells have when it comes to conducting operations or striking targets of opportunity, Levitt relates the assessment of Israeli intelligence officials who believe that within Hamas, "there are no rogue operations, but cells do push the boundaries," though Levitt's own assessment is that it is not uncommon for Hamas cells to operate on their own, or at least independent from sister cells and some leaders.[86]

Ideology

As mentioned earlier in the chapter, Hamas has political and ideological linkages with the Muslim Brotherhood as well as "shared ideological roots" with both the Egyptian Islamic Group (al-Gama'a al-Islamiyya)[87] and Egyptian Islamic Jihad,[88] a group which once claimed Al-Qaida's current leader Ayman al-Zawahiri among its members. Since its inception, Hamas has maintained a hard-line toward Israel while representing the rejectionist strand of Palestinian politics.

Hamas focuses on the importance of traditional Islamic values and has called for the elimination of Israel and the establishment of an Islamic state in Palestine. It considers the conflict with Israel an existential struggle, rather than a mere dispute over borders.[89] According to Meir Litvak, in the Hamas Charter of 1987, Hamas makes clear that its purpose is to elevate the concept of "Jihad of the Sword" into its efforts to mobilize Palestinians behind its politico-military efforts.[90] The group, which blends Palestinian nationalism with religious ideology and believes that both offensive and defensive jihad are duties of Hamas fighters, does not reserve its scorn for Israel along. In April 2003, Rantissi published an article titled "Why Shouldn't We Attack the United States?" to which be argued that striking the United States was a moral, national, and religious duty.[91]

The group's decision to sit for elections, always a controversial decision point for an insurgent or terrorist group was highly controversial. Organizing for elections costs money and in the eyes of some members, diverts precious resources from the overarching goal—attacking Israel. Many of the group's leaders remain skeptical of the efficacy of diplomacy and the peace process.[92] Still, there have been some benefits. Similar to the PIRA, Hamas has made gains from its intransigence at certain points throughout the conflict, painting negotiations as a fraud and arguing that only through violence (what the PIRA dubbed "armed struggle") could Palestinian land be liberated. In 2015, Hamas has reached in a phase where both violence and political participation are part of its platform. This evolution could be regarded as a display of pragmatism.

Without question, Hamas's ideology has changed over time. Like Hezbollah, despite inflammatory rhetoric on occasion, Hamas's ideology is pragmatic and the group has demonstrated "ideological flexibility," though some themes have remained constant. The organization has consistently emphasized the closely related themes of the legitimation of violent tactics as a form of resistance while also stressing the temporary nature of its compromises. Through its numerous Web sites, Hamas engages in "ideological marketing" in an attempt to appeal to a wide range of audiences—Palestinian, Arab, Islamist, and so on.[93]

A more recent phenomenon in Gaza is the rise of radical Islamist groups associated with Al-Qaida's brand of Salafist Islam, groups that Hamas has gone to great lengths to distance itself from, especially from an ideological standpoint.[94] Israeli Prime Minister Benjamin Netanyahu consistently conflates the Al-Qaida threat with that from Hamas, perhaps to elicit sympathy from the United States, its population, and especially its elected officials. Nevertheless, Hamas has continuously disassociated itself from Al-Qaida ideologically, even as other Salafist groups continue to pledge fealty to Al-Qaida or the even more radical Islamic State in Iraq and Syria (ISIS).

Human Resources and Recruitment

By the late 1980s, Israel had arrested over 1,000 Hamas militants and less than three percent of Palestinians in Gaza were considered supporters of the organization.[95] This support has changed dramatically over the past two decades as Hamas has demonstrated its ability to confront Israel while also vying for leadership of the Palestinian people. Hamas is undoubtedly more popular in Gaza than it is in the West Bank, where it remains weak organizationally. Still, despite this reality, some scholars speculate that popular support for Hamas in the West Bank has increased exponentially over the last decade and that, were an election for the presidency to be held today, Hamas would beat out Fatah.[96]

As the organization has grown over time, Hamas has begun to recognize the inescapable fact that maintaining such a vast social services infrastructure necessarily requires a rather robust bureaucracy. Hamas openly acknowledges that some of the money it receives from Iran goes toward helping pay the salaries of teachers, police officers and doctors in Hamas-ruled territories.[97] The internal leadership is tasked with recruiting, which it does on campuses, in mosques and through its many social service organizations. In line with the growing culture of martyrdom, a major part of the Hamas recruitment pitch is the opportunity to become a martyr, or *Shaheed*, a figure glorified in broader Palestinian society. There is also an economic incentive—payments to the families of suicide bombers are typically between $12,000 and $15,000.[98]

In addition to shouldering the responsibilities of a vast social services infrastructure, Hamas needed to further develop its human resource capabilities before contesting elections. Hamas first began reconsidering its stance on electoral participation in 1992 although this process took years to mature. Hamas eschewed participation in the 1995 elections. According to Brathwaite, one of the main reasons that Hamas changed its stance on running for elections was financial. Just after the Oslo Accords, an Israeli intelligence estimate put Hamas's annual budget at between $10 and $20 million, while Fatah was bringing in $1.5 billion each year. Hamas saw political participation as an avenue to expand its support base and with that base, the group's war chest.[99] Collectively, Hamas's leadership decided to send representatives to the municipal elections between December 2004 and May 2005, where Hamas candidates won majority seats in 7 out of 26 councils in the West Bank and 7 out of 9 councils in Gaza, before moving on to win elections for the Palestine Legislative Council the following year.

Media, PR, Propaganda, and Publicity

Hamas maintains an extensive media and public relations element as it attempts to control the narrative in its fight against Israel. One of the group's most important periodicals is *Filastin al-Muslimah,* which is released monthly and features Hamas propaganda, reaching supporters in the Middle East, as well as further abroad in Europe, the United States, Canada, and Australia.[100] Weekly newspapers include *Al Watan* and *A Risala, Sawt al Aksa* is the group's legal radio station (which broadcasts in addition to the many illegal radio stations associated with Hamas) and shortly before the 2006 general elections, Hamas acquired a license to operate a television channel, al-Aqsa TV, which offers a variety of shows including children's programs and productions focused on religion and world news. Hamas also runs numerous Web sites which vary in sophistication and content.[101]

Because it has only been in power for a short time, Hamas has been able to successfully portray itself as the non-corrupt alternative to the PA. Indeed, Hamas owes much of its popularity to the ineptitude of the PA, which failed in its promise to deliver transparent, democratic, and efficient governance. Hamas has been able to remain popular in Gaza despite repeated Israeli attacks in response to repeated provocations by the militants, from kidnappings to rocket attacks. Historically, the group's use of suicide bombings has not caused its popularity to ebb—in May 2002, one survey revealed that nearly 70 percent of Palestinians believed that suicide bombing was a perfectly legitimate tactic in the conflict with Israel.[102] Some pamphlets, posters, and CDs sold in the West Bank and Gaza feature Hamas leaders alongside figures from the Iraqi insurgency as well as with Chechen militants.[103]

HOW HAMAS FINANCING WAS COUNTERED

Through a combination of kinetic and non-kinetic actions, Israel, the United States, and the European Union have each targeted the financing of Hamas at various points. Since Hamas emerged in 1987, Israel has remained in an almost near state of constant warfare with the group, with the intensity of the conflict ebbing and flowing over time and punctuated by spasms of extremely violent periods of conflict varying in duration. Over the past decade, Israel launched countless kinetic actions against Hamas, including Operation Rainbow and Operation Days of Penitence in 2004, Operation Summer Rain and Operation Autumn Clouds in 2006, Operation Hot Winter in 2008, Operation Cast lead in 2009, Operation Returning Echo and Operation Pillar of Defense, which was an eight day Israeli offensive that killed Hamas military chieftain Ahmed Jabari, in 2012 and Operation Protective Edge in July 2014.

Kinetic Activities

As detailed throughout this chapter, Hamas has developed into a fierce politico-military organization capable of waging an ongoing guerilla war against Israel while consolidating power in Gaza and establishing linkages with foreign sponsors such as Iran. With a robust funding stream and tactical skills honed from both the First and Second Intifada, Hamas and its never ending barrage of increasingly more sophisticated Qassam rockets threaten the security of Israel like never before. In the mid-2000s, the Israeli army and intelligence services increased kinetic activities against Hamas specifically designed to hinder affiliated charities that served as a conduit for funding. Frequent raids were launched against organizations suspected of working closely with Hamas.[104] During Operation Cas Lead in 2009, the IDF attacked Hamas bases (including the University of Gaza, which the Israelis claimed was a paramilitary base and thus a fair target), rocket launch sites, the homes of some of the group's leadership and its overall infrastructure, including police training camps, offices and any hospitals, mosques, or schools suspected of doubling as military site.[105]

Non-kinetic Activities

Israeli and Fatah security operations against Hamas in the 1990s left the group weak organizationally.[106] During the Second Intifada, the Israelis convinced the PA to freeze the bank accounts of Hamas-affiliated charities in both Gaza and the West Bank.[107] In 1997, the United States designated Hamas a FTO and then two weeks after the 9/11 attacks, the militant group was labeled as a Specially Designated Global Terrorist (SDGT) under executive order (EO) 13224. This order was intended to assist the American government in blocking the assets of individuals and entities, and their subsidiaries, front organizations, agents and associates.[108] The U.S. Treasury designated six Hamas commanders under this order: Sheikh Ahmed Yassin, Imad Khalil al-Alami, Usama Hamdan, Khaled Meshall, Musa Abu Marzouq, and Abdel Aziz Rantissi. But the group's level of cohesion has fluctuated over time. Between 2003 and 2005, during a time of internecine Palestinian violence, Hamas remained above the fray, demonstrating a "high degree of internal unity and discipline" during a three year span that saw 325 fatalities related to Palestinian internal violence.[109] After years of deliberating, the European Union finally banned all Hamas wings, including the group's charitable and political factions (the EU proscribed the Izz ad-Din al-Qassam wing in 2001 and the entire organization in 2003). Charities in France, Switzerland, Britain, Austria and Lebanon had their American assets frozen.[110]

CONCLUSION

In its current incarnation, Hamas is heading down the path of Hezbollah—a daunting prospect to the Israelis and perhaps its Palestinian rivals as well. Through robust state sponsorship of funding and weapons, Hamas has emerged as a lethal non-state actor with growing political clout. With a charity network that is firmly entrenched and an ability to collect taxes from the tunnels running below its territory, Hamas has displayed a sophisticated understanding of the gray and dark economies.[111] Much like Hezbollah in Lebanon, it is no longer feasible to disarm Hamas, now that it has grown into a full-blown politico-military force in Palestine.[112] The options for the international community seeking to counter Hamas's activities are limited, although targeting the group's main sources of support will continue to remain a priority for the Israelis and other nations attempting to limit its influence.

CHAPTER 6

Afghan Taliban: From Strugglers to Smugglers

BACKGROUND

The Taliban first emerged in Kandahar province in 1994 as a vigilante group comprised of *madrassa* students, or Talibs. Unlike the Northern Alliance or the various militias led by former *mujahedin* turned warlords, Taliban fighters were "students," or "seekers," to use the religious connotation.[1] Led by Mullah Mohammed Omar, this group of religious students initially rose to prominence after providing security to local Afghans being preyed upon by warlords and militia commanders. In the spring of 1994, the Taliban freed two young girls who had been kidnapped and abused by a militia commander in Singesar. The commander was killed and hung from the barrel of a tank as an example to others. Later that year, the Taliban rescued a young boy whom two local commanders were fighting over—in order to determine who would get to sodomize him.[2] By 1996, the Taliban controlled the southern Pashtun heartland of Afghanistan, as well as Herat and Kabul.[3]

It is important to note, however, that *Taliban* is far from a monolithic entity. Indeed, there are many differences to be cognizant of—Afghan versus Pakistani Taliban, "old" Taliban versus "neo-Taliban," and stark divisions within the Taliban itself, between Durrani and Ghilzai Pashtuns.[4] Throughout this chapter, I have used the terms *Taliban*, *Afghan Taliban*, *neo-Taliban*, and *Quetta Shura Taliban (QST)* to refer to the same group, led by Mullah Mohammad Omar.[5]

HOW TALIBAN FUNDED ITS ACTIVITIES

The Taliban's two primary sources of funding are the narcotics trade and money donated by sympathizers in the Middle East.[6] Though figures vary widely, the narcotics trade generates a profit between $70 million and $500 million per year for the Taliban.[7] Even after the costs of sustaining an insurgency are debited, this is hardly a "rainy day fund." How an insurgent group finances itself has a major impact on the motivation of its members, overall group morale, political legitimacy, and the trajectory of the conflict.[8] The Taliban does not rely solely upon narcotics as a means of funding its insurgent activities in Afghanistan and indeed maintains diverse sources of financing, coupled with a robust support network that offers both active and passive support.[9] Part of the Taliban's war chest is derived from a multibillion dollar trade in goods smuggled from Dubai to Pakistan.[10]

Gray Economy

Since Afghanistan has been a nation at war continuously for over three decades, much of the formal economy has been destroyed and is only now being rebuilt, albeit slowly. As such, much of the country's economic activity resides in a space somewhere between licit and illicit, which is a boon to the insurgency. Accordingly, "the Taliban is able to pursue financial practices beyond the reach of the enforceable state regulation and without being subjected to any sort of tax or other state induced cost occurrence."[11] The "Warlord Economy" of Afghanistan is conducive to fraud, money laundering, and the financing of terrorism through charities, which all serve to complement the Taliban's criminal and insurgent activities.

Diaspora Support

Perhaps the most significant event to affect the modern day Afghan diaspora was the Soviet invasion in 1979. Since that time, Afghanistan has been embroiled in some type of conflict, which has led many refugees to flee the country and settle elsewhere, both in the region (Pakistan and Iran) as well as further abroad. The diaspora has been linked to illicit transnational trade networks that include smuggling and trafficking groups connected to the narcotics trade.[12] In other words, the Afghan diaspora is linked with what Barnett Rubin labels the "Afghan war economy," which has "generated a pattern of regional economic activity and associated social and political networks that compete with and undermine legal economies and states."[13] This war economy is facilitated by porous borders and a lack of customs enforcement throughout the country and the region. In addition to organized criminal activities, the Taliban has also relied on expertise from the Afghan diaspora to help it develop its media messaging strategy.[14]

Charities

In addition to the money funneled through charities, some of the Taliban's funding comes from a network of sympathizers located throughout Pakistan and the Gulf. At one point, the Taliban was thought to earn approximately 15 percent of its overall income from donors in the Gulf.[15] This network is comprised of businessmen from Karachi, goldsmiths in Peshawar, Saudi oil tycoons, Kuwaiti traders and members of the Pakistani military and intelligence services who sympathize with the jihadist ideology.[16] Charities from Kuwait, Saudi Arabia, and other Islamic countries have operated in Afghanistan both during and after Taliban rule. While some are known for social welfare and humanitarian assistance, others, like the Al-Rashid Trust, exploited its status as a charity to raise funds for the Taliban.[17]

Fraud

Throughout much of the war in Afghanistan, there have been allegations of massive fraud in United States contracting, including an estimate that (at a minimum) 10 percent of the Defense Department's logistics contracts (in the hundreds of millions of dollars) consist of payments to insurgents.[18] One of the companies implicated in this fraud is the Watan Group, a consortium that includes telecommunications, logistics, and security. Another Afghan security company, NCL Holdings, was one of six companies that were paid to bring supplies to U.S. bases and outposts dotted throughout Afghanistan. Afghan International Trucking (AIT), another component of the Host Nation Trucking contract, paid $20,000 a month in kickbacks to a U.S. Army contracting official. The money that trickles down to the insurgents is intended as a *quid pro quo*—payments are made to ensure that the Taliban refrains from attacking the convoys delivering toilet paper, water, fuel, guns, and vehicles.[19]

Legal Businesses

Taliban operations were organized horizontally across the narcotics trade, with money invested in transport businesses and import-export companies in order to hide the drug shipments while also laundering the profits.[20] Over 3,500 import-export "firms" pockmark the Chaman border-crossing between Afghanistan and Pakistan. The UAE is a common destination for Afghan front companies, where totally fabricated companies move millions of dollars in laundered money each year. Establishing a front company is surprisingly easy. First, the firm is registered, next, an employment visa is procured for the director of the company, and finally, an account is opened "where the boss supposedly would receive a generous salary."[21]

Money Laundering

The Taliban launders money from its drug proceeds through myriad pipelines, including commodities, *hawala* money transfers, overpricing goods, real estate, shell businesses, and the stock exchange. Trade-based money laundering is another common activity in the narcotics trade, as two traders agree to misprice a deal by overvaluing it by a certain amount so that the extra money is undetectable by authorities. The lack of a single operational trade transparency unit between the Middle East and South Asia has further hampered efforts to counter money laundering between these regions.[22] In addition to a popular destination for establishing front companies, Dubai has also become known for its burgeoning real estate market, which is another way that Afghan drug traffickers have laundered money. Finally, a significant amount of drug money is likely laundered through the stock market, including the Karachi Stock Exchange (KSE), where wealthy brokers have expanded their operations into private banking, real estate, and energy (oil and natural gas) exploration.[23] Because there is so little paperwork involved in the movement of funds, there is little government oversight, which means less of a chance that the money can be interdicting using standard AML/CFT anti-money laundering tools.[24]

Dark Economy

Are the Taliban strugglers, or merely smugglers?[25] Though the group's staunch Islamic ideology would suggest the former, its panoply of criminal activities might lend some to label it the latter. To be sure, the Taliban's reliance on the dark economy provides the majority of the revenue it needs to sustain the insurgency.[26] In Kandahar, each commander is tasked with raising funds for his group and there are no regular salaries, per se. Instead, between fifty dollars and several hundred dollars are distributed to fighters on a semi-regular basis roughly each month.[27]

Kidnapping for Ransom (KFR)

The Taliban's reliance on kidnapping for ransom as a form of revenue generation can be traced back to early 2008 when the group officially altered its code of conduct to allow for the practice. The code of conduct states that with the permission of Taliban leadership, fighters can kidnap individuals and seek money for the release of government, non-government organization (NGO), and private sector staff working on government projects (this was extended to include truck drivers affiliated with Coalition forces or the Afghan government).[28] The Taliban's reliance on KFR includes several high-profile incidents, including the kidnappings of Italian journalist Gabriele Torsello in 2006, Italian-Swiss journalist Daniele Mastrogiacomo in 2007, and 19 South Korean missionaries that same year. The Italian government has refused to confirm reports that a $2.8 million ransom was paid for the release of Torsello and a $2 million ransom paid for Mastrogiacomo, though the Taliban acknowledged shortly after those crimes that the group had been handsomely remunerated for kidnapping.[29] Because the kidnapping business has been so lucrative, the Taliban began to "sub-contract" these operations to decentralized kidnapping rings, which would sell the individuals they kidnapped to the Taliban, who would then exchange them for an even greater ransom. Some estimates are that the Taliban makes more than $10 million a year from kidnappings.[30] In 2010, Kandahar City and other locations experienced a major increase in kidnappings, prompting the Taliban to reconsider how this tactic was affecting the group's popular support throughout Afghanistan.[31]

Armed Robbery and Theft

The Taliban ascended to power in part for its ability to curb the behavior of rogue warlords and highway bandits that preyed upon Afghans as they traveled throughout the country. Yet, after the U.S. invasion in 2001, as the Taliban sought to consolidate all possible streams of revenue, the insurgents turned to this very behavior themselves in order to finance their activities. As detailed in the section on extortion and protection payments, trucking convoys that hope to avoid being attacked by the insurgents pay a steep fee.[32] Those that eschew these payments, however, are considered "fair game," and their convoys are attacked, pillaged, and plundered by Taliban insurgents. During these attacks, not only are the goods stolen, but the vehicles are burned and the personnel are often killed or kidnapped. By planting IEDs along transportation routes, those vehicles that are not destroyed are disabled, making robbery and theft an even easier chore for the insurgents turned bandits.

Smuggling, Trafficking, and Counterfeiting

The Taliban has knowingly (and skillfully) suppressed the cultivation of poppy in Afghanistan in order to manipulate the international market price. At one point, a Taliban ban on poppy cultivation suppressed the supply by 90 percent, thus increasing the value of the group's stocks by ten times the price.[33] Besides deriving significant financial profits from the drug trade in Afghanistan, the Taliban also gains political capital from its sponsorship of the illicit economy.[34] The Taliban's involvement with the narcotics trade has increased steadily over time. In 2004, the group was sending small teams to attack checkpoints or make diversionary strikes in order to protect opium cultivation. Three years later, by 2007, insurgent commanders were operating mobile laboratories to process heroin.[35] Some reports have also indicated that the Taliban has engaged in heroin-for-arms trades with members of Russian organized crime.[36]

On narcotics, the Taliban's position has evolved considerably throughout the years. As described above, the Taliban flip flopped back and forth on its stance toward narcotics between 1994 and 2001. Keeping in line with its renewed offensive to win "hearts and minds," the Taliban now actively promotes the growing of poppy and provides protection to farmers growing the crop.[37] As Coalition forces continue to target the nexus between narcotics and the insurgency, the Taliban portrays itself as a defender of Afghans' livelihoods, while attempting to paint Coalition forces as an occupying force intent on destroying the crop most important to the Afghan economy. More recently, a report in May 2012 surfaced suggesting that Taliban fighters destroyed fields of opium poppies in eastern Afghanistan, the first time since 2001.[38]

Extortion and Protection

In Afghanistan the Taliban has extorted truck convoys through the imposition of transit taxes.[39] Its ally, the Haqqani Network (HQN) "collects regular security payments from local, regional, and international businesses that operate in its zone of influence, effectively selling insurance against itself.[40] The Haqqanis are extremely opportunistic, appearing to collect money from small local shopkeepers up to large international firms."[41] The Haqqani network is also a major player in the Afghan insurgency. Although the network is part of the insurgency, it also functions like a mafia, motivated by profits but also by issues such as honor, revenge, and ideology.[42] An in-depth analysis of HQN funding is beyond the scope of this chapter, but it is worth noting that recent assessments suggest that high levels of violence, rampant criminality, and indiscriminate brutality could mean that the group has descended into more of a criminal operation than an insurgent group. It is believed that the Taliban collects approximately $100 million per year from *ushr*, which is an Islamic tax, or tithe, levied on local businesses and farms. *Kharaj*, an Islamic land tax, also provides funding to the insurgency.[43] As Gordon and Conway recognize, Taliban taxation of the poppy harvest is not merely an issue of *either* counter-narcotics *or* COIN but rather "a threat finance and counterinsurgency issue—it both funds the Taliban and establishes the Taliban as the legitimate source of governance for the people."[44] The Taliban also targets Afghanistan's telecommunications firms, wrong placement receiving payments in exchange for not attacking cell phone towers and kidnapping the firms' employees.

External State Support

Historically, Taliban fighters received support from several states, chief among them Pakistan and Saudi Arabia. This support has come in the form of weapons, ideological support, safe haven, and funding; in the case of the Saudis, much of this money was provided for mosques and *madrassas* in Pakistan, the students of which served as "an important military reserve" for the Taliban.[45] More recently, the U.S. Treasury Department has accused Iran of supporting the insurgents, providing them with small arms and ammunition, RPGs, mortar rounds, 107mm rockets, plastic explosives and most likely MANPADs.[46] But even more extensive (and important) support to the Taliban has come from Pakistan. Logistical support and military training provided by Pakistan have been critical to the Taliban's longevity.[47]

Exactly what type of insurgency the Taliban is waging in Afghanistan in 2012 is still a matter of debate. While some would term the conflict an example of a "local-global" insurgency, because of the Taliban's links to Al-Qaida (which are now acknowledged to be quite limited, at least within Afghanistan proper), others, like Peter Dahl Thruelsen, argue that the Taliban is a localized insurgency with a local objective. Perhaps the most accurate characterization would be a "local-regional" insurgency encompassing various parts of South Asia. The majority of the Taliban's military operations are conducted by insurgents operating within their home provinces.[48] Still, the influence of Siraj Haqqani and his links to both Al-Qaida and the TTP, or Pakistani Taliban, indicate that as the conflict continues, the Afghan Taliban could be influenced by actors with more regional and even global ambitions.[49] As of late 2014, Afghan government officials were openly accusing Pakistan of supporting the Taliban with money, fighters, and technical expertise.[50]

WHAT THE TALIBAN ACHIEVED WITH THESE FUNDS

Funding has been valuable because it has allowed the Taliban to sustain the insurgency for over a decade. Giustozzi estimates that the Taliban retains an annual surplus of between $110 and $130 million.[51] Gretchen Peters does a comprehensive job mapping out the Taliban's funding streams in southern, southeastern, northern, and northeastern Afghanistan.[52] Money generated through crime, extortion, and fundraising is devoted to paying Taliban insurgents and obtaining weapons for the group's fighters. At various times, particularly when relations between the two groups were more cordial, the Afghan Taliban siphoned funds off for Baitullah Mehsud and the Pakistani Taliban over the border.[53]

Operational Capabilities

The impetus to maintain the ability to conduct attacks, including raids and bombings, is the driving force behind the funding that bolsters the Taliban's operational capabilities. The more effectively the counterinsurgents target the Taliban's supply lines, the more the International Security Assistance Force (ISAF) is able to disrupt crucial tangible support to the insurgents. This makes access to weapons, intelligence, sanctuary, and training even that much more valuable. A group that cannot fight, cannot win. The Taliban's operational capabilities are key to the group's momentum on the battlefield, as well as its ability to delegitimize the Afghan government and Afghan security forces.

Weapons

The Taliban's approach is a mixture of rural-urban insurgency, depending on which regional command of the country is being analyzed. Overall, the insurgency is rural, protracted, and funded through rents acquired from illicit economies.[54] Its approach, or fighting strategy, has alternatively been described as asymmetric, "Fourth Generation," Maoist, and that of the "war of the flea."[55] While there are certainly elements of each of these fighting styles apparent in the Taliban's approach, the most accurate characterization is probably closest to Maoism.

In the opening stages of the conflict, insurgents infiltrated the population and gained control over key areas before moving on to consolidate base areas, organize guerilla war, and create rudimentary political structures. Before the Taliban escalated its activities between late 2005 and 2007, its fighters relied mainly on AK-47 assault rifles, RPG-7 rocket launchers, BM-1 field rockets, machine guns, suicide bombers, and improvised explosive devices.[56] The fighting is asymmetric and the Taliban function primarily as a guerilla army, relying on sniping and ambushes. The insurgents operate in small units and strike logistical convoys, lightly guarded outposts, and other targets of opportunity.[57] At times, the Taliban has relied on human wave attacks, specifically in the south and east of Afghanistan. This kind of "open warfare" is rare and is mostly used to counter the effectiveness of Coalition air strikes.[58]

As a fighting force, the Taliban has proved capable of evolution and adaptation, conducting sophisticated attacks which require competency in a wide range of weaponry. As relayed by Thomas Johnson, United States Marine Corps (USMC) After Action Reports from Helmand province detail Taliban tactics including fire control, fire discipline, interlocking fields of fire, combined arms, fire and maneuver, anti-armor tactics, cover and concealment, and defense in depth.[59] These kinds of tactics reflect the insurgents' ability to use RPGs, heavy machine guns, rockets, and mortars. Perhaps even more impressive, the insurgents possess a sober understanding of their own limitations using different weapons systems, which allows them to specialize and tailor their attacks.[60]

Between 2010 and 2012, the Taliban began conducting urban attacks in major cities like Kabul, including bombings, drive-by assassinations, and raids.[61] The change in tactics by Taliban units throughout Afghanistan was not a coincidence. Rather, it was a deliberate strategic shift driven by a Quetta military commission general order that urged insurgents to rely more on IEDs, sniper attacks, and traditional guerilla warfare tactics.[62]

Intelligence

Even prior to the insurgency, the Afghan Taliban maintained a robust intelligence structure on both sides of the border, cooperating often with the Inter-Services Intelligence (ISI) as well as the Pakistani political party Jamiat Ulema-e-Islam (JUI). In the early stages of the conflict, Taliban intelligence operatives bribed Northern Alliance commanders to infiltrate the ranks of their comrades to conduct assassinations.[63] Taliban intelligence networks are strong at the village and neighborhood level, which allows the insurgents to control large segments of the Pashtun population in the south and east.[64] Over the past several years, both the Taliban and the Haqqani Network have placed spies inside the ranks of the Afghan Ministry of Interior (MoI) and Ministry of Defense (MoD), which has allowed the insurgents to strike at the heart of the Afghan security services.

The Taliban rely on intelligence and counterintelligence to mitigate the overwhelming U.S. firepower and technological advantage. Intelligence has been used in several capacities, from intelligence preparation of the battlefield (IPB) to military deception (MILDEC) to high value-targeting (HVT).[65] The Taliban intelligence network is also largely responsible for the successful jail break in Kandahar city in the spring of 2011. Although it is impossible to know how many fighters went directly back to the battlefield, the spate of attacks immediately following the incident indicated an increased capability for Taliban units operating in the area.[66]

The removal of key leaders in the Taliban's intelligence apparatus—Khairullah Khairkhwa, Qari Ahmadullah, and Abdul Haq Wasiq have all been captured or killed since the conflict began—has enervated the insurgents, but overall the network has proved resilient.[67] ISAF operations in Afghanistan and U.S. drone strikes in Pakistan have kept the insurgents off balance. Evidence suggests that the Taliban's attempt to share intelligence has been made more onerous as the network is forced to reorganize and replace its commanders.[68] From a COIN perspective, the most alarming trend has been the increase in incidents since early 2009 where coalition troops were executed by Taliban insurgents posing as Afghan security force personnel.

Sanctuary, Safe Haven, and Operational Space

The worst kept secret throughout the insurgency has been the Afghan Taliban's Pakistani safe haven, both in the Federally Administered Tribal Areas (FATA) as well as in major cities like Karachi, Quetta, Lahore, and Peshawar. In more recent years, the Taliban has also enjoyed sanctuary in parts of Iran. Pakistan remains the preferred locale, however, as it is geographically proximate to southern and eastern Afghanistan and is home to approximately 25 million Pashtuns, twice as many as live in Afghanistan. Furthermore, the rugged terrain of the AfPak border region make it ideally suited for avoiding detection.[69] At the height of the Taliban's comeback in 2007, the border provinces between Afghanistan and Pakistan were designated as either "extreme risk/hostile" or "high risk/ hostile" environments.[70]

Throughout history, insurgents who have enjoyed relatively unfettered access to safe haven, either internal or external, have fared more successful than those insurgents without such access.[71] Besides the popular support enjoyed by Taliban insurgents in their Pakistani sanctuary, fighters have been able to plot, recruit, proselytize, fund-raise, and communicate with each other.[72] Obviously, the most valuable aspect of the Taliban's Pakistani sanctuary is that it allows the insurgents to evade ISAF counterinsurgency operations.[73] The border stretches for 2,450 km and is almost impossible for Coalition troops to patrol.[74] This challenge is compounded by a less capable and mostly reluctant Pakistani military, which deployed its paramilitary Frontier Corps and regular army elements from the Twelfth Corps to the FATA in 2004.[75] Pakistan's FATA have been a generous safe haven to Al-Qaida as well.

Training

Between 2004 and 2011, of the 32 "serious" terrorist plots against the West, more than half (53 percent), had operational or training links to established jihadist groups in Pakistan.[76] The Taliban has maintained a sanctuary in Pakistan since being chased over the border by U.S. Special Forces on horseback in November 2001. In 2003 and 2004, the ISI operated training camps for Afghan Taliban insurgents in Pakistan, just north of Quetta.[77] U.S. drone strikes have limited the ability of insurgents in Pakistan's Northwest Frontier Province (NWFP) and FATA to operate freely. This is true not only of the Afghan Taliban, but also of the TTP. The issue of Taliban sanctuary in Pakistan has been perhaps the most vexing obstacle facing ISAF in Afghanistan. In what should probably qualify as somewhat of an understatement, former U.S. Director of National Intelligence Dennis C. Blair conceded that the safe haven in Pakistan "is an important Taliban strength."[78] In addition to safe haven provided by Pakistan, the Taliban has also bolstered its support on the western front by strengthening its ties with the mullahs in Tehran in the past few years.[79]

A Department of Defense Report to Congress on Afghanistan from April 2012 states that, "the insurgency's safe haven in Pakistan, as well as the limited capacity of the Afghan Government, remains the biggest risks to the process of turning security gains into a durable and sustainable Afghanistan. The insurgency benefits from safe havens inside Pakistan with notable operational and regenerative capacity."[80] The continuing ability of the Taliban to use Pakistan as sanctuary provides it with a clear advantage should the insurgency's goal be to "wait out" the United States before returning to Afghanistan after an American withdrawal to retake the country by force. At the end of the day, there is little the United States can do militarily to force the Pakistanis to eliminate this safe haven. After all, Pakistan is an "ally" with six times the population of Iraq, in addition to a growing arsenal of nuclear weapons.[81]

Organizational Capabilities

Fighting against other warlords and violent non-state actors in Afghanistan is completely different than trying to defeat the United States and ISAF forces that have such a pronounced military advantage over the Taliban. To stand a chance, the insurgents must maintain annual expenditures directed toward operational costs, maintaining (and adapting) organizational infrastructure, growth and recruiting initiatives, and savings. These organizational costs, which comprise the bulk of the finances, include administrative functions, provisions, and logistical support like fuel, transportation, and so on.[82]

Leadership

Even 10 years after the start of the insurgency, it remains difficult to present an accurate depiction of the Taliban's group composition. As of 2012, Tier I of the Taliban is comprised of the strategic leadership, the Quetta Shura, province shadow governors and old fighters from the 1990s. These are thought to be the most hardcore ideologues of the entire group and those most inimical to negotiating. Of course, these are the individuals most removed from the actual fighting, so they are the least likely to be affected by ISAF kinetic operations. Local leaders, fill-time fighters, and active supporters make up most of Tier II. While it is

difficult to gauge the political commitment of this tier, the full-time fighters are undoubtedly suffering the brunt of the COIN force military offensive. Finally, Tier III is composed of part-time fighters (to include those
fighting for remuneration), less committed local supporters, and those
that sympathize with the Taliban's cause.[83]

Ideology

Over time, the Taliban has increasingly recognized the utility of alienating the population from the government and acquiring its active support, an indispensable outcome for any insurgent group involved in an
asymmetric conflict against far superior military forces.[84] In 2009, the
Taliban released a 69 page "Code of Conduct," which was updated a
year later. The two main purposes of the booklet were to rein in unruly
commanders and win back segments of the population that were disenfranchised by the Taliban's harsh tactics. The Taliban's ideological transformation has addressed the group's continuing effort to garner
legitimacy, as well as changes in its organizational structure. Finally, it
includes a concerted effort to portray the group as a national movement
whose appeal extends beyond the traditional Pashtun strongholds of
southern Afghanistan and into parts of the country dominated by Tajiks,
Hazaras, and Uzbeks.

An analysis of the Taliban's ideology would not be complete without
addressing the group's changing tactics over the course of the insurgency.
During the early stages of the insurgency, those Taliban fighters who
remained in Afghanistan organized into small pockets of resistance
throughout the south and east of the country. They fought U.S. forces in
the P2K region (Paktia, Paktika, Khost), and Kunar province.[85] At least
initially, the Taliban relied on rocket attacks, small arms fire, and
ambushes as its main tactics. However, beginning in 2005 and increasing
exponentially over the next several years, the Taliban conducted a campaign of suicide attacks and roadside bombings through the use of IEDs
unseen before in the Afghan conflict.

While it is difficult to pinpoint precisely when the Taliban began to
reconsider the more austere elements of its ideology, some scholars argue
that the genesis of the "neo-Taliban" harkens back to 2002.[86] Like the Coalition, the Taliban also realizes the importance of gaining the trust and
support of the population, although the increased use of IEDs, suicide
bombing, and the targeting of civilians might suggest otherwise.[87] The
driving force behind the switch to the use of suicide bombing was Mullah
Dadullah, a leading Taliban military commander who adopted suicide
bombing as a tactic after watching DVDs of similar attacks by Iraqi insurgents.[88] Suicide attacks in Afghanistan increased each year from 2003
until 2007, the year that the Dadullah was killed by U.S. forces in

Helmand province.[89] After Dadullah's death, suicide attacks began to decline steadily, and in 2009 the Taliban's Code of Conduct provided guidance on the subject. The document suggested that suicide attacks were only acceptable in the case of high-value targets and that civilian casualties should be avoided with great care.[90]

Even with the guidance offered to avoid civilian casualties, a 2011 United Nations Report estimated that nearly three-quarters of all civilian deaths in Afghanistan are caused by the Taliban and other insurgents. Possibly in response to this report and an increasing perception in Afghanistan that Taliban fighters are undisciplined, often showing wanton disregard for the lives of their fellow Afghans, the group publicly announced the start to its spring offensive in late April 2011, the first time such an announcement has been made since the beginning of the insurgency.[91] In its statement, the Taliban mentioned the protection of civilians as a priority, claiming that every effort would be made to avoid harming or killing Afghan civilians.

The most important component of the Taliban's evolution is the group's shift to an inclusive and less draconian political platform. In sum, the Taliban still values power over profit, even if as many believe, the group's ideological shift is disingenuous and a byproduct of political expedience. Indeed, while comparisons of insurgent groups often oversimplify the complexities inherent in these organizations, comparative historians know that *sequence matters* and will always look to the past for answers.

In 2007 and 2008, an element of the insurgency that came to be called "pious Taliban," came out against the group's use of suicide bombing as a tactic. This group of insurgents, a sub-element of the "Kandahari mainstream" Taliban, recognized that victory through military means was not possible. Splintering and spoiling both remain acute possibilities with respect to a negotiated settlement. Like most insurgent groups, the Taliban has its share of hardcore fighters who will refuse to give up the fight, especially those who see it as a religious obligation to retake the country and implement *sharia* in an Islamic Emirate governed by religious leaders.

The Taliban has already moderated its position on several fronts. This moderation is largely superficial and is mostly an attempt to avoid alienating potential supporters in its quest for legitimacy. If negotiations do take place, ideological hardliners could seek to play the role of spoiler, as they did in the post-Bonn period.[92] To that end, radical splinter groups aligned with the HQN or Al-Qaida is almost guaranteed to emerge following a negotiated settlement.

The Taliban, or the "neo-Taliban," as it is sometimes referred to, has developed a more nuanced understanding of the political dynamics of the insurgency since 2001 and is currently engaged in a struggle with the Afghan government to gain the allegiance of the Afghan people.

The group's focus on affecting public opinion, demonstrates that the Taliban has political goals and is using economic gain to further these goals. With so much attention paid to how the insurgency is funded, the Taliban's ideological evolution has been misinterpreted. By temporarily shelving some of its more austere policies, the Taliban is angling to position itself as a legitimate political actor in Afghanistan.

Organizations change over time and adapt to new circumstances. Insurgent groups are no different. The changes implemented by the Taliban have been deliberate and carefully calculated. The willingness to put certain objectives on hold in the short-term is nothing more than misdirection. Once in power, it is possible the Taliban will return to these goals. Having an idea about what the group's objectives are will go a long way toward fashioning a peace deal amenable to all sides. As Shinn and Dobbins point out, in any negotiation there are "must haves" and "want to haves." Taliban "must haves" include the removal of foreign forces from Afghanistan (with no presence other than *temporary* peacekeepers), a guarantee of security for the insurgents, and the prospect of political legitimacy, both internal and external.[93]

One of the most important questions is whether or not the Taliban remains committed to building an Islamic state in Afghanistan. To this point, all indications have suggested that this is the case, although just how much Afghanistan would move toward the institutionalization of Islamic law is likely an area of compromise.

Human Resources and Recruitment

The Afghan Taliban is a decentralized network comprised of four regional *shuras* located in Quetta, Peshawar, Miramsha, and Gerdi Jangal.[94] Three overlapping networks, including the HQN, Hizb-i-Islami Gulbuddin, and the Mansur network are also associated with the group.[95] The Taliban maintain both formal and informal structures, with the former consisting of the Leadership Council, provincial leadership councils, and a host of different commissions.[96] In addition to regional *shuras*, the Taliban maintains four "regional commands," covering southern Afghanistan, eastern Afghanistan, southeastern Afghanistan, and western Afghanistan. Each "regional command" has a different relationship with the group's leadership in Pakistan as well as with the Pakistani Army and ISI.[97]

Since each of the four regional *shuras* is located across the border in Pakistan, the Taliban created shadow governments in each of Afghanistan's provinces, mainly as an alternative to the corrupt Afghan government. Taliban shadow governance includes a mechanism for land dispute resolution and a provincial level commission where civilians can file formal complaints against local commanders. This stands in stark contrast to an Afghan government that takes months to resolve disputes, is widely viewed as both corrupt and inept, and operates with little fear of consequence for accepting bribes and preying on the population.[98] The Taliban shadow government rules through *sharia*, or Islamic law.[99] According to Dressler and Forsberg, the Taliban's parallel institutions "are more effective than anything the Afghan government or international community has been able to muster."[100]

Each province has its own Taliban shadow governor responsible for civil and military matters, including financial oversight and judicial processes.[101] In some areas, the Taliban dispenses licenses, collects a form of taxation known as *zakat*, and is preferred over the Afghan government because it is perceived as more reliable and less corrupt.[102] These provincial level commissions were established to make the Taliban's shadow governance competitive with Kabul's administrative ability, which in many cases it either equals or surpasses in efficiency. The shift toward structural reorganization, rather than merely "tactical and financial in motive," appears to be a strategic move aimed at gaining support over the medium to long-term.[103]

Minimizing the financial exploitation of the population and creating the mechanisms that allow for censure against those Taliban members convicted of wrongdoing places the group in juxtaposition to the corrupt and unaccountable Karzai government.[104] In the "Code of Conduct," one passage follows that "the Taliban must treat civilians according to Islamic norms and morality to win over the hearts and minds of the people."[105] From the standpoint of basic strategic approaches to insurgency, these directives should not be seen as revolutionary. In fact, many of these same tenets were laid out by Mao in "Six Main Points for Attention," which provided his troops with directions on how to treat the population as they marauded through the countryside.[106] These basic guidelines for maintaining the goodwill of the population have become more important to the Taliban's campaign as the group's ideology has evolved to include a more nuanced view of the importance of the population in fighting an insurgency.

If the population is truly the sea in which insurgents (the fish) swim, then the popular support of the population is critical to their success.[107] The Taliban has picked up on the Americans' insistence on a population-centric counterinsurgency strategy and has countered with its own campaign to win over the population, making critical changes to its approach over the past several years of the insurgency, including its views regarding narcotics.

In 2006, at about the same time the Taliban placed a higher priority on earning legitimacy in the eyes of the Afghan people, the group also greatly expanded recruitment efforts throughout Afghanistan, including at the village level.[108] One of the main driving forces behind local recruitment of Afghans into the insurgency was the influence of the clergy.[109] While the Taliban undoubtedly draws recruits from *madrassas* along the Afghan-Pakistani border, after 2006 the group expanded efforts to recruit in urban areas, especially in universities, and began to reconnect with former mujahedin commanders to grow its fighting force.[110] The Taliban recruitment process also relies on family and clan loyalties, tribal lineage, personal friendships, and social networks.[111]

Taliban recruitment efforts are bolstered by continuing corruption in the Afghan government, which extends from the highest reaches of the Karzai government all the way down to provincial, district, and village officials and security forces.[112] Indeed, a desire to respond to grievances is a commonly cited factor motivating the radicalization of individuals who make the decision to join an insurgent or terrorist group.[113] By exploiting the narratives of oppression, occupation, and corruption, the Taliban can appeal to both theological justifications and nationalist sentiments at the same time.[114] Thomas Ruttig believes that the current U.S. strategy of degrading the Taliban to force it to the negotiating table is having unintended effects. The most serious of these is contributing to the rise of younger, more radical Taliban commanders who are filling the ranks of the "neo-Taliban," an iteration of the insurgency with a more "jihadist internationalist" worldview.[115]

Media, PR, Propaganda, and Publicity

For a group comprised largely of illiterate and rural fighters, the Taliban has displayed an effective propaganda effort by taking advantage of the full range of media outlets—radio, Internet, DVDs, audio cassettes, magazines, and traditional songs and poems.[116] Through its propaganda, the Taliban attempts to portray itself as the only legitimate actor in the conflict, the vanguard of not just the Pashtun population, but of the Afghan people as a whole. The Americans are cast as just the next wave of foreign occupiers, no different than the Russians before them and the British before them.

Taliban propaganda routinely points out ISAF and Afghan government shortcomings. Frequent themes include civilian casualties resulting from Coalition air strikes and the rampant corruption of the Karzai government. In addition to these messages, Taliban propaganda assails the American-run prison at Guantanamo Bay and also provides justifications for the use of suicide bombings in Afghanistan. A significant component of the organization's propaganda machine, which former commander of NATO forces in Afghanistan David Richards characterized as the most sophisticated he's ever seen, is the group's public relations activities. Taliban spokesmen eagerly address the press by arranging meetings with journalists and satellite phone calls to explain their side of the story.[117]

While public relations and propaganda would not play much of a role in influencing the Taliban's decision to negotiate or keep fighting, they will certainly affect the course of negotiations should the insurgents pursue this option. Taliban spokesmen control the group's message and influence its followers through carefully crafted public relations. This skill carries over to the realm of politics, where these same insurgents will attempt to position the Taliban as the most legitimate and representative entity of the Afghan people.

The Taliban's efforts to present itself as the most legitimate actor in the Afghan conflict require buttressing its own credentials while simultaneously discrediting the ISAF and the Afghan government. In this sense, legitimacy is a zero-sum game. Beginning in 2006, as the insurgency increased in strength, the Taliban portrayed itself as a broad-based independence movement.[118] Public statements drew attention to the American occupation, egregious corruption within the Afghan government, and even attempted to offer commentary on political events.[119] Furthermore, the Taliban crafted its public statements in a way that avoided mentioning specific tribes or ethnic groups and even softened its anti-Shia rhetoric.[120]

Another departure from past views includes a different approach to women's rights and female education, which the Taliban no longer opposes as fervently as it once did.[121] In Taliban-controlled areas, there has been an easing of social restrictions, including a toleration of television, music, and movies.[122] Finally, the Taliban's shadow governance has imbued the group with a sense of legitimacy because the judicial arm of the group's parallel government is credited with offering swift justice in areas including disputes over land, family issues, loans, and crime.[123] The Taliban's "hearts and minds" offensive has been girded by an attempt to distance itself from Al-Qaida, although any separation is likely more rhetoric than reality. To be sure, several senior Taliban leaders, including Mullah Omar and Mullah Zakir, continue to have working relationships with senior Al-Qaida leaders.

HOW TALIBAN FINANCING WAS COUNTERED

Prior to September 11th and in the nascent stages of the insurgency, the Taliban was able to rely on a steady stream of income from Osama bin Laden and Al-Qaida's financial network.[124] Furthermore, while the Taliban once relied heavily on extorting transportation companies and other privately-hired contractors, as the Western footprint in Afghanistan diminishes, the funding is drying up along with it.[125] As this source of internal revenue declines, the Taliban will continue to solicit donations from Middle Eastern sheikhs with deep pockets and sympathizers from the Persian Gulf and elsewhere to keep its bankroll steady. Overall, however, figuring out how the Taliban financed its organization did not become a priority for Coalition forces until several years into the conflict, by which point the Taliban had already become well entrenched in both the gray and dark economies.[126]

Kinetic Activities

By 2012, after a decade of ISAF forces in Afghanistan, it became clear that there was a different strategic scenario in each of Afghanistan's regional commands (RCs). Regional commands North and West, commanded by Germany and Italy respectively, were relatively pacified compared to the rest of the country. In RCs South, Southwest, East, and Capital (Kabul), Taliban and insurgent activity was still an everyday reality. For the countries operating in these RCs—the United States, France, Holland, Britain, and several others—the insurgent threat showed little sign of abating. According to Ruttig, "despite the significant number of casualties the Taliban have suffered, including among commanders, there is no sign that their momentum has been stopped, in spite of U.S. military assertions to the contrary. Instead, their geographic reach, ethnic inclusiveness, and potential for intimidation seem to be growing."[127]

The decision by the Obama administration to go ahead with the troop surge and increased drone strikes across the border in Pakistan were supposed to be the great equalizers, however, neither has been able to crush the Taliban in the manner that many expected. Cutting off the Taliban's primary sources of funding should be one of the highest priorities of any line of effort, especially as the decision on whether or not to sustain a significant counterterrorism capability looms on the horizon.

Non-kinetic Activities

One of the primary task forces created to counter threat financing in Afghanistan is the Afghan Threat Finance Cell (ATFC), a unit comprised of agents from the FBI, the DEA, Treasury, and the DoD. The ATFC was organized in 2008 to investigate the Taliban's financial structure and how the insurgency was funded.[128] Perhaps the most significant victory of the ATFC was its exposure of the Kabul Bank scandal, a fiasco that involved characters so nefarious that the plot unfolded like a Hollywood-style mafia movie, with insurgents connected to warlords, Afghan government officials, and economic powerbrokers from the Persian Gulf to South Asia.

Since 2001, and mostly as a result of international pressure, Afghanistan (as well as countries like the UAE, and Pakistan) has drafted money laundering legislation and stricter regulations and oversight on bank transfers. The United Nations has passed a series of resolutions dating back to 1999 directed at freezing Taliban assets and resources. In the United States, Executive Order 13129 blocks any property and prohibits transactions with the Taliban, while Executive Order 13224 allows the United States to attack the broader terrorist group infrastructure, to include the ability to block U.S. assets of, and deny access to U.S. markets to, foreign banks who fail to comply with U.S. authorities' continued attempts to freeze terrorists assets throughout the globe.[129]

Still, tracking the money is complicated because narcotics coming from Afghanistan are traded for commodities (e.g., automobiles, electronics) with no money trail to follow.[130] Some important steps in Afghanistan include the creation of a National Drug Control Strategy (NDCS) as well as efforts to build the capacity of the Sensitive Investigative Unit (SIU) and Technical Investigative Unit (TIU) as the investigative branches of the National Interdiction Unit (NIU). Accordingly, the enforcement capabilities of these units are also being bolstered, in part by further strengthening Afghanistan's formal legal processes and the ability of the Criminal Justice Task Force (CJTF) to successfully prosecute guilty parties.[131] The Government of the Islamic Republic of Afghanistan (GIRoA) has begun working to introduce regulation, transparency and trade controls at the border while government agencies like the Afghanistan Investment Support Agency (AISA) is working to attract FDI, though much of this depends on the stability or fluidity of the security situation in the country.

CONCLUSION

Taliban insurgents who fight against the United States and ISAF troops in late 2015 are motivated by a different set of factors than the group of young *madrassa* students that initially comprised the movement in the mid-1990s. Then, the Taliban was primarily motivated by the desire to establish an ideal Islamic state governed by *sharia* law. After all, the Taliban's ranks were made up of young Afghans who grew up in the refugee camps of Pakistan, displaced from the fighting of the Soviet-Afghan War. Today, the Taliban fight first and foremost to expel foreign troops from Afghan soil.

Following 14 years of fighting against Coalition forces, the Taliban has been seriously degraded. Estimates put the number of insurgents somewhere between 60,000 and 70,000, of which approximately 15,000 insurgents are full-time fighters.[132] American airpower, ISAF counterinsurgency warfare, and special operations night raids have damaged the organization and caused it to disperse throughout Afghanistan and across the border in Pakistan. However, this is the same group that claims membership in the *mujahedin* that drove the Soviets out of Afghanistan in the late 1980s. Despite suffering major losses, elements of the insurgency remain confident that if its fighters are able to muddle along, the Taliban can survive until U.S. troops are withdrawn from Afghanistan. This could potentially set the stage for a return to violence and yet another Afghan civil war.

If the Taliban were to lose its two primary sources of revenue— donations from wealthy sponsors abroad and money obtained through the drug trade—it could have a significant impact on the insurgents' ability to continue fighting. Neither of these two outcomes is likely, however. Moreover, the Taliban maintains a diversified revenue stream, with other income garnered through various organized crime rackets, to include KFR and extortion. In short, the only way funding will play a role is in possible financial incentives offered to insurgents as part of a reintegration package.

The majority of Afghans want peace.[133] Inevitably, the longer the conflict drags on, the more Afghan civilians are killed. This affects the level of popular support for the Taliban, even when the casualties are caused by the COIN force.[134] Understandably, Afghans are war weary following over 30 years of constant conflict. If the Taliban is seen as a force for stability in the country, its members may be able to concentrate significant support among the Pashtun population. When translated into a political context, this bodes well for a negotiated settlement.

Of all the seminal events in Afghanistan over the past decade—Quran burnings, civilian casualties, the Kabul Bank scandal—none will be more important than the phases immediately following the withdrawal of United States, NATO, and ISAF troops from Afghanistan. Then, and only then, will the international community have a hint at what the future may hold. The ANSF, to include the Afghan National Army (ANA) and the Afghan National Police (ANP) will be left with the difficult task of providing security throughout the country, likely with the assistance of a small footprint of U.S. Special Forces and other counterterrorist capabilities.[135]

CHAPTER 7

Al-Qaida: 9/11, Franchise Groups, and the Future after Bin Laden

BACKGROUND

The origins of Al-Qaida[1] can be traced back to an organization called Maktab al-Khidamat, or MAK, established by a Palestinian jihadist named Abdulla Azzam. The organization's early efforts focused on recruiting Arab fighters to join the resistance in Afghanistan, where the so-called mujahedin, or holy warriors, were fighting to expel Soviet troops from the country.[2] Early members of MAK, which was founded in 1984, included Azzam, Osama bin Laden, and the Algerian, Abdullah Anas. In the mid-1980s, bin Laden met and joined forces with Ayman al-Zawahiri, the current leader of "core" Al-Qaida. Zawahiri eventually merged key members of his group, Egyptian Islamic Jihad (EIJ), with Al-Qaida, once it emerged as its own entity in the late 1980s, at which point MAK had become more focused on humanitarian efforts rather than actual fighting.[3] Al-Qaida has continued to evolve over the years. Now entering its third decade, Al-Qaida is many things—terrorist organization, global jihadist network, brand and franchise group for Salafist jihadists throughout the world. This chapter will focus primarily on what is known as Core Al-Qaida,[4] but will also touch upon several Al-Qaida affiliates,[5] including Al-Qaida in the Arabian Peninsula (AQAP) and Al-Qaida in the Islamic Maghreb (AQIM), as well as, Al-Shabaab, and Jabhat al-Nusra.[6]

HOW AL-QAIDA FUNDED ITS ACTIVITIES

Al-Qaida raises funds through a variety of activities, ranging from donations from charitable organizations to KFR, drug trafficking, and robbery, among other methods. The group's fund-raising methods have evolved over time, beginning with the Soviet Afghan War (1979–1989) and adapting with each subsequent conflict (Bosnia, Chechnya, Tajikistan, etc.) in which Al-Qaida operatives fought. Some methods of raising funds are crude, while others are more sophisticated. More recently, Al-Qaida members have utilized "anonymisers" that replace Internet Protocol (IP) addresses by an Internet service provider with an "anonymiser" address unable to be traced.[7] The Internet remains an avenue that Al-Qaida and other terrorist groups can use to facilitate logistical and financial support of their organizations, which in turn enable them to conduct operations.[8]

As Rabasa et al. have noted about Al-Qaida, "The organization is constrained largely by the limits of its own imagination. Many fund-raising criminal activities exist to which Al-Qaida could turn if it wants."[9] This is not to suggest that Al-Qaida maintains a consistent, steady supply of funding. On the contrary, like most terrorist or insurgent groups, the funding ebbs and flows. In 2008, Al-Qaida was struggling to raise money and sustain a high operational tempo.[10] It was during this time that Al-Qaida sympathizers from Bahrain arranged to transfer money to Al-Qaida's senior leadership in Pakistan, in an example of a reverse directional flow of funds. Only a few years earlier, in 2005, Al-Qaida's then number two, Ayman al-Zawahiri, reached out to AQI chief Abu Musab al-Zarqawi to request $100,000 in financial assistance.[11]

Gray Economy

In response to pressure exerted by state governments, Al-Qaida has diversified its fund-raising portfolio to include money raised using a bottom-up approach, wherein some of the onus for donating money has shifted from wealthy donors and organizations to local efforts, supported by grassroots financing. Still, the group relies on money from the worldwide Muslim diaspora, funds sent to the group through various charities, multiple types of fraud, and a range of legal businesses, which are also responsible for laundering funds gained through illicit ventures. Funds flow from and through the Persian Gulf, especially countries like Saudi Arabia, Qatar, and Kuwait. Al-Qaida's sectarian strategy is partly designed to appeal to its donor base in these and other Gulf countries with Sunni majorities.

Diaspora Support

Just as other groups have done, including the PIRA and the LTTE, Al-Qaida's leadership has reached out to the *ummah* for financial assistance to allegedly help sustain the families of those Al-Qaida members imprisoned or dead.[12] In Syria, jihadists receive a steady provision of financial contributions from wealthy individuals throughout the Persian Gulf.[13] Pakistani jihadists living in Spain have sent millions of dollars to terrorists in Pakistan, money earned from petty crime.[14] According to Rohan Gunaratna, Salafism has endured throughout the Islamic world, as well as through the growing Muslim diaspora across Europe, North America, and Australia.[15]

As wars and instability continue to ravage predominantly Muslim countries, more refugees seek and are granted asylum in the United States, Scandinavia, and other Western nations. This trend is coupled by a worldwide increase in Salafist jihadist groups, as Seth Jones has noted.[16] This trend is troubling for the counterterrorism apparatus of many Western nations. Many Muslims feel obliged to donate money to humanitarian assistance and disaster relief organizations, most of which are run by religious parties and organizations. *Zakat* is a form of obligatory almsgiving and a main tenet of the Islamic faith.[17] Collections can be particularly hefty during the Muslim holy month of Ramadan. For those who can afford to give more, *sadaqah* are voluntary donations to the neediest recipients. Foreign diasporas are a major node in this fund-raising network.

Charities

Al-Qaida and affiliated groups have established a bevy of charities, humanitarian organizations, and religious associations to help with financial support.[18] These charities collect, comingle, mask, maintain, transfer, and distribute the funds necessary to support the organization. Charities that fund terrorism and perform good deeds are not necessarily mutually exclusive. For example, a Kuwaiti charity called Lajnat al Daawa Al Islamiya (LDI) was linked to Al-Qaida, but was also known for its medical clinics and orphanages in Afghanistan and Pakistan.[19]

Sometimes funds are solicited surreptitiously, while other times they are brazenly demanded. A December 2003 edition of *al Hilal*, a militant magazine published by Harakat-ul-Mujahideen (HUM) leader Maulana Fazlur Rehman Khalil, implored those Muslims who could not travel abroad to conduct jihad to contribute money to jihadists fighting in Iraq.[20] In 2006, the U.S. Department of Treasury designated Abd al-Hamid al-Mujil as a terrorist financier. Al-Mujil served as the executive director of the Eastern Province office of the International Islamic Relief Organization (IIRO).[21] Based in Jeddah, Saudi Arabia, the IIRO has established an Endowment Fund (*Sanabil al Khair*) and works closely with the Global Islamic League. Along with several of its subsidiaries, the IIRO has been accused of financing Al-Qaida and terrorist operations. Another Saudi-based charity, Al Haramain Islamic Foundation,[22] has also been accused of financially supporting Al-Qaida and other jihadist groups, such as JI, Lashkar-e-Taiba (LeT), the Pakistani Taliban, and Al Itihaad al Islamia, a Somali group aligned with Al-Qaida.[23] The Blessed Relief (Muwafaq) Foundation and the Rabita Trust were also linked to Al-Qaida.[24]

A Kuwaiti charity called the Revival of Islamic Heritage Society (RIHS) has been accused of providing material and financial support to Al-Qaida and its affiliates,[25] while some of its subsidiaries have been shut down by the governments of the countries[26] in which these subsidiaries have operated. As Levitt notes, "Even with the proliferation of local and self-led terrorist cells, traditional methods of terrorist financing—such as the abuse of charities, individual major donors and organized facilitation and financial support networks—remain a mainstay of al-Qa'ida financing."[27]

Fraud

Similar to revenue generating activities like petty crime and robbery, fraud is typically committed more frequently at the grassroots level of Al-Qaida, where small cells of sympathizers not directly connected to the group raise funds in the few ways they can. Fraud tends to be a crime with low barriers to entry, which is one of the reasons it is favored by terrorist fund-raisers. Al-Qaida has remained active in acquiring money through online fraud.[28] Al-Qaida cells have raised money through the abuse of government welfare benefits. While welfare fraud may only raise limited amounts of money, even small amounts of money can be used to conduct a narrowly-focused terrorist attack.[29] One of the British jihadists who conducted the suicide attacks of July 7, 2005, committed bank fraud by deliberately defaulting on a £10,000 loan and overdrawing on his multiple bank accounts.[30] In Italy, tax fraud has generated funding for Al-Qaida-linked militants,[31] while in France, stolen credit card information has been used by Islamist militants to commit fraud online and finance attacks with the proceeds.[32]

The 1993 attack on the World Trade Center was funded with money stolen through credit card and other low-level fraud, as was the December 1999 "Millennium Plot" to attack the Los Angeles International Airport, a case in which the plotters committed check fraud, credit card fraud, and identity theft.[33]

Legal Businesses

Controlling legal businesses becomes a must at some point for most terrorist and insurgent groups that eventually grow their operating budgets to finance operational and organizational goals. These businesses allow groups like Al-Qaida to disguise the transfer of currency through international trade. The over- and under-invoicing of goods and services, anticipated payments never delivered, and re-invoicing through free-trade areas are ways in which Al-Qaida could mask its movement of money. Front companies located in "high-risk jurisdictions" further complicate the challenge.[34] In many cases, front organizations and legitimate businesses have provided cover for charitable organizations with more nefarious aims.[35]

While based in Sudan, Al-Qaida was able to earn money through a range of legal businesses, including construction, manufacturing, currency trading, import-export companies, and agriculture.[36] At one point, it was believed that bin Laden owned 80 companies scattered throughout the globe.[37] Several of these businesses were located in Yemen, including the Al Hamati Sweet Bakeries, Al Nur Honey Press Shops, and Al Shifa Honey Press for Industry and Commerce. Al-Qaida's network of businesses and shell corporations around the world also included Wadi al-Aqiq, the Laden International firm, Hijra Construction, the Themar al-Mubaraka Company, Khalifa Trading Industries, the Safa Group, ET Dizon Travel Pyramid Trading, NASCO conglomerate, Manpower Services, Daw al-Iman al-Shafee Inc., and the Konsojaya Trading Company, among others.[38] Al Taqwa, with offices in Switzerland, Liechtenstein, Italy, and the Caribbean, helped Al-Qaida launder money while also providing important indirect investment services for bin Laden and co.[39]

Al-Barakaat is a network of companies founded in Mogadishu, Somalia with headquarters in Dubai. This conglomerate was used by Al-Qaida in as many as 40 different countries, with services as diverse as telecommunications, construction, money remittance and other banking services. Al-Barakaat managed, invested, and distributed funds for Al-Qaida, while simultaneously functioning as a source of financing and cash transfers for bin Laden, during his tenure as the organization's boss.[40] On an annual basis, it is believed that this Al-Qaida front dealt with upwards of $140 million a year in transmitted payments, while skimming fees to the tune of 2 to 5 percent, a service that blessed Al-Qaida with millions of dollars.[41]

Money Laundering

Following the attacks of September 11, 2001, international banking transfers inevitably came under greater scrutiny. As a result, Al-Qaida began relying more on moving its money through *hawala,* which is an ancient form of money dealing and funds transfer that competes with state-governed finance in developing countries across the globe.[42] *Hawala* is used because it is a known quantity throughout the Middle East and South Asia. It is mostly secure, relatively anonymous, and convenient for those who do not wish to deal with the scrutiny or due diligence procedures of banks. Furthermore, it is personal—linked to extended families, tribes, clans, and sub-clans. Al-Qaida's reliance on *hawala* is not a new phenomenon. Historically, the international hawala transfer system has been Al-Qaida's most effective and reliable means of smuggling cash around the world and remains the group's "fallback" system of moving money.[43]

Another method to move money is through the use of "mules," which are couriers used to physically transport large quantities of bulk cash, valuable commodities (gemstones, precious metals), and other valuable items that can be converted to cash or used in nonmonetary barter transactions. These couriers can link up with other couriers to exchange money and goods, creating a complex chain in an attempt to obfuscate both the origin and final destination of the money. In Europe, terrorists and their supporters have utilized the hassle-free bus and rail system to transport cash throughout the continent with ease.

Al-Qaida has favored Mogadishu, Dubai, Mombassa, and Nairobi for much of its money laundering ventures.[44] Persian Gulf countries like the UAE and Yemen are both source and destination countries for funds transferred through hawala networks. The takeaway for law enforcement and those attempting to curb Al-Qaida's flow of money is that the group evolves and consistently seeks and finds workarounds to efforts to combat its money laundering. The group and its affiliates have implemented innovative techniques to hide and launder money, including the use of online gambling sites.[45] Indeed, Al-Qaida even once attempted to invest in a Chicago futures brokerage house.[46]

Dark Economy

In addition to raising money through the gray economy, Al-Qaida's criminal activities also provide a significant portion of its operating budget. The combination of ways in which Al-Qaida raises money in the dark economy is not static. To be sure, this mix changes over time as terrorists adopt an approach to fund-raising that has been described as "eclectic and opportunistic."[47] In Afghanistan and Pakistan, Al-Qaida works closely with the Haqqani Network to raise funds through a range of criminal activities.[48] In Yemen, AQAP colludes with local tribes to earn money through kidnapping and other illicit means.[49] In short, Al-Qaida and its affiliates have successfully adapted to their surroundings to raise money through an array of illegal ventures, which will be detailed throughout the remainder of this section.

Kidnapping for Ransom (KFR)

Al-Qaida Central and each of the Al-Qaida affiliates rely on kidnapping for ransom as a form of fund-raising, although certain affiliates—particularly AQIM and AQAP—rely on this tactic more than others. Throughout the

Maghreb, a sparsely populated stretch of arid desert territory stretching throughout Northwest Africa, AQIM fighters have continuously kidnapped Westerners, especially European citizens, and exchanged them for hefty ransoms paid by governments including Germany, Switzerland, Austria, Sweden, Holland, France, and Spain. According to a July 2014 investigative report by *The New York Times*, Al-Qaida and its affiliates have pulled in at least $125 million from KFR since 2008, with $66 million paid in 2013 alone.[50]

Another Al-Qaida affiliate, AQAP, also relies on KFR as a primary revenue stream to finance its operations, with at least half of the group's operating budget funded through kidnapping. Local Yemenis work on commission for AQAP, scouring the streets of San'a searching for foreigners to abduct.[51] Indeed, KFR has become such a central tactic of these groups that AQAP, AQIM and Al-Shabaab in Somalia have coordinated efforts through the establishment of a common kidnapping protocol. These groups work closely with local criminal groups who conduct the actual kidnapping and then exchange the hostages for a percentage of the ultimate fee.[52] Kidnapping is a crime of opportunity and successful kidnappings that generate revenue encourage more kidnappings. Local cells of Al-Qaida sympathizers utilize KFR to raise funds as well. Pakistanis jihadists living in Spain have engaged in so-called "express kidnappings," which are quick hit snatch and grab jobs that end once the victim's family in Pakistan pays the ransom.[53]

Armed Robbery and Theft

Like fraud, independent or grassroots Al-Qaida cells often rely on petty crime, armed robbery and theft to support their operations. An Al-Qaida cell in France robbed automatic teller machines (ATMs), while a separate French cell attempted to rob a cash distribution center by blowing a hole in the wall of the building as it attempted (and failed) to steal 4 million Euros.[54] Terrorists inspired by Al-Qaida in Spain and Switzerland committed robberies to finance armed attacks and terrorist training abroad. The theft and sale of designer watches, gold bracelets, and emerald necklaces stolen by a Salafist group calling itself the "Group of Truth," and operating in Costa del Sol, generated funds which were used to fund assassinations in Algeria and Mauritania.[55] Al-Qaida cells have also been known to support operations through credit card theft. Stolen credit cards have been used to purchase items such as GPS, night vision goggles, sleeping bags, telephones, knives, tents, and other supplies for jihadists operating in Iraq.[56]

Smuggling, Trafficking, and Counterfeiting

Al-Qaida and its affiliated groups have engaged in smuggling, trafficking and counterfeiting of numerous commodities in order to raise cash for their respective organizations. In African countries including Sierra Leone, Liberia, and the DRC, Al-Qaida has profited from the sale of gold, gemstones, tanzanite and so-called conflict diamonds or blood diamonds. Douglas Farah estimates that Al-Qaida invested approximately $50 million in the West African illicit diamond market.[57] Participation in the illicit diamond market likely brought Al-Qaida in contact with members of Lebanese Hezbollah, also active in the trade through a dense network of contacts from the Lebanese diaspora living in West Africa.

As the noose was tightened around charities that funded Al-Qaida after 9/11, the group attempted to diversify its revenue sources, to include allegedly garnering money earned through drug trafficking, possibly through an alliance with the IMU in Central Asia, but also in North Africa by one of its affiliates. In the latter case, AQIM has been linked to Colombian cocaine traffickers in a quid pro quo relationship that brings cash to the terrorists while providing the traffickers with access (and in some cases, heavily armed escorts) across the desert region between Mauritania, Mali, and Algeria, where narcotics transit through on their way to the European market. In addition to money obtained through KFR, AQIM earns significant sums of money from trafficking tobacco, cocaine and synthetic drugs between Spain and Algeria.[58]

By operating on the black market, terrorists and insurgents come into contact with a panoply of shadowy figures, including assassins, arms dealers, human traffickers, document forgers and others who exist on the margins of society. These contacts with the criminal underworld are crucial to many of the logistical needs of violent non-state actors.

Extortion and Protection

In Afghanistan and Pakistan, Al-Qaida has forged a working criminal relationship with another terrorist group, the Haqqani Network, in which the two organizations collaborate to extort businesses in zones under the control of militants.[59] Other business owners offer protection payments, sometimes referred to as "security investments," to make sure that jihadists do not destroy or interfere with the properties and businesses they manage and own.[60] The Pakistani Taliban also engages in extortion and is known to work closely with Al-Qaida in this area, as they do with KFR. In fact, cooperation between Al-Qaida, the Haqqani Network, and the Pakistani Taliban has been characterized as "seamless," indicating that these groups maintain a close working relationship.[61]

External State Support

External state support to terrorism can come in a variety of ways: financial, logistical, political, etc. During the height of the Cold War, the United

States and the Soviet Union funded proxy actors throughout the globe and indeed, in an ironic twist, the United States provided support for the *mujahedin* fighting the Soviets in Afghanistan, some portion of whom would go on to form the core of Al-Qaida. States can be active supporters of terrorism, knowingly allowing groups to occupy parts of their sovereign territory, as Sudan did with Al-Qaida. States can also be what Byman calls passive sponsors of terrorism, where their inaction proves in some way to be vital to the group's success.[62] No state formally sponsors Al-Qaida today.[63] Some scholars find it far-fetched that elements of the Pakistani government were unaware that Osama bin Laden was hiding in Abbottabad, but a review of documents captured in the raid that ultimately killed Al-Qaida's chieftain "do not *explicitly* point to any institutional Pakistani support to Bin Ladin."[64] According to Seth Jones, over the past several years, Iran has been willing to expand its relationship with Al-Qaida.[65]

WHAT AL-QAIDA ACHIEVED WITH THESE FUNDS

Al-Qaida uses funding to pay the salaries of its members, to maintain training camps, to secure weapons and explosives, and to conduct the mundane day-to-day operations of a transnational terrorist group. One of its main challenges is to utilize the strengths of its networked structure, without losing unity, cohesion, and collective action capacity.[66] Prior to the terrorist attacks of September 11, 2001, Al-Qaida was, in the words of terrorism scholar Bruce Hoffman, "a lumbering bureaucracy."[67] But following the U.S. invasion of Afghanistan, the group has dispersed like mercury, fanning out to different parts of the globe. In addition to Al-Qaida's more formal affiliates, the group maintains contact with a broader network of jihadist organizations, including Boko Haram in Nigeria, JI in Southeast Asia, the ASG in the Philippines, TTP),[68] LeT in Pakistan, the Libyan Islamic Fighting Group, the Islamic Jihad Union, and the IMU, just to name a few. "Global Jihad" fighters have traveled to fight alongside insurgents in places like Tajikistan, Bosnia, Chechnya, Kashmir, Mindanao, Indonesia, Somalia, and many others.[69] Most recently, Afghanistan and Syria have been among the most popular destinations for jihadists.

Operational Capabilities

Al-Qaida's operational capabilities help contribute to its ability to plan and execute attacks. And while the group has not been able to successfully strike the U.S. homeland since September 11, 2001, it has, along with its affiliated groups, conducted attacks throughout the world. Prominent Al-Qaida strikes have killed citizens in the Bali attacks in Indonesia in

2002, the Casablanca attacks in Morocco in 2003, the Madrid attacks in Spain in 2004, the London attacks in England in 2005, and so on.[70] Moreover, there have been innumerable failed plots and attacks, which demonstrate both the competence of those organizations countering Al-Qaida, but also Al-Qaida's will to strike the West.

Weapons

Al-Qaida relies on a range of weapons to execute its attacks, from small arms to vehicle-borne improvised explosive devices (VBIEDs) and just about everything else in between. Moreover, the methods of delivery are diverse, relying on land, sea, and air. The East Africa embassy attacks of 1998 were conducted on land using truck bombs, pistols, and stun grenades. The 2000 USS Cole bombing involved a small boat packed with hundreds of pounds of explosives. The 9/11 attacks involved the use of civilian passenger aircraft to fly into the World Trade Center and the Pentagon. According to data analyzed by Robert Pape, Al-Qaida employs teams of suicide attackers, as opposed to single, one-off attackers, more often than any other group that also employ suicide bombing as a tactic.[71] Suicide attacks are considered to be effective because they deliver multiple benefits on various levels without incurring significant costs to an organization as a whole.[72]

In Afghanistan, Al-Qaida attacks against ISAF forces usually consist of IEDs, rocket and mortar attacks, ground assaults, and suicide bombings. Al-Qaida is able to acquire weapons from the Taliban, which in some cases is obtaining weapons from Pakistan's ISI. Proximity to Peshawar and leftover weapons from Soviet-Afghan War; as well as extensive use of the worldwide black market in arms and munitions also stocks Al-Qaida's arsenal. The group's fighters deliberately seek out failed states and ungoverned areas, which are already awash in weaponry, from small arms to more sophisticated weapons like shoulder-fired surface to air missiles. In addition to guns and ammunition, Al-Qaida also needs vehicles, technology (GPS, surveillance material, etc.), and bomb-making materials to carry out attacks.

According to Moisés Naim, of the roughly 80 million AK-47s in circulation today, most are in the wrong hands. Naim cites a United Nations statistic that only 18 million (or about 3 percent) of the 550 million small arms and light weapons in circulation today are used by government, military, or police forces. Illicit trade accounts for almost 20 percent of the total small arms trade and generates more than $1 billion a year.[73] Weak states simultaneously serve as the source, transition, and destination countries for the illegal arms trade.[74] Al-Qaida militants tend to travel lightly, which enables the jihadists to function as a parasite, attaching themselves to local groups, exploiting parochial grievances, and taking advantage of instability in countries or regions where conflict is ripe and weapons aplenty. To this end, Al-Qaida is particularly adept at linking up with warlords, as it has in North Africa, Central Asia, and East Africa, where it has supported and exploited relationships with a range of other violent non-state actors in order to acquire the weaponry needed for its own fighters.

Al-Qaida has used MANPADS several times while attempting to destroy aircraft. One attempt occured in May 2002 when militants used a shoulder-fired missile to take out a U.S. military aircraft in Saudi Arabia, although the missile misfired. Just a few months after that attempt, Al-Qaida terrorists in Mombasa, Kenya, tried to shoot down an Israeli charter aircraft using two shoulder-fired SA-7 Strela-2Ms, although this attempt also failed because the plane was beyond the range of the missiles.[75]

The ultimate attack would be an Al-Qaida plot where terrorists detonate a chemical, biological, radiological, nuclear and explosives (CBRNE) weapon on U.S. soil. While acquiring this material and successfully employing it would be difficult, the results would be disastrous. Indeed, as Al-Qaida has made clear time and again, the will to conduct an attack is not lacking.[76] U.S. authorities must remain vigilant and be prepared to deal with a worst-case scenario in the event of an Al-Qaida CBRNE attack.

Intelligence

Before it conducts operations, especially spectacular attacks, Al-Qaida seeks high levels of certainty and operational control. The group's use of intelligence and counterintelligence in executing the 9/11 attacks demonstrate the importance of tradecraft in both the preparation of a detailed plan and the process of identifying and vetting targets. Moreover, intelligence greatly informed both the conceptualization and planning phases.[77]

As a complement to its intelligence and counterintelligence activities, Al-Qaida also conducts surveillance and reconnaissance to prepare for its operations. Several of the 9/11 hijackers engaged in reconnaissance flights in both New York and Washington D.C. Dry-runs of flights were executed in order to carry out surveillance of the airplane, boarding process, cockpit access, and so on. Finally, Al-Qaida members relied on open source intelligence to compile data from Western aviation magazines, airline materials, and web searches of U.S. flight schools.[78] Commenting on Al-Qaida's use of counterintelligence protocols in the lead up to the 9/11 attacks, Ilardi believes that it "revealed a detached objectivity that allowed it [Al Qaeda] to form and respond to accurate and highly detailed assessments of its operating environment."[79]

Al-Qaida's predecessor, MAK, produced an eleven volume encyclopedia of jihad, replete with an entire section dedicated to the importance of insurgent intelligence.[80] In training manuals, large portions of jihadist literature are dedicated to how to resist interrogation methods and techniques commonly employed by governments and intelligence services. As Bill Rosenau has noted, insurgent intelligence is an auxiliary activity, as it seeks to reduce risk while reinforcing confidence in the insurgents that the planned operation or operations will succeed. Even more importantly, there is an obvious cost-benefit tradeoff involved with respect to intelligence—"funds, personnel, training, and other resources that are employed for intelligence purposes are resources that cannot be applied to other important insurgent activities."[81]

In Europe, to evade technical methods of monitoring by counterterrorism officials, Al-Qaida members have focused on operational security, honing their tradecraft and discipline. Al-Qaida cells have familiarized themselves with governmental security measures, including phone monitoring, and have adapted in kind to circumvent these measures intended to detect terrorist activity and plots.[82]

Sanctuary, Safe Haven, and Operational Space

In terms of geopolitics, failed states usually make for poor neighbors, but can serve as welcome hosts to non-state actors, including transnational terrorist groups and violent insurgencies. Al-Qaida has enjoyed sanctuary in Afghanistan and Pakistan (1984–1991), Sudan (1991–1995), Afghanistan again (1995–2001) and finally, Pakistan (2001–present), which seems to be somewhat hospitable terrain for the militants, while providing them with access to other jihadists. After the U.S. led war against the Taliban, Al-Qaida operatives fled Afghanistan and found refuge in Pakistan's Pashtun-majority FATA.[83] Covering some 27,220 square kilometers of mountainous, rugged, and unforgiving landscape, the FATA offered an ideal location for the defeated Taliban and Al-Qaida forces to regroup.[84] As Gunaratna has noted, "Al Qaeda members, with the help of the Taliban, have created FATA as the global headquarters of like-minded groups."[85]

By establishing a safe haven in the FATA, Al-Qaida has been able to take advantage of the jihadist infrastructure already in place. Indeed, Chechens, Uzbeks, Algerians, Tunisians, Libyans, Egyptians, and Chinese jihadists known as Uighurs and representing the East Turkestan Islamic Movement (ETIM) were already living and training in Pakistan's tribal belt. The tribal regions are populated primarily by ethnic Pashtuns, who also constitute the majority of the population in eastern and southern Afghanistan and live by a code of pashtunwali, a pre-Islamic concept of living or philosophy regarded as an honor code, or unwritten law.[86]

The most dangerous and lawless areas of the tribal belt of the FATA comprises seven agencies bordering Afghanistan, which include Bajaur, Mohmand, Khyber, Kurram, Orakzai, North Waziristan, and South Waziristan.[87] In October 2006, in an audacious snub of government authority, Al-Qaida declared the establishment of the "Islamic Emirate of Waziristan" and organized a governing shura council to rule the area.[88] Al-Qaida and its affiliated groups have sought and established sanctuaries and safe havens in areas governed by religious leaders or tribal laws and norms conducive to the Salafist jihadist ideological worldview. With a rugged terrain and a sympathetic population, Pakistan's tribal areas are ideally suited for Al-Qaida. Pakistan's clumsy counterinsurgency effort in the FATA and seminal events like the siege of the disregard; Lal Masjid, or Red Mosque, in 2007, have only served to push Pashtun warlords and tribal leaders closer to Al-Qaida.

In Pakistan, Al-Qaida has used its safe haven to deepen its connections to a growing network of jihadist groups and militant movements within the country, including Tehrik, Nifaz Shariat Muhammadi (TNSM), Jamiat ul-Ansar, Jamiat ul-Furqan, Harakat ul-Jihad ul-Islami, Jaish Muhammad, LeT and Lashkar e-Jhangvi, among others. Local power brokers like the Ahmadzai-Wazir tribe and members of the Yargulkhel sub-clan of the Zalikhel clan also welcomed Al-Qaida militants as guests.[89] In addition to the FATA, core Al-Qaida enjoys safe haven in Pakistan's major cities like Karachi, Peshawar, Lahore, and Quetta. Its offshoots continue to control large chunks of ungoverned space in parts of the Levant, the Maghreb, the Sinai Peninsula, West Africa, Yemen, Somalia, and elsewhere.[90]

In Yemen, AQAP has expanded at the expense of a chronically weak central government which struggles to control territory outside of the capital, Sanaa. Al-Qaida is always on the lookout for new opportunities to establish a safe haven. While failed states present some opportunities, they are often inhospitable in terms of security, stability, and the infrastructure necessary to function as an effective terrorist organization in the twenty-first century. At one point, bin Laden expressed interest in South Africa, which he saw as an "open territory" with a stable, growing economy and a place where Al-Qaida members had used off and on for planning, fund-raising, and logistics over the years.[91]

Still, it is important to note that all sanctuary comes at some cost. When Al-Qaida was based in Sudan and Afghanistan, respectively, to operate openly as a "guest" of the government, bin Laden doled out tens of millions of dollars a year to his hosts.[92] This is not to say that the cost was not a worthwhile return on investment. The money bought carte blanche sanctuary, which was essential to Al-Qaida's ability to train, plot attacks, and grow its organization.

Training

Following the end of the Soviet–Afghan War, Al-Qaida established a large complex of training camps throughout Sudan, where bin Laden was invited by Hassan al-Turabi.[93] After a failed assassination attempt on Egyptian president Hosni Mubarak in Ethiopia, Al-Qaida was forced out of Sudan and eventually made its way to Afghanistan, as a guest of the Taliban. Between 1996 and 2001, it is believed that approximately 18,000 individuals trained in Al-Qaida training camps in Afghanistan.[94] Between 2002 and 2004, Abu Faraj al-Libi spearheaded the rebuilding of Al-Qaida's training facilities in the Shakai Valley of South Waziristan.[95] In late 2004/early 2005, Al-Qaida moved its training infrastructure from South to North Waziristan, based in and around the towns of Mir Ali and between Miran Shah and Shawal Valley, at Sedgi and Data Khel. Al-Qaida's relationship with the Pashtun tribes in this area has been instrumental to its ability to rebuild a sufficient training infrastructure.[96]

While some of the terrorists receiving training in the FATA are dispatched to fight against ISAF forces in Afghanistan, others are part of what Cruickshank has labeled the "militant pipeline" between Pakistan's tribal areas and the West. According to his analysis, between 2004 and 2010, in the majority of the 21 "serious" plots against the West, plotters either received direction from or trained with Al-Qaida or its allies in Pakistan.[97] In 2003, it was well-known that Al-Qaida was operating mobile training camps throughout South Asia. Reports surfaced of Al-Qaida militants trained in Pakistan-administered Kashmir, eastern Afghanistan, and camps in both Pakistan's tribal areas as well as close to major cities like Islamabad, the Pakistani capital.[98]

In Yemen, AQAP established training camps throughout the Shabwah region where fighters, including the failed "underwear bomber" Umar Farouk Abdulmutallab, were provided with military and religious instruction.[99] Indeed, training is one of the primary reasons why groups ultimately choose to partner with Al-Qaida. Historically, Al-Qaida has offered comprehensive training facilities to a range of jihadist offshoots, which is "an attractive service" for those groups whose fighters lack experience and a physical place to conduct training.[100]

Organizational Capabilities

While it started as a single, monolithic entity, Al-Qaida today is a decentralized, networked, transnational terrorist organization. In addition to the costs of conducting operations, Al-Qaida also needs a healthy budget to maintain its rather substantial structural costs. This includes money for subsistence living for its members (as well as for some of those who have families), communications, travel expenses, media and propaganda, and the provision of social services to selected constituents in an effort to buoy its popular support.[101] As groups grow more networked, it can be challenging to retain the cohesiveness of the group. Maintaining lines of communication, agreeing on shared goals and objectives, and remaining relevant in the increasingly crowded universe of global jihad is a time consuming and expensive undertaking, especially when law enforcement and intelligence services around the world are seeking to combat this network wherever it pulses.

Leadership

For some time, being the number three leader in Al-Qaida was the most dangerous job in the jihadist world. Top lieutenants including Ilyas Kashmiri, Atiyah abd al-Rahman, and Abu Yahya al-Libi have all been killed by U.S. counterterrorism forces. Still, this organization has proved nothing if not resilient. Indeed, noted terrorism scholar and Al-Qaida expert Bruce Hoffman concludes that "For more than a decade, it has withstood arguably the greatest international onslaught directed against a terrorist organization in history."[102]

The group has expanded beyond its base in South Asia to encompass wide swaths of Africa and the Middle East. It has ensured longevity by devolving power to its local franchises.[103] Throughout the group's evolution, its leadership has continued to play a major role in its longevity. The *Amir* is the overall leader of Al-Qaida and is tasked with a broad array of responsibilities, including planning on multiple levels (operational, strategic, tactical, logistical, and organizational), approving annual plans and budgets, and just like any corporate chief executive office, serving as the face of the organization.[104]

As the founder of Al-Qaida and leader of the organization until his death at the hands of U.S. Special Forces in May 2011, there is still debate over exactly how important he was to the movement.[105] Though Bin Laden fancied himself part "lecturer-businessman" part "activist theologian," his leadership style has been described as "soft-mannered, long-winded, project-oriented, media conscious."[106] On the other hand, his former deputy and now overall *Amir* of core Al-Qaida Ayman al-Zawahiri has been described as "a formidable figure," "committed revolutionary," who is simultaneously "pious, bitter, and determined," and since its early days had been "the real power behind Al-Qaida."[107]

Just as concerning as Zawahiri's leadership, Al-Qaida affiliated groups are also led by highly capable veteran jihadists. AQIM has been led by trained engineer and explosives expert Abdelmalek Droukdel since 2004,[108] while AQAP is currently headed by Zawahiri loyalist Nasir al-Wuhayshi.[109]

Ideology

In many ways, Al-Qaida's ideology reflects that it sees itself as a defender of the Islamic world and vanguard of Muslims everywhere, the *ummah*. In declaring jihad on the United States, bin Laden argued that the West, and in particular the United States, is hostile to Islam and the only way to respond to this aggression is with force or violence, which is the only language that America understands. In his speeches, bin Laden exhorts his followers to fight back and defend Muslims from the United States, which has perpetrated against Muslims "an ocean of oppression, injustice, slaughter and plunder."[110] Therefore, the next logical step is jihad. In essence, the core of Al-Qaida's ideology is individual jihad fused with collective revenge.[111]

From an intellectual standpoint, David Aaron has noted that jihadi totalitarian ideology is a closed system, but it also allows for disagreements over strategy, tactics, and other critical issues.[112] Not as draconian as some scholars make it out to be. Cragin agrees, observing that an analysis of the group's internal documents reveal a group at ease with allowing for internal disagreement and debate amongst its members and the leadership.[113] One well-known ideological divide in Al-Qaida is between those who desire to strike "the far enemy" and those whose interests are more parochial and prefer to target what they perceive as apostate regimes throughout the Muslim world.

Primarily, and almost exclusively, the bulk of guidance on contemporary insurgency is manufactured by Salafist ideologues. Individuals like Ayman al-Zawahiri, Abu Musab al Suri,[114] Anwar al-Awlaki (deceased),[115] and Abu Yahya al-Libi (deceased)[116] serve as Al-Qaida's main insurgent theorists, proffering advice on strategy, operations, and tactics (in addition to a host of other issues including diet, grooming, and marriage).[117] These modern day insurgency theorists are highly adept at propagating the narrative that the Muslim *ummah* is being oppressed by an American-Israeli (or "Crusader-Zionist") nexus.[118] According to Bruce Hoffman, Al-Qaida is "more an idea or a concept than an organization" and "an amorphous movement tenuously held together by a loosely networked transnational constituency rather than a monolithic, international terrorist organization with either a defined or identifiable command and control apparatus."[119]

Human Resources and Recruitment

One of the core missions of a terrorist organization's bureaucracy is to fulfill a human resources function, to include recruiting new members. Despite the image conjured when envisioning a dark network dispersed throughout 60 countries worldwide and forced to communicate covertly,

Al-Qaida remained a highly bureaucratic organization throughout most of the 1990s and 2000s. In the lead up to the attacks of September 11, 2001, Al-Qaida could accurately be characterized as a "unitary organization" with many of the trappings of a "lumbering bureaucracy," according to Hoffman.[120]

In Al-Qaida's training camps in Afghanistan, recruits were required to take a written exam and sign a contract before acceptance into the group. The contract detailed the moral responsibilities of would-be Al-Qaida members, as well as the stipulations of remuneration, including marital and family allowances, vacation time, and reimbursements for expenses incurred.[121] The group's organizational structure included the following components in addition to the top leadership: the Secretary, the Command Council, the Military Committee, the Documentations Unit, the Political Committee, the Media Committee, the Administrative and Financial Committee, the Security Committee, and the Religious Committee.[122]

On the recruitment front, Al-Qaida's core demographic is disenfranchised, disillusioned, marginalized youth that are vulnerable to radicalization and the message of violent religious extremism. And while the group's recruiting approach has always been global, more recently it has urged potential followers to conduct "DIY terrorism," or do-it-yourself attacks against soft targets in the West.[123] These "stray dogs," as Jenkins calls them, can be non-affiliated jihadists who simply share Al-Qaida's worldview and accept its ideology. Recruiting in diaspora communities is another favored method.[124] Al-Qaida has been particularly successful rallying European-born Muslims to its cause and in the past decade, there have been plots and attacks in the United Kingdom, Germany, Spain, Netherlands, France, and Belgium.

Media, PR, Propaganda, and Publicity

Al-Qaida uses thousands of Web sites to convey its messages and its production company, As-Sahab, releases dozens of videos each year. In March 2004, a document titled the "Camp al Battar [the sword] Magazine," was released, offering information on jihadist attacks in Saudi Arabia and Iraq.[125] In 2006, an Al-Qaida media distribution wing known as the Global Islamic Media Front released "Jihad Academy," which included footage showing attacks on U.S. troops, Al-Qaida militants assembling IEDs, and suicide bombers martyrdom tapes, complete with anti-American and anti-Israeli vitriol.[126] At the time of this writing, in 2015, the three most important, password-protected/access-controlled jihadist Web sites—al Shumukh al Islam, al Fida, and Ansar al Mujahideen—have recently been focused almost exclusively on the deteriorating situation in Syria.[127]

Throughout his tenure as Al–Qaida's leader, bin Laden consistently used AlQaida's media platforms to emphasize issues that many across the Arab and Islamic world are passionate about, including the liberation of Palestine, the American occupation of Iraq, and the corruption of apostate governments and regimes throughout the Middle East and South Asia.[128] Al-Qaida's media production is sophisticated, both aesthetically and historically. Propaganda routinely references colonial injustices of the past, including the Sykes-Picot Agreement, which carved up the Middle East between France and Britain. If Al-Qaida's media production seems high quality and refined, that is because the group has been producing media since its inception, although over the years, the themes have changed and its presentation has grown more nuanced.[129]

In February 2012, al-Zawahiri addressed the "Lions of the Levant," peppering his message with themes that railed against Alawites, Hezbollah, and Iran. In March 2013, a new e-journal was created, named *Balagh* ("Message"), the group promoting the journal called itself the "Levant News Battalion" and urged its followers to join the fight and send money to support those already fighting.[130] Sawt al-Jihad, or Voice of Jihad, is an Al-Qaida online magazine aimed at mobilizing public support for the group and justifying its actions to its core constituency.[131] As Evan F. Kohlman notes, in countering the media strategies of terrorist groups, foremost among them Al-Qaida, "technological sophistication is no longer a luxury," but instead, "a basic survival skill" for law enforcement and intelligence agencies.[132]

HOW AL-QAIDA FINANCING WAS COUNTERED

Al-Qaida financing was countered through a combination of kinetic and non-kinetic activities, aimed at preventing the group from acquiring and spending the funds needed to maintain its vast operational and organizational infrastructure. The response, at least from the United States, was swift and forceful. Laws were passed, task forces formed, and regulatory bodies commissioned to prevent terrorists from raising, storing and moving funds.[133]

One of the main challenges of countering Al-Qaida's financial network is that U.S. expertise in combating the financing of terrorism is more suited to dealing with financial transfers across borders than within them.[134] However, more government agencies have realized the importance of targeting terrorists' financial networks. The U.S. Department of Treasury is just one of several entities that continue to craft measures and laws that are aimed at freezing terrorist assets and targeting their traditional sources of income.[135] Nevertheless, Al-Qaida members are aware of government efforts to combat fund-raising schemes and how individual terrorists might be identified through bank transactions, money transfer services, credit cards, and online Web sites.[136] As related by Gretchen Peters, Osama bin Laden once noted that Al-Qaida was as "aware of the cracks inside the Western financial system as they are aware of the lines in their hands."[137]

Kinetic Activities

Before 9/11, numerous financial institutions were responsible for moving millions of dollars of Al-Qaida's money—some aware of what they were doing, others not.[138] Some analysts have speculated that during the 2000s, Al-Qaida earned as much as $1 billion per year from the entirety of its financing efforts.[139] Others suggest that before the 9/11 attacks, Al-Qaida sustained itself on roughly $30 million annually.[140] In an article published in 2004, Mark Basile claimed that Al-Qaida operated a significant financial network valued at over $300 million, although it disbursed between $30 and $40 million per year to run the organization.[141] The CIA estimated that prior to September 11, 2001, the cost of sustaining Al-Qaida was approximately $30 million per year.[142] Despite the fact that the Bank Secrecy Act mandates U.S. financial institutions to file currency transaction reports on transactions of $10,000 or more, terrorists nevertheless felt secure in using the formal banking system to move funds with relative impunity.

The March 2003 arrest of Al-Qaida's accountant, Saudi born-Mustafa Ahmed Hawsawi, set the group back in the short term. Hawsawi was the group's primary money man, responsible for managing day-to-day finances, and even in charge of wiring the money used to conduct the 9/11 attacks.[143] Over the next decade, U.S. counterterrorism efforts in Pakistan have included increased covert assets against Al-Qaida as well as a relentless onslaught of armed drone strikes targeted the organization's senior leadership. In Pakistan, U.S. counterterrorism strikes have been successful in removing senior level Al-Qaida members from the battlefield, including Osama bin Laden, external operations chief Ab Abd al-Rahman al-Najdi, and chief financial officer, Shaykh Sa'aid al-Masri.[144]

Non-kinetic Activities

Some of the non-kinetic responses aimed at cracking down on Al–Qaida fund-raising include a series of federal regulations that were designed to impose stricter requirements on financial institutions, the implementation of rules and guidelines by national and international regulatory and standards-setting organizations stressing the importance of due diligence KYC laws, as outlined by the FATF's recommendations.[145] Government-regulated official financial systems have tightened controls on bank-based money transfers across borders. Charitable organizations supporting Al-Qaida have been shuttered. Others have been hampered after being added to the UN list of organizations that support terrorism. These charities have been disrupted or deterred from continuing their activities.[146]

The government of Saudi Arabia "took some counter-terrorism measures immediately after 9/11," but American authorities remain concerned about the ability of religious charities to support terrorism beyond Riyadh's watch, as these organizations use money transfers to move funds to remote locations around the globe.[147] The government of the UAE has taken some steps to regulate hawala transactions, requiring users to register and provide background information about the identity of the remitters and beneficiaries on forms submitted to the Central Bank.[148] In Afghanistan, businesses that offer hawala services have to hold a license and report transactions to a financial intelligence agency that operates as part of the Central Bank.[149]

CONCLUSION

When thinking about the difficulty of countering terrorism financing in a globally connected, increasingly borderless world, consider the following: An Algerian citizen and AQIM member living in Spain with banks accounts in Palma de Mallorca in the name of an American company formed in Delaware transmitted funds to allegedly pay invoices for the services of an information technology company with branches in Holland and Germany. The invoices turned out to be false, while the Fiscalia of the High Court (Audiencia Nacional) in Spain determined that the money was transported to Algeria and Syria and used for "other purposes."[150] Financial crimes that support terrorism are increasingly occurring across countries, continents, cultures, and companies, spanning jurisdictions, legal regimes, and national governments in a complex web of transactions. Responding to this challenge requires a nimble, adaptive, and resilient counterthreat finance architecture that is willing to share information and relinquish sovereignty in some cases. According to Hoffman, "while bin Laden's death inflicted a crushing blow on Al-Qaida, it is still not clear that it has necessarily been a lethal one. He left behind a resilient movement that, although seriously weakened, has nonetheless been expanding and consolidating its control in new and far-flung locales."[151]

CHAPTER 8

The Islamic State of Iraq and Syria (ISIS): Building a Caliphate in the Levant

BACKGROUND

The Islamic State of Iraq and Syria[1] grew out of its predecessor organization, Al-Qaida in the Land of Two Rivers or AQI, which itself was an outgrowth of a group named Jama'at al-Tawhid wali-Jihad (JTWJ), headed by Abu Musab al-Zarqawi.[2] The group currently known as ISIS began metastasizing following the United States withdrawal of troops from Iraq in 2011 and continued to rest, rearm, and resupply its ranks until mid-2014, when it began its offensive throughout Iraq.[3] In an effort to build up its operational and organizational capabilities, ISIS took advantage of chaos in neighboring Syria while gaining recruits as a result of the marginalization of Iraqi Sunnis by Iraq's then-Prime Minister Nouri al-Maliki.

Under the Maliki regime, sectarianism intensified, pushing Iraqi Sunnis, many of whom were formerly associated with Saddam Hussein's Baath Party, into the arms of ISIS.[4] At the same time, foreign fighters from around the globe flocked to join the group, emboldened by its recent string of successful military victories and a slickly marketed media campaign unrivaled in its sophistication, technical prowess, and reach. The estimates vary widely, but some intelligence officials believe that there are currently approximately 15,000 citizens from 80 countries fighting with ISIS in Syria and Iraq, making it the most significant transnational jihadist conflict of all time.[5] Fighters have traveled from far afield, including many fighters from the United States, various European countries, Australia, and even other countries not normally associated with global jihad, like Chile and Cambodia.

HOW ISIS FUNDED ITS ACTIVITIES

For the most part, ISIS is locally funded. Unlike other terrorist groups that rely on external state support, ISIS funds its operations through various crimes, ranging from oil theft to bank robbery to extortion. The group has been described as a "ruthless and entrepreneurial enterprise run by bosses determined to squeeze out every penny of profit."[6] Some estimates put ISIS's *daily* income as of July 2014 at an astonishing $1 million per day.[7] Another self-described "conservative" estimate of this group that has been described as having "built its organization using a financial strategy characterized by ruthless efficiency and pragmatism" is that ISIS will earn between $100 to $200 million this year.[8]

The group "inherited" tens of millions of dollars from the criminal activities it undertook while known as AQI, which was so well-endowed at certain points that Al-Qaida senior leadership was requesting that AQI kick up funds to core Al-Qaida in Pakistan, instead of the other way around.[9] Indeed, during the insurgency against U.S. forces in Iraq, much of AQI's logistical apparatus operated out of neighboring Syria, including the Abu Ghadiyah, network which was responsible for managing the flow of men, money, and material back and forth along the Iraqi–Syrian border.[10] One report even suggested that ISIS militants paid for their English language Web site using the virtual currency Bitcoin, a claim which if true, could have serious implications for how the group's financing is countered.[11]

Gray Economy

In an interesting twist, ISIS is now thought to be the most financially well-endowed insurgent group ever, though the group's finances are almost exclusively raised and spent locally.[12] To be sure, the lion's share of ISIS's funds is generated through the dark economy. However, as moneymaking ventures like the smuggling and trafficking of oil are curtailed, the group will inevitably be forced to broaden its aperture to focus more closely on raising money through the gray economy. If ISIS is able to maintain a hold on territory throughout both Iraq and Syria, this will provide more opportunities for it to generate money from fraud and perhaps even the establishment of legal businesses. To be sure, ISIS's mafia mentality when it comes to finances ensures that its members will continue to engage in any activity necessary to keep the group fully resourced.

Diaspora Support

While perhaps not part of an Iraqi or Syrian diaspora in the traditional sense, ISIS has nonetheless managed to receive support from radical elements within the broader *ummah*, to include financial and logistical support from foreign terrorist fighter facilitators in countries including Georgia, Indonesia, Qatar, Kuwait, Turkey, and Jordan.[13] Still, ISIS's leadership realizes that funds donated from external states, wealthy patrons, and diaspora communities[14] are more vulnerable to law enforcement than funds generated *within* Iraq and Syria. To date, there has been no evidence that the Syrian diaspora has been supporting ISIS with funding or material support.[15]

To the extent that one considers the Muslim diaspora worldwide, the vision of reestablishing some semblance of a caliphate has long appealed to young Muslim (mostly) men from the Middle East, North Africa, South Asia and many Western countries as well.[16] This partly explains the large number of Westerners, especially Europeans, who have traveled to Iraq and Syria to join ISIS.[17] As David S. Cohen, the Under Secretary for Terrorism and Financial Intelligence at the U.S. Treasury Department has noted, although ISIS does not rely heavily on donations from abroad to fund its operations, "as ISIL gains additional prominence in the global terrorist movement, we must be prepared for the possibility that wealthy extremists will increasingly seek to fund it."[18]

Charities

The sheer magnitude of the funding provided by some states to different groups in Syria is worth considering. For example, in addition to more than $300 million in Kuwaiti government grants, independent charities in that country raised $183 million for humanitarian aid work in Syria. As Dickinson observes, in what seems like somewhat of an understatement, "It is [also] possible that at least some private Kuwaiti donors do not know exactly where the funds they raise will be channeled, entrusting logistics to existing groups or donor networks who share their ideology or political views."[19]

When operating under authoritarian regimes, many Islamic charities have demonstrated a predilection toward ambiguity and in some cases secrecy.[20] But even more challenging than operating under the watchful eye of an authoritarian government is operating in an active conflict zone, as evidenced by the work of Islamic charities in places like Afghanistan, Chechnya, and the Balkans. In war-torn Syria, the truth about which charities are cooperating with specific groups may not surface for years to come, if ever. Although core Al-Qaida has historically eschewed social service provision, the Islamic State controls large swaths of territory, which could potentially allow the group to set up charities in areas it controls.[21] If charities are established within insurgent-held territory, this could provide ISIS with another avenue to fund its activities, although such charities would be extremely vulnerable to disruption.

Fraud

In a country as chaotic as Iraq, the anarchic conditions provide numerous opportunities for fraud of various kinds. One fraud perpetrated by AQI was a real estate scam in which the insurgents stole 26 ledgers that contained the deeds to approximately $88 million worth of property, which were later resold.[22] Furthermore, the insurgents likely take a cut from the various frauds connected to the fraudulent diversion of imported fuel and crude oil. As Williams notes, in 2005 alone, approximately 200,000 trucks entered Iraq from Turkey, which "provided all sorts of opportunities for abuse and exploitation, especially theft, fraud, and smuggling."[23] The insurgents also engaged in document fraud, which served as a facilitator of human smuggling and the trafficking of women in Iraq. The high levels of violence created a massive refugee problem and a market for those Iraqis who wished to flee the country. Forged passports and fake identifications could fetch in the tens of thousands of dollars.[24]

Legal Businesses

While much of the attention on ISIS activities in Iraq has focused on extortion and other criminal activities, the group's involvement with legal businesses and front companies has received far less scrutiny. In Mosul in 2011, a dip in violence was in part attributed to the direct involvement of both ISIS (at the time known as ISI) and other jihadist elements with construction companies operating in the area.[25] Indeed, ISIS has worked through front companies to conceal its activities for several years, beginning at some point in the mid- to late-2000s and continuing to the present day.[26] ISIS has been able to insert itself into Iraqi owned businesses because of the group's control of territory throughout northern Iraq. Its leadership is well aware that the massive revenues it earns from oil will not continue unabated.[27] As such, it is seeking to diversify its portfolio across both the gray and dark economies in order to sustain the organization well into the future.

Money Laundering

The money the Islamic State generates from smuggling oil throughout Iraq and Kurdistan and into Syria, Jordan, and Turkey is laundered back into Iraq through trade-based schemes and informal financial institutions, including money exchanges like hawalas.[28] While much is still unknown about exactly how the group is moving its millions, some anti-money laundering professionals have speculated that the group could attempt to keep its money "liquid," as in cash form, or move it to gold. Moreover, even when ISIS moves its money into the formal financial system, it will attempt to obfuscate the origins of the money and will almost certainly insulate its leadership from being tracked by having a shadowy network of operatives, agents and front companies in its employ.[29] In what amounts to a form of passive support for ISIS, states in the Persian Gulf with notoriously loose financial regulations (e.g., Kuwait, Qatar, and the UAE) essentially offered the militants a "tacit nod of approval" by allowing the group to take advantage of its poor money laundering protections.[30] According to a 2013 U.S. Department of State *Country Reports on Terrorism*, "despite a strong legal framework, judicial enforcement and effective implementation of Qatar's anti-money laundering/counter-terrorist the financing of terrorism [sic] (AML/CFT)[31] law(s) are lacking."[32]

Dark Economy

In many ways, ISIS has benefited from its predecessor organization, AQI. But of all the capabilities inherited, the well-funded networks of raising money are perhaps the most important. Through KFR, armed robbery and theft, money gained from extortion and racketeering, as well as the sale of oil smuggled and trafficked across the region, ISIS has separated itself from the other jihadist groups fighting in Syria on a financial level. It remains likely that even if what small percentage of funding ISIS does receive from wealthy patrons in the Gulf dries up, the group is well positioned to keep earning money through a wide array of criminal activities.

Kidnapping for Ransom (KFR)

Although ISIS is perhaps most notorious for executing the individuals it kidnaps, in particularly gruesome fashion by beheading them and then sending the video around on social media, the group also relies on KFR as a form of revenue generation. This is not a new tactic, as AQI earned approximately $36 million a year by ransoming foreign reporters and aid workers it had kidnapped.[33] ISIS has continued relying on this tactic for a number of reasons, including that it remains an activity with a low barrier to entry, but also because it is undeniably lucrative. In 2013, ISIS earned approximately $20 million from ransoms generated through kidnapping.[34]

In an effort to curb ISIS's revenue from this tactic, the U.S. Treasury Department is attempting to gain broad consensus with other nations that adopting and implementing a no-ransom policy will help persuade terrorist groups like ISIS to jettison KFR as a means of raising money, since a no-ransom policy means no remuneration from groups and perhaps opprobrium from those who might criticize the group as illegitimate for preying on civilians.

Armed Robbery and Theft

Perhaps the most legendary tale of ISIS's sudden rejuvenation is the armed bank robbery of Mosul's central bank that allegedly netted the group approximately 500 billion Iraqi dinars, or $425 million dollars. In addition to the money, ISIS fighters also pilfered large quantities of gold bullion.[35] Without even considering ISIS's finances from the range of other rackets described within this chapter, the Mosul heist immediately made the group the richest terrorist outfit in history.[36] Robbery has helped make the group financially independent, while helping improve its ability to pay its fighters and further expand its territory throughout both Iraq and Syria. In Aleppo, ISIS has made money from stealing industrial machinery from plants and factories and selling them on the black market.[37]

Throughout the areas it occupies, ISIS has stolen livestock and crops from farmers.[38] In the lead up to the Anbar Awakening, many prominent scholars believe that it was AQI's heavy reliance on criminal activities, including robbery and theft from the Iraqi population in the country's Anbar province that led Sunni tribal sheikhs to turn against the group and begin working with the Americans to provide intelligence and then manpower to combat the insurgents.[39] If the coalition of nations aligned against ISIS is able to significantly curtail the group's financing, especially the money it earns through the smuggling and trafficking of oil, the militants may find themselves faced with the difficult decision to make do with much less or to return to the predatory forms of criminality that caused the Iraqi Sunni tribes to turn against it back in the late 2000s.

Smuggling, Trafficking, and Counterfeiting

A significant portion of the money raised by ISIS between June 2014 and September 2014 came from the group's capture of key oil fields and refineries in northeastern Syria as well as parts of Northern Iraq, in addition to its control of key arterial roads and other centers of commerce.[40] Indeed, the smuggling and trafficking of oil—which is smuggled out in tanker trucks before it is sold on the black market in Turkey and Syria (including to the Assad regime)—provides ISIS with tens of millions of dollars of steady funding each month. ISIS sells crude at a discounted price of between $20 to $35 a barrel to either truckers or middlemen.[41] The money ISIS has earned from the sale of oil has helped the group "to establish a significant level of self-reliance and financial autonomy," notes Keatinge.[42]

The territory ISIS controls, as of late 2014, had a total production capacity of more than 150,000 barrels per day, although actual production was estimated to be much lower than that.[43] When ISIS takes over a refinery, it keeps the technical workers in their jobs and replaces the top management with its own people.[44] The black market oil smuggling routes are well-established, dating back to the reign of Saddam Hussein and the oil-for-food scam he ran in response to sanctions.[45] In addition to oil, ISIS has made money trafficking antiquities[46] and kidnapped women from minority communities.[47]

Extortion and Protection

Of all the Al-Qaida affiliates, perhaps no group relied more on extortion to fund its activities than AQI. In the anarchic situation that developed throughout Iraq following the 2003 United States-led invasion, Baghdad and its surrounding areas fell victim to AQI fighters that extorted individuals and businesses, large and small. Around Mosul, insurgents extorted between 5 and 20 percent of the value of contracts local businessmen obtained from the Iraqi government.[48] Payments also had to be made to insurgents in order for trucks to pass along on the highways. In all, AQI likely garnered millions of dollars from extortion, where "taxes" were paid for commerce, reconstruction, and the transportation of oil.[49]

ISIS's extortion practices demand between 10 and 20 percent of revenue from businesses in its territories and operates other "mafia-style" rackets that help the group bring in as much as $1 million a day.[50] According to Jonsson, ISIS couches its extortion related activities in terms of *jizya*, which is traditionally a tax paid by non-Muslims living in Muslim lands and is similar to other forms of "revolutionary" taxes collected by a number of other insurgent groups.[51] In Mosul alone, ISIS earned an estimated $8 million a month from its extortion activities in 2012 and 2013,[52] with the bulk of funding coming from commercial, reconstruction, and oil sectors of northern Iraq,[53] including taxes collected on trucks and cell phone towers.[54] ISIS also extorts individuals or groups moving back and forth through critical border crossings between Syria and Iraq.[55] The group has even extorted the Syrian government, as was the case in February 2013 when ISIS militants seized control of the Tabqa Dam in eastern Syria and sold electricity back to the Assad regime.[56]

External State Support

Similar to the *modus operandi* of AQI, there has been no hard evidence that ISIS has received funding directly from states in the Gulf, especially "the usual suspects," Sunni states like Saudi Arabia, Kuwait, and Qatar.[57] Elizabeth Dickinson agrees that countries like Qatar, which is closely tied to many prominent Salafist groups, likely have not provided ISIS with direct financial support; however, some of the jihadists who have benefited from Qatari funds have left their respective groups to join more radical organizations like ISIS, taking their money and weapons with them.[58] Furthermore, even if no evidence has surfaced of direct government sponsorship of ISIS, a prominent analyst of terrorist financing does believe that wealthy sympathizers and individuals from Qatar and Kuwait are indeed donating money to the group.[59]

WHAT ISIS ACHIEVED WITH THESE FUNDS

Since storming through Iraq from a base in eastern Syria in the summer of 2014, ISIS militants have secured control over large swaths of eastern Syria and western Iraq, although this territory takes different forms at different times. Money does not always directly translate to legitimacy, but it does help bolster the insurgents' operational and organizational capabilities. In the case of ISIS, the group now seeks to build and maintain a caliphate in the heart of the Middle East. State building is an expensive endeavor, though, so for all of the money ISIS brings in, it also has a significant number of debits for providing a range of services to those living within its proclaimed territory.[60]

Operational Capabilities

When AQI operated in Anbar province throughout the mid to late 2000s, financial documents recovered by the U.S. military indicate that fighters were paid for food, accommodations, and other expenses described as "assistance." During this time, fighters were paid approximately 60,000 Iraqi dinars (IQD), roughly $41 USD, and an additional 30,000 IQD for each dependent. Furthermore, as long as AQI remained viable, payments continued even after a fighter was killed or captured.[61] While it is unclear how much ISIS fighters are being paid in early 2015, the group consists of an estimated 31,000 fighters and also maintains on-again off-again alliances with other Sunni factions including the Ba'thist Jaysh Rijal al-Tariqa al-Naqshbandiyya (JRTN).[62]

Weapons

Not only is ISIS one of the most well-funded terrorist groups in history, it is also one of the most well-equipped.[63] And unlike many terrorist and insurgent groups that operated during the Cold War, ISIS does not rely upon external states to provide it with weaponry. Instead, the group has forcibly looted hundreds of millions of dollars' worth of weapons and equipment from Iraqi and Syrian military installations in those two countries.[64] The group has diversified its weapon sources, which include weapons acquired from other insurgents in Syria who have defected to ISIS, weapons purchased from other insurgents that receive them from foreign donors, weapons captured from vanquished enemies, and weapons purchased or traded for with corrupt members of the security forces in both Syria and Iraq.[65] ISIS has even acquired sophisticated antiaircraft weaponry like the Chinese-made FN-6, though to have been provided by the Qataris (and possibly the Saudis, too) to Syrian rebels before falling under ISIS's control.[66]

In addition to armored vehicles purchased on the black market or acquired when the Iraqi security forces retreated from the battlefield,[67] ISIS militants also have M79 antitank rockets made in the former Yugoslavia, American made M16 and M14 rifles, small arms and ammunition.[68] The weapons and equipment that ISIS militants now have in their possession were intended to give the Iraqi Army both a qualitative and quantitative edge over its adversaries.[69] In October 2014, reports suggested that U.S. planes dropped weapons in ISIS territory that were intended for Kurdish fighters near Kobani, but were instead commandeered by the militants.[70]

In August 2014, ISIS fighters used a mini-surveillance drone in preparation for an attack on a Syrian army base near Raqaa province in northern Syria. Footage from the drone shows two suicide bombers detonating vehicle borne improvised explosive devices (VBIEDs) at the gate of the base before its fighters stormed the compound.[71] The use of "technicals," which are pickup trucks modified with machine guns or anti-aircraft weaponry, provides the militants freedom of movement and much-needed mobility. ISIS fighters have used artillery and RPGs in Syria while also making use of Humvees and T-55 tanks captured from the Iraqi security forces.[72]

Intelligence

ISIS relies on subversion and clandestine operations to carry out attacks in both Syria and Iraq, including suicide bombings, assassinations, and offensive raids on critical military targets, such as Syrian Army bases. In response to U.S. airstrikes in the fall of 2014, ISIS fighters began to stress the importance of operational security, assuming a "covert posture submerged within the population," donning masks that cover fighters' faces, and even eschewing any identifying information while operating in public.[73] As he assumed power, Baghdadi relied on ISIS's internal security apparatus to purge the organization of suspected informants.[74] When new recruits arrive from abroad, especially from Western countries but also from the broader region, they are screened by ISIS fighters through a series of interviews during which personal information is obtained, passports are examined and donations are accepted.[75]

ISIS's counterintelligence is robust—a captured ISIS computer revealed a downloaded copy of the U.S. Army and Marine Corps Counterinsurgency Field Manual (FM) 3-24.[76] What is extremely worrisome to Western intelligence and law enforcement officials is that in addition to receiving training in guerilla warfare skills, ISIS fighters could be receiving skills that would prepare them to return to their countries of origins to conduct a terrorist attack. These skills include how to conduct surveillance, how to avoid detection, and how to build a clandestine network.[77]

Sanctuary, Safe Haven, and Operational Space

More than any other insurgent group in recent memory, the Islamic State now holds a significant amount of territory across Syria and Iraq. In Syria, ISIS maintains a sanctuary in Ayn Isa, Raqqa City, and parts of Idlib and Aleppo provinces where they established training camps. In Aleppo, as of late 2014, the group controlled the Jarabulus crossing to the west and the Tal Abayd crossing to the east, critical chokepoints that regulate the flow of men, money, and materiel coming into Syria from Turkey.[78]

Unlike core Al-Qaida based in Pakistan, ISIS enjoyed safe haven in Syria for long enough to allow it to really hold territory that it could use to train, produce media, and begin implementing a preview of how it might govern a caliphate.[79] ISIS is so confident in some parts of the territory it holds that it has allowed municipal workers and civil servants to remain in their jobs, including some mayors of cities and other top local officeholders who have been allowed to keep their posts in return for acknowledging ISIS's supremacy. ISIS may have recognized the success of a true hybrid group like Hezbollah, the Shiite terrorist organization that maintains a quasi-army and vast social service network while also controlling seats in the Lebanese parliament.[80]

Accordingly, the control of territory means the control of resources, including oil, wheat, water and ancient artifacts, all of which can be sold to further ISIS's financial portfolio.[81] Perhaps just as important as the territory and resources the group commands are its human capital. As it continued to grow, ISIS took over territory inhabited by JRTN, Sunni tribes and Iraqi Islamist "resistance groups" such as Jaysh Muhammad and Ansar al-Sunnah.[82] As of mid-October 2014, ISIS controlled swaths of territory in Iraq and Syria that were on par with the size of the state of Maryland.[83] In the areas in Syria under its control, ISIS has stood up an electricity office that monitors electricity-use levels, installs new power lines and instructs workshops on how to repair damaged ones.[84] Furthermore, ISIS checkpoints throughout the territory it controls provide the militants with multiple opportunities to "tax" those attempting to pass through.[85]

Another frightening scenario is the spread of ISIS's virulent ideology beyond the Middle East and into North Africa, South Asia and other jihadist hot spots around the world. In late January 2015, a group linked to ISIS attacked a luxury hotel in Tripoli, Libya, killing eight people, five of whom were foreigners, including one American.[86] There are also reports of ISIS flags flying in Afghanistan and Pakistan.[87] Moreover, even the Chinese are now concerned that ISIS's ideology could influence the minority Uighur population: an estimated 300 Chinese citizens are allegedly fighting alongside ISIS in Syria in Iraq, many of whom are linked to the East Turkestan Islamic Movement (ETIM), responsible for an increasing number of attacks in China's restless Xinjiang province.[88] Nor are there are any signs that the flow of Westerners, especially from European countries, has abated.[89]

Training

By the summer of 2014, ISIS had established logistical hubs, headquarters, training camps and other vital infrastructure throughout Syria, with a significant portion of its operations based in Raqqa.[90] Training for ISIS recruits, especially foreign fighters, is important because it builds a militant's practical skills, but also "imbues him with a sense of solidarity with a larger cause."[91] Upon passing screening from ISIS intelligence operatives, new recruits spend several weeks undergoing both religious and military training, primarily on how to fire pistols, assault rifles, RPGs and mortars. Some recruits that prove especially proficient or might have prior training are occasionally selected to receive further training on more sophisticated weapons.[92] Because ISIS holds territory and maintains a sanctuary in Syria, it is able to train more effectively than core Al-Qaida ever could while hiding in the mountains of Waziristan. Even before U.S. airstrikes commenced in late September 2014, ISIS dispersed its forces and resources to avoid exposing its fighters to American bombs.[93]

Organizational Capabilities

In line with the ISIS's stated goal of establishing an Islamic caliphate, the group has devoted a robust portion of its funding to the nascent stages of state building. In August 2014, ISIS paid municipal salaries, provided public works, maintained electric, trash and sewage services, offered health care and education to its supporters and even attempted to enforce parking laws and regulations in areas it controlled or claimed to control.[94] ISIS dedicates attention and resources to spreading its message and diffusing its propaganda, exemplified by its pervasive use of social media, including active Twitter campaigns in each of the provinces where it operates and promotes its activities and the battles it fights.[95] As one commentator noted, "Gulf state fundamentalists, battle-hardened Chechens, and middle-class Londoners were all drawn into ISIS by its powerful messaging and the promise to, in a twist on an old phrase, be the evil you want to see in the world."[96]

Leadership

ISIS is led by Abu Bakr al-Baghdadi, an Iraqi also known as Ibrahim Awad Ibrahim al-Badry, thought to have been born in Samarra in 1971.[97] Al-Baghdadi is widely viewed as the most ruthless jihadist leader since AQI's former chieftain, Abu Musab al-Zarqawi. Al-Baghdadi is rumored to have received a doctorate in Islamic Studies from the Islamic University in Baghdad, the ISIS leader combines theological credentials with tactical success on the battlefield. Captured by U.S. forces near Fallujah in 2004, al-Baghdadi spent years at Camp Bucca, a detention facility where he is thought to have grown even further radicalized and anti-American, while also broadening his network among aggrieved Iraqi Sunni Arabs, including many from Anbar and Nineveh provinces.[98]

While the group's leadership does include some prominent foreign fighters, such as a Chechen named Omar al-Shishani,[99] most of ISIS's leadership cadre consist of former Baath party military and intelligence officers that held high-ranking positions during Saddam Hussein's regime, including Abu Ali al-Anbari and Abu Muslim al-Turkmani.[100] Two other former regime loyalists are Fadel al-Hayali and Adnan al-Sweidawi, both of whom served as military officers and Baath party insiders.[101] Indeed, ISIS maintains a leadership council, a cabinet, and has ties to local leaders. The leadership council helps deal with religious issues and doctrine, but also apparently makes decisions about executions. The cabinet maintains oversight on finance, security, media, prisoners, and recruitment, while local leaders are comprised of roughly a dozen deputies spread between Iraq and Syria.[102] ISIS operates in a more decentralized fashion than Al-Qaida ever did, with operations carried out by a network of regional commanders that each maintain responsibility for subordinates, who have their own autonomy, but find time to collaborate and coordinate with the regional commanders on a variety of tactical issues.[103]

Ideology

The brand of Islam practiced by the Islamic State has been described, perhaps most accurately, as "untamed Wahhabism" that views the killing of those deemed unbelievers as a necessity to furthering its mission of purifying the community of the faithful.[104] The group's ideology, defined by a very narrow interpretation of *sharia* on social and criminal issues, explains its use of beheading as a way of murdering its victims, which have included several Westerners, Christian, and Yazidi religious minorities, Shiite Muslims (considered apostates), Kurds, Alawites, and even other Sunni Muslims who ISIS deems worthy of elimination.[105] It has been labeled "the most elaborate and militant jihad polity in modern history."[106] After it seized Mosul in June 2014, ISIS publicized a "city charter" that called for the amputation of thieves' hands, mandatory prayers, the banning of all drugs and alcohol and the desecration of shrines and graves considered to be polytheistic.[107] Some scholars believe that ISIS's ideology is an even more nefarious threat than its military capabilities.[108]

The group's adherence to such an austere, unforgiving brand of Islam was partly responsible for its split with Al-Qaida senior leadership, including Ayman al-Zawahiri, who viewed the group's extreme violence as ultimately counterproductive.[109] The overarching goal of the Islamic State is to establish a caliphate throughout parts of "al-Sham," or the Levant, to include land stretching from Lebanon across Syria and into Iraq. Moreover, the very public split with Al-Qaida has seemingly forced jihadists to choose sides,[110] although in an interesting twist, some ISIS fighters likely get some of their ideological guidance on building an Islamic State from "The Management of Savagery," a manifesto penned by one of core Al-Qaida's main ideologues, Abu Bakr Naji.[111]

Several groups have already sided with ISIS and its harsher ideology, including fighters (though not the entire organization) from AQIM, AQAP, Ansar-al Sharia branches in both Libya[112] and Tunisia, as well as jihadists in Gaza/Sinai and Indonesia.[113] Its ideology has been described as "aggressive" and "expansionist" with no recognition of modern-day political borders.[114] To be sure, ISIS regards state boundaries as "artificial creations of colonial powers designed to divide the Muslim world."[115] The fact that ISIS has announced the establishment of an Islamic state— referred to by Aaron Zelin as the *khilafa* project—is proof in the eyes of many Muslims worldwide that Baghdadi will be able to resurrect the caliphate, a feat unable to be accomplished by the Khilafat Movement in British India and the Sharifian Caliphate in modern-day Saudi Arabia.[116] In all of its public announcements, ISIS refers consistently to "the Prophetic methodology," which governs how its members live and how the organization rules the territory it controls.[117]

Human Resources and Recruitment

Though the numbers are murky, in September 2014 the CIA estimated that ISIS had approximately 31,000 fighters in Iraq and Syria, nearly three times as high as its original estimate.[118] Thousands of Europeans have flocked to Syria to fight alongside Al-Qaida linked Jabhat al-Nusra or ISIS.

In fact, the conflict in Syria has attracted more Westerners than any other conflict in the modern era, to include the 1979–1989 anti-Soviet jihad.[119] The lion's share of these fighters is from the Middle East, North Africa, and other regions typically associated with global jihad, like the Caucasus and Central Asia. However, there are also a significant number of Westerners counted among ISIS's ranks, including fighters from the United States,[120] the United Kingdom, Australia, Scandinavia, and many European countries.[121] Some estimates peg the number of foreign fighters in Syria and Iraq at around 15,000 individuals from as many as 80 different countries. Most of these jihadists have joined to fight with ISIS.[122] Moreover, the group has deliberately recruited extremely young fighters, including many teenagers.[123]

Besides foreign fighters and militants from Saudi Arabia, Tunisia, Lebanon, and Jordan, ISIS is comprised of thousands of Iraqis and Syrians.[124] After the initial U.S. invasion of Iraq in 2003, a radical Salafi cleric from Aleppo named Abu al-Qaqaa became the primary point of contact for Syrian recruits eager to join AQI under the leadership of Zarqawi.[125] Many of those contacts likely remain in place today. The group has also won recruits following large-scale prison breaks throughout Iraq, replenishing its ranks with hardened jihadists, violent sociopaths, and career criminals.[126] Included in the panoply of individuals recruited by ISIS are children as young as six years old, some of whom are trained to become suicide bombers.[127]

Perhaps in an effort to avoid repeating the mistakes of AQI in Anbar province throughout the late 2000s, especially the violence against local Sunni Iraqis that led in part to the Anbar Awakening, ISIS has displayed an awareness of winning the hearts and minds of Iraqi and Syrian Sunnis. In areas that ISIS claims to control, it ensures the availability of basic necessities like gas and food.[128] In Mosul, ISIS has held a "fun day" for kids, distributed gifts and food during Eid al-Fitr, held Quran recitation competitions, started bus services and opened schools. More so in Iraq than in Syria, ISIS has been more aware of dealing with the local population in Sunni-predominant towns, villages, and cities.[129]

An analysis of Al-Qaida in Iraq reveals that that group, too, was a bureaucratic and hierarchical organization that tried to keep an ironclad grip over the money it earned from a series of rackets.[130] So, it should come as little surprise than its progeny is as well. ISIS may be wealthy, especially when compared to other terrorist groups, but it also maintains a vast human resources type network to deal with medical expenses for fighters (and their families), legal support, safe houses, administrative expenses (e.g., utilities) in the areas under its control and other logistical requirements of clandestine organizations.[131] In what may be a sign that ISIS has learned from its mistakes in Anbar Province during the "Awakening," when ISIS has removed some civil servants from their leadership positions, it has consistently compelled mid-level bureaucrats and technocrats to remain in their positions in order to ensure continuity.[132] ISIS's use of former Assad regime loyalists displays a pragmatism that has been vital to its success holding onto territory it has captured.[133] The lessons from America's disastrous de-Baathification policy in Iraq under L. Paul Bremer's Coalition Provisional Authority (CPA) during the initial invasion apparently have not been lost on ISIS.

Media, PR, Propaganda, and Publicity

When ISIS reemerged on the radar of the Obama administration in the summer of 2014, much hyperbole surrounded the group's military capabilities. Indeed, its blitzkrieg-like offensive throughout northern Iraq was well executed, but insurgent groups with conventional military capabilities are not a new phenomenon (e.g., LTTE, PIRA, the Afghan Taliban, etc.). What was new, however, was ISIS's sophisticated use of media, especially social media, in spreading its message, sowing terror and fear, recruiting new members, and countering Western efforts to shape the narrative.[134] Perhaps most impressive has been the speed with which ISIS is able to produce its media campaigns, responding in real-time (by "live tweeting") to events as they unfold on the ground. This mode of communication has been described as a "swarmcast" for its interconnected, dispersed, and resilient form.[135]

ISIS did use social media to broadcast the beheading of several Westerners it had kidnapped, but it also used Twitter,[136] Instagram, YouTube, and Facebook to show its humanitarian efforts, including fighters handing out ice cream cones to children, in an attempt to appeal its constituents. It has even developed its own video game modeled after "Grand Theft Auto."[137] ISIS has produced several popular series such as "Knights of Martyrdom" and "Risen Alive," which emphasize the camaraderie of jihad by showing militants fighting together on the battlefield.[138] *Dabiq* is ISIS's magazine, which is an English-language production used to help lure more recruits.[139] The magazine is multifaceted, reporting battlefield statistics, but also laying out a thoroughly detailed religious explanation for its actions, especially its attempt to establish an Islamic caliphate in Syria and Iraq.[140]

Just like other millennials, the concept of "oversharing" extends to terrorists as well. The use of multiple media platforms has served as a source of open source intelligence (OSINT) for intelligence and law enforcement authorities attempting to track, monitor, and combat ISIS.[141] Simply from monitoring jihadists' use of social media, Western authorities have been able to gain insight into foreign fighters traveling to Syria and Iraq to fight with the group, as well as mapping the rift that developed and eventually led to a split between ISIS and Jabhat al-Nusra.[142]

Even though ISIS militants communicate openly on some social media forums, its media wing remains incredibly agile. When its accounts on Twitter and other sites are shuttered, new accounts appear almost immediately. It relies on services like JustPaste to distribute battle summaries, SoundCloud for the release of audio reports, Instagram to share photos, and WhatsApp to swap graphics and videos.[143]

HOW ISIS FINANCING WAS COUNTERED

It should be noted that at the time of this writing, late 2014/early 2015, the fight against ISIS is merely in its nascent stage. U.S. strategy is currently comprehensive in nature, primarily focused on disrupting ISIS revenue streams, restricting ISIS's access to the international financial system and targeting ISIS leaders, facilitators, and supporters with a range of kinetic and non-kinetic actions, from kill/capture operations to sanctions, where appropriate. Convincing our allies not to indirectly fund ISIS is part of this strategy. In his work on ISIS, Philipp Holtmann has noted that some European oil companies, with the knowledge of European governments and worried about Russian unreliability, have purchased oil through proxies at dumping prices. Until the oil fields are recaptured, international companies should be prohibited from buying crude oil through middlemen.[144] At present, the U.S. Treasury Department is seeking to blacklist any purchaser or facilitator purchasing oil from ISIS, no matter how high or low on the value chain.[145]

Another key element of the CFT strategy against ISIS is working to identify middlemen and buyers for the smuggled fuel and stop those transactions by any means required. Mobile refineries should be targeted and roads and other pathways that tanker trucks use to transport oil to and from fields should be made impassable by military means.[146] And with respect to recapturing the oil fields, to avoid market perturbations and regional disarray, the tap cannot be shut off overnight. Rather, as Charles Lister notes, "Though necessitating a gargantuan effort in minimal time, the provision of large quantities of diesel fuel and oil for generators into opposition areas of northern Syria should be an immediate policy priority."[147]

Kinetic Activities

Curbing ISIS's revenue from the sale of smuggled oil meant pressuring Ankara to assist with stemming money laundering and stopping traders in Turkey from purchasing smuggled oil from ISIS.[148] In September 2014, U.S. airstrikes targeted oil refineries controlled by ISIS in Syria. U.S. Central Command (CENTCOM) estimated that the refineries targeted were responsible for producing between 300 and 500 barrels of oil per day.[149] Western law enforcement agencies, including the FBI have attempted to prevent ISIS recruits from leaving the country, arresting those individuals suspected of traveling to join the group and charging them with providing material support to a terrorist organization. If convicted, an individual could face a maximum of 15 years in prison and a $250,000 fine.[150]

Non-kinetic Activities

In September 2014, the UN Security Council passed Resolution 2178 on policies and security measures to better track and deter terrorist travel activity, which requires member countries to implement improved border controls and to disrupt or prevent financial support to terrorists, though enforcement of these policies will be more difficult in reality.[151] Later that same month, the U.S. Treasury Department stepped up its efforts to crack down on Al-Qaida and Islamic State funding by designating several individuals with links to Qatar. One of the designated individuals was Tariq Bin-Al-Tahar Bin Al Falih Al-Awni Al-Harzi, accused of gathering support from Qatar and arranging for ISIS to receive approximately $2 million from a Qatar-based financial facilitator who expressly stated the money should be used for military operations.[152] Though ISIS is not acquiring a serious amount of funding from the Gulf States that could change in the future. "To date, implementation and enforcement have not been a component of Qatar's approach" to combating terrorist financing, according to Levitt. Indeed, he notes that "Qatar routinely stresses to investors and critics alike the passage of laws that, on paper, appear robust but are almost never implemented or enforced."[153] It is not as much about the passing of laws in countries like Kuwait and Qatar but more about the implementation and enforcement of those laws.

The other primary line of effort against ISIS is attempting to identify and sanction those who benefit from the oil trade as well as working with governments in the region to devote more resources to shutting down existing smuggling networks and securing porous borders.[154] Every node in the network—middlemen, traders, refiners and transport companies, to name a few—are targets of United States efforts to deny ISIS the ability to raise funds through the sale of black market oil.[155]

CONCLUSION

From 2003 through 2009, Syria was a safe haven for AQI fighters battling U.S. troops in Iraq. During this period, western Iraq, particularly Anbar province became a sanctuary for many AQI fighters. Tensions between AQI and the Sunni tribes resulted from the former's attempt to take control over the traditional smuggling and black market activities of the latter. What followed was the Anbar Awakening and in turn, the defeat of AQI in Anbar province.[156] Those nations countering ISIS hope that as the United States targets ISIS's control of oil refineries, the group may be forced to rely more on criminal activities to fund its activities. In turn, this could provide an opening, as the group may repeat its mistakes by usurping traditional Sunni smuggling routes, thus opening the door for an "Anbar Awakening Part II". But challenges lay ahead. As Levitt laments, "the problem is that we have tools—from military force to Treasury designations and more in between—to deal with oil smuggling and extensive sugar daddies in the Gulf, but our ability to counter ISIL's local criminal enterprises is severely limited."[157] And though the fate of ISIS in Iraq and Syria is still to be determined, the group's war chest makes it the wealthiest insurgent group in history and one seemingly determined to fight to its death.[158]

CHAPTER 9

Conclusion

In his work on countering the financing of terrorism, Michael Freeman concludes that "without money, terrorists can neither function as organizations nor conduct attacks."[1] This rather simple statement of fact has been the basis for much of this book. Only by truly understanding how terrorist and insurgent groups raise money and how these funds are spent, can states and governments begin to formulate a strategy for countering the financing of terrorism. This book examines the challenges of combating the financing of terrorism through the analytic lens of the gray and dark economies. It also presents an assessment of how terrorist and insurgent financing bolstered operational and organizational capabilities. It concludes with implications from this examination and assessment that are relevant not only to the U.S. government, but to governments and nation-states throughout the world that recognize the importance of countering the financing of terrorism, insurgency and irregular warfare.

CHALLENGES IN COMBATING THE FINANCING OF TERRORISM AND IMPLICATIONS

As the case studies demonstrate, tremendous progress has been made in combating the financing of terrorism, insurgency and irregular warfare, though many challenges remain and new challenges are certain to arise. Some of these challenges will be more manageable than others, but no matter what obstacles present themselves, it is crucial to remember the lessons learned and best practices of the past several decades of CFT and to apply these lessons to confronting emerging threats like the Islamic State in Iraq and Syria (ISIS), the constellation of Al-Qaida franchises like Al-Qaida in the Arabian Peninsula (AQAP), Al-Qaida in the Islamic Maghreb (AQIM) and other terrorist and insurgent groups including Al-Shabaab in Somalia and Boko Haram in Nigeria.

TERRORIST GROUPS ARE RESILIENT AND ADAPTIVE
IN THEIR ABILITY TO RAISE FUNDS

As demonstrated by the longevity of groups like the PIRA, the LTTE, and Hezbollah, it is clear that terrorist and insurgent groups can be highly capable and adaptive adversaries. With diversified portfolios, these groups demonstrated an impressive resiliency that made them more difficult to counter. Hezbollah is entering its third decade, with seats in Lebanon's parliament and a sub-state military apparatus the envy of most states. Although a decapitation strike can be a highly effective approach to dealing with some insurgent groups,[2] Hamas has survived the targeted assassination of several of its key leaders, due in no small part to its relatively high level of cohesion, underwritten by consistent if not always overwhelming levels of funding. In Afghanistan, the Taliban has now survived against the U.S. military for well over a decade and shows no signs of being defeated anytime soon. Even where the organization is fracturing, the most consistent threat of continuity remains the insurgents' ability to raise money through taxing and sale of opium.[3]

Combating terrorist financing, and in particular the financing of groups like Al-Qaida and ISIS, is challenging because these groups and their fund-raising schemes are ever moving targets in many cases. In response to government counter-measures, the methods of financiers and cells adjust in kind. It is a continuous cycle of adaption and counteradaptation. Even with improved financial regulations designed to combat these groups, terrorists "have simply become more adept at masking these transactions and at using intermediaries to act on their behalf."[4] Moreover, as Gomez notes, "the speed and ease with which money can be moved via the international financial system enables terrorists to move funds efficiently, unfortunately often still with relatively small risk of detection."[5] Accordingly, these groups are more adaptive *because* of their financing but they are also resilient and adaptive in the way that they raise funds.

As detailed throughout the case studies, successful terrorists and insurgent organizations develop an agile organizational structure and when the opportunity arises, they turn to new technologies and other nonstate actors like criminals, which in many cases can act as force multipliers. Moreover, there is evidence that terrorists and insurgents are considering and in some cases already using digital currencies like Bitcoin to launder or conceal their funds.[6] Even with all of the tools that Western powers have at their disposal it remains difficult, especially as an external actor, to significantly influence local or regional economies firmly entrenched in gray and dark sectors. Western nations are structured to deal in the legal financial system. Financial measures enacted by the U.S. Department of State and U.S. Department of Treasury can be ineffective at times because those individuals designated for targeting are also in the best position to evade the tangible effects of these sanctions.[7]

Terrorist and insurgent groups have also learned to diversify their funding portfolios, to the extent possible, a lesson that several prominent groups learned the hard way following the end of the Cold War, when external state sponsorship of these groups declined significantly. The PIRA overcame the loss of Libya as an external state sponsor by focusing on a range of criminal activities, a lesson not lost on both Hamas and Hezbollah as those groups attempt to deal with shrinking annual donations from Iran. Diversification provides groups with the flexibility and dexterity to shift from one method of financing to another. In some cases, terrorist groups have deliberately reduced their infrastructure to alleviate stress on their financial needs.[8] As the revenue ISIS earns from the smuggling and trafficking of oil continues to dwindle, that organization may need to seriously recalibrate considerable elements of its quixotic (and costly) struggle to build a caliphate.

While states correctly focus on countering the ability of terrorists and insurgents to raise funds, another element of the CFT challenge is dealing with the difficulties inherent in tracing money that is transferred and stored through online entities like Cash-U or E-Gold.[9] New methods of payment are constantly emerging and new developments in information technology mean that governments seeking to combat the financing of terrorism must try to remain one step ahead. Furthermore, when charities are implicated in the funding of terrorism, it is rather easy for these organizations to simply channel funds through another organization or change the name of the subsidiary in order to avoid the suspicious of the authorities.[10] A group like Hamas is able to rely on a decentralized network of charities, so if authorities in Western Europe or North America successfully curtail funds raised in those locales, Hamas can simply seek to shift the onus to raise funds to charities in Africa or Asia.

In the case of Al-Qaida, even after fund-raisers are identified and their assets frozen, the group has been able to replace these individuals with still unknown figures in a "next man up" type environment that allows its terror network to continue operating.[11] Al-Qaida takes its finances seriously and has a section of its manual, sometimes referred to as the "Manchester Document," dedicated to topics like "Financial Security Precautions" that emphasize the need to divide operational funds into two parts, one for investment and another for active operations.[12] Indeed, as discussed throughout the individual case studies, *every* terrorist or insurgent organization analyzed in this book dedicated some portion of its manpower to raising, storing, moving, and managing funds.

Al-Qaida and its sympathizers have taken an interest in cyber-crime, as stolen credit cards gained through phishing have enabled terrorists to purchase millions of dollars worth of much- needed supplies, including plane tickets and prepaid mobile telephones which can be used and then disposed of quickly before authorities have an opportunity to trace any calls made to or from these "burners." In a post-Snowden environment, it is likely that terrorists have resorted to even more surreptitious methods of communication. Furthermore, rigged transactions between two companies controlled by the same organization, the use of falsified documents, and the diversity of payment methods (personal and bank checks, transfers, payment orders, banking remittances and credits, etc.) all contribute to the difficulty of countering groups adept at these processes.[13] Terrorists continue to transfer funds through a variety of means, including the use of cash couriers and *hawalas* but also electronically in real-time. In the past, when methods including Western Union, credit cards, or online payment sites like PayPal have come under scrutiny, terrorists and their sympathizers post warning messages on a variety of online forums.[14] Issues like this should remain a priority for the intelligence community and Congress, including the House Financial Services Subcommittee on Oversight and Investigations.

It is critical to deny money to terrorists and insurgents by disrupting and destabilizing operations, which causes them to expend more effort devoted to financing, in turn leaving them with less time to train and recruit or to plot, plan, and execute attacks. As Shapiro and Siegel note, "seizing funds, and thereby tightening terrorists' budget constraints can increase friction within an organization to the point where leaders choose to spend on activities other than attacks."[15] Addressing fund-raising through crime remains essentially a law enforcement challenge, suggesting the need to devote more resources to border security and customs enforcement and the agencies that are responsible for these issues, as well as local and federal police. In many countries, this remains an issue of both capacity and will. Furthermore, it is important to recognize that this is a multi-player game. The efficacy of these programs depends not only on the resources marshaled by the host-nation government (and in some cases the resources of its neighbors, allies and/or the international community), but also on the nature and severity of the threat. What worked in Colombia may not necessarily be realistic in Somalia.

And, while the ability to kill, capture, arrest and prosecute depends on actionable intelligence and a capable kinetic force, terrorist and insurgent groups are not comprised solely of "trigger pullers," as demonstrated throughout the case studies. Therefore, neither should those agencies working to counter these groups be purely kinetic. Employing smart financial power means being able to "follow the money" and conduct sound financial network analysis. In many ways, success breeds further challenges. Success in focusing on funds generated by Al-Qaida has had an atomizing effect on the organization, thus fracturing the group's fund-raising arm into many smaller pieces, which are in turn, more difficult to track. The more vulnerable terrorists feel in using the international financial system, the more likely they will be to rely upon more informal means of raising and moving money. "With greater restraints on international money transfers, a 'ceiling' may have been established under which terrorist funds may begin to pool," note Rabasa et al. When funding flows are stagnant between the core and the periphery, with no money sent in either direction, local cells are forced to finance their own activities and indeed may be called upon to send money from the periphery back to the core.[16] As the case studies related, local cells in both the PIRA and the Afghan Taliban demonstrated considerable success in raising money, part of which was in turn used to support both groups' leadership cadre. If ISIS is able to successfully expand beyond Iraq and Syria, its local cells will be required to do the same.

Just as terrorist and insurgents are resilient and adaptive, so too do nation-states need to strive for agility in responding to current and emerging threats. This includes being prepared to take advantage of changing geopolitical dynamics. As the attacks of September 11, 2001 demonstrated, major international events can impact how governments view national security issues. While the Sri Lankan government struggled to influence governments in the United States, United Kingdom, and Canada to take action on the LTTE before 9/11, all three nations eventually agreed to clamp down on this group in the years following the attacks. Similarly, in the wake of the Arab Spring, the Israelis have seized the opportunity provided by a new government in Egypt to restrict the flow of resources to Hamas in Gaza.

THE UNITED STATES AND ITS ALLIES CANNOT SUCCEED ALONE

Even with all of the resources that the United States and its allies are able to marshal, there is still the issue of getting other states to cooperate. Some countries have made little to no effort to curb the activities of informal money transfer systems, which can then be used by terrorists to move and launder money obtained through the gray and dark economies.[17] For a variety of reasons, cooperation from states can be, and often is, somewhat limited due to domestic political concerns and differing opinions of what constitutes a threat to national security. While the Kuwaitis and Qataris may say one thing privately, public actions could be much different, leading to accusations of "two-facedness," or "playing a double game."[18]

This dilemma should not be surprising, however. For two decades, the United States largely decided to look the other way with respect to PIRA activity on U.S. soil, much to the chagrin of London. The Tamils in Canada maintained sufficient political clout and enough influence to avoid being proscribed a terrorist organization for many years. Even now, with ISIS threatening to destabilize much of the Middle East, countries like Turkey remain undecided on whether or not to fully cooperate with the United States and its allies. Regarding Al-Qaida, shift away from its original "business model" and toward a more grassroots financing system will present a challenge to authorities that are still attempting to perfect the art of combating large donors and more obvious transmission mechanisms.[19]

The American experiences in Iraq and Afghanistan have led to the realization that it takes time and a sophisticated understanding of the operational environment in order to piece together a comprehensive and accurate intelligence picture of what local network structures look like on the ground. Only with the help of the host-nation governments will it be possible to improve the transparency and accountability of indigenous institutions, locate and positively identify the bankers and financiers who comprise critical nodes in the business cycle of a particular network, and seize cash as it flows into and out of a country's borders, although another major challenge is that most of this funding can be raised and spent locally. Even with the active assistance of a partner nation, affecting terrorist and insurgent networks and preparing for second and third order effects is a tenuous proposition. Countering the financing of terrorism is not a linear problem set and is frequently plagued by a lack of robust metrics, a dearth of international cooperation, and poor information sharing.[20] Because there are widely varying perceptions of the severity of the threat, the result is a half-hearted approach to monitoring suspicious transactions in financial institutions throughout the globe. This remains an issue of capacity as well as an issue of will.

It is worth noting, however, that there have been some bright spots in this area. In late 2000, an Al-Qaida attack on the Strasbourg Christmas market was foiled partly due to German cooperation with a British surveillance team focused on the attack's primary logistician and financier, Abu Doha.[21] Then in 2002 in Sarajevo, following a raid, the security services discovered a list with the names of twenty-three individuals, including some prominent Arab businessmen, who were identified as primary donors to Al-Qaida. The list became known as "the Golden Chain" and it provided law enforcement and intelligence authorities with a solid foundation for unraveling Al-Qaida's fund-raising network.[22] In 2003, the Society for Worldwide Interbank Financial Telecommunications (SWIFT), an electronic system by which banks send transfer instructions to each other, was credited with providing information which helped lead to the capture of Jemaah Islamiyah's operational commander.

Basile makes an argument that the United States should continue its foreign policy push for banking oversight and regulation in the Middle East as well as pressure on local governments in the region to crackdown on unregulated charities.[23] Diplomatic efforts should focus on strengthening bilateral relations with the individual countries of concern, which includes not only countries like Kuwait, Qatar, Saudi Arabia, and Pakistan but also countries that provide offshore havens and money laundering hubs such as the Cayman Islands, Cyprus, and the UAE, among others. Progress is possible working by, with and through embassies in the country of concern and also with financial institutions and major multinational banks.

Combating the financing of terrorism and insurgency in the modern era requires governments to cooperate, share intelligence and information and a whole-of-government approach, information and intelligence sharing among countries and their security services as well as multilateral cooperation both within and between agencies. Often times, as happened with the British government pressuring the Americans or the Sri Lankan government's diplomatic offensive to persuade the Canadians and British, states must encourage foreign governments to take action against terrorists and insurgents that enjoy sanctuary on foreign soil. Furthermore, countering corruption can also unearth evidence of illicit funds tied to the insurgency, although any successful counter-corruption campaign must involve significant cooperation between a broad range of actors, which is not always feasible or realistic. As the case study on the Afghan Taliban showed, building local institutions and capacity (NDCS, SIU, TIU, and the NIU) can be a step in the right direction but these efforts can be extremely costly, in terms of both money and time, and they can be politically risky since there is no guarantee of progress, much less success.

FAILED AND FRAGILE STATES AND UNGOVERNED SPACES REMAIN ISSUES OF CONCERN OVER A DECADE AFTER 9/11

More than a decade after U.S. forces beat Al-Qaida militants across the Afghan border into Pakistan, failed states and ungoverned or poorly governed spaces continue to serve as a breeding ground for terrorists, insurgents, violent drug trafficking organizations and transnational criminal networks. In areas where insurgents have carved out sanctuary, they can exert control over local economies, including any businesses operating in this territory. Weak states often lack the ability to maintain proper oversight of the financial institutions operating within their borders and even less ability to control or monitor the informal institutions like hawalas and other informal value-transfer institutions.

Where governments suffer from capacity gaps and functional holes, alternative sources of governance will fill the void.[24] Insurgents are just one form of alternative governance that often emerge in response to centralized political collapse, where a government either cannot or will not provide its citizens with basic services. The result is that governments can suffer from a dearth of legitimacy, thus allowing non-state entities to act both financially and politically without interference from the state in which they are based. These organizations flourish where cultural identities are fragmented, political space is in flux, and where the absence of traditional governance mechanisms is apparent.

Weak governance and corruption contribute to weak, failing, failed, and collapsed states, which in turn become a haven for terrorists, insurgents and transnational criminal organizations that engage in money laundering, kidnapping for ransom, counterfeiting, and the smuggling and trafficking of humans, weapons, and narcotics. Failed and weak states are plagued by corruption, which attenuates the rule of law and makes police and border security officials more prone to bribery, increasing the porosity of borders and thus facilitating the flow of illicit goods into and out of the territory. Other challenges faced by failed states are too numerous to list, but include at least the following: insurgency, terrorism, energy insecurity, climate change, resource deprivation, brain drain, transnational crime, corrupt patronage networks, religious extremism and radicalization, piracy (both digital and maritime), cyber-warfare, weapons of mass destruction, global economic slowdown, and the spread of pandemics or disease. While strong states also face many of these same challenges, the primary difference is vulnerability to the threat and the ability (or inability) to respond.

Strong states have more robust institutions that are capable of mitigating many of these dangers before the threat is able to overwhelm the government. In turn, it is rather obvious why malevolent actors gravitate toward weak states. Terrorists, insurgents and criminals prefer to operate in the shadow, deliberately seeking out underground banking networks and unregulated offshore jurisdictions where banking supervision is limited, anti-money laundering legislation does not exist or is not enforced, and a culture of no-questions-asked banking secrecy is the rule, not the exception.[25]

Dealing with the threat posed by failing states and alternatively governed spaces will require international efforts to promote the rule of law and encourage good governance and transparency although as mentioned above, issues of both capacity and will continue to plague efforts in this area. Through a host of security cooperation activities, the international community, regional bodies, and/or individual nation-states should seek to build the partner capacity of failed states to help these nations counter transnational organized crime, as criminal activities are often a major funding stream for terrorist and insurgent groups.[26] Before deciding on a course of action to assist states with CFT, it is important to recognize that "analysis of terrorist finance is easy to do badly and hard to do well," which suggests the need to identify and work with "true experts on small topics," such as indigenous financial systems and traditions and the economics of relevant value chains.[27]

In what Moises Naim has dubbed "mafia states," organized crime has a corrupting influence on state institutions, including the government, parliament, and the judiciary.[28] It is in these kinds of states that the provision of technical assistance in combating the financing of terrorism and insulating their vulnerable financial institutions against fraud and crime is most necessary.[29] (It is less clear whom to work with if the state has been corrupted). This assistance can be offered by the World Bank, IMF, FATF, the UN and others and should be focused on improving countries' legal, regulatory, and enforcement capabilities. Unfortunately, these programs too often emphasize individual training courses and due to inconsistencies with funding, are rarely long-term in nature.[30] Increased capacity in the financial sector could even help some weak states recoup some of the estimated $120–$160 billion that is lost each year in tax revenues that are hidden in offshore accounts and shell companies.[31]

Building partner capacity to counter transnational organized crime and the financing of terrorism can be accomplished through focusing security cooperation efforts in weak and failed states on ministerial capacity, institution building, and defense reform, all of which are foundational to other forms of capacity. Furthermore, ministerial capacity can be improved even when the partner nation's absorptive capacity is generally low. This is a self-reinforcing cycle since ministerial capacity building can itself improve a partner's absorptive capacity, thus enabling future capacity building in other areas. With sufficient ministerial capacity, countries plagued by high levels of non-state violence will be better prepared to plan and integrate strategy and operations against the range of threats arrayed against them. Not all countries begin from the same starting point and many face issues of absorptive capacity—improving ministerial capacity is far more feasible in Northern Ireland than in Afghanistan, Iraq, or even Lebanon.

As demonstrated in the case studies of Hamas, Hezbollah, and Al-Qaida, security services need to be able to rely on actionable intelligence to conduct kinetic strikes including raids, targeted crackdowns and large-scale sweeps against terrorist fund-raising networks. In cases where resources provide terrorists with funding, as in Afghanistan, it is essential to understand the nuances involved between counterinsurgency and counterterrorism on the one hand and counternarcotics and countertrafficking on the other. These should not be "pick and choose" strategies but rather all part of an overarching and comprehensive plan to defeat the enemy.

NON-STATE ACTORS, THEIR GOALS, AND HOW STATES PERCEIVE THEM, MATTER

Throughout the majority of the Cold War, American policymakers and military leadership were understandably locked into a worldview dominated by nation-states. But after the 9/11 attacks, many within the U.S. government awoke to the notion that non-state actors can play an outsized role in accordance with either the experience and skills of the organization or the resources at its disposal. While the announcement of a Global War on Terrorism (GWOT) might have been a victim of poor nomenclature, the general concept underpinning the GWOT was successful in elevating the importance of non-state actors on the international security agenda. There is a growing consensus among analysts that, whether they are terrorists, insurgents, warlords, militias, paramilitaries, vigilante groups, organized criminal organizations, soldier-rebels ("sobels") or even pirates, violent non-state armed groups have become a major security concern.[32] The United States currently finds itself searching for footing in uncertain times of Russian aggression and Chinese military modernization, while seemingly somewhat flummoxed by a panoply of violent non-state actors, including insurgent groups with conventional military capabilities like ISIS, violent transnational drug trafficking organizations like Los Zetas, hacktivists and cyber criminals, diaspora populations, and NGOs that provide support to terrorists and insurgents.

Highly capable sub-state actors like the PIRA and LTTE are gone, only to be replaced by Al-Qaida, the Taliban, and ISIS. Perhaps even more troubling, terrorist groups like Hamas and Hezbollah have transformed into hybrid organizations that challenge the legitimacy of the state through military means whilst also providing essential social services to their respective constituencies and successfully contesting elections. Some scholars have labeled the rise of non-state actors *BlackFor*, or Black Force, defined as a "postmodern form of societal cancer," and "a confederation of illicit non-state actors linked together by means of a network of criminalized and criminal (narco) cities."[33] Components of the BlackFor are likely to be inextricably intertwined with, and indeed aided by, symbiotic relationships with the leadership of corrupt states, although some scholars caution falling victim to hyperbole in affording these actors with more power than they actually yield in reality.

One of the major factors that make non-state actors so dangerous is the use of fictitious, shell, and offshore fiduciary companies, which all pose a challenge to those organizations attempting to regulate business transactions and provide terrorists and insurgents with financial safe havens where they can conceal their funds. Gomez relates the difficulty of companies, funds, entities, or businesses that are registered in an extraterritorial financial center, such as International Business Corporations (IBC) which can be used to construct complex financial structures (the issue here becomes the degree of transparency of beneficial owners). Commenting on these entities, he suggests that "they can be established using bearer shares and do not have to publish accounts. Residents of financial centers can act as fictitious directors or shareholders in order to disguise the genuine directors or owners. These entities are attractive to investors who seek anonymity or wish to carry out their activities beyond the official scrutiny of their national government."[34]

In the effort to choke off funding to terrorist and insurgent groups, the U.S. response has been criticized widely as "profoundly state-centered," which has hampered its overall effectiveness.[35] It is precisely this state-centered approach that plagues efforts to collect and analyze high-fidelity intelligence. According to Bunker, one of the main takeaways from U.S. experiences in Iraq and Afghanistan is that "it takes a network to defeat a network."[36] However, as Chad C. Serena argues persuasively, "this overly simplified yet widely accepted view ignores the point of organizational adaptation" because "being a network or acting like a network does not ensure that an organization can or will adapt appropriately to achieve its goals."[37] This finding dovetails nicely with another of Serena's most poignant observations—an insurgency might not be an insurgency. In essence, this argues for the need to discern between terrorists groups, insurgent organizations, militias, and criminal networks.

When dealing with combating the finances of non-state actors, it is also important to recognize that in certain cases—as with ISIS—the international banking system will be of little help. Instead, the local economies of these groups must be the primary focus and the priority should remain developing the capacity of local and regional actors while also targeting the insurgent group's financial facilitators and local sources of revenue. By working with interagency partners to cultivate financial intelligence, the United States and its allies can create leverage and shape her adversaries. Again, even if it proves impossible to defeat a group like ISIS, targeting the group's financing can provide valuable information and intelligence on the group and its broader network, including its organizational structure, alliances, sources of popular support and legitimacy, and technological prowess. This kind of approach is best when used as part of a comprehensive strategy that includes all facets of statecraft, from kinetics to diplomacy.

Particularly in the non-kinetic realm, there are many opportunities for governments to make progress against countering the financing of terrorism and insurgency. Some of the case studies highlighted the importance of establishing committees and task forces specifically designed to work on CFT issues, which often means pulling in resources from across the spectrum of law enforcement, intelligence, the judicial branch, academia, the private sector, and so on. With concrete evidence to draw upon, it is easier to craft, pass, implement and where the political will is present, to enforce the legislation in an effort to designate and proscribe terrorists while freezing and seizing their assets and conducting a more robust financial analysis of the network and its critical nodes.

TERRORISM IS INEXPENSIVE AND INSURGENCY CAN BE TOO, DEPENDING ON A GROUP'S GOALS

Comparatively, terrorism is inexpensive while insurgency requires more funding if a group intends to legitimately challenge the sovereignty of an incumbent regime. As demonstrated in the case studies, groups can survive for long periods of time with a combination of active and passive sponsorship from civilian populations, or through a reliance on petty criminal activities. Terrorist attacks can be inexpensive and funds are easy to move because it is extremely difficult, even in developed countries, to distinguish suspicious or illicit activity from the routine.[38] Al-Qaida has responded by raising larger numbers of small donations from a wider array of sources while also moving money in more diverse ways as well.[39] Terrorists and insurgents can raise, move, or store funds using bulk cash smuggling, traditional banking, wire transfers, money exchange services, trade-based money laundering, storage with value cards or prepaid instruments, mobile and electronic payments (including via mobile phones), and diversion of funds from charities and nongovernmental organizations.[40] Naim reinforces this concern when he declares, "never in the field of human conflict have so few had the potential to do so much damage to so many at so little cost."[41] The following figure demonstrates just how inexpensive terrorist attacks have been over time.

A study by Emilie Oftedal of the Norwegian Defence Research Establishment (FFI) looked at data on the financing of 40 jihadi cells that have plotted attacks against European targets between 1994 and 2013 and concluded that three-quarters of the plots cost less than $10,000 to plan.[42]

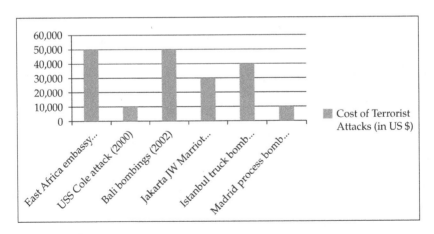

Figure 9.1

Cost of Terrorist Attacks (in US $)[43]

The 2004 Madrid train bombings killed 191 people and injured another 1,600 in an attack financed primarily by the leader of a small, yet effective drug trafficking network that smuggled hash from Morocco and ecstasy from Holland to Spain.[44]

While the connection between making money from the illicit trade in illegal narcotics to sustain an insurgent organization is well-documented—Revolutionary Armed Forces of Colombia (FARC), Afghan Taliban, Kurdish Workers' Party (PKK)—what is less well explored and understood if the use of petty crime to fund small scale attacks in the West. In addition to low-level drug dealing, terrorist attacks can be funded through myriad sectors of both the licit and illicit economy, including the sale of counterfeit clothing, illicit whites (cigarettes), pirated software, DVDs, stolen smartphones, and phone cards. In February 2015, an investigation revealed that a network of over 250 butchers and phone shops in Spain were helping to fund jihadists in Syria.[45] This money could just as easily be used to plot and conduct a terrorist attack in Western Europe similar to the Charlie Hebdo attacks in Paris in January 2015. And while that attack was allegedly funded with $20,000 from AQAP, it is easy to see why some terrorists planning similar types of attacks would follow the Madrid model—small sums of money collected over time through the use of somewhat banal criminal activities like drug dealing, various types of fraud and petty theft.[46]

For myriad reasons, terrorists and insurgent groups are turning to crime to raise funds more than ever before. To be sure, some credit must be given to the success of the CFT in combating terrorists and insurgents' ability to move money through the formal banking sector and through NGOs. The increasing reliance of terrorists and insurgents on the organized criminal activities of the dark economy is also partly a post-Cold War phenomenon accelerated due to the withdrawal of external state sponsorship, but also a result of the advances of globalization—it is easier now, more so than at any point in history, for non-state actors to communicate and cooperate. Terrorist groups are often able to raise the necessary cash by methods that would be extremely difficult to identify as related to terrorism or other serious criminality. Since attacks can be so inexpensive, even if they fail to kill or wound large numbers of individuals, attacks still cost Western nations billions of dollars in security expenditures and fit into the overall narrative of waging economic warfare on the West. But with this increasing reliance on criminal activities comes a new set of risks and in turn, more opportunities for law enforcement and the intelligence community to identify, arrest, and prosecute these individuals or to simply sit back and gather more intelligence about the group, its activities, and overall objectives before moving against it.[47] Having to raise cash, resources, and so on, diverts individual and organizational focus, raises profiles, and causes myriad weaknesses. In short, it exposes the group and can create an influence chain (particularly in the case of external sponsors) where those providing resources can be leveraged appropriately.

ALTHOUGH WESTERN NATIONS "PLAY BY DIFFERENT RULES" THAN THEIR ADVERSARIES, MANY LEGAL AVENUES REMAIN VIABLE TO COMBAT THE FINANCING OF TERRORISM, INSURGENCY, AND IW

The essence of irregular or asymmetric warfare is that one side fights in a manner that is unconventional and also enjoys the freedom to operate relatively unconstrained from the laws of war and most widely agreed upon legal strictures governing combat. Just as the behavior of nation-states are constrained in warfare, so too does this regulation extend to combating the financing of terrorism. There is a well-established firewall between the private sector and the government in the United States and many other developed nations. Beyond achieving success, it is believed to be just as critical for the action of nation-states to remain well within the boundaries of mature legal frameworks and to maintain the integrity of the global financial system.

Terrorists and insurgents, on the other hand, are less restricted by laws and borders and thus more capable of working across domains more fluidly and developing hybrid capabilities and relationships with a range of illicit actors and enterprises. For its part, the CFT side is beset by strict rules governing public-private collaboration. One side is agile, while the other is compartmentalized, stove-piped, protective of rice bowls, and at the mercy of temporary freezes in funding due to partisan rancor and legislative cacophony. Nation-states face the uphill battle of making a bureaucracy nimble and proactive, no easy tasks. Closer cooperation between the public and private sector is critical and as Zarate points out, in some cases multinational corporations like Paypal, Amazon, and Mastercard can be swifter and more effective than government bureaucracies in responding to emerging issues.[48] The governments of those nations seeking to curb the illicit financing of terrorist and insurgent groups need to view the private sector as an ally, not an adversary, and vice versa. In certain cases, private sector institutions and multinational corporations should be able to leverage the experience of armed services reservists or members of the National Guard. These "weekend warriors" might be bankers, accountants, or software engineers in their everyday lives while also privy to the emerging threats to national security faced by the military on the front lines.

Like most bureaucracies, the effort of nation-states to combat the financing of terrorism can be marked by redundancy, insufficient collaboration and coordination, internal disagreements, and inadequate information sharing. No system is perfect and no single tool provides a silver bullet. Rather than starting from scratch, it is important to improving the money-laundering and anticorruption financial systems that already exist. One area for improvement should be an attempt to be more parsimonious in the reporting of suspicious activity, as suspicious activity reports (SARs) have proliferated exponentially since 9/11, inundating analysts with a deluge of data that is so voluminous to almost be meaningless.[49] According to Gomez, "the enforcement of due diligence with bank clients has been helpful in detecting some terrorist operations, although in general reports of suspicious financial transactions made by financial institutions are currently of limited value in actually seizing assets of terrorist organizations."[50] While generating SARs might serve to help protect financial institutions from hefty fines, this practice may actually encourage terrorists to transfer money through the system in hopes of "hiding in plain sight."

One of the consequences of this new era of financial warfare has been an increase in "de-risking," which is a phenomenon by which financial firms exit problematic markets where clients are less capable of meeting "know-your-customer" requirements, causing compliance officials to grow concerned about an institution's reputational risk.[51] Several high profile banks—HSBC, Barclays, ING, Standard Chartered and BNP Paribas, to name a few—have already been fined for offenses ranging from money laundering to sanctions-busting.[52] But as Tom Keatinge points out, "Money always finds a way to its intended recipient. Restrictive regulations have simply pushed large pools of funds outside formal channels—encouraging criminals and terrorists to finance their activities in the shadows."[53]

At its core, one of the main issues from a counter-terrorism perspective is that of intelligence gain/loss (IGL). Put simply, when information about an adversary is disclosed, this alerts adversaries and forces them to change their tactics, techniques, and procedures (TTPs). Restrictions on banks could encourage terrorists to avoid the formal financial system altogether and so the crux of the issue remains, is it better to move against an adversary when an opportunity arises or is it more beneficial to allow the adversary to continue any actions that are traceable and can thus provide even more valuable intelligence on a terrorist or insurgent group's intentions, to possibly include details of an attack? When banks exit problematic markets and de-risk their operations, what entity fills the void?

For Future Study

This book has examined a range of terrorist and insurgent groups, how those groups raise and move funds, how those funds are spent, and the challenges in combating the financing of these organizations. Yet, despite the in-depth analysis undertaken throughout this book, much work remains to be done.

Now that a sufficient amount of time has passed, it would be valuable to conduct comprehensive assessments of the effectiveness of both the Afghan Threat Finance Cell (ATFC) and the Iraq Threat Finance Cell (ITFC) to gauge how vital these elements are to the war effort.[54] Another area that is indispensable to determining progress (or lack thereof) is the improvement of metrics to better understand what has worked, what has not worked, and methods to improve CFT. Relying on a strategy able to leverage metrics is the equivalent of targeted (as opposed to blanket) sanctions—this is smart financial intelligence and there is always room for improvement. As Perl laments, "one potential pitfall plaguing measurements of success is an over-reliance on quantitative data at the expense of its qualitative significance."[55] Indicators could include the successful conviction rate of terrorist sympathizers responsible for supplying money or the level within these networks of those apprehended as a result of financial strictures.[56] Eckert and Biersteker suggest that as a starting point, "perhaps we should begin by accepting that there are no definitive metrics by which success or effectiveness can be assessed, but rather a variety of information and indicators that can help paint an overall picture."[57]

At the same time, even perfect metrics are useless against a network that has not been properly mapped. Only after developing a comprehensive picture of the network, to include the identification of key nodes, can the network then be probed, disrupted, and monitored. For example, when attempting to analyze a network comprised of terrorists and criminals, the first step might be to develop a list of major transnational smugglers suspected of involvement with the network, which could be accomplished through consultations with law enforcement agencies such as the Drug Enforcement Administration (DEA), Immigrations and Customs Enforcement (ICE), the Customs Border Protection, and myriad open source reporting on transnational criminal activity.[58] From there, an analyst must consider terrorist or insurgent finance as an interaction with value chains by examining how the non-state actor in question accesses, influences, controls or otherwise interacts with flows of value within existing local, regional, or global political economies.[59] Tracking funds through an organization can identify key elites, organizational function, and network structure/alliances with states or other insurgent groups as well as shed some light on how these networks operate, how they have evolved over time, and perhaps offer insight on how they are likely to adapt once challenged.[60] Moreover, as Shima Keene points out, combating the financing of terrorism and insurgency is about much more than just "following the money" but can prove useful as both a forensic tool and a psychological weapon.[61]

Staying one step ahead of adaptive adversaries is a challenge. It is difficult to be anticipatory, predictive, and accurate. Prior to 9/11, most money laundering controls were designed to detect narcotics trafficking and large-scale financial fraud. Similarly, with the move toward virtual currencies such as Bitcoin, and the ever-present evolution of anonymous transactions, it is nearly impossible for governments and international bodies like the United Nations to remain current in all possible arenas of information technology and financial transfers. Gomez puts it thusly, "the sheer volume and speed with which sums of money rush through the computer-linked international financial system make watertight CFT measures impossible."[62] However, by providing government agencies with the resources, authorities and manpower necessary to engage in this fight, and by anticipating and preparing for future trends, states and law enforcement agencies can at least adversely impact the ability of terrorists and insurgents to raise funds through the gray and dark economies while working to restrict their operational and organizational capabilities and thus their capacity to do harm.

Notes

CHAPTER 1

1. Kevin D. Stringer, "Tackling Threat Finance: A Labor for Hercules or Sisyphus" *Parameters*, Vol. 41, No. 1, Spring 2011, pp. 101–119.

2. Assaf Moghdam et al., "Say Terrorist, Think Insurgent: Labeling and Analyzing Contemporary Terrorist Actors," *Perspectives on Terrorism*, Vol. 8, No. 5, October 2014, pp. 2–17.

3. The most comprehensive treatment of irregular warfare is found in the Irregular Warfare Joint Operating Concept, 2007.

4. Alan Vick et al., *Airpower in the New Counterinsurgency Era: The Strategic Importance of USAF Advisory and Assist Missions*, Santa Monica, CA: RAND Corp., 2007, p. 11.

5. In *Trends in Outside Support for Insurgent Movements*, Byman et al. note that the LTTE and Hezballah could be considered *both* terrorists and insurgents because of their relentless use of terrorism *in addition to* a host of other tactics used to control territory. The authors go on to note that size can also be a useful distinguishing characteristic, commenting, "terrorist groups often consist of a small number of individuals, sometimes no more than a handful. Insurgent organizations, like Hizballah or the LTTE, in contrast, number in the thousands." See Daniel Byman et al., *Trends in Outside Support for Insurgent Movements*, Santa Monica, CA: RAND Corp, 2001, p. 5. Also, in his research on proto-insurgencies, Byman notes that "many of the most important 'terrorist' groups in the world—including the Lebanese Hizballah, the Liberation Tigers of Tamil Eelam (LTTE), and the Revolutionary Armed Forces of Colombia (FARC)—are better described as insurgencies that use terrorism than as typical terrorist movements." Daniel Byman, "Understanding Proto-Insurgencies," Santa Monica, CA: RAND Corp, 2007, p. 1.

6. Bard E. O'Neill, *Insurgency and Terrorism: Inside Modern Revolutionary Warfare*, Washington DC: Brassey's Inc., 1990, p. 24.

7. As Michael Marks correctly points out, there is a lack of a universally accepted definition of "failed states" and much of the international security literature has lacked nuance in its explanation. See Michael P. Marks, *Metaphors in International Relations Theory*, New York: Palgrave MacMillan, 2011, pp. 120–124. While it is beyond the scope of this research to delve into the debate here, suffice to say there is some literature that this author does believe goes into nuance on the differences between weak states, failed states, failing states, and collapsed states and why it matters. See Stewart Patrick, "Weak States and Global Threats: Fact or Fiction," *Washington Quarterly*, Vol. 29, No. 2, 2006, pp. 27–53; Robert I. Rotberg, ed., *When States Fail: Causes and Consequences*, Princeton: Princeton University Press, 2004; Robert I. Rotberg, ed., *State Failure and State Weakness in a Time of Terror*, Washington DC: Brookings Institution Press, 2003; and I. William Zartman, ed., *Collapsed States: The Disintegration and Restoration of Legitimate Authority*, Boulder: Lynne Rienner, 1995.

8. For more, see Nick Vaughan-Williams, *Border Politics: The Limits of Sovereign State Power*, Edinburgh: Edinburgh University Press, 2012.

9. Michael Freeman, "Introduction to Financing Terrorism: Case Studies," in Michael Freeman, ed., *Financing Terrorism: Case Studies*, Farnham: Ashgate, 2012, p. 3.

10. Many terrorist groups operate legal businesses for a profit, including Al-Qaida. When bin Laden's organization was based in Sudan during the early to mid-1990s, it operated several legitimate businesses, including farms that produced peanuts and honey, trading companies, a tannery, a furniture making company, a bakery, and an investment company.

11. Daniel Byman et al., *Trends in Outside Support for Insurgent Movements*, Santa Monica, Calif.: RAND Corporation, 2001, p. 88.

12. Jason Burke, *Al-Qaeda: The True Story of Radical Islam*, London: I.B. Tauris, 2003, p. 45.

13. Phil Williams, "Warning Indicators and Terrorist Financing," in Jeanne K. Giraldo and Harold A. Trinkunas, *Terrorism Financing and State Responses: A Comparative Perspective*, Stanford: Stanford University Press, 2007, pp. 76–77.

14. Sidney Weintraub, "Disrupting the Financing of Terrorism," *Washington Quarterly*, Vol. 25, No. 1, Winter 2002, pp. 53–60.

15. Louise I. Shelley and John T. Picarelli, "Methods Not Motives: Implications of the Convergence of International Organized Crime and Terrorism," *Police Practice and Research*, Vol. 3, No. 4, 2002, p. 308.

16. Byman et al., *Outside Support*, p. 41. Latin America is accepted as an outlier since diaspora support largely tends to be directed at ethnic insurgencies, which are rare in Latin America.

17. Ibid., p. 57.

18. Gabriel Sheffer, "Diasporas and Terrorism," in Louise Richardson, ed., *The Roots of Terrorism*, London: Routledge, 2006, pp. 118–119.

19. Terrence Lyons and Peter Mandaville, eds., *Politics from Afar: Transnational Diasporas and Networks*, New York: Columbia University Press, 2012, p. 19.

20. Steve Kiser, *Financing Terror: An Analysis and Simulation for Affecting Al Qaeda's Financial Infrastructure*, RAND Pardee School dissertation, Santa Monica, Calif.: RAND Corporation, 2005, p. 70.

21. Evan F. Kohlmann, "The Role of Islamic Charities in International Terrorist Recruitment and Financing," Danish Institute for International Studies, DIIS Working Paper, 2006.

22. Daveed Gartenstein-Ross and Aaron Y. Zelin, "Uncharitable Organizations," *Foreign Policy*, February 26, 2013.

23. "Risk of Terrorist Abuse in Non-Profit Organizations," Report of the Financial Action Task Force (FATF), June 2014.

24. Kevin Stringer, "Counter Threat Finance (CTF): Grasping the Eel," *Military Power Revue*, No. 2, 2013.

25. Jay S. Albanese, *Transnational Crime and the 21st Century: Criminal Enterprise, Corruption, and Opportunity*, Oxford: Oxford University Press, 2011, p. 66.

26. Ibid., p. 73.

27. Shelley and Picarelli, "Methods Not Motives," p. 311.

28. Phil Williams, "Insurgencies and Organized Crime," in Phil Williams and Vanda Felbab-Brown, eds., *Drug Trafficking, Violence, and Instability*, Carlisle Barracks, PA: U.S. Army War College Strategic Studies Institute, April 2012, p. 61.

29. Malcolm Beith, "HSBC Report Shows Difficulty of Stopping Money Launderers," *The Daily Beast*, July 19, 2012.

30. Michael Levi and Peter Reuter, "Money Laundering," in Michael Tonry, ed., *The Oxford Handbook of Crime and Public Policy*, Oxford University Press, 2011, p. 290.

31. "Global Surveillance of Dirty Money: Assessing Assessment of Regimes to Control Money Laundering and Combat the Financing of Terrorism," Center on Law & Globalization, January 30, 2014, p. 9.

32. U.S. Comptroller General, *Money Laundering: Extent of Money Laundering through Credit Cards Is Unknown*, Washington DC: U.S. Government Accountability Office (GAO), 2002.

33. Svante Cornell, "Narcotics and Armed Conflict: Interaction and Implications," *Studies in Conflict & Terrorism*, Vol. 30, No. 3, 2007, p. 208.

34. Thomas Mockaitis, "Resolving Insurgencies," *Strategic Studies Institute (SSI)* U.S. Army War College, June 2011, pp. 37–48.

35. Tamara Makarenko, "The Crime-Terror Continuum: Tracing the Interplay between Transnational Organized Crime and Terrorism," *Global Crime*, Vol. 6, No. 1, 2004, pp. 129–145.

36. Chris Dishman, "Terrorism, Crime, and Transformation," *Studies in Conflict & Terrorism*, Vol. 24, No. 1, 2001, p. 52.

37. McKenzie O'Brien, "Fluctuations Between Crime and Terror: The Case of Abu Sayyaf's Kidnapping Activities," *Terrorism and Political Violence*, Vol. 24, No. 2, 2012, p. 320.

38. Thomas M. Sanderson, "Transnational Terror and Organized Crime: Blurring the Lines," *SAIS Review*, Vol. 24, No. 1, Winter-Spring 2004, p. 52.

39. Williams, "Insurgencies and Organized Crime," in Williams and Felbab-Brown, *Drug Trafficking, Violence, and Instability*, p. 41.

40. Phil Williams and Colin P. Clarke, "Terrorist Financing and Organized Crime" in Amit Kumar and Dennis Lormel, eds., *Understanding and Combating Terrorist Financing*, London: Taylor and Francis, *forthcoming*.

41. Jam Hajjad Hussain, "Son-in-Law of Gen Tariq Wins Freedom for Rs 300 m," *The Nation*, March 16, 2012.

42. Catherine Collins with Ashraf Ali, "Financing the Taliban: Tracing the Dollars Behind the Insurgencies in Afghanistan and Pakistan," New America Foundation *Counterterrorism Strategy Initiative Policy Paper*, April 2010, p. 7.

43. Ibid.

44. Sami Yousafzai, "For the Taliban, A Crime that Pays," *The Daily Beast*, September 5, 2008.

45. Arabinda Acharya et al., "Making Money in the Mayhem: Funding Taliban Insurrection in the Tribal Areas of Pakistan," *Studies in Conflict & Terrorism*, Vol. 32, No. 2, 2009, pp. 95–108.

46. Vanda Felbab-Brown, "Fighting the Nexus of Organized Crime and Violent Conflict While Enhancing Human Security," in Williams and Felbab-Brown, eds., *Drug Trafficking, Violence, and Instability*, p. 1.

47. John Rollins and Liana Sun-Wyler, "Terrorism and Transnational Crime: Foreign Policy Issues for Congress," Congressional Research Service (CRS), October 19, 2012, p. 11.

48. Williams, "Insurgencies and Organized Crime," in Williams and Felbab-Brown, eds., *Drug Trafficking, Violence, and Instability*, p. 54.

49. James J. F. Forest, "Kidnapping by Terrorist Groups, 1970–2010: Is Ideological Orientation Relevant?" *Crime & Delinquency*, Vol. 58, No. 5, 2012, pp. 769–797.

50. Mark Galeotti, "Spirited Away—The Rise of Global Kidnapping Trends," *Jane's Intelligence Review*, April 27, 2010.

51. Phil Williams, "Terrorist Financing and Organized Crime: Nexus, Appropriation, or Transformation?" In Thomas J. Biersteker and Sue E. Eckert, eds., *Countering the Financing of Terrorism*, New York: Routledge, 2008, pp. 130–131.

52. Albanese, *Transnational Crime*, pp. 27–28.

53. John M. Martin and Anne T. Romano, *Multinational Crime: Terrorism, Espionage, Drug & Arms Trafficking*, Los Angeles: Sage, 1992, pp. 67–68.

54. Kim Cragin and Bruce Hoffman, *Arms Trafficking and Colombia*, Santa Monica, Calif.: RAND Corp., 2003, pp. 10–11.

55. Alissa J. Rubin, "U.S. Patrols Smuggling Routes to Macedonia: Balkans: American Peacekeepers in Kosovo Intercept Weapons on Way to Rebels," *Los Angeles Times*, August 20, 2001.

56. Esther Bacon, "Balkan Trafficking in Historical Perspective," in Kimberley L. Thachuk, *Transnational Threats: Smuggling and Trafficking in Arms, Drugs, and Human Life*, Westport, CT: Praeger Security International, 2007, p. 80.

57. Peter Andreas, *Blue Helmets and Black Markets: The Business of Survival in the Siege of Sarajevo*, Ithaca: Cornell University Press, 2008, pp. 54–55.

58. For more on the network aspect of drug trafficking, see Phil Williams, "The Nature of Drug-Trafficking Networks," *Current History*, April 1998, pp. 154–159.

59. Rollins and Sun Wyler, "Terrorism and Transnational Crime" p. 10; see also, Vanda Felbab-Brown, *Shooting Up: Counterinsurgency and the War on Drugs*, Washington DC: Brookings Institution Press, 2010.

60. Chris Dishman, "The Leaderless Nexus: When Crime and Terror Converge," *Studies in Conflict & Terrorism*, Vol. 28, No. 3, 2005, p. 246.

61. Williams, "Insurgencies and Organized Crime," in Williams and Felbab-Brown, *Drug Trafficking, Violence, and Instability*, p. 32.

62. Ibid, p. 33.

63. Dishman, "Terrorism, Crime, and Transformation," p. 43.

64. Sanderson, "Blurring the Lines," p. 52; see also Williams, "Insurgencies and Organized Crime," in Williams and Felbab-Brown, eds., *Drug Trafficking, Violence, and Instability*, p. 44.

65. Sanderson, "Blurring the Lines," p. 51.

66. Nick McKenzie and Richard Baker, "Terrorists Taking Cut of Millions in Drug Money," *The Canberra Times*, January 23, 2014.

67. Felbab-Brown, "Fighting the Nexus," in Williams and Felbab-Brown, eds., *Drug Trafficking, Violence, and Instability*, p. 5.

68. Shelley and Picarelli, "Methods Not Motives," p. 313.

69. Sanderson, "Blurring the Lines," p. 53.

70. Jay Albanese and Philip Reichel, eds., *Transnational Organized Crime: An Overview from Six Continents*, Los Angeles: Sage, 2014, p. 77; see also, Maggy Lee, *Trafficking and Global Crime Control*, Los Angeles: Sage, 2011.

71. Katja Franko Aas, *Globalization & Crime*, Los Angeles: Sage, 2013, p. 38.

72. Ibrahim Abdullah and Patrick Muana, "The Revolutionary United Front of Sierra Leone: A Revolt of the Lumpenproletariat," in Christopher Clapham, ed., *African Guerillas*, Oxford: James Currey, 1998, p. 179.

73. Jeffrey Gettleman and Nicholas Kulish, "Somali Militants Mixing Business and Terror," *New York Times*, September 30, 2013.

74. Albanese, *Transnational Crime*, p. 93.

75. Seth G. Jones and Patrick B. Johnston, "The Future of Insurgency," *Studies in Conflict & Terrorism*, Vol. 36, No. 1, 2013, p. 8.

76. Brian J. Philippes, "Terrorist Group Cooperation and Longevity," *International Studies Quarterly*, Vol. 58, No. 2, 2014, p. 338.

77. Daniel Byman, "Talking with Insurgents: A Guide for the Perplexed," *Washington Quarterly*, Vol. 32, No. 2, 2009, p. 126.

78. Kim Cragin et al., *The Dynamic Terrorist Threat: An Assessment of Group Motivations and Capabilities in a Changing World*, Santa Monica, Calif.: RAND Corporation, 2004, p. 25.

79. Ibid.

80. Richard H. Shultz and Andrea J. Dew, *Terrorists, Insurgents, and Militias: The Warriors of Contemporary Combat*, New York: Columbia University Press, 2007, p. 124.

81. Byman et al., *Trends in Outside Support*, p. 93.

82. Ibid., p. 117.

83. Ibid., p. 91.

84. Cragin et al., *Dynamic Threat*, pp. 50–51.

85. Ibid., p. 53.

86. William Rosenau, "Understanding Insurgent Intelligence Operations," *Marine Corps University Journal*, Vol. 2, No. 1, Spring 2011, pp. 15–18.

87. Ibid., p. 47.

88. Christopher Tuck, "Northern Ireland and the British Approach to Counter-Insurgency," *Defense & Security Analysis*, Vol. 23, No. 2, 2007, pp. 165–183.

89. Bard E. O'Neill, *Insurgency and Terrorism: Inside Modern Revolutionary Warfare*, Washington DC: Brassey's Inc., 1990, p. 117.

90. Angel Rabasa et al., *Beyond Al-Qaeda: The Global Jihadist Movement, Part I*, Santa Monica, Calif.: RAND Corp., 2006, p. 62.

91. Ben Connable and Martin Libicki, *How Insurgencies End*, Santa Monica, Calif.: RAND Corp., 2010, pp. 34–49.

92. Paul Staniland, "Defeating Transnational Insurgencies: The Best Offense Is a Good Fence," *Washington Quarterly*, Vol. 29, No. 1, pp. 22–23.

93. Anne L. Clunan and Harold A. Trinkunas eds., *Ungoverned Spaces: Alternatives to State Authority in Era of Softened Sovereignty*, Stanford: Stanford University Press, 2010.

94. Rabasa et al., *Ungoverned Territories*, pp. 15–19.

95. Dennis Gormley, "Silent Retreat: The Future of U.S. Nuclear Weapons," *Nonproliferation Review*, Vol. 14, No. 2, July 2007, p. 201.

96. Ibid.

97. Michael Kenney, "Organizational Learning and Islamist Militancy," National Institute of Justice, NIJ Journal No. 265, 2010.

98. Daniel Byman and Kenneth M. Pollack, "Let Us Now Praise Great Men: Bringing the Statesman Back In," *International Security*, Vol. 25, No. 4, pp. 107–146.

99. Cragin et al., *Dynamic Threat*, p. 25.

100. Headquarters, U.S. Department of the Army, and Headquarters, U.S. Marine Corps, *Counterinsurgency Field Manual*, Field Manual 3-24/Marine Corps Warfighting Publication 3–33.5, Chicago, Ill.: University of Chicago Press, 2007, pp. 20–25.

101. Cragin et al., *Dynamic Threat*, p. 40.

102. G. H. McCormick and G. Gown, "Security and Coordination in Clandestine Organization," *Mathematical and Computer Modeling*, No. 31, 2000, pp. 175–192; J. Bowyer Bell, "Revolutionary Dynamics: The Inherent Inefficiency of the Underground," *Terrorism and Political Violence*, Vol. 2, No. 4, 1990, pp. 193–211.

103. For more on the effectiveness of decapitation of leadership in counter-insurgency, see Patrick B. Johnston, "Does Decapitation Work? Assessing the Effectiveness of Leadership Targeting in Counterinsurgency Campaigns," *International Security*, Vol. 36, No. 4, 2012, pp. 47–79.

104. Field Manual 3–24, 2007.

105. Eric Hobsbawm, *Primitive Rebels*, Manchester, England: Manchester University Press, 1959.

106. Raj Desai and Harry Eckstein, "The Transformation of Peasant Rebellion," *World Politics*, Vol. 42, No. 4, July 1990, p. 454.

107. Thomas Marks, "Ideology of Insurgency: New Ethnic Focus or Old Cold War Distortions?" *Small Wars & Insurgencies*, Vol. 15, No. 1, Spring 2004, p. 110.

108. See Marks, "Ideology of Insurgency"; Nicholas I. Haussler, *Third Generation Gangs Revisited: The Iraq Insurgency*, Monterey, Calif.: Naval Postgraduate School, Thesis, September 2005; see also, Martin C. Libicki et al., *Byting Back: Regaining Information Superiority Against 21st Century Insurgents*, Santa Monica, Calif.: RAND Corporation, 2007. The phrase "disproportionate" use of force is a

widely contested term and is often the cause of serious debate, especially in regards to Israeli responses to Palestinian or Lebanese violence.

109. Nichole Argo, "The Role of Social Context in Terrorist Attacks," *The Chronicle of Higher Education*, January 13, 2006.

110. On the intensity of the resistance, see Metz and Millen, *Insurgency and Counterinsurgency in the 21st Century* and Louise Richardson *What Terrorists Want*, New York: Random House, 2006. On the increase in the likelihood of suicide attacks, see Robert Pape, *Dying to Win: The Strategic Logic of Suicide Terrorism*, New York: Random House, 2006; For a theoretical and empirical treatment of military occupations, see David M. Edelstein, "Occupational Hazards: Why Military Occupations Succeed or Fail," *International Security*, Vol. 29, No. 1, pp. 49–91.

111. Christopher Paul, "How Do Terrorists Generate and Maintain Support?" in Paul K. Davis and Kim Cragin, eds., *Social Science for Counterterrorism: Putting the Pieces Together*, Santa Monica, Calif.: RAND Corporation, 2009, pp. 113–150.

112. Hilal Khashan, "Collective Palestinian Frustration and Suicide Bombings," *Third World Quarterly*, Vol. 24, No. 6, December 2003, pp. 1049–1067.

113. On a lack of economic opportunity, see Richard Clutterbuck, "Peru, Cocaine, Terrorism, and Corruption," *International Relations*, Vol. 12, No. 5, 1995, pp. 77–92 and Robert Looney, "The Business of Insurgency: The Expansion of Iraq's Shadow Economy," *The National Interest*, Fall 2005, pp. 1–6.

114. C. Christine Fair and Bryan Shepherd, "Who Supports Terrorism? Evidence from Fourteen Muslim Countries," *Studies in Conflict & Terrorism*, Vol. 29, 2006, pp. 51–74.

115. Michael P. Boyle et al., "Expressive Responses to News Stories about Extremist Groups: A Framing Experiment," *Journal of Communication*, Vol. 56, No. 2, 2006, pp. 271–288.

116. Todd C. Helmus, "Why and How Some People Become Terrorists," in Davis and Cragin, eds., *Social Science for Counterterrorism*, p. 77.

117. Thomas Hegghammer, "Terrorist Recruitment and Radicalization in Saudi Arabia," *Middle East Policy*, Vol. 13, No. 4, 2006, pp. 39–60; see also, Robert F. Worth, "Hezbollah Seeks to Marshal the Piety of the Young," *New York Times*, November 20, 2008.

118. On Saudi recruits for Iraq, see Thomas Hegghammer, *Saudi Militants in Iraq: Backgrounds and Recruitment Patterns*, Norwegian Defence Research Establishment (FFI), February 5, 2007 and Alexandrea Zavis, "Foreign Fighters in Iraq Seek Recognition, US Says," *Los Angeles Times*, March 17, 2008; on Jemmah Islamiyah recruitment see Helmus, "Why and How Some People Become Terrorists"; on the PKK, see Ami Pedahzur, *Suicide Terrorism*, Cambridge, United Kingdom: Polity Press, 2005.

119. Brynjar Lia and Ashild Kjok, *Islamist Insurgencies, Diaspora Support Networks, and Their Host States: The Case of the Algerian GIA in Europe 1993–2000*, Kjeller, Norway: Forsvartes Forskningsinstitutt, FFI/APPORT-2001/03789, August 8, 2001.

120. On clan and tribal connections see William S. McCallister, "The Iraq Insurgency: Anatomy of a Tribal Rebellion," *First Monday*, Vol. 10, No. 3, March 2005; on the use of social services see Teresa Shawn Flanigan, "Charity as Resistance: Connections Between Charity, Contentious Politics, and Terror," *Studies in Conflict &*

Terrorism, Vol. 29, 2006, pp. 641–655 and Alexus G. Grynkewich, "Welfare as Warfare: How Violent Non-State Groups Use Social Services to Attack the State," *Studies in Conflict & Terrorism*, Vol. 31, 2008, pp. 350–370; Erik A. Claessen, "S.W.E.T. and Blood: Essential Services in the Battle Between Insurgents and Counterinsurgents," *Military Review*, November/December 2007.

121. Kelly M. Greenhill and Paul Staniland, "Ten Ways to Lose at Counterinsurgency," *Civil Wars*, Vol. 9, No. 4, 2007, p. 407.

122. Byman et al, *Trends in Outside Support*, pp. 88–89.

123. "Terrorist Financing," Council on Foreign Relations, Report of an Independent Task Force, 2002, p. 2.

124. Anne L. Clunan, "U.S. and International Responses to Terrorist Financing," in Jeanne K. Giraldo and Harold A. Trinkunas, *Terrorism Financing and State Responses: A Comparative Perspective*, Stanford: Stanford University Press, 2007, pp. 271–272.

125. Kathryn L. Gardner, "Fighting Terrorism the FATF Way," *Global Governance*, Vol. 13, No. 3, July–Sept 2007, p. 329.

126. Clunan, "U.S. and International Responses," p. 270.

127. Interestingly, neither the Treasury Department nor its Financial Crimes Enforcement Center (FinCEN) designated analysts for the FTATG. Ibid., p. 275.

128. Aimen Dean et al., "Draining the Ocean to Catch One Type of Fish: Evaluating the Effectiveness of the Global Counter-Terrorism Financing Regime," *Perspectives on Terrorism*, Vol. 7, No. 4, 2013.

129. Jonathan M. Winer and Trifin J. Roule, "Fighting Terrorist Finance," *Survival*, Vol. 44, No. 3, 2002, p. 91.

130. Jeffery M. Johnson and Carl Jensen, "The Financing of Terrorism," *The Journal of the Institute of Justice & International Studies*, No. 10, 2010, p. 111.

131. Financial Action Task Force (FATF) IX Special Recommendations, October 2001. These recommendations were significantly revised again in 2012.

132. Clunan, "U.S. and International Responses," p. 267.

133. Author interview with anonymous United States Government (USG) official, December 2014.

134. Juan C. Zarate, *Treasury's War: The Unleashing of a New Era of Financial Warfare*, New York: Public Affairs, 2013, p. 46.

CHAPTER 2

1. On the origins of the Provisional Irish Republican Army (PIRA) and a historical background to Irish terrorism, see Tim Pat Coogan, *The IRA*, New York: Palgrave, 2000.

2. Coogan, *The IRA*, p. 5.

3. James Adams, *The Financing of Terror: How the Groups That Are Terrorizing the World Get the Money to Do It*, New York: Simon and Shuster, 1986, p. 131; p. 164.

4. John Horgan and Max Taylor, "Playing the 'Green Card'—Financing the Provisional IRA: Part 2," *Terrorism and Political Violence*, Vol. 15, No. 2, Summer 2003, p. 6.

5. John Horgan and Max Taylor, "Playing Green Card—Financing the Provisional IRA: Part I," *Terrorism and Political Violence*, Vol. 11, No. 2, Summer 1999, p. 2.

6. Horgan and Taylor, " 'Green Card'—Part 2," pp. 38–41.

7. According to Adams, although sources of financial support from the Irish-American diaspora once accounted for over half of the PIRA's budget in the early 1970s, by the mid-1980s these funds comprised no more than £135,000 ($200,000). Adams, *The Financing of Terror*, p. 136.

8. Ibid., pp. 142–143.

9. Ibid., p. 134.

10. Daniel Byman, *Deadly Connections: States that Sponsor Terrorism*, Cambridge: Cambridge University Press, 2005, pp. 246–258.

11. Daniel Byman, "Passive Sponsors of Terrorism," *Survival*, Vol. 47, No. 4, Winter 2005, p. 134.

12. In many of these cities, NORAID maintained what it called "Century Clubs," which were groups of 10 individuals who would be called on to donate $100 at a moment's notice. Each "Century Club" produced $1,000.

13. Adams, *Financing of Terror*, p. 143.

14. Richard English, *Armed Struggle: The History of the IRA*, Oxford: Oxford University Press, 2004, p. 117.

15. Adams, *Financing of Terror*, p. 137.

16. Ibid., p. 141.

17. Ibid., p. 136.

18. Ibid., p. 131.

19. Ibid., p. 142.

20. Peter Taylor, *Provos: The IRA & Sinn Fein*, London: Bloomsbury, 1997, pp. 84–85.

21. John Horgan and Max Taylor, "The Provisional Irish Republican Army: Command and Functional Structure," *Terrorism and Political Violence*, Vol. 9, No. 3, 1997, p. 13. According to Adams, tax exemption scams earned upwards $60 m a year. Adams, p. 180.

22. Keith Maguire, "Fraud, Extortion and Racketeering: The Black Economy in Northern Ireland," *Crime, Law, and Social Change*, Vol. 20, No. 4, 1993, pp. 284–285.

23. Horgan and Taylor, " 'Green Card'—Part 2," p. 8.

24. Maguire, "Fraud, Extortion, Racketeering," p. 285.

25. Horgan and Taylor, " 'Green Card'—Part 1," p. 8.

26. Horgan and Taylor, " 'Green Card'—Part 2," p. 4.

27. Adams, *Financing Terror*, p. 175.

28. Keith Maguire, "Policing the Black Economy: The Role of C.13 of the R.U.C. in Northern Ireland," *The Police Journal*, Vol. 66, No. 2, April–June 1993, p. 133.

29. Adams, *Financing Terror*, p. 177.

30. Author interview with John Horgan, October 2014.

31. Horgan and Taylor, " 'Green Card'—Part 2," pp. 17–32.

32. Ibid., p. 33.

33. Horgan and Taylor, "Command and Functional Structure," p. 13.

34. *Riding shotgun* is a term used for providing an armed escort on international drug shipments.

35. Coogan, *The IRA*, p. 522.

36. Ibid., p. 523.

37. James Dingley, *The IRA: The Irish Republican Army*, Santa Barbara: Praeger Security International, 2012, p. 194.

38. The Active Service Unit (ASU) is made up of PIRA insurgents who are directly responsible for executing military operations such as shootings or bombings. A typical ASU was trained for a specific task (e.g., bombing, intelligence, robberies, etc.) and consisted of 4 Volunteers and had one OC, with 3–4 ASUs in each Brigade.

39. Horgan and Taylor, " 'Green Card'—Part 1," p. 13.

40. Adams, *Financing Terror*, p. 179.

41. By the 1990s, only armed robberies that were thought to have the potential to net large sums of money were sanctioned, as scores of 100,000 pounds or more were capable of funding specific projects. Dingley, *The IRA*, p. 194.

42. There is a fierce debate in the literature over whether or not the PIRA engaged in drug trafficking. Because a consensus has never been reached, this chapter eschews further analysis of the issue. For a thoughtful and balanced analysis of the debate, see Horgan and Taylor, " 'Green Card'—Part 1," pp. 24–30.

43. Horgan and Taylor, "Command and Functional Structure," p. 13.

44. Dingley, *The IRA*, p. 196.

45. Ibid.

46. Horgan and Taylor, " 'Green Card'—Part 1," pp. 20–21.

47. Dingley, *The IRA*, p. 194.

48. Adams, *Financing Terror*, p. 171.

49. In August 1972, two members of the PIRA's ruling body, Joe Cahill and Denis McInerney, met with members of Libyan intelligence in Warsaw, Poland. Ed Moloney, *A Secret History of the IRA*, New York: WW Norton & Company, 2003, p. 9.

50. English, *Armed Struggle*, p. 344. Coogan puts the group's annual income in the early 1980s at over 1.5 million pounds. Coogan, *The IRA*, p. 430. Nevertheless, it should be noted that many scholars, including Horgan and Taylor, stress that most of the estimates on the PIRA's income are mere "guesstimates." Horgan and Taylor, " 'Green Card'—Part 2," p. 46. By definition, the nature of a clandestine organization makes an accurate assessment extremely difficult.

51. Horgan and Taylor, " 'Green Card'—Part 1," p. 4.

52. Ibid., p. 5.

53. Still, as the expertise of the "Engineers" grew, the group relied on low-cost detonators that could be fashioned out of everyday devices like garage door openers.

54. Though this is not an exhaustive list, some IRA explosive device innovations included: radar detectors, police radar guns, photographic unites triggered by flashes of light, infrared transmitters from garage door openers, projectile detonators, Memopark timers, and electromagnetic traps. See Brian Jackson et al., *Aptitude for Destruction, Volume 2: Case Studies of Organizational Learning in Five Terrorist Groups*, Santa Monica, CA: RAND Corp., 2005, pp. 100–104.

55. Ibid., p. 107.

56. Horgan and Taylor, " 'Green Card'—Part 1," p. 5.

57. Toby Harnden, *Bandit Country: The IRA & South Armagh*, London: Hodder & Stoughton, 2000, p. 53. For a thorough analysis of the PIRA's intelligence capabilities, see also, Gaetano Joe Ilardi, "IRA Operational Intelligence: The Heartbeat of the War," *Small Wars & Insurgencies*, Vol. 21, No. 2, June 2010, pp. 331–358.

58. For an in-depth explanation of each department, see Horgan and Taylor, "Command and Functional Structure," pp. 9–18.

59. Ilardi, "IRA Operational Intelligence," p. 333.

60. Horgan and Taylor, " 'Green Card'—Part I," p. 6.

61. Ibid.

62. Brian Jackson, "Training for Urban Resistance: The Case of the Provisional Irish Republican Army," p. 123, in James J. F. Forest, ed., *The Making of a Terrorist, Volume II: Training*, Santa Barbara: Praeger, 2005.

63. Horgan and Taylor, "Command and Functional Structure," p. 7.

64. Training camps were located throughout the entire ROI even as far south as Cork and took the form of farms, beaches, and wooded areas. Jackson, "Training for Urban Resistance," p. 128.

65. Jackson, "Training for Urban Resistance," p. 127.

66. Jackson et al., *Aptitude for Destruction*, Vol. 2, p. 124.

67. Ibid., p. 103.

68. Brian Jackson, "Training for Urban Resistance," p. 131.

69. Don Mansfield, "The Irish Republican Army and Northern Ireland," in Bard E. O'Neill, William R. Heaton, and Donald J. Alberts, eds., *Insurgency in the Modern World*, Boulder: Westview Press, 1980, p. 73.

70. Horgan and Taylor, " 'Green Card'—Part I," p. 7.

71. Adams, *Financing Terror*, pp. 164–166

72. Author Interview with John Horgan, October 2014.

73. Dingley, *The IRA*, p. 191.

74. Ibid., p. 192.

75. English, *Armed Struggle*, p. 107.

76. Gerry Adams cited in Taylor, *Provos*, pp. 283–284.

77. English, *Armed Struggle*, p. 216.

78. Peter Neumann, *Old & New Terrorism*, Cambridge: Polity Press, 2009, pp. 33.

79. Rogelio Alonso, "Irish Republican Thinking Toward the Utility of Violence," *Studies in Conflict and Terrorism*, Vol. 24, No. 2, 2001, p. 141.

80. *Óglaigh na hÉireann* is an Irish-language title for the Irish Volunteers of 1913.

81. Interview with John Horgan, October 2014.

82. Horgan and Taylor, " 'Green Card'—Part I," p. 7.

83. This was a common tactic of the security services in Northern Ireland. Individuals would be arrested and promised steady payments and freedom from prosecution for agreeing to become a "tout," or informer of PIRA activities and operations. Martin McGartland, *Fifty Dead Men Walking: The Heroic True Story of a British Secret Agent Inside the IRA*, London: John Blake, 2009.

84. *Handbook for Volunteers of the Irish Republican Army: Notes on Guerrilla Warfare*, Boulder: Palladin Press, 1985, pp. 17–18.

85. Cronin provides examples of active support, such as hiding members, raising money, and joining the organization. Passive support includes ignoring obvious signs of terrorist activity, declining to cooperate with police investigations, sending money to organizations that act as fronts for the group, and expressing support of the group's objectives. Audrey Kurth Cronin, "How al-Qaida Ends:

The Decline and Demise of Terrorist Groups," *International Security*, Vol. 31, No. 1, Summer 2006, p. 27.

86. Coogan, *The IRA*, p. 581.

87. English, *Armed Struggle*, p. 115.

88. Quoted in Patrick Bishop and Eamonn Mallie, *The Provisional IRA*, London: Corgi Books, 1992, p. 330.

89. English, *Armed Struggle*, p. 181.

90. In Adams' description of a 1979 NORAID benefit dinner, he lists among the guests a chairman of the House Judiciary Committee, former ambassadors, an Under Secretary of State, treasure of an AFL-CIO branch, an Attorneys General from the State of New York and Long Island respectively, several congressmen, AOH leaders, and influential union representatives. Adams, *Financing Terror*, p. 137.

91. Ibid., p. 136.

92. These politicians included Edward Kennedy, Thomas "Tip" O'Neill, Daniel Patrick Moynihan, and Hugh Carey, who were subsequently dubbed "The Four Horsemen." Ibid., p. 138.

93. Moloney, *A Secret History of the IRA*, p. 16.

94. Ibid., p. 101.

95. Adams, *Financing Terror*, p. 145.

96. Ibid., p.183.

97. Maguire, "Fraud, Extortion, Racketeering," p. 284.

98. Maguire, "Policing the Black Economy," p. 134.

99. Adams, *Financing Terror*, p. 146; pp. 151–152.

100. Maguire, "Fraud, Extortion, Racketeering," p. 288.

101. Adams, pp. 165–166; see also, Horgan and Taylor, " 'Green Card'—Part 1," pp. 21–22.

102. Maguire, "Fraud, Extortion, Racketeering," p. 283.

103. Ibid.

104. Paul Norman, "The Terrorist Finance Unit and the Joint Action Group on Organised Crime: New Organisational Models and Investigative Strategies to Counter 'Organised Crime' in the UK," *The Howard Journal*, Vol. 37, No. 4, November 1998, p. 379.

105. Ibid., p. 380.

106. See John Horgan and John F. Morrison, "Here to Stay? The Rising Threat of Violent Dissident Republicanism in Northern Ireland," *Terrorism and Political Violence*, Vol. 23, No. 4, pp. 642–669, 2011; see also, Martyn Frampton, "The Return of the Militants," "Violent Dissident Republicanism," "International Centre for the Study of Radicalisation and Political Violence," 2010.

CHAPTER 3

1. Robert I. Rotberg, ed., *Creating Peace in Sri Lanka: Civil War & Reconciliation*, Washington DC: Brookings Institution Press, 2005, p. 4. A 2001 census notes that Sri Lanka's main ethnic populations are Sinhalese (82 percent), Tamil (9.4 percent), and Sri Lanka Moor (7.9 percent). Jayshree Bajoria, Council on Foreign Relations Backgrounder: The Sri Lankan Conflict, May 18, 2009.

2. Rotberg, *Creating Peace*, p. 43.

3. Ibid., p. 47.

4. Ibid., pp. 44–50.

5. Rohan Gunaratna, "International and Regional Implications of the Sri Lankan Tamil Insurgency," December 2, 1998.

6. Rotberg, *Creating Peace*, p. 7.

7. By the mid-1990s, it is estimated that the LTTE has cells in as many as 38 countries throughout Europe, the Middle East and North America. These cells could collect donations from the Tamil diaspora, or obtain money through coercion and extortion. Phil Williams, "Insurgencies and Organized Crime," in Phil Williams and Vanda Felbab-Brown, *Drug Trafficking, Violence, and Instability*, Carlisle Barracks, PA: U.S. Army War College Strategic Studies Institute, April 2012, p. 50.

8. Personal interview with Peter Chalk, October 2014. Gunaratna estimates that by late 1995, 40 percent of the LTTE's war budget was generated abroad until the loss of the Jaffna peninsula in 1996, when this number rose to 60 percent.

9. Peter Chalk, "Liberation Tigers of Tamil Eelam's (LTTE) International Organization and Operations—A Preliminary Analysis," Canadian Security Intelligence Service, Commentary No. 77, Winter 1999.

10. Peter Chalk, "The Liberation Tigers of Tamil Eelam Insurgency in Sri Lanka," in Rajat Ganguly and Ian MacDuff, *Ethnic Conflict and Secessionism in South and Southeast Asia*, London: Sage, 2003, p. 146.

11. Ibid., p. 131.

12. Gunaratna, "International and Regional Implications."

13. Frederic Lemieux and Fernanda Prates, "Entrepreneurial Terrorism: Financial Strategies, Business Opportunities, and Ethical Issues," *Police Practice and Research: An International Journal*, Vol. 12, No. 5, p. 371.

14. S. T. Flanigan, "Nonprofit Service Provision by Insurgent Organizations: The Cases of Hizballah and the Tamil Tigers," *Studies in Conflict & Terrorism*, Vol. 31, No. 6, p. 515.

15. Samantha Bricknell, "Misuse of the Nonprofit Sector for Money Laundering and Terrorist Financing," *Trends & Issues in Crime and Criminal Justice*, No. 424, September 2011.

16. A. Abocar, "Canada Police Say Tamil Gangs Funding Rebels," *Reuters*, March 28, 2000.

17. Phil Williams, "Crime, Illicit Markets, and Money Laundering," in P. J. Simmons and Chantel Ouderen, *Challenges in International Governance*, Washington: Carnegie Endowment for International Peace, 2001, p. 115.

18. Gunaratna, "International and Regional Implications."

19. Rohan Gunaratna, "Sri Lanka: Feeding the Tamil Tigers," in Karen Ballentine and Jake Sherman, eds., *The Political Economy of Armed Conflict: Beyond Greed and Grievance*, Boulder: Lynne Rienner, 2003, p. 192.

20. Ibid.

21. Ibid., p. 209.

22. Ravinatha Aryasinha, "Terrorism, the LTTE and the Conflict in Sri Lanka," *Conflict, Security, & Development*, Vol. 1, No. 2, 2001, p. 35.

23. Aurel Croissant and Daniel Barlow, "Following the Money Trail: Terrorist Financing and Government Responses in Southeast Asia," *Studies in Conflict & Terrorism*, Vol. 30, No. 2, 2007, pp. 134–135.

24. Chalk, "LTTE in Sri Lanka," p. 144.

25. Manoj Joshi, "On the Razor's Edge: The Liberation Tigers of Tamil Eelam," *Studies in Conflict and Terrorism*, Vol. 19, No. 1, 1996, p. 37.

26. Louise I. Shelley, *Dirty Entanglements: Corruption, Crime and Terrorism*, New York: Cambridge University Press, 2014, p. 186.

27. James J. F. Forest, "Kidnapping by Terrorist Groups, 1070–2010: Is Ideological Orientation Relevant?," *Crime & Delinquency*, Vol. 58, No. 5, September 2012, p. 770.

28. Janine Lilja, "Trapping Constituents or Winning Hearts and Minds? Rebel Strategies to Attain Constituent Support in Sri Lanka," *Terrorism and Political Violence*, Vol. 21, No. 2, April 2009, p. 313.

29. Phil Williams, "Transnational Criminal Enterprises, Conflict and Instability," in Chester A. Crocker, Fen Osler Hampson and Pamela Aal, *Turbulent Peace: The Challenges of Managing International Conflict*, Washington DC: United States Institute of Peace Press, 2001, pp. 97–112.

30. Steven Hutchinson and Pat O'Malley, "A Crime-Terror Nexus? Thinking Some on the Links Between Terrorism and Criminality," *Studies in Conflict & Terrorism*, Vol. 30, No. 12, p. 1104.

31. Gordon Weiss, *The Cage: The Fight for Sri Lanka and the Last Days of the Tamil Tigers*, London: Bodley Head, 2011, p. 89.

32. Williams, "Insurgencies and Organized Crime," in Williams and Felbab-Brown, *Drug Trafficking, Violence, and Instability*, p. 46.

33. The mid-1980s were probably the apex of Tamil drug trafficking arrests. In 1984, 317 drug traffickers were arrested. The next year, that number increased to 374, only to drop by 1986 to 218 arrests and flatline in 1990 at around 37. G. H. Peires, "Clandestine Transactions of the LTTE and the Secessionist Campaign in Sri Lanka," Ethnic Studies Report, Vol. 19, No. 1, 2001.

34. Phil Williams, "Terrorist Financing and Organized Crime: Nexus, Appropriation, or Transformation?" in Thomas J. Biersteker and Sue E. Eckert eds., *Countering the Financing of Terrorism*, London: Routledge, 2008, p. 139.

35. "Sri Lanka: Sri Lanka's Rebels Involved in Trafficking Human Cargo," *Xinhua News Agency*, April 7, 2000.

36. Louise I. Shelley and John T. Picarelli, "Methods Not Motives: Implications of the Convergence of International Organized Crime and Terrorism," *Police Practice and Research*, Vol. 3, No. 4, 2002, p. 313.

37. John Rollins and Liana Sun-Wyler, "Terrorism and Transnational Crime: Foreign Policy Issues for Congress," Congressional Research Service (CRS), October 19, 2012, p. 14.

38. Williams, "Insurgencies and Organized Crime," in Williams and Felbab-Brown, *Drug Trafficking, Violence, and Instability*, p. 50.

39. Weiss, *The Cage*, p. 89

40. Williams, "Insurgencies and Organized Crime," in Williams and Felbab-Brown, *Drug Trafficking, Violence, and Instability*, p. 56.

41. Shelley and Picarelli, "Methods Not Motives," p. 314.

42. Rotberg, *Creating Peace*, p. 32.

43. Cecile Van de Voorde, "Sri Lankan Terrorism: Assessing and Responding to the Threat of the Liberation Tigers of Tamil Eelam," *Police Practice and Research*, Vol. 6, No. 2, 2005.

44. Both Mozambique and Angola experienced serial insurgencies during this period. In Mozambique, separate insurgencies occurred in 1962–1974 and 1976–1995. In Angola, serial insurgencies wracked that country from 1962–1974 and from 1975–2002.

45. Chalk, "The LTTE in Sri Lanka," p. 143.

46. Byman, *Outside Support*, "Appendix B: The LTTE's Military-Related Procurement," p. 121.

47. Ibid., p. 120.

48. IHS Jane's World Terrorism and Insurgency, "Liberation Tigers Tamil Eelam."

49. Ibid.

50. These groups include The Tamil National Retrieval Force, People's War Group, Liberation Cuckoos, Peasants and People Party, MGF Anna Dravida Munethra Kalaham of Thirunavakarasu, Tamil National Movement of Nedumaran, Indian People's Party, Center for the Campaign of Tamil Education, Thaliai Nagar Tamil Society, Movement of the Educated Front, Tamil Nadu People's Movement, Thileepan Society, People's Education Center, Tamil Nadu Socialist Party, Republic Party of India, People's Democratic Youth Front, Liberation Organization of the Oppressed People, World People's Progressive Front, Human Rights Organization, Organization for Social History, and the Marxist Periyar Socialist Party. Van de Voorde, "Sri Lankan Terrorism," p. 192.

51. IHS Jane's World Terrorism and Insurgency, "Liberation Tigers Tamil Eelam."

52. Gunaratna, International and Regional Implications."

53. Joshi, "On the Razor's Edge," p. 33.

54. Weiss, *The Cage*, p. 88.

55. IHS Jane's World Terrorism and Insurgency, "Liberation Tigers Tamil Eelam."

56. Joshi, "On the Razor's Edge," p. 33.

57. Rotberg, *Creating Peace*, p. 33.

58. Ibid., p. 18

59. Byman, *Outside Support*, "Appendix B: The LTTE's Military-Related Procurement," p. 117.

60. Rotberg, *Creating Peace*, p. 32.

61. Byman, *Outside Support*, "Appendix B: The LTTE's Military-Related Procurement," p. 117.

62. Ibid., p. 119.

63. Chalk, "LTTE in Sri Lanka," p. 144.

64. Rotberg, *Creating Peace*, p. 33.

65. IHS Jane's World Terrorism and Insurgency, "Liberation Tigers Tamil Eelam."

66. Lionel Beecher, "What Sri Lanka Can Teach Us about COIN," *Small Wars Journal*, August 27, 2010, p. 3.

67. Brendan O'Duffy, "The Liberation Tigers of Tamil Eelam (LTTE): Majoritarianism, Self-Determination and Military-to-Political Transitions in Sri Lanka," in M. Heiburg, B. O'Leary and J. Tirman (eds.), *Terror, Insurgency and States*, Philadelphia, PA: Univ. of Pennsylvania, 2007, p. 266.

68. Ibid.

69. Ibid.

70. Gunaratna, "International and Regional Implications."

71. Joshi, "On the Razor's Edge," p. 27

72. IHS Jane's World Terrorism and Insurgency, "Liberation Tigers Tamil Eelam."

73. Rotberg, *Creating Peace*, p. 18.

74. Ibid.

75. According to Chalk, the most specialized training was conducted at Chakrata, India's elite military academy. Here, Research and Analysis Wing (RAW) trainers worked with a range of insurgent groups, including Bangladeshi, Pakistani, and Tibetan dissidents. Chalk, "LTTE in Sri Lanka," p. 131.

76. Joshi, "On the Razor's Edge," p. 23.

77. Tamil militant groups trained in the Middle East in the 1980s and beginning in the 1990s, small numbers of insurgents were trained in underwater sabotage techniques in camps located in Thailand by former Norwegian naval instructors. Other insurgents received training in Sudan to learn how to use global positioning systems (GPS) while member of South Africa's African National Congress imparted lessons to LTTE cadres on the political element of insurgency. IHS Jane's World Terrorism and Insurgency, "Liberation Tigers Tamil Eelam."

78. IHS Jane's World Terrorism and Insurgency, "Liberation Tigers Tamil Eelam."

79. Kevin A. O'Brien, "Assessing Hostile Reconnaissance and Terrorist Intelligence Activities: The Case for a Counter Strategy," *RUSI Journal*, Vol. 153, October 2008, p. 53.

80. Joshi, "On the Razor's Edge," p. 26. For details on the activities conducted by Indian intelligence services during this period, see Anirudhya Mitra, "Rajiv Assassination: Conspiracy Surfaces" *India Today,* December 15, 1992, pp. 57–60.

81. IHS Jane's World Terrorism and Insurgency, "Liberation Tigers Tamil Eelam."

82. Interview with Peter Chalk, October 2014.

83. Weiss, *The Cage*, p. 8.

84. Kristian Stokke, "Building the Tamil Eelam State: Emerging State Institutions and Forms of Governance in LTTE-controlled Areas in Sri Lanka," *Third World Quarterly*, Vol. 27, No. 6, 2006, p. 1022.

85. Ibid.

86. Weiss, *The Cage*, pp. 74–75.

87. Jerrold M. Post, *The Mind of the Terrorist: The Psychology of Terrorism from the IRA to al-Qaida*, New York: Palgrave Macmillan, 2007, p. 92.

88. Andrew Perrin, "Tiger Country: Whatever the outcome of peace talks between Colombo and the separatist Tigers, a Tamil nation in all but law already exists in Sri Lanka's battle-scarred northeast," *Time*, September 16, 2002.

89. Mia Bloom, *Dying to Kill: The Allure of Suicide Terror*, New York: Columbia University Press, 2005, p. 71.

90. According to Brendan O'Duffy, the LTTE always rejected the notion that the conflict was simply about ethnicity at its core. According to this line of thinking, if full civil and political rights were to be restored to the Tamils and other minority communities, then the conflict would cease. However, the LTTE regarded the conflict as *ethno-national* in scope, which included the indispensable element of national self-determination to be recognized. O'Duffy, p. 264.

91. Marks, "Ideology of Insurgency," p. 112.

92. Ibid. On p. 114, Marks notes that of the main Marxist groups, the PLOTE were the most sophisticated politically.

93. Ibid., p. 114.

94. Marks, *Maoist Insurgency Since Vietnam*, p. 188.

95. A. S. Balasingham, *Liberation Tigers and Tamil Eelam Freedom Struggle*, Madras: Political Committee, LTTE, 1983, p. 42.

96. Marks, *Maoist Insurgency Since Vietnam*, p. 192.

97. Marks, "Ideology of Insurgency," p. 114.

98. Ibid., p. 54.

99. Ibid., p. 53.

100. Ibid., p. 71.

101. Lilja, "Trapping Constituents," pp. 314–318.

102. Ibid., p. 266.

103. C. Christine Fair, *Urban Battlefields of South Asia: Lessons Learned from Sri Lanka, India, and Pakistan*, Santa Monica, Calif.: RAND Corp., 2004, p. 25.

104. *Jane's World Insurgency and Terrorism*, Vol. 15 (2002), available at www.janes.com

105. Fair, *Urban Battlefields*, p. 29.

106. Chalk, "LTTE International Organization and Operations—A Preliminary Analysis." In addition to these Western nations, the LTTE also had representatives working in Cambodia, Myanmar, South Africa, and Botswana.

107. John C. Thompson and Jon Turlej, *Other People's Wars: A Review of Overseas Terrorism in Canada*, Toronto: The Mackenzie Institute, 2003, p. 21.

108. According to Gunaratna, the LTTE has established, absorbed, or infiltrated a number of LTTE front or pro-LTTE organizations in the United Kingdom, including the Tamil Information Center at Tamil House in Romford Road in London, The Tamil Rehabilitation Organization in Walthamstow in London, and the International Federation of Tamils (IFT) in Birchiew Close in Surrey.

109. Chalk, "LTTE International Organization and Operations—A Preliminary Analysis."

110. C. Van de Voorde, "Sri Lankan Terrorism," p. 192.

111. Gunaratna, "International and Regional Implications."

112. IHS Jane's World Terrorism and Insurgency, "Liberation Tigers Tamil Eelam."

113. For more on this, see Shyam Tekwani, "The LTTE's Online Network and its Implications for Regional Security," Singapore: Institute of Defense and Strategic Studies, January 2006.

114. Stewart Bell, "Canada a Key Source of Tamil Tiger Funding," *National Post*, July 20, 2009.

115. Somini Sengupta, "Take Aid From China and Take a Pass on Human Rights," *The New York Times*, March 9, 2008; see also, Robert Kaplan, "To Catch a Tiger," *The Atlantic*, July 2009.

116. Niel A. Smith, "Understanding Sri Lanka's Defeat of the Tamil Tigers," *Joint Forces Quarterly*, No. 59, 4th quarter, 2010, pp. 40–44.

117. Paul Staniland, "Between a Rock and a Hard Place: Insurgent Fratricide, Ethnic Defection, and the Rise of Pro-State Paramilitaries," *Journal of Conflict Resolution*, Vol. 56, No. 1, 2012, p. 30.

118. IHS Jane's World Terrorism and Insurgency, "Liberation Tigers Tamil Eelam."

119. Christian Chung, "The Killer Tiger Roared: A Strategic Analysis of Sri Lankan "Kinetic" Counterinsurgency and its Theoretical Implications," *Small Wars Journal*, December 15, 2010, p. 6.

120. In an interesting paper, Albert Wesley Harris utilized prospect theory to analyze the LTTE's decision to mount a stand at Kilinochchi. He concludes that the insurgents preferred to accept the risk of losing the battle, incurring significant casualties, and potentially losing the war in return for the chance that they could win the battle and turn the tide of the war. See Albert Wesley Harris, "Insurgency Decision-making under Conditions of Risk," *International Journal of Psychological Studies*, Vol. 4, No. 3, 2012, pp. 43–47.

121. Author interview with Peter Chalk, November 2014.

122. Author interview with Peter Chalk, November 2014.

123. Sengupta, "Take Aid From China," July 2009.

124. Peter Chalk notes that after being designated as a FTO by the United States in 1997, other states began to review their own practices with regard to LTTE activity in their country. The United Kingdom, for example, has struggled with first PIRA terrorism and then Islamist militancy, so has moved to make the incitement of terrorism an illegal activity and connected to this, publicity and fund-raising has become a criminal offense. Chalk, Commentary No. 77.

CHAPTER 4

1. This particular transliteration—Hezbollah—will be used throughout this study. Note that there are other common transliterations including: Hezbollah, Hizbullah, Hezballah, Hisbollah, and Hizb Allah.

2. For a detailed discussion of the Lebanese civil war, see Dilip Hiro, *Lebanon Fire and Embers: A History of the Lebanese Civil War*, New York: St. Martin Press, 1992; Marwan George Rowayheb, "Political Change and the Outbreak of Civil War: The Case of Lebanon," *Civil Wars*, Vol. 13, No. 4, 2011, pp. 414–436; and Walid Khalidi, *Conflict and Violence in Lebanon: Confrontation in the Middle East*, Harvard University: Center for International Affairs, 1979.

3. Augustus Richard Norton, *Hezbollah: A Short History*, Princeton: Princeton University Press, 2007, p. 6.

4. Kenneth M. Pollack, *The Persian Puzzle: The Conflict Between Iran and America*, New York: Random House, 2004, p. 201.

5. Jeffrey Goldberg, "A Reporter at Large: In the Party of God," Part II, *The New Yorker*, October 28, 2002.

6. Magnus Ranstorp, "The Hezbollah Training Camps of Lebanon," in James J. F. Forest, ed., *The Making of a Terrorist, Volume II: Training*, Santa Barbara: Praeger, 2005, p. 247. In 1994, Hezbollah militants were stopped before they could detonate a bomb at the Israeli Embassy in Bangkok, Thailand.

7. Ibid., pp. 246–247.

8. Ibid., p. 247.

9. Matthew Levitt, "Hezbollah Finances: Funding the Party of God," in Jeanne K. Giraldo and Harold A. Trinkunas, eds., *Terrorism Financing and State Responses: A Comparative Perspective*, Stanford: Stanford University Press, 2007, pp. 141–142.

10. Matthew Levitt, "The Hezbollah Threat in Africa," The Washington Institute, Policywatch, No. 283, January 2, 2004.

11. Angel Rabasa et al., *Beyond al-Qaeda, Pat II: The Outer Rings of the Terrorist Universe*, Santa Monica, CA: RAND Corp., 2006, p. 147.

12. In addition to financial and operational support, the Martyrs Foundation, an offshoot of an institution created in Iran, provides ideological support. Thanassis Cambanis, *A Privilege to Die: Inside Hezbollah's Legions and Their Endless War Against Israel*, New York: Simon and Schuster, 2010, p. 195.

13. Matthew Levitt, *Hezbollah: The Global Footprint of Lebanon's Party of God*, Washington DC: Georgetown University Press, 2013, p. 83.

14. Ibid., p. 154.

15. Cambanis, *Privilege to Die*, p. 226.

16. Levitt, *Global Footprint*, p. 233.

17. Rachel Ehrenfeld, *Funding Evil: How Terrorism Is Financed and How to Stop It*, Chicago: Bonus Books, 2003, p. 141.

18. Levitt, *Global Footprint*, p. 320.

19. Ibid., pp. 318–323.

20. Ibid., p. 223.

21. Ibid.

22. David Kilcullen, *Out of the Mountains: The Coming Age of the Urban Guerrilla*, New York: Oxford University Press, 2013, p. 142–144.

23. Jo Becker, "Beirut Bank Seen as a Hub of Hezbollah's Financing," *New York Times*, December 13, 2011, p. A1.

24. Ibid.

25. Jessica Hume, "U.S. Seizes $150 million from Hezbollah-linked Lebanese Canadian Bank," *Toronto Sun*, August 21, 2012. As noted in Louise Shelley, *Dirty Entanglements: Corruption, Crime, and Terrorism*, New York: Cambridge University Press, 2014, fn 181, p. 214.

26. Levitt, p. 265 (fn 126).

27. Norton, *Hezbollah*, pp. 13–14.

28. Levitt, *Global Footprint*, pp. 246–247.

29. Nicholas Blanford, *Warriors of God: Inside Hezbollah's Thirty-Year Struggle Against Israel*, New York: Random House, 2011, pp. 73–76.

30. Ibid., p. 88.

31. Ibid., pp. 290–294.

32. In January 2004, Tannenbaum and the bodies of the three soldiers abducted and killed during the cross-border raid in Sheba Farms in 2000, were exchanged

for 23 Lebanese detainees, 400 Palestinian prisoners, and 12 other Arabs. Further-more, as part of the exchange, Israel agreed to repatriate the bodies of 59 Lebanese fighters, provide information on 24 Lebanese missing since Israel's 1982 invasion, and provide Hezbollah with the maps of land mines planted throughout southern Lebanon during Israel's 18 year occupation. Ibid., p. 365.

33. Ibid., pp. 375–376.

34. Levitt, *Global Footprint*, pp. 336–339.

35. Ibid., p. 338.

36. Thomas M. Sanderson, "Transnational Terror and Organized Crime: Blurring the Lines," *SAIS Review*, Vol. 24, No. 1, Winter-Spring 2004, p. 52.

37. Martin Ewi, "A Decade of Kidnappings and Terrorism in West Africa and the Trans-Sahel Region," *African Security Review*, Vol. 19, No. 4, p. 68.

38. Gail Wannenburg, "Organised Crime in West Africa," *African Security Review*, 2005, Vol. 14, No. 4, p. 10.

39. Levitt, "Hezbollah Threat in Africa."

40. Douglas Farah, "Digging Up Congo's Dirty Gems," *The Washington Post*, December 30, 2001, pp. A1–A16.

41. Matthew Levitt, "Hezbollah Finances: Funding the Party of God," The Washington Institute, February 2005.

42. Douglas Farah, *Blood from Stones: The Secret Financial Network of Terror*, New York: Broadway Books, 2004, pp. 33–34.

43. Eric Denece and Alain Rodier, "The Security Challenges of West Africa," in OECD, *Global Security Risks and West Africa: Development Challenges*, OECD Publishing, 2012.

44. James Cockayne and Phil Williams, "The Invisible Tide: Towards an International Strategy to Deal with Drug Trafficking Through West Africa," New York: International Peace Institute, October 2009, p. 4.

45. Levitt, *Global Footprint*, p. 320.

46. Ibid., p. 227.

47. Ibid., p. 250.

48. Ibid., pp. 258–261.

49. Ibid., p. 12.

50. Some of these private charities include the Al Aqsa International Founda-tion, the Martyr's Organization, the Institute of the Palestinian Martyrs, and the al Mabarrat Charity Association.

51. For more on this so-called shadow war, see Yaakov Katz and Yoaz Hendel, *Israel vs. Iran: The Shadow War*, Washington DC: Potomac Books, 2012.

52. Seymour Hersh, "Iran and the Bomb," *The New Yorker*, June 6, 2011; on Jun-dallah, see William Lowther and Colin Freeman, "US Fund Terror Group to Sow Chaos in Iran," *The Telegraph*, February 25, 2007.

53. Charlie Savage, "Iranians Accused of a Plot to Kill Saudis' U.S. Envoy," *New York Times*, October 11, 2011.

54. Daniel Byman, "The Lebanese Hezbollah and Israeli Counterterrorism," *Studies in Conflict and Terrorism*, Vol. 34, No. 12, p. 936.

55. ICG Report, "Rebel without a Cause," p. 4.

56. Graham E. Fuller, "The Hezbollah-Iran Connection: Model for Sunni Resis-tance," *The Washington Quarterly*, Vol. 30, No. 1, Winter 2006–2007, p. 143.

57. Robert Grace and Andrew Mandelbaum, "Understanding the Iran-Hezbollah Connection," United States Institute of Peace, September 2006.

58. Joby Warrick, "Attack on Israeli Tourists Prompts Fears of Escalating 'Shadow War,'" *Washington Post*, July 19, 2012.

59. Norton, "The Role of Hezbollah in Lebanese Domestic Politics," p. 482.

60. Judith Harik, "Syrian Foreign Policy and State/Resistance Dynamics in Lebanon," *Studies in Conflict & Terrorism*, Vol. 20, No. 3, pp. 249–265.

61. Andrew Exum, "Hezbollah at War: A Military Assessment," The Washington Institute for Near East Policy, Policy Focus #63, December 2006, p. 7.

62. Steven Erlanger and Richard A. Oppel, "A Disciplined Hezbollah Surprises Israel with Its Training, Tactics and Weapons," *The New York Times*, August 7, 2006.

63. Ibid.

64. Cragin, *Aptitude for Destruction Volume 2*, p. 49.

65. Thomas M. Sanderson, "Transnational Terror and Organized Crime: Blurring the Lines," *SAIS Review*, Vol. 24, No. 1, Winter 2004, p. 52.

66. Exum, "Hezbollah at War," p. 6. From Figure 1, "Weaponry Used by Hezbollah During the July War."

67. Thannassis Cambanis, "Stronger Hezbollah Emboldened for Fights Ahead," *New York Times*, October 6, 2010.

68. Frederic Wehrey, "A Clash of Wills: Hezbollah's Psychological Campaign Against Israel in South Lebanon," *Small Wars and Insurgencies*, Vol. 13, No. 2, 2001, p. 54.

69. Ibid.

70. Ron Schleifer, "Psychological Operations: A New Variation on an Age Old Art: Hezbollah versus Israel," *Studies in Conflict and Terrorism*, Vol. 29, No. 1, 2006, p. 5.

71. Clive Jones, "'A Reach Greater Than the Grasp': Israeli Intelligence and the Conflict in South Lebanon, 1990–2000," *Intelligence and National Security*, Vol. 16, No. 3, p. 10.

72. Ranstorp, "Hezbollah Training Camps in Lebanon," pp. 256–257.

73. Ibid., p. 260.

74. Ibid., p. 254.

75. Ibid., p. 251.

76. Ibid.

77. Cragin, *Aptitude for Destruction Volume 2*, p. 51.

78. Byman, "Lebanese Hezbollah and Israeli Counterterrorism," p. 931.

79. Steven Erlanger and Richard A. Oppel, Jr., "A Disciplined Hezbollah Surprises Israel with Its Training, Tactics, and Weapons," *New York Times*, August 7, 2006.

80. "European Union Must Respond to Hezbollah's Attack in Bulgaria," *The Washington Post*, February 5, 2013.

81. For more on the tri-border area, also known as the triple frontier, see Angel Rabasa, et al., *Ungoverned Territories: Understanding and Reducing Terrorism Risks*, Santa Monica, CA: RAND Corp., 2007; and Enrique Desmond Arias, "Understanding Criminal Networks, Political Order, and Politics in Latin America," in Anne L. Clunan and Harold A. Trinkunas, eds., *Ungoverned Spaces: Alternatives to State Authority in Era of Softened Sovereignty*, Stanford: Stanford University Press, 2010, pp. 115–135.

82. In addition to the tri-border region, Hezbollah operatives have enjoyed sanctuary in Panama and Venezuela. Levitt, *Global Footprint*, p. 103.

83. "Hezbollah: Financing Terror Through Criminal Enterprise," Testimony of Matthew Levitt, Committee on Homeland Security and Government Affairs, United States Senate, May 25, 2005, p. 7.

84. "Fighting Terrorism in Africa," Testimony of Douglas Farah, Committee on International Relations, Subcommittee on Africa, United States House of Representatives, April 1, 2004.

85. Frederic Wehrey et al., *Dangerous but Not Omnipotent: Exploring the Reach and Limitations of Iranian Power in the Middle East*, Santa Monica, CA: RAND Corp., 2009, p. 88.

86. The Iranian Revolutionary Guards Corps (IRGC) is also known as the *Pasdaran* (Persian for "Guards"). For more information, see Frederic Wehrey et al., *The Rise of the Pasdaran: Assessing the Domestic Roles of Iran's Islamic Revolutionary Guards Corps*, Santa Monica, CA: RAND Corp., 2009.

87. Magnus Ranstorp, "The Hezbollah Training Camps of Lebanon," in James J.F. Forest, ed. *The Making of a Terrorist, Volume II: Training*, p. 244. Of the 1500 IRGC members sent to Lebanon, 800 were deployed in Baalbek and the remaining 700 were spread throughout villages and town in the eastern Bekaa region, mostly in Brital, Nabisheet, and Ba'albek. The Guards headquarters was located in the Syrian border village of Zebdani.

88. Cragin and Daly, *Dynamic Threat*, p. 68.

89. Cragin, *Aptitude for Destruction Volume 2*, p. 47. The BGM-71 TOW is a tube-launched, optically tracked and wire-guided anti-tank missile. It is American made and has a maximum range of 3.75 kilometers. According to Cragin, this weapon most likely came to Hezbollah from Iran via Damascus and likely included some initial training by the IRGC in how to use the weapon effectively. In an interesting historical twist, Richard Norton has alleged that the TOWS used were originally supplied in the 1980s to Iran by Israel as part of the Iran-Contra deal. See Norton, "Hezbollah and the Israeli Withdrawal from Southern Lebanon," *Journal of Palestine Studies*, Vol. 30, No. 1, Autumn 2000, p. 30.

90. Ranstorp, "Hezbollah Training Camps," p. 246.

91. Ibid., p. 47.

92. In Chapter 2 of their study *The Dynamic Terrorist Threat: An Assessment of Group Motivations and Capabilities in a Changing World*, Kim Cragin and Sara A. Daly construct an assessment framework for evaluating both the intentions and the capabilities of various terrorist and insurgent groups, including Hezbollah. According to the capabilities portion of the framework, Hezbollah did not follow a linear development and indeed was able to "skip a number of steps" that other insurgents groups suffer through. They credit the training provided by the IRGC as being one of the key factors enabling this rapid development.

93. Ranstorp, "Hezbollah Training Camps," p. 255.

94. Ibid.

95. Norton, *Hezbollah*, p. 116.

96. "Hizbollah: Rebel Without a Cause?" International Crisis Group Middle East Briefing Paper, July 30, 2003, p. 2.

97. Amal Saad-Ghorayeb, *Hizbu'llah: Politics and Religion*, London: Pluto Press, 2002, p. 43.

98. Joe Klein, "The Hezbollah Project," *New York Times*, September 30, 2010.

99. Klein, "The Hezbollah Project."

100. Wehrey, "Clash of Wills," p. 55.

101. Magnus Ranstorp, "The Strategy and Tactics of Hezbollah's Current 'Lebanonization Process'," *Mediterranean Politics*, Vol. 3, No. 1, Summer 1998, p. 121.

102. Ranstorp, "Lebanonization," pp. 121–122.

103. Noe, *Voice of Hezbollah*, p. 23.

104. Wehrey, "Clash of Wills," pp. 59–60.

105. Ibid.

106. Norton, *Hezbollah*, pp. 117–118.

107. Jerrold Green, *Understanding Iran*, Santa Monica, CA: RAND Corp., 2008, p. 120.

108. Joseph Alagha, *The Shifts in Hizbullah's Ideology: Religious Ideology, Political Ideology, and Political Program*, Leiden: Amsterdam University Press, 2006, pp. 13–15.

109. Ranstorp, "Hezbollah Training Camps," p. 249.

110. Ranstorp, *Hizb'Allah in Lebanon*, New York: St. Martin's Press, 1997, pp. 34–35.

111. Adam Shatz, "In Search of Hezbollah," *The New York Review of Books*, April 29, 2004.

112. Judith Palmer Harik, *Hezbollah: The Changing Face of Terrorism*, London: I.B. Tauris, 2004, p. 71.

113. Norton, *Hezbollah*, p. 17.

114. As'ad Abu Khalil, *Middle Eastern Studies*, Vol. 27, No. 3, July 1991, pp. 390–403.

115. Norton, *Hezbollah*, p. 35.

116. Hajjar, "Hezbollah: Terrorism, National Liberation, or Menace?" p. 10.

117. Norton, *Extremist Ideals vs. Mundane Politics*, p. 12.

118. Saad-Ghorayeb, *Hizbu'llah: Politics and Religion*, pp. 16–17.

119. Hajjar, "Hezbollah: Terrorism, National Liberation, or Menace?" p. 11.

120. The *ummah* is the global Muslim community.

121. Shatz, "In Search of Hezbollah."

122. Norton, Middle East Policy, Vol. 5, No. 4, January 1998, p. 152.

123. Judith Palmer Harik, *Hezbollah: The Changing Face of Terrorism*, London: I.B. Tauris, 2004.

124. Ranstorp, "Hezbollah Training Camps," p. 254.

125. Ibid., pp. 257–259.

126. Norton, *Hezbollah*, p. 6.

127. Mohamad Bazzi, "Lebanon: Hezbollah's Way," *Global Post*, August 7, 2010.

128. Simon Haddad, "The Origins of Popular Support for Lebanon's Hezbollah," *Studies in Conflict and Terrorism*, Vol. 29, No. 1, 2006, pp. 21–34.

129. Alexus G. Grynkewich, "Welfare as Warfare: How Violent Non-State Groups Use Social Services to Attack the State," *Studies in Conflict and Terrorism*, 31, 2008, p. 363.

130. Ilene R. Prusher, "Through Charity, Hezbollah Charms Lebanon," *Christian Science Monitor*, April 19, 2000.

131. Martin Kramer, "The Moral Logic of Hezbollah," in I. Cronin, ed., *Confronting Fear: A History of Terrorism*, New York: Thunder's Mouth Press, pp. 282–293.

132. S. T. Flanigan, "Charity as Resistance: Connections between Charity, Contentious Politics, and Terror," *Studies in Conflict and Terrorism*, 29, 2006.

133. Ibid., pp. 646–648.

134. Jaber, *Born with a Vengeance*, p. 147.

135. Ibid., 149–150.

136. Gabriel Weimann, "Hezbollah Dot Com: Hezbollah's Online Campaign," *New Media and Innovative Technologies*, Ben-Gurion University Press, 2008, p. 5. See also, A. Jorisch, "Al-Manar: Hezbollah TV, 24.7," *Middle East Quarterly*, Winter 2004, pp. 17–31.

137. Ibid., p. 7. To put Al-Manar's budget in perspective, the PIRA's entire operating budget was $15 million a year until the 1990s. Horgan, "Playing the Green Card Part I," p. 10.

138. Ron Schleifer, "Psychological Operations: A New Variation on an Age Old Art: Hezbollah versus Israel," *Studies in Conflict and Terrorism*, Vol. 29, No. 1, 2006, pp. 11–12.

139. For more on Hezbollah's all-around technology use, see A. J. Dallal, "Hezbollah's Virtual Civil Society," *Television and New Media*, Vol. 2, No. 4, 2001, pp. 367–372.

140. Weimann, "Hezbollah Dot Com," p. 11.

141. Elisabeth Ferland, "Hezbollah and the Internet," Center for Strategic and International Studies, March 4, 2010.

142. Hillary Hylton, "How Hezbollah Hijacks the Internet," *Time*, August 8, 2006.

143. Levitt, *Global Footprint*, p. 157.

144. Ibid., pp. 102–103.

145. Ibid., p. 119.

146. Ibid., pp. 317–318. The scheme was run out of Toledo, OH, by a Dearborn, MI, resident named Ali Nasrallah.

147. Doug Philippone, "Hezbollah: The Organization and Its Finances," in Michael Freeman, ed., *Financing Terrorism: Case Studies*, Surrey: Asghate, 2012, p. 58.

148. Author interview with Matthew Levitt, December 2014.

149. Addis and Blanchard, CRS Report, January 3, 2011, p. 22.

150. Juan Zarate, *Treasury's War: The Unleashing of a New Era of Financial Warfare*, New York: Public Affairs, 2013, p. 118.

151. James Kanter and Jodi Rudoren, "European Union Adds Military Wing of Hezbollah to List of Terrorist Organizations," *New York Times*, July 22, 2013.

152. Philippone, "Organization and Finances," in Freeman *Case Studies*, p. 59.

153. Wiegand, "Support of a Terrorist Group," p. 674.

154. Naim Qaseem, *Hizbullah: The Story from Within*, trans. D. Khalil, London: Saqi, 2005, p. 190.

155. Bilal Y. Saab, "Rethinking Hezbollah's Disarmament," *Middle East Policy*, Vol. 15, No. 3, 2008, p. 96.

CHAPTER 5

1. There is some confusion about the various Palestinian militant organizations and how these groups have evolved over time. Fatah is the largest guerilla organization, the group once headed by Yasser Arafat and formed in early 1960s as part of the Palestine Liberation Organization (PLO), which was an umbrella organization that brought together all of the various guerilla groups, including Fatah, the Palestinian Front for the Liberation of Palestine (PFLP), the Democratic Front for the Liberation of Palestine (DFLP) and several other smaller and lesser known groups. The PLO was established by Egyptian leader Gamel Abdel Nasser in an attempt to exert some form of control over the Palestinian militant groups that were proliferating at the time. The Palestinian Authority (PA) was established in the wake of the Oslo as a civilian organization to rule over Gaza and the West Bank, since many of the aforementioned guerilla groups were too closely associated with violence. Arafat was the first President of the PA, followed by Mahmoud Abbas (Abu Mazen) in 2005.

2. When Hamas first emerged, it was viewed by Israel as "a temporary nuisance with no real capacity to present a threat, and with little popular legitimacy." Beverley Milton-Edwards, "Islamist versus Islamist: Rising Challenge in Gaza," *Terrorism and Political Violence*, Vol. 26, No. 2, 2014, p. 261.

3. Matthew Levitt, *Hamas: Politics, Charity and Terrorism in the Service of Jihad*, New Haven: Yale University Press, 2006, pp. 23–24.

4. For more, see Sara Roy, *Hamas and Civil Society in Gaza: Engaging the Islamist Social Sector*, Princeton: Princeton University Press, 2011.

5. Daniel Byman, *A High Price: The Triumphs & Failures of Israeli Counterterrorism*, Oxford: Oxford University Press, 2011, p. 102.

6. Helena Lindholm Shulz with Juliane Hammer, *The Palestinian Diaspora: Formation of Identities and Politics of Homeland*, London: Routledge, 2003.

7. Thomas M. Sanderson, "Transnational Terror and Organized Crime: Blurring the Lines," *SAIS Review*, Vol. 24, No. 1, Winter-Spring 2004, p. 53.

8. Are Knudsen, "Islamism in the Diaspora: Palestinian Refugees in Lebanon," *Journal of Refugee Studies*, Vol. 18, No. 2, 2005, p. 223.

9. Shaul Mishal and Avraham Sela, *The Palestinian Hamas: Vision, Violence, and Coexistence*, New York: Columbia University Press, p. 162.

10. Matthew Levitt, "Could Hamas Target the West?" *Studies in Conflict & Terrorism*, Vol. 30, No. 11, 2007, pp. 928–929.

11. Levitt, *Hamas*, pp. 38–39.

12. Beverley Milton-Edwards and Stephen Farrell, *Hamas: The Islamic Resistance Movement*, Cambridge: Polity Press, 2010, p. 164.

13. Levitt, "Target the West?," pp. 930–931.

14. Levitt, *Hamas*, p. 57.

15. Louise I. Shelley and John T. Picarelli, "Methods Not Motives: Implications of the Convergence of International Organized Crime and Terrorism," *Police Practice and Research*, Vol. 3, No. 4, 2002, p. 311.

16. Levitt, *Hamas*, p. 59.

17. Levitt, "Target the West?," p. 932.

18. Levitt, "Target the West?," p. 933.

19. Levitt, *Hamas*, pp. 70–71.

20. Levitt, *Hamas*, p. 44.

21. Patrick Poole, "Mortgage Fraud Funding Jihad?" *Front Page Magazine*, April 11, 2007.

22. Frank S. Perri and Richard G. Brody, "The Dark Triad: Organized Crime, Terror and Fraud," *Journal of Money Laundering Control*, Vol. 14, No. 1, 2011, p. 53.

23. Gregory F. Treverton et al., *Film Piracy, Organized Crime, and Terrorism*, Santa Monica, CA: RAND Corp., 2009, p. 23.

24. Edward F. Mickolous and Susan L. Simmons, *The Terrorist List*, Santa Barbara: ABC-CLIO, 2011, p. 67.

25. Mathew Levitt, "Palestinian Authority Minister of Economy Tied to Hamas?" Washington Institute for Near East Policy, Policy Watch No. 496, March 4, 2005.

26. Jodi Vittori, *Terrorist Financing and Resourcing*, Palgrave Macmillan, 2011, p. 73.

27. Levitt, *Hamas*, p. 77.

28. Levitt, *Hamas*, p. 69.

29. Milton-Edwards and Farrell, *Hamas*, p. 140.

30. Jodi Vittori, "Idealism Is Not Enough: The Role of Resources in the Autonomy and Capability of Terrorist Groups," PhD dissertation, University of Denver, June 2008, p. 199.

31. Triffin J. Roule, "Post-911 Financial Freeze Dries Up Hamas Funding," *Jane's Intelligence Review*, April 19, 2002.

32. Claudia Rosett, "Can We Give to Gaza Without Giving to Hamas?" *Forbes*, March 5, 2009.

33. Chaim Levinson, "Shin Bet Probe Reveals Scope of Hamas Money Laundering Through Chinese Banks," *Haaretz*, September 29, 2013.

34. Levitt, "Target the West?," p. 937.

35. James J. F. Forest, "Kidnapping by Terrorist Groups, 1970–2010: Is Ideological Orientation Relevant?" *Crime & Delinquency*, Vol. 58, No. 5, pp. 769–797.

36. According to Matthew Levitt, a longtime Hamas operative from the West Bank and now living in Turkey is responsible for formulation of Hamas's kidnapping strategy. Matthew Levitt, "Hamas' Not-So-Secret Weapon," *Foreign Affairs*, July 9, 2014.

37. "Gaza Banks Close in Protest at Hamas Cash Seizure," *Reuters*, reprinted online in the *Jerusalem Post*, March 3, 2011.

38. John Rollins and Liana Sun-Wyler, "Terrorism and Transnational Crime: Foreign Policy Issues for Congress," Congressional Research Service (CRS), October 19, 2012, p. 10.

39. Clare Ribando Seelke et al., "Latin America and the Caribbean: Illicit Drug Trafficking and U.S. Counterdrug Programs," Congressional Research Service (CRS), May 12, 2011, p. 6.

40. Matthew Levitt, "Hezbollah: Financing Terror Through Criminal Enterprise," Testimony presented to United States Senate Committee on Homeland Security and Governmental Affairs, May 25, 2005, p. 10.

41. Gerard DeGroot, "The Enemy Below: Why Hamas Tunnels Scare Israel So Much," *Washington Post*, Monkey Cage blog, July 25, 2014; Jodi Rudoren, "Tunnels

Lead Right to the Heart of Israeli Fear," *New York Times*, July 28, 2014; and Jodi Rudoren and Ben Hubbard, "Despite Gains, Hamas Sees a Fight for Its Existence and Presses Ahead," *New York Times*, July 27, 2014.

42. Daniel Byman, "Is Hamas Winning?" *Washington Quarterly*, Vol. 36, No. 3, Summer 2013, p. 67.

43. Yezid Sayigh, "Hamas Rule in Gaza: Three Years On," Brandeis University Crown Center for Middle East Studies, Middle East Brief, No. 41, March 2010, p. 6.

44. Dennis Lormel, "Identifying and Disrupting Funding Streams to Thwart Terrorist Financing and Organized Criminal Activities," IPSA International, 2009, p. 8.

45. "Hamas Extortion Ring Uncovered in Israel," *Xinhua*, September 24, 2012.

46. "Hamas Leaders Worth Millions of Dollars from Allegedly Skimming Donations and Extortion: Is Anyone Surprised?" *Inquisitr*, July 18, 2014.

47. David B. Carter, "A Blessing or a Curse? State Support for Terrorist Groups," *International Organization*, Vol. 66, No. 1, January 2012, p. 138.

48. Milton-Edwards and Farrell, *Hamas*, p. 224.

49. Ibid., p. 140.

50. Ibid., p. 133.

51. Hillel Frisch, "Strategic Change in Terrorist Movements: Lessons from Hamas," *Studies in Conflict & Terrorism*, Vol. 31, No. 12, 2009, p. 1059.

52. Iran temporarily cut financial support to Hamas, while increasing aid to PIJ and the Popular Resistance Committees. There is also now tension between Hamas and Hezbollah, a key ally of the Assad regime.

53. Adam Dolnik and Anjali Bhattacherjee, "Hamas: Suicide Bombings, Rockets, or WMD?" *Terrorism & Political Violence*, Vol. 14, No. 3, Autumn 2002, p. 109; 125.

54. Triffin J. Roule, "Post-911 Financial Freeze Dries Up Hamas Funding," *Jane's Intelligence Review*, April 19, 2002.

55. Byman, "Hamas Winning?," p. 71.

56. Levitt, "Target the West?," p. 935.

57. Byman, "Hamas Winning?," p. 63.

58. Yoav Appel, "Israel: Bombers Tried to Use Cyanide," *The Associated Press*, June 5, 2002.

59. Dolnik and Bhattacherjee, "Suicide Bombings, Rockets, or WMD?," p. 113.

60. Dolnik and Bhattacherjee, "Suicide Bombings, Rockets, or WMD?," p. 113.

61. Byman, "Hamas Winning?," p. 66.

62. Levitt, "Target the West?," p. 931.

63. Hillel Frisch, "Strategic Change in Terrorist Movements: Lessons from Hamas," *Studies in Conflict & Terrorism*, Vol. 31, No. 12, 2009, p. 1057.

64. Levitt, *Hamas*, pp. 55–56.

65. Brian A. Jackson, *Breaching the Fortress Wall: Understanding Terrorist Efforts to Overcome Defensive Technologies*, Santa Monica, CA: RAND Corp., 2007, p. 25.

66. Ioana Emy Matesan, "What Makes Negative Frames Resonant? Hamas and the Appeal of Opposition to the Peace Process," *Terrorism and Political Violence*, Vol. 24, No. 5, 2012, p. 688.

67. Milton-Edwards, "Islamist versus Islamist," p. 269.

68. Levitt, *Hamas*, p. 49.

69. Levitt, "Target the West?," p. 930.

70. Shaul Mishal and Avraham Sela, *The Palestinian Hamas: Vision, Violence, and Coexistence*, New York: Columbia University Press, p. 58.

71. Levitt, *Hamas*, p. 26.

72. Byman, *A High Price*, pp. 102–103.

73. Levitt, "Target the West?," pp. 928–929.

74. Byman, *A High Price*, p. 355.

75. Dolnik and Bhattacherjee, "Suicide Bombings, Rockets, or WMD?," p. 109.

76. Throughout the Second Intifada, the four main themes emphasized by Hamas were the untrustworthiness of the Israelis, the need for revenge, maintaining Palestinian unity, and the tangible gains made by the intifada. Joas Wagemakers, "Legitimizing Pragmatism: Hamas' Framing Efforts from Militancy to Moderation and Back?" *Terrorism and Political Violence*, Vol. 22, No. 3, 2010, p. 360.

77. Cragin et al., *Sharing the Dragon's Teeth*, pp. 59–66. The physical technology exchanges included Ketusha rockets (both 122 m and 107 mm), AT-3 Sagger missiles, and YM-III Iranian antitank missiles.

78. Ranstorp, "Hezbollah Training Camps," p. 259.

79. Cragin et al., *Sharing the Dragon's Teeth*, p. 53. According to Ranstorp, Hezbollah is credited with introducing suicide bombing as a tactic into the Palestinian theater.

80. Kim Cragin, "Al Qaeda Confronts Hamas: Divisions in the Sunni *Jihadist* Movement and Its Implications for U.S. Policy," *Studies in Conflict & Terrorism*, Vol. 32, No. 7, 2009, p. 583.

81. Levitt, *Hamas*, p. 36.

82. Tavishi Bhasin and Maia Carter Hallward, "Hamas as a Political Party: Democratization in the Palestinian Territories," *Terrorism and Political Violence*, Vol. 25, No. 1, 2013, p. 81.

83. Daniel Baracskay, "The Evolutionary Path of Hamas: Examining the Role of Political Pragmatism in State Building and Activism," *Terrorism & Political Violence*, 2014, p. 2.

84. Dolnik and Bhattacherjee, "Suicide Bombings, Rockets, or WMD?," p. 125.

85. Levitt, *Hamas*, p. 34.

86. Levitt, "Target the West?," p. 933; p. 936.

87. Levitt, "Target the West?," p. 926.

88. Kim Cragin, "Al Qaeda Confronts Hamas: Divisions in the Sunni *Jihadist* Movement and Its Implications for U.S. Policy," *Studies in Conflict & Terrorism*, Vol. 32, No. 7, 2009, p. 583.

89. Litvak, "'Martyrdom Is Life," p. 718.

90. Meir Litvak, "Martyrdom Is Life: *Jihad* and Martyrdom in the Ideology of Hamas," *Studies in Conflict & Terrorism*, Vol. 33, No. 8, 2010, p. 716.

91. Levitt, "Target the West?," p. 934.

92. Ioana Emy Matesan, "What Makes Negative Frames Resonant? Hamas and the Appeal of Opposition to the Peace Process," *Terrorism and Political Violence*, Vol. 24, No. 5, 2012, p. 674.

93. Tomer Mozes and Gabriel Weimann, "The E-Marketing Strategy of Hamas," *Studies in Conflict & Terrorism*, Vol. 33, No. 3, 2010, p. 224.

94. Some of these groups include *Jund Ansar Allah, Jaysh Tawheed wa Jihad, Jund Allah Popular Resistance Committee, Jaysh Arafat as-Sunnah,* and *Jaysh Ansar as-Sunnah.* Milton-Edwards, "Islamist versus Islamist," p. 261; p. 268.

95. Byman, "Hamas Winning?," p. 63.

96. Byman, "Hamas Winning?," p. 72.

97. Milton-Edwards and Farrell, *Hamas,* p. 225.

98. Dolnik and Bhattacherjee, "Suicide Bombings, Rockets, or WMD?," p. 113.

99. Robert Brathwaite, "The Electoral Terrorist: Terror Groups and Democratic Participation," *Terrorism and Political Violence,* Vol. 25, No. 1, 2013, pp. 66–67. To put things in perspective, compared with the group's operating budget in the early 1990s, by the mid-2000s, U.S. government estimates put the figure at approximately $50 million annually. Haim Malka, "Forcing Choices: Testing the Transformation of Hamas," *Washington Quarterly,* Vol. 28, No. 4, 2005, p. 39. Levitt provides a broader range, between $30 million and $90 million annually. Levitt, *Hamas,* p. 54.

100. Tomer Mozes and Gabriel Weimann, "The E-Marketing Strategy of Hamas," *Studies in Conflict & Terrorism,* Vol. 33, No. 3, 2010, pp. 212–213.

101. Tomer Mozes and Gabriel Weimann, "The E-Marketing Strategy of Hamas," *Studies in Conflict & Terrorism,* Vol. 33, No. 3, 2010, pp. 213–214.

102. Dipak K. Gupta and Kusum Mundra, "Suicide Bombing as a Strategic Weapon: An Empirical Investigation of Hamas and Islamic Jihad," *Terrorism and Political Violence,* Vol. 17, No. 4, 2005, p. 590. According to Mia Bloom, Palestinian acceptance of suicide bombings resulted from the continued televised killing of Palestinians by Israelis, a poor economy, disillusionment with the peace process and Ariel Sharon's visit to the Temple Mount. Mia Bloom, *Dying to Kill: The Allure of Suicide Terror,* New York: Columbia University Press, 2005.

103. Levitt, "Target the West?," p. 927.

104. Milton-Edwards and Farrell, *Hamas,* p. 170.

105. Byman, *A High Price,* p. 194.

106. Byman, "Hamas Winning?," p. 64.

107. Milton-Edwards and Farrell, *Hamas,* p. 108.

108. Ibid., pp. 164–165.

109. Hillel Frisch, "Strategic Change in Terrorist Movements: Lessons from Hamas," *Studies in Conflict & Terrorism,* Vol. 31, No. 12, 2009, p. 1056.

110. Ibid.

111. Author interview with Jean-Marc Oppenheim, December 2014.

112. Haim Malka, "Forcing Choices: Testing the Transformation of Hamas," *Washington Quarterly,* Vol. 28, No. 4, 2005, p. 43.

CHAPTER 6

1. Stephen Tanner, *Afghanistan: A Military History from Alexander the Great to the War Against the Taliban,* revised edition, Philadelphia, PA: De Capo Press, 2009, p. 279.

2. Ahmed Rashid, *Taliban,* New Haven: Yale University Press, 2001, p. 25.

3. Daniel P. Sullivan, "Tinder, Spark, Oxygen, and Fuel: The Mysterious Rise of the Taliban," *Journal of Peace Research,* Vol. 44, No. 1, January 2007, p. 96.

4. For more on the differences between "old" Taliban and "neo-Taliban," see Antonio Giustozzi, ed., *Decoding the New Taliban: Insights from the Afghan Field*, New York: Columbia University Press, 2009. On meaningful differences between Durrani and Ghilzai Pashtuns, see Thomas Barfield, *Afghanistan: A Cultural and Political History*, Princeton, NJ: Princeton University Press, 2010, pp. 285–336.

5. It should also be noted here that the Afghan Taliban is a separate group from the Pakistani Taliban, otherwise known as Tehrik-e-Taliban (TTP), which is an umbrella organization of roughly 40 smaller insurgent groups active in Khyber-Pakhtunkhwa's 24 districts, 7 tribal agencies, and 6 provincial regions. The Afghan Taliban considers Pakistan as a benefactor, while the Pakistani Taliban has been waging an insurgency against the Pakistani state and its security forces since 2002. For more, see Shehzad H. Qazi, "Rebels of the Frontier: Origins, Organization, and Recruitment of the Pakistani Taliban," *Small Wars & Insurgencies*, Vol. 22, No. 4, October 2011, pp. 574–602 and Zachary Laub, "The Taliban in Afghanistan," Council on Foreign Relations Backgrounder, February 25, 2014. This chapter focuses on the Afghan Taliban, although it also touches briefly upon other insurgent and terrorist groups active in the Afghanistan–Pakistan (AfPak) region, including the Haqqani Network and others.

6. Catherine Collins and Ashraf Ali, "Financing the Taliban: Tracking the Dollars Behind the Insurgencies in Afghanistan and Pakistan," New America Foundation Counterterrorism Strategy Initiative Policy Paper, April 2010, p. 1.

7. Collins and Ali, "Financing the Taliban," p. 5. The CIA and the DIA estimate that the Taliban receives $70 million a year from the drug trade. According to the former U.S. director of national intelligence Dennis Blair, the Taliban made $100 million from the drug trade in 2008. The DEA puts the number at around $300 million, while Gretchen Peters asserts that the number is much higher, probably $500 million.

8. See the considerable body of literature devoted to the effect of resources on conflict. Paul Collier and Anke Hoeffler, "Greed and Grievance in Civil War," *Oxford Economic Papers*, Vol. 56 (2004): pp. 563–595; Richard Snyder, "Does Lootable Wealth Breed Disorder? A Political Economy of Extraction Framework," *Comparative Political Studies*, Vol. 39, No. 8 (October 2006): pp. 943–968; Michael L. Ross, "How Do Natural Resources Influence Civil War? Evidence from Thirteen Cases," *International Organization*, Vol. 58, No. 1 (Winter 2004): pp. 35–67; Michael L. Ross, "What Do We Know About Natural Resources and Civil War?" *Journal of Peace Research*, Vol. 41, No. 3, 2004, pp. 337–356.

9. For a discussion of active versus passive support in terrorism and insurgency, see Christopher Paul, "As a Fish Swims in the Sea: Relationships Between Factors Contributing to Support for Terrorist or Insurgent Groups," *Studies in Conflict and Terrorism*, Vol. 33, No. 6, 2010, pp. 488–510.

10. Barnett R. Rubin, "The Political Economy of War and Peace in Afghanistan," *World Development*, Vol. 28, No. 10, 2000, pp. 1789–1803.

11. Justin Y. Reese, "Financing the Taliban," in Michael Freeman, *Financing Terrorism: Case Studies*, Surrey: Ashgate, 2012, p. 104.

12. Matthew Fielden and Jonathan Goodhand, "Beyond the Taliban? The Afghan Conflict and United Nations Peacemaking," *Conflict, Security & Development*, Vol. 1, No. 3, 2001, p. 12.

13. Barnett Rubin, "The Political Economy of War and Peace in Afghanistan," *World Development*, Vol. 28, No. 10, 2000, p. 1791.

14. Kristian Berg Harpviken, "The Transnationalization of the Taliban," *International Area Studies Review*, Vol. 15, No. 3, 2012, p. 221.

15. Collins and Ali, p. 9.

16. Giustozzi, Koran, Kalashnikov, and Laptop, p. 86.

17. Howell and Lind, p. 724.

18. Aram Roston, "How the U.S. Funds the Taliban," November 11, 2009; also see, Aram Roston, "How the U.S. Army Protects Its Trucks—By Paying the Taliban," *The Guardian*, November 12, 2009, In full disclosure, a header at the top of *The Guardian* article notes that the article is the subject of a legal complaint from lawyers acting on behalf of NCL holdings and its principal, Hamed Wardak.

19. Roston, "U.S. Funds the Taliban."

20. Gretchen Peters, Seeds of Terror, p. 42.

21. Seeds, p. 183.

22. Peters, Seeds, p. 183.

23. Seeds, pp. 184–185.

24. Freeman, p. 106.

25. Jihad is literally translated as "to struggle," hence the term *strugglers* used in lieu of jihadists. See BBC, "Religions: Islam," *BBC.com*, 2009.

26. A in-depth analysis on some of the Taliban's criminal activities can be found in Farhana Schmidt, "From Islamic Warriors to Drug Lords: The Evolution of the Taliban Insurgency," *Mediterranean Quarterly*, Vol. 21, No. 2, Spring 2010, pp. 61–77.

27. Anand Gopal, "The Taliban in Kandahar," in Peter Bergen with Katherine Tiedemann, *Talibanistan: Negotiating the Borders Between Terror, Politics, and Religion*, Oxford: Oxford University Press, 2013, p. 41.

28. Mohammad Osman Tariq Elias, "The Resurgence of the Taliban in Kabul, Logar, and Wardak," in Giustozzie, *Decoding the New Taliban*, p. 52.

29. Collins and Ali, p. 7.

30. Sami Yousafzai, "For the Taliban, A Crime that Pays," *The Daily Beast*, September 5, 2008.

31. Thomas Johnson and Matthew C. Dupee, "Analyzing the New Taliban Code of Conduct (*Layeha*): An Assessment of Changing Perspectives and Strategies of the Afghan Taliban," *Central Asian Survey*, Vol. 31, No. 1, March 2012, p. 82; see also, Asim Qadeer Rana, "Mullah Omar Wars Taliban Leaders of Action Over Abductions," *The Nation*, April 3, 2013.

32. For more, see *Warlord Inc.: Extortion and Corruption Along the U.S. Supply Chain in Afghanistan*, Report of the Majority Staff, Subcommittee on National Security and Foreign Affairs, U.S. House of Representatives, June 2010.

33. Vanda Felbab-Brown, "Kicking the Opium Habit? Afghanistan's Drug Economy and Politics Since the 1980s," *Conflict, Security, and Development*, Vol. 6, No. 2, Summer 2006, pp. 127–149.

34. Vanda Felbab-Brown, "Fighting the Nexus of Organized Crime and Violent Conflict While Enhancing Human Security," in Phil Williams and Vanda Felbab-Brown, *Drug Trafficking, Violence, and Instability*, Carlisle Barracks, PA: U.S. Army War College Strategic Studies Institute, April 2012, p. 13.

35. Peters, *Seeds of Terror*, pp. 116–123.

36. Phil Williams, "Insurgencies and Organized Crime," in Phil Williams and Vanda Felbab-Brown, *Drug Trafficking, Violence, and Instability,* Carlisle Barracks, PA: U.S. Army War College Strategic Studies Institute, April 2012, p. 45.

37. Brahimi, "Evolving Ideology," p. 9.

38. Emma Graham-Harrison, "Taliban Destroy Poppy Fields in Surprise Clampdown on Afghan Opium Growers," *The Guardian*, May 20, 2012.

39. Gretchen Peters, *Haqqani Network Financing: The Evolution of an Industry,* Combating Terrorism Center at West Point, Harmony Program, 2012, p. 40.

40. For more on the Haqqani Network, see Vahid Brown and Don Rassler, *Fountainhead of Jihad: The Haqqani Nexus, 1973–2012,* Oxford: Oxford University Press, 2013.

41. Peters, p. 39

42. Gretchen Peters, "Haqqani Network Financing: The Evolution of an Industry," *Combating Terrorism Center,* West Point, NY: Harmony Program, August 2012, p. 2.

43. Shivan Mahendrarajah, "Conceptual Failure, the Taliban's Parallel Hierarchies, and America's Strategic Defeat in Afghanistan," *Small Wars & Insurgencies,* Vol. 25, No. 1, 2014, p. 109.

44. Brian A. Gordon and J. Edward Conway, "Cost Accounting: Auditing the Taliban in Helmand Province, Afghanistan," in David M. Blum and J. Edward Conway, eds., *Counterterrorism and Threat Finance Analysis During Wartime,* Lanham, MD: Lexington Books, 2015, p. 82.

45. Thomas H. Johnson, "Financing Afghan Terrorism," in Jeanne K. Giraldo and Harold A. Trinkunas, *Terrorism Financing and State Responses: A Comparative Perspective,* Stanford: Stanford University Press, 2007, p. 101. For more on madrassa students as recruits for the insurgency in Afghanistan, see Carlotta Gall, *The Wrong Enemy: America in Afghanistan, 2001–2014,* New York: Houghton Mifflin Harcourt, 2014.

46. Justin Y. Reese, "Financing the Taliban," in Michael Freeman, *Financing Terrorism: Case Studies,* Surrey: Ashgate, 2012, p. 99.

47. Thomas H. Johnson, "Financing Afghan Terrorism," in Jeanne K. Giraldo and Harold A. Trinkunas, *Terrorism Financing and State Responses: A Comparative Perspective,* Stanford: Stanford University Press, 2007, pp. 97–98.

48. Christia and Semple, "Flipping the Taliban," p. 41.

49. Shezhad H. Qazi, "Rebels of the Frontier: Origins, Organization, and Recruitment of the Pakistani Taliban," *Small Wars & Insurgencies,* Vol. 22, No. 4, pp. 574–602.

50. Jason Lyall, "A (Fighting) Season to Remember in Afghanistan," *Washington Post,* Monkey Cage Blog, October 20, 2014.

51. Giustozzi, "Negotiating with the Taliban," pp. 12–13.

52. See Gretchen Peters, "Crime and Insurgency in the Tribal Areas of Afghanistan and Pakistan," Combating Terrorism Center, October 2010.

53. Arabinda Acharya, Syed Adnan Ali Shah Bukhari, and Sadia Sulaiman, "Making Money in the Mayhem: Funding Taliban Insurrection in the Tribal Areas of Pakistan," *Studies in Conflict & Terrorism,* Vol. 32, No. 2, 2009, p. 104.

54. Francisco Gutierrez Sanin and Antonio Giustozzi, "Networks and Armies: Structuring Rebellion in Colombia and Afghanistan," *Studies in Conflict & Terrorism*, Vol. 33, No. 9, 2010, pp. 838–839.

55. Antonio Giustozzi, *Koran, Kalashnikov, and Laptop: The Neo-Taliban Insurgency in Afghanistan*, New York: Columbia University Press, 2008, pp. 98–99.

56. Ibid., p. 147.

57. Thomas H. Johnson, "Taliban Adaptations and Innovations," *Small Wars & Insurgencies*, Vol. 24, No. 1, 2013, p. 5.

58. Giustozzi, p. 156.

59. Johnson, "Adaptations," pp. 7–8.

60. Ibid., pp. 7–8.

61. David Kilcullen, *Out of the Mountains: The Coming Age of the Urban Guerilla*, Oxford: Oxford University Press, 2013, p. 27.

62. Theo Farrell and Antonio Giustozzi, "The Taliban at War: Inside the Helmand Insurgency, 2004–2012, *International Affairs*, Vol. 89, No. 4, 2013, p. 865.

63. Ben Brandt, "The Taliban's Conduct of Intelligence and Counterintelligence," *Combating Terrorism Center Sentinel*, Vol. 4, No. 6, June 2011, p. 20.

64. C. J. Chivers, "Afghanistan's Hidden Taliban Government," *New York Times*, February 6, 2011.

65. Ibid., p. 19.

66. Paraag Shukla, "ISW in Brief: Jailbreak Spurs Attacks in Kandahar City," *Institute for the Study of War*, May 12, 2011.

67. Brandt, "The Taliban's Conduct of Intelligence," p. 20.

68. Borzou Daraghi, "Afghan Intelligence Network Embraces the New," *Los Angeles Times*, April 13, 2011.

69. Seth G. Jones, *In the Graveyard of Empires: America's War in Afghanistan*, New York: W.W. Norton & Co., 2009, p. 99.

70. Thomas H. Johnson, "On the Edge of the Big Muddy: The Taliban Resurgence in Afghanistan," *China and Eurasia Forum Quarterly*, Vol. 5, No. 2, 2007, p. 101.

71. In a 2011 RAND Corporation Delphi exercise, respondents consistently cited the COIN forces' inability to prevent cross-border smuggling of weapons, narcotics, and fighters as one of the factors most likely to contribute to a potential victory for the Taliban. See Christopher Paul, *Counterinsurgency Scorecard: Afghanistan in Early 2011 Relative to the Insurgencies of the Past 30 Years*, Santa Monica, Calif.: RAND Corp., 2011. This finding is consistent with that of other expert elicitations, including one chaired by Richard L. Armitage and Samuel R. Berger and directed by Daniel S. Markey, "U.S. Strategy for Pakistan and Afghanistan," Council on Foreign Relations Independent Task Force Report No. 65, November 2010.

72. Jones, *In the Graveyard of Empires*, p. 99.

73. Paul Staniland, "Caught in the Muddle: America's Pakistan Strategy," *The Washington Quarterly*, Winter 2011, p. 137.

74. For an in-depth analysis of the difficulty of operating along the AfPak border, see Thomas H. Johnson and M. Chris Mason, "No Sign Until the Burst of Fire: Understanding the Pakistan-Afghanistan Frontier," *International Security*, Vol. 32, No. 4, Spring 2008, pp. 41–77.

75. Thomas H. Johnson and M. Chris Mason, "Understanding the Taliban and Insurgency in Afghanistan," *Orbis*, Winter 2007, p. 83.

76. Paul Cruickshank, "The Militant Pipeline: Between the Afghanistan-Pakistan Border Region and the West," New America Foundation National Security Studies Program Policy Paper, second edition, July 2011.

77. Ahmed Rashid, *Descent into Chaos: How the War against Islamic Extremism Is Being Lost in Pakistan, Afghanistan, and Central Asia*, London: Allen Lane, 2008, p. 222.

78. Dennis C. Blair, "Annual Threat Assessment of the U.S. Intelligence Community," Testimony before the Senate Select Committee on Intelligence, 2 February 2010.

79. For more on the relationship between the Taliban and Iran, see Sajjan M. Gohel, "Iran's Ambiguous Role in Afghanistan," *Combating Terrorism Center Sentinel*, Vol. 3, No. 3, March 2010, pp. 13–16; Alireza Nader and Joya Laha, *Iran's Balancing Act in Afghanistan*, Santa Monica, Calif.: RAND Corp., 2011; and Seth G. Jones, "Al Qaeda in Iran: Why Tehran Is Accommodating the Terrorist Group," *Foreign Affairs*, January 29, 2012.

80. Department of Defense Report on Progress Toward Stability and Security in Afghanistan: United States Plan for Sustaining the Afghan National Security Forces, April 2012, p. 1.

81. James F. Dobbins, *After the Taliban: Nation-Building in Afghanistan*, Washington DC: Potomac, 2008, p. 166.

82. Justin Y. Reese, "Financing the Taliban," in Michael Freeman, *Financing Terrorism: Case Studies*, Surrey: Ashgate, 2012, p. 96.

83. Peter Dahl Thruelsen, "The Taliban in Southern Afghanistan: A Localized Insurgency with a Local Objective," *Small Wars & Insurgencies*, Vol. 21, No. 2, June 2010, p. 264.

84. Seth Jones, *Counterinsurgency in Afghanistan*, Santa Monica, CA: RAND Corporation, 2008, p. 13.

85. Anne Stenersen, "The Taliban Insurgency in Afghanistan—Organization, Leadership, and Worldview," Norwegian Defense Research Establishment (FFI), 5 February 2010, p. 24.

86. Brahimi, "Evolving Ideology," p. 4.

87. In fact, a United Nations report attributed 75 percent of civilian casualties to the Taliban and other insurgents. See Alissa J. Rubin, "Taliban Causes Most Civilian Deaths in Afghanistan," *New York Times*, March 9, 2011.

88. Brian Glyn Williams, "Mullah Omar's Missiles," *Middle East Policy*, Vol. 15, No. 4, Winter 2008, p. 28.

89. Stenersen, "Organization, Leadership, Worldview," p. 27.

90. Ibid., p. 27.

91. Alissa J. Rubin, "Taliban Say Offensive Will Begin Sunday," *New York Times*, April 30, 2011.

92. Mohammad Masoom Stanekzai, *Thwarting Afghanistan's Insurgency: A Pragmatic Approach toward Peace and Reconciliation*, United States Institute of Peace, September 2008, pp. 9–10.

93. Shinn and Dobbins, *Afghan Peace Talks*, p. 24.

94. All locations listed are in Pakistan.

95. Shinn and Dobbins, p. 19.

96. Giustozzi, "Negotiating with the Taliban," p. 8.

97. For example, the "southeastern command" is dominated by the Haqqani Network and therefore maintains close relations with the ISI. Ibid., p. 14.

98. Jeffrey Dressler and Carl Forsberg, "The Quetta Shura Taliban in Southern Afghanistan: Organization, Operations, and Shadow Governance," Institute for the Study of War Backgrounder (December 21, 2009), 8.

99. Fotini Christia and Michael Semple, "Flipping the Taliban: How to Win in Afghanistan," *Foreign Affairs*, Vol. 88, No.4, July/August 2009, p. 34.

100. Dressler and Forsberg, "Quetta Shura Taliban," p. 7.

101. Ibid.

102. Ibid.

103. Peters, *Seeds of* Terror, pp. 15–16.

104. Peters, "Crime and Insurgency," pp. 18–19.

105. Matiullah Achakzai, "Taliban Code of Conduct Seeks to Win Heart, Minds," *Associated Press*, August 3, 2010.

106. Among the strictures proffered by Mao were: replace straw bedding and wooden bed-boards after sleeping at peasant homes overnight; return whatever was borrowed; pay for any item damaged; remain courteous and humane; and be fair in any business dealings. Philip Short, *Mao: A Life*, New York: Holt, 1999, p. 222; another great source on Mao is Jung Chang's *Mao: The Unknown Story*, New York: Knopf, 2005.

107. Christopher Paul, "As a Fish Swims in the Sea: Relationships Between Factors Contributing to Support for Terrorist or Insurgent Groups," *Studies in Conflict and Terrorism*, Vol. 33, No. 6, 2010, p. 488.

108. Stenersen, "Organization, Leadership, Worldview," p. 30.

109. Antonio Giustozzi, *Koran, Kalashnikov, Laptop: The New-Taliban Insurgency in Afghanistan*, New York: Columbia University Press, 2008, pp. 38–39.

110. Ibid., pp. 71–72.

111. Shahid Asfar, Chris Samples, Thomas Wood, "The Taliban: An Organizational Analysis," *Military Review*, May/June 2008, p. 67.

112. Najibullah Lafraie, "Resurgence of the Taliban Insurgency in Afghanistan: How and Why?" *International Politics*, Vol. 46 (2009), pp. 102–113. For more on the provincial and district levels of governance in Afghanistan, see Michael Shurkin, *Subnational Government in Afghanistan*, Santa Monica, Calif.: RAND Corp., 2011; Colin Cookman and Caroline Wadhams, "Governance in Afghanistan: Looking Ahead to What We Leave Behind," Center for American Progress, May 2010; and Thomas H. Johnson and M. Chris Mason, "All Counterinsurgency Is Local," *The Atlantic*, October 2008.

113. Todd Helmus, "Why and How Some People Become Terrorists," in Paul K. Davis and Kim Cragin, eds., *Social Science for Counterterrorism: Putting the Pieces Together*, Santa Monica, CA: RAND Corporation, 2009, p. 86.

114. Florian Broschk, "Inciting the Believers to Fight: A Closer Look at the Rhetoric of the Afghan Jihad," Afghanistan Analysts Network, February 2011.

115. Thomas Ruttig, "The Battle for Afghanistan: Negotiations with the Taliban: History and Prospects for the Future," New America Foundation, National Security Studies Program Policy Paper, May 2011, p. 5.

116. International Crisis Group Report, "Taliban Propaganda: Winning the War of Words?" Asia Report No. 158, July 24, 2008.

117. Giustozzi, *Koran, Kalashnikov, and Laptop*, p. 120.

118. Alia Brahimi, "The Taliban's Evolving Ideology," London School of Economics Global Governance Working Paper, February 2010, p. 4.

119. Stenersen, "Organization, Leadership, and Worldview," p. 32.

120. Brahimi, "Evolving Ideology," p. 11.

121. Ibid., p. 9.

122. Ibid., p. 8.

123. Ibid.

124. Mark Basile, "Going to the Source: Why Al-Qaeda's Financial Network Is Likely to Withstand the Current War on Terrorist Financing," *Studies in Conflict & Terrorism*, Vol. 27, No. 3, 2004, p. 170.

125. See Aram Roston, "How the U.S. Funds the Taliban," *The Nation*, November 11, 2009 and Karen DeYoung, "U.S. Trucking Funds Reach Taliban, Military-Led Investigation Concludes," *Washington Post*, July 24, 2011.

126. Author interview with Gretchen Peters, October 2014.

127. Ruttig, "The Battle for Afghanistan," p. 4.

128. Dexter Filkins, "The Afghan Bank Heist," *The New Yorker*, February 14, 2011.

129. Freeman, pp. 108–109.

130. Gretchen Peters, Seeds of Terror, p. 178.

131. Freeman, p. 107.

132. Giustozzi, "Negotiating with the Taliban," p. 4.

133. Shinn and Dobbins, *Afghan Peace Talks*, p. 5.

134. Ruttig, "The Battle for Afghanistan," p. 7.

135. For more on the challenges of training and equipping ANSF, see Anthony H. Cordesman, Adam Mausner, and David Kasten, *Winning in Afghanistan: Creating Effective Afghan Security Forces*, Washington DC: Center for Strategic and International Studies, May 2009.

CHAPTER 7

1. Al Qaeda, Al-Qaida, Al-Qa'ida and several other variants are often used interchangeably in the literature. Al-Qaeda has been translated variously as the "base of operation," "foundation," "precept," or "method." Bruce Hoffman, "The Changing Face of Al Qaeda and the Global War on Terrorism," *Studies in Conflict & Terrorism*, Vol. 27, No. 6, 2004, p. 551.

2. R. Kim Cragin, "Early History of Al-Qaida," *The Historic Journal*, Vol. 51, No. 4, December 2008, pp. 1051–1052.

3. Cragin, "Early History of Al-Qaida," p. 1056.

4. Core Al Qaeda is sometimes referred to as the Al Qaeda Core, Al Qaeda Central, or the Al Qaeda Senior Leadership (AQSL).

5. It is important to note that these groups are constantly in a state of flux.

6. Al Qaeda in Iraq (AQI), once considered an Al Qaeda Affiliate, is now known as ISIS and is outside the orbit of Al Qaeda. As such, it will receive separate, in-depth treatment in Chapter 9.

7. John Roth et al., *Monograph on Terrorist Financing*, Staff Report to the National Commission on Terrorist Attacks Upon the United States, Washington DC: U.S. Government Printing Office, 2004, pp. 119–120.

8. Matthew Levitt, "Al-Qa'ida's Finances: Evidence of Organizational Decline?" *CTC Sentinel*, Vol. 1, No. 5, April 2008, p. 7.

9. Angel Rabasa et al., *Beyond Al-Qaeda: The Global Jihadist Movement, Part I*, Santa Monica, CA: RAND Corp., 2006, p. 59.

10. Hearing of the House Permanent Select Committee on Intelligence, "Annual Worldwide Threat Assessment," February 7, 2008.

11. Levitt, "Al-Qa'ida's Finances," p. 8.

12. Reuters, "Saudi Says Arrests Qaeda Suspects Planning Attacks," *Washington Post*, March 3, 2008.

13. Bruce Hoffman, "Al Qaeda's Uncertain Future," *Studies in Conflict & Terrorism*, Vol. 36, No. 8, 2013, p. 644.

14. Levitt, "Al Qaida's Finances," p. 8.

15. Gunaratna and Oreg, "Al Qaeda's Organizational Structure," p. 1047.

16. Seth G. Jones, *A Persistent Threat: The Evolution of Al Qaida and Other Salafist Jihadists*, Santa Monica, CA: RAND Corp., 2014.

17. Under *zakat*, Muslims are encouraged to donate approximately 2.5% of their savings and assets annually, if possible.

18. Rohan Gunaratna, "The Post-Madrid Face of Al Qaeda," *The Washington Quarterly*, Vol. 27, No. 3, 2004, p. 95.

19. Victor Comras, "Al Qaeda Finances and Funding to Affiliated Groups," in Jeanne K. Giraldo and Harold A. Trinkunas, *Terrorism Financing and State Responses: A Comparative Perspective*, Stanford: Stanford University Press, 2007, pp. 122–123.

20. Paul Watson and Mubashir Zaidi, "Militants Flourish in Plain Sight," *Los Angeles Times*, January 25, 2004.

21. Levitt, "Al-Qa'ida's Finances," p. 8.

22. In March 2002, the U.S. and Saudi Arabia jointly designed the Bosnia and Herzegovina and Somalia offices of al Haramain as Al Qaeda funding sources. Other branches were also implicated, including those in Albania, Croatia, Ethiopia, Kenya, Kosovo, Indonesia, Pakistan, and Tanzania. Comras, "Al Qaeda Finances," in Giraldo and Trinkunas, *Terrorism Financing and State Responses*, p. 121.

23. Juan Miguel del Cid Gomez, "A Financial Profile of the Terrorism of Al-Qaeda and Its Affiliates," *Perspectives on Terrorism*, Vol. 4, No. 4, October 2010, pp. 8–9.

24. Comras, "Al Qaeda Finances," in Giraldo and Trinkunas, *Terrorism Financing and State Responses*, p. 118.

25. Including associated groups like Lashkar-e-Taiba and Jamaat Mujahidin Bangladesh (JMB).

26. These countries include Albania, Azerbaijan, Bangladesh, Bosnia, Cambodia, and Russia. Gomez, "A Financial Profile of Al-Qaeda and Its Affiliates," p. 10.

27. Levitt, "Al-Qa'ida's Finances," p. 7.

28. Rabasa et al., *Beyond Al-Qaeda, Part I*, p. 57.

29. Levitt, "Al-Qa'ida's Finances," p. 7.

30. *Terrorist Financing*, Financial Action Task Force, February 29, 2008, p. 14.

31. Gomez, "A Financial Profile of Al-Qaeda and Its Affiliates," p. 13.

32. Timothy L. Thomas, "Al Qaeda and the Internet: The Danger of 'Cyberplanning,'" *Parameters*, Spring 2003, p. 117.

33. Jeffrey Robinson, "The Money Trail: How Petty Crime Funds Terror," *New York Times*, August 13, 2004.

34. Gomez, "A Financial Profile of Al-Qaeda and Its Affiliates," p. 18.

35. Ibid., p. 7.

36. Peter Bergen, *Holy Terror, Inc.: Inside the Secret World of Osama bin Laden*, New York: Free Press, 2001, pp. 47–49.

37. Hoffman, "Changing Face," p. 553.

38. Comras, "Al Qaeda Finances," in Giraldo and Trinkunas, *Terrorism Financing and State Responses*, pp. 123–124.

39. Ibid., p. 128.

40. Gomez, "A Financial Profile of Al-Qaeda and Its Affiliates," p. 10.

41. Comras, p. 128.

42. Edwina A. Thompson, "An Introduction to the Concept and Origins of *Hawala*," *Journal of the History of International Law*, Vol. 10, 2008, p. 83.

43. Mark Basile, "Going to the Source: Why Al Qaeda's Financial Network Is Likely to Withstand the Current War on Terrorist Financing," *Studies in Conflict & Terrorism*, Vol. 27, No. 3, 2004, p. 170.

44. Gomez, "A Financial Profile of Al-Qaeda and Its Affiliates," p. 11.

45. Ibid., p. 14.

46. Annie Sweeney, "Al-Qaida Operative Invested with Chicago Brokerage House in 2005," *Chicago Tribune*, June 21, 2011.

47. Phil Williams, "Terrorist Financing," in Paul Shemella, ed., *Fighting Back: What Governments Can Do About Terrorism*, Stanford: Stanford University Press, 2011, p. 45.

48. For more, see Vahid Brown and Don Rassler, *Fountainhead of Jihad: The Haqqani Nexus*, 1973–2012, Oxford: Oxford University Press, 2013.

49. For more, see Gregory D. Johnsen, *The Last Refuge: Yemen, Al Qaeda, and America's War in Arabia*, New York: W.W. Norton & Co., 2013.

50. Rukmimi Callimachi, "Ransoming Citizens, Europe Becomes Al Qaeda's Patron," *The New York Times*, July 29, 2014.

51. Ellen Knickmeyer, "Al Qaeda-Linked Groups Increasingly Funded by Ransom," *The Wall Street Journal*, July 29, 2014.

52. Rukmimi Callimachi, "Ransoming Citizens, Europe Becomes Al Qaeda's Patron," *The New York Times*, July 29, 2014.

53. Gomez, "A Financial Profile of Al-Qaeda and Its Affiliates," p. 14.

54. Levitt, "Al-Qa'ida's Finances," p. 7.

55. Gomez, "A Financial Profile of Al-Qaeda and Its Affiliates," pp. 12–13.

56. Ibid., pp. 13–14.

57. Douglas Farah, *Blood from Stones: The Secret Financial Network of Terror*, New York: Broadway Books, 2004, p. 4.

58. Gomez, "A Financial Profile of Al-Qaeda and Its Affiliates," pp. 12–13.

59. Gretchen Peters and Don Rassler, "Crime and Insurgency in the Tribal Areas of Afghanistan and Pakistan," Center for Combating Terrorism (CTC) at West Point, 2010, pp. ii–iii.

60. Ibid., p. 36

61. Gretchen Peters, "Haqqani Network Financing," Center for Combating Terrorism (CTC) at West Point, 2012, p. 47.

62. Daniel Byman, "Passive Sponsors of Terrorism," *Survival*, Vol. 47, No. 4, Winter 2005–06, p. 117. Byman notes that Al-Qaida recruited and raised money in Germany, enjoyed financial support from major financiers in Saudi Arabia, and planned operations in Malaysia.

63. Daniel Byman, *Deadly Connections: States that Sponsor Terrorism*, New York: Cambridge University Press, 2005, p. 322.

64. Letters from Abbottabad, p. 42.

65. Seth G. Jones, "Al Qaeda in Iran," *Foreign Affairs*, January 29, 2012.

66. Mette Eilstrup-Sangiovanni and Calvert Jones, "Assessing the Dangers of Illicit Networks," *International Security*, Vol. 33, No. 2, Fall 2008, p. 34.

67. Hoffman, "The Changing Face," p. 551.

68. Also known as the Pakistani Taliban.

69. Gunaratna and Oreg, "Al Qaeda's Organizational Structure," pp. 1048–1049.

70. One of the most comprehensive treatments of Al-Qaida attacks worldwide can be found in Bruce Hoffman and Fernando Reinares, eds., *The Evolution of the Global Terrorist Threat: From 9/11 to Osama Bin Laden's Death*, New York: Columbia University Press, 2014.

71. Paper, Dying to Win, pp. 185–186.

72. Mia Bloom, Dying to Kill, p. 76.

73. Moises Naim, "Five Wars of Globalization," *Foreign Policy*, November 3, 2009.

74. Stewart Patrick, Weak States, p. 37.

75. Rabsa et al., Beyond Al Qaeda, pp. 48–50.

76. Brian Michael Jenkins, *Will Terrorists Go Nuclear?*, pp. 127–129.

77. Gaetano Joe Ilardi, "The 9/11 Attacks—A Study of Al Qaeda's Use of Intelligence and Counterintelligence," *Studies in Conflict & Terrorism*, Vol. 31, No. 1, 2009, pp. 171–173.

78. Ibid., p. 176.

79. Ibid., p. 178.

80. William Rosenau, "Understanding Insurgent Intelligence Operations," *Marine Corps University Journal*, Vol. 2, No. 1, Spring 2011, p. 23.

81. Ibid., p. 12.

82. Gunaratna, "Post-Madrid Al Qaeda," pp. 92–94.

83. "Pakistan's Tribal Areas: Appeasing the Militants," *International Crisis Group*, Asia Report No. 125, December 11, 2006, p. 1.

84. James Revill, "Militancy in the FATA and the NWFP," *Pakistan Security Research Unit*, Brief No. 23, November 19, 2007, p. 3.

85. Rohan Gunaratna and Anders Nielsen, "Al Qaeda in the Tribal Areas of Pakistan," *Studies in Conflict & Terrorism*, Vol. 31, No. 9, 2008, p. 777.

86. The main tenets of pashtunwali include hospitality, asylum, justice, revenge, and strict defense of honor, land, women, nation, and Pashtun culture Palwasha Kakar, "Tribal Law of Pashtunwali," *Harvard University School of Law*.

87. "Pakistan's Tribal Areas," Council on Foreign Relations, October 26, 2007.

88. Eric Sayers, "The Islamic Emirate of Waziristan and the Bajaur Tribal Region: The Strategic Threat of Terrorist Sanctuaries," *The Center for Security Policy*, No. 19, February 2007, p. 3.

89. Rohan Gunaratna and Anders Nielsen, "Al Qaeda in the Tribal Areas of Pakistan," *Studies in Conflict & Terrorism*, Vol. 31, No. 9, 2008, pp. 781–782.

90. Hoffman, "Al Qaeda's Uncertain Future," p. 636.

91. Scott Helfstein with John Solomon, "Risky Business: The Global Threat Network and the Politics of Contraband," West Point: Combating Terrorism Center, May 2014, p. 55.

92. During its years in Afghanistan, bin Laden paid the Taliban approximately $20 million a year. In Sudan, a five year stay resulted in approximately $150 million paid to the Sudanese government. Rabasa et al., *Beyond Al-Qaeda, Part I*, p. 61.

93. Gunaratna and Oreg, "Al Qaeda's Organizational Structure," p. 1049.

94. Hoffman, "The Changing Face," p. 551.

95. Rohan Gunaratna and Anders Nielsen, "Al Qaeda in the Tribal Areas of Pakistan," *Studies in Conflict & Terrorism*, Vol. 31, No. 9, 2008, p. 783.

96. Ibid., p. 788.

97. Paul Cruickshank, "The Militant Pipeline: Between the Afghanistan-Pakistan Border Region and the West," New America Foundation, February 2010.

98. Carlotta Gall, "The Wrong Enemy," p. 83.

99. Seth Jones, "Hunting in the Shadows," pp. 351–352.

100. Daniel L. Byman, "Breaking the Bonds Between Al-Qa'ida and Its Affiliate Organizations," Brookings Institution Analysis Paper, No. 27, August 2012, p.v.

101. Gomez, "A Financial Profile of Al-Qaeda and Its Affiliates," pp. 4–5.

102. Hoffman, "Al Qaeda's Uncertain Future," p. 636.

103. Ibid., p. 639. Also see Brian Michael Jenkins, "Al Qaeda in Its Third Decade: Irreversible Decline or Imminent Victory?" Santa Monica, CA: RAND Corp., 2012 as well as Rick Nelson and Thomas M. Sanderson, "A Threat Transformed: Al Qaeda and Associated Movements in 2011," Center for Strategic and International Studies (CSIS), February 2011.

104. Gunaratna and Oreg, p. 1054.

105. Some of this debate played out in the pages of *Foreign Affairs* while bin Laden was still alive. See Bruce Hoffman, "The Myth of Grass-Roots Terrorism: Why Osama bin Laden Still Matters," *Foreign Affairs*, Vol. 87, No. 3, May–June 2008, pp. 133–138. For a synopsis of his importance after his death, see Brian Michael Jenkins, "Al Qaeda After Bin Laden: Implications for American Strategy," Testimony presented before the House Armed Services Committee, Subcommittee on Emerging Threats and Capabilities, June 22, 2011.

106. Steve Coll, Ghost Wars, p. 269; p. 380.

107. Lawrence Wright, Looming Tower, p. 60; p. 264.

108. Zachary Laub, "Backgrounders: Al Qaeda in the Islamic Maghreb (AQIM)," Council on Foreign Relations, January 8, 2014.

109. Eli Lake, "Meet Al Qaeda's New General Manager: Nasser al-Wuhayshi," *The Daily Beast*, August 9, 2013.

110. Anonymous, *Imperial Hubris: Why the West if Losing the War on Terror*, Washington DC: Brassey's, Inc., 2004, p. 129.

111. Bruce Hoffman, "Al Qaeda Trends in Terrorism and Future Potentialities: An Assessment," paper presented at a meeting of the Council on Foreign Relations, Washington DC Office, May 8, 2003, p. 5.

112. David Aaron, *In Their Own Words: Voices of Jihad*, Santa Monica, CA: RAND Corp., 2008, p. 73.

113. Cragin, "Early History of Al-Qa'ida," p. 1066.

114. Also known as Mustafa Setmariam Nasar.

115. Al-Awlaki's significance has been questioned by Gregory Johnsen in "A False Target in Yemen," *New York Times*, November 19, 2010. Johnsen argues that by authorizing the killing of Al-Awlaki, an American citizen reported to be hiding in Yemen, the Obama administration has afforded him undue influence far beyond his true position as a "midlevel religious functionary." Johnsen goes on to point out that far more dangerous individuals should be a priority, including the leader of Al-Qaida in the Arabian Peninsula (AQAP) Nasir al-Wuhayshi, deputy commander Said Ali-al Shihri, AQAP's top religious scholar Adil al-Abab, its chief of military operations Qassim al-Raymi, its bomb maker Ibrahim Hassan Asiri, and its leading ideologue Ibrahim Suleiman al-Rubaysh.

116. Declan Welsh and Eric Schmitt, "Drone Strike Killed No. 2 in Al Qaeda U.S. Officials Say," *New York Times*, June 5, 2012.

117. A great source for Salafist jihadist writings is Cronus Global LLC, which can be found in addition to the three insurgent theorists listed above, there are also a number of emerging jihadi pundits in the virtual arena. Some of the most prolific Internet authors include Asad al-Jihad, Abd al-Rahman al-Faqir, Hafid al-Hussain, Shaykh abu-Abd-al Rahman al-Yafi'I, Abu Shadiyah, Ziyad Abu Tariq, Shaykh Abu Ahmad and al-Rahman al-Masri, and Yaman Mukhaddab. For more information see Jarret Brachman, "The Worst of the Worst," *Foreign Policy*, January 22, 2010.

118. For more on narratives, see William D. Casebeer and James A. Russell, "Storytelling and Terrorism: Towards a Comprehensive 'Counter-Narrative Strategy'," *Strategic Insights*, Vol. 4, No. 3, March 2005.

119. Hoffman, "The Changing Face," p. 551.

120. Ibid., pp. 551–552.

121. Cragin, "Early History of Al-Qa'ida," pp. 1063–1064.

122. Gunaratna and Oreg, pp. 1054–1064.

123. Brian Michael Jenkins, "The al Qaeda-Inspired Terrorist Threat: An Appreciation of the Current Situation," Testimony presented before the Canadian Senate Special Committee on Anti-terrorism on December 6, 2010, p. 6.

124. Brian Michael Jenkins, Stray Dogs and Virtual Armies, p. 14; see also, Steven Simon and Jonathan Stevenson, "Al-Qaeda's New Strategy: Less Apocalypse, More Street Fighting," *The Washington Post*, October 10, 2010.

125. Hoffman, "The Changing Face," p. 553.

126. Philip Seib, "The Al-Qaeda Media Machine," *Military Review*, May/June 2008, pp. 75–75.

127. Hoffman, "Al Qaeda's Uncertain Future," p. 643.

128. Marc Lynch, "Al Qaeda's Media Strategies," *The National Interest*, Spring 2006 Vol. 83, pp. 50–52.

129. Michael Scheuer, "Al Qaeda's Media Doctrine," The Jamestown Foundation, Vol. 4, No. 5, May 30, 2007; see also, Manuel R. Torres et al., "Analysis and Evolution of Global Jihadist Media Propaganda," *Terrorism & Political Violence*, Vol. 18, No. 3, 2006, pp. 399–421.

130. Hoffman, "Al Qaeda's Uncertain Future," p. 643.

131. Yariv Tsfati and Gabriel Weimann, "www.terrorism.com: Terror on the Internet," *Studies in Conflict and Terrorism*, Vol. 25, No. 5, pp. 317–332.

132. Evan F. Kohlmann, "The Real Online Terrorist Threat," *Foreign Affairs*, Vol. 85, No. 5, 2006, p. 124.

133. Tom Keatinge, "The Price of Freedom: When Governments Pay Ransoms," *Foreign Affairs*, August 13, 2014.

134. Rabasa et al., *Beyond Al-Qaeda*, Part I, p. 60.

135. Gomez, "A Financial Profile of Al-Qaeda and Its Affiliates," p. 6.

136. Ibid.

137. Seeds, p. 187

138. Rabasa et al., *Beyond Al-Qaeda*, Part I, p. 58.

139. Ibid., p. 59.

140. Gomez, "A Financial Profile of Al-Qaeda and Its Affiliates," p. 3.

141. Basile, "Going to the Source," p. 170.

142. Victor Comras, "Al Qaeda Finances and Funding to Affiliated Groups," in Jeanne K. Giraldo and Harold A. Trinkunas, *Terrorism Financing and State Responses: A Comparative Perspective*, Stanford: Stanford University Press, 2007, p. 115.

143. Gunaratna and Nielsen, p. 782.

144. Seth G. Jones, "The Future of Al Qa'ida," Congressional Testimony, presented before the House Foreign Affairs Committee, Subcommittee on Terrorism, Nonproliferation and Trade, May 24, 2011.

145. The FATF is the de facto international standard for countering financial crime and the illicit use of the global financial system Scott Helfstein with John Solomon, "Risky Business: The Global Threat Network and the Politics of Contraband," West Point: Combating Terrorism Center, May 2014.

146. Levitt, "Al-Qa'ida's Finances," p. 8.

147. Gomez, "A Financial Profile of Al-Qaeda and Its Affiliates," p. 9.

148. Ibid., p. 15.

149. Ibid.

150. Ibid., p. 11.

151. Hoffman, "Al Qaeda's Uncertain Future," p. 641.

CHAPTER 8

1. Al Qaeda in Iraq/Al Qaeda in the Land of the Two Rivers (which was originally known as Jamaat al-Tawhid wali-Jihad, or "Monotheism and Holy War Group") has undergone several transformations in recent years, becoming the Islamic State in Iraq, the Islamic State in Iraq and the Levant (ISIL)/the Islamic State in Iraq and al-Sham (ISIS), and then finally, the Islamic State, which is the group's current name at the time of this writing.

2. In between the time it was AQI and ISIS, the group was alternatively known as Majlis Shura al-Mujahedin (MSM) and the Islamic State of Iraq (ISI). Aaron Y. Zelin, "The War Between ISIS and al-Qaeda for Supremacy of the Global Jihadist Movement," *The Washington Institute for Near East Policy*, No. 20, June 2014, p. 1.

3. William Young et al., *Spillover from the Conflict in Syria: An Assessment of the Factors that Aid and Impede the Spread of Violence*, Santa Monica, CA: RAND Corporation, 2014.

4. Tim Arango, "Uneasy Alliance Gives Insurgents an Edge in Iraq," *New York Times*, June 18, 2014. See also, Anthony Cordesman, "The Real Center of Gravity in the War Against the Islamic State," *Center for Strategic and International Studies (CSIS)*, September 30, 2014.

5. "A New Focus on Foreign Fighters," *The New York Times*, September 24, 2014.

6. Jamie Detmer, "How to Cut Off ISIS Terror Tycoons," *Daily Beast*, September 26, 2014

7. Vivienne Walt, "How Guns and Oil Net ISIS $1 Million A Day," *Fortune*, July 24, 2014.

8. Patrick B. Johnston and Benjamin Bahney, "Hit the Islamic State's Pocketbook," *Newsday*, October 5, 2014.

9. Matthew Levitt and Lori Plotkin Boghardt, "Funding ISIS," The Washington Institute for Near East Policy, September 12, 2014.

10. Matthew Levitt, "Foreign Fighters and Their Economic Impact: A Case Study of Syria and Al Qaeda in Iraq," *Perspectives on Terrorism*, Vol. 3, No. 3 pp. 13–24, 16, 2009.

11. "Did Islamic State Militants Use Bitcoin To Fund Their English-Language Website?" *Radio Free Europe/Radio Liberty*, October 13, 2014.

12. Johnston and Bahney, "Hitting ISIS Where It Hurts," August 13, 2014.

13. Matthew Levitt, "Show Me the Money: Targeting the Islamic State's Bottom Line," *Homeland Security Policy Institute*, October 1, 2014.

14. As Daniel Byman notes, intelligence services can more easily penetrate diasporas that are based in Western countries in order to curtail fund-raising. Daniel L. Byman, "Breaking the Bonds Between Al-Qa'ida and Its Affiliate Organizations," Brookings Institution Analysis Paper, No. 27, August 2012, p. 43.

15. One of the largest Syrian diaspora communities is in Germany, with an estimated 33,000 Syrians living in Germany. "The Engagement of the Syrian Diaspora in Germany in Peacebuilding," United Nations University Migration Network, *IS Academy Policy Brief*, No. 13.

16. Peter K. Waldmann, "Radicalisation in the Diaspora: Why Muslims in the West Attack Their Host Countries," Real Instituto Elcano Working Paper, September 2010, p. 17.

17. See Petter Nesser, "Jihadism in Western Europe After the Invasion of Iraq: Tracing Motivational Influences from the Iraq War on Jihadist Terrorism in Western Europe," *Studies in Conflict & Terrorism*, Vol. 29, No. 4, 2006, pp. 323–342 and Peter R. Neumann, "Europe's Jihadist Dilemma," *Survival*, Vol. 48, No. 2, 2006, pp. 71–84.

18. "Attacking ISIL's Foundation," Remarks of Under Secretary for Terrorism and Financial Intelligence David S. Cohen at The Carnegie Endowment for International Peace, October 23, 2014.

19. Elizabeth Dickinson, "Playing with Fire: Why Private Gulf Financing for Syria's Extremist Rebels Risks Igniting Sectarian Conflict at Home," *Brookings Analysis Paper*, No. 16, December 2014, p. 3; p. 10.

20. Marc Lynch, "Islamists and Their Charities," *Washington Post* Monkey Cage Blog, October 15, 2014.

21. Steven Brooke, "Assumptions and Agendas in the Study of Islamic Social Service Provision," in *Islamist Social Services*, Project on Middle East Political Science (POMEPS), October 15, 2014, p. 14.

22. Amit R. Paley, "Iraqis Joining Insurgency Less for Cause Than Cash," *Washington Post*, November 20, 2007

23. Phil Williams, *Criminals, Militias, and Insurgents: Organized Crime in Iraq*, Carlisle, PA: U.S. Army War College Strategic Studies Institute (SSI), June 2009, pp. 83–84.

24. Ibid., pp. 186–188.

25. Ahmad Salama, "Kidnapping and Construction: Al Qaeda Turns to Big Business, Mafia-Style," *Niqash*, April 6, 2011.

26. Michael Jonsson, "Following the Money: Financing the Territorial Expansion of Islamist Insurgents in Syria," Swedish Defense Research Agency, FOI Memo #4947, May 2014.

27. Indeed, as of February 2015, the Pentagon reported that airstrikes were effective in diminishing ISIS's overall revenues from oil smuggling. Kate Brannen, "Pentagon: Oil No Longer the Islamic State's Main Source of Revenue," *Foreign Policy*, February 3, 2015.

28. Patrick B. Johnston and Benjamin Bahney, "Hit the Islamic State's Pocketbook," *Newsday*, October 5, 2014.

29. Rachel Louise Ensign, "Will Anti-Money Laundering Efforts Work Against the Islamic State?" *Wall Street Journal*, August 29, 2014.

30. Josh Rogin, "America's Allies Are Funding ISIS," *Daily Beast*, June 14, 2014. For more on Qatar and Kuwait, specifically, see Lauri Plotkin Boghardt, "The Terrorist Funding Disconnect with Qatar and Kuwait," *Washington Institute for Near East Policy*, Policywatch 2247, May 2, 2014.

31. The CFT in AML/CFT stands for "Combating the Financing of Terrorism," rather than "counterterrorist the financing of terrorism," as reported by the State Department in its report.

32. United States Department of State Country Reports on Terrorism 2013, Bureau of Counterterrorism, released April 2014.

33. Michael Jonsson, "Following the Money: Financing the Territorial Expansion of Islamist Insurgents in Syria," Swedish Defense Research Agency, FOI Memo #4947, May 2014.

34. Remarks of Under Secretary for Terrorism and Financial Intelligence David S. Cohen at The Carnegie Endowment for International Peace, "Attacking ISIL's Financial Foundation," October 23, 2014.

35. Terrence McCoy, "ISIS Just Stole $425 Million, Iraqi Governor Says, And Became the 'World's Richest Terrorist Group.'" *The Washington Post*, June 12, 2014.

36. In January 2015, the Islamic State released its 2015 budget of $2 billion. Damien Sharkov, "ISIS 'Releases 2015 Budget Projections' of $2bn with $250m Surplus," *Newsweek*, January 5, 2015.

37. Jamie Detmer, "How to Cut Off ISIS Terror Tycoons," *Daily Beast*, September 26, 2014. See also, Richard Barrett, "The Islamic State," The Soufan Group, November 2014, p. 10.

38. Remarks of Under Secretary for Terrorism and Financial Intelligence David S. Cohen at The Carnegie Endowment for International Peace, "Attacking ISIL's Financial Foundation," October 23, 2014.

39. Jacob Shapiro, "Bureaucratic Terrorists: Al-Qa'ida in Iraq's Management and Finances," in Brian Fishman, ed., *Bombers, Bank Accounts & Bleedout: Al Qa'ida's Road In and Out of Iraq*, West Point, NY: Combating Terrorism Center (CTC), 2008, p. 70; see also, Austin Long, "The Anbar Awakening," *Survival*, Vol. 50, No. 2, April-May 2008, pp. 67–94.

40. Tom Keatinge, "How the Islamic State Sustains Itself: The Importance of the War Economy in Syria and Iraq," *RUSI Analysis*, August 29, 2014.

41. The crude then gets sold to refiners for approximately $60 a barrel. Louise Shelley, "Blood Money: How ISIS Makes Bank," *Foreign Affairs*, November 30, 2014.

42. Tom Keatinge, "The Importance of Financing in Enabling and Sustaining the Conflict in Syria," *Perspectives on Terrorism*, Vol. 8, No. 4, August 2014.

43. Howard J. Shatz, "To Defeat the Islamic State, Follow the Money," *Politico*, September 10, 2014.

44. Howard J. Shatz, "How ISIS Funds Its Reign of Terror," *New York Daily News*, September 8, 2014.

45. David E. Sanger and Julie Hirschfield Davis, "Struggling to Starve ISIS of Oil Revenue, U.S. Seeks Assistance from Turkey," September 13, 2014.

46. "ISIS Selling Iraq's Artifacts in Black Market: UNESCO," *Al Arabiya News*, September 30, 2014. See also, Justine Drennan, "The Black Market Battleground," *Foreign Policy*, October 17, 2014; see also, Janine di Giovanni et al., "How Does ISIS Fund Its Reign of Terror," *Newsweek*, November 6, 2014.

47. Nick Cumming-Bruce, "5,500 Iraqis Killed Since Islamic State Began Its Military Drive, U.N. Says," *New York Times*, October 2, 2014.

48. Williams, *Criminals, Militias, and Insurgents*, p. 158.

49. Ibid., p. 159.

50. David E. Sanger and Julie Hirschfield Davis, "Struggling to Starve ISIS of Oil Revenue, U.S. Seeks Assistance from Turkey," September 13, 2014.

51. Michael Jonsson, "Following the Money: Financing the Territorial Expansion of Islamist Insurgents in Syria," Swedish Defense Research Agency, FOI Memo #4947, May 2014.

52. Harith Hasan, "Al Qaeda Sinks Roots in Mosul," *Al-Monitor*, October 24, 2013.

53. Patrick B. Johnston and Benjamin Bahney, "Hitting ISIS Where It Hurts: Disrupting ISIS's Cash Flow in Iraq," *New York Times*, August 13, 2014.

54. Ariel I. Ahram, "Can ISIS Overcome the Insurgency Resource Curse?" *Washington Post* Monkey Cage, July 2, 2014.

55. Ben Hubbard, Clifford Kraus and Eric Schmitt, "Rebels in Syria Claim Control of Resources," January 28, 2014.

56. Ariel Ahram, "The Dangerous Mixture of Oil and Water in Iraq," *Political Violence @ a Glance*, August 18, 2014. See also, Hwaida Saad and Rick Gladstone, "Syrian Insurgents Claim to Control Large Hydropower Dam," *New York Times*, February 11, 2013.

57. Howard J. Shatz, "How ISIS Funds Its Reign of Terror," *New York Daily News*, September 8, 2014. Between 2005 and 2010, when the group was known as

AQI, it is estimated that no more than 5 percent of its funding came from external donors. Matthew Levitt, "Show Me the Money: Targeting the Islamic State's Bottom Line," *Homeland Security Policy Institute*, October 1, 2014.

58. Elizabeth Dickinson, "The Case Against Qatar," *Foreign Policy*, September 30, 2014.

59. Scott Bronstein and Drew Griffin, "Self-Funded and Deep-Rooted: How ISIS Makes Its Millions," *CNN.com*, October 7, 2014.

60. Cam Simpson, "The Banality of the Islamic State: How ISIS Corporatized Terror," *Bloomberg Business Week*, November 20, 2014.

61. Benjamin W. Bahney et al., "Insurgent Compensation: Evidence from Iraq," *American Economic Review: Papers & Proceedings*, Vol. 103, No. 3, 2013, p. 519.

62. Charles Lister, "Profiling the Islamic State," Brookings Institution Doha Center Analysis Paper, No. 13, November 2014, p. 20.

63. An analysis of ISIS's weaponry reveals that China, the Soviet Union/Russian Federation and the United State are the top three manufacturing states represented in the sample of ammunition used by ISIS in Iraq and Syria. "Islamic State Ammunition in Iraq and Syria: Analysis of Small-Calibre Ammunition Recovered from Islamic State Forces in Iraq and Syria," London: Conflict Armament Research, October 2014, p. 5.

64. "How ISIS Works," *New York Times*, September 16, 2014.

65. C. J. Chivers, "ISIS Ammunition is Shown to Have Origins in U.S. and China," *The New York Times*, October 5, 2014. See also, Julia Harte and R. Jeffrey Smith, "Where Does the Islamic State Get Its Weapons?" *Foreign Policy*, October 6, 2014.

66. Kirk Semple and Eric Schmitt, "Missiles of ISIS May Pose Peril for Aircrews," *New York Times*, October 26, 2014.

67. Many of the Iraqi soldiers who refused to fight blamed their failure to stand their ground on officers, saying they were deliberately denied the resupply of basic necessities like food and water. C. J. Chivers, "After Retreat, Iraqi Soldiers Fault Officers," *New York Times*, July 1, 2014.

68. Gina Harkins, "5 Things to Know About Islamic State's Military Capabilities," *Army Times*, September 16, 2014.

69. "Arms Windfall for Insurgents as Iraq City Falls," *The New York Times*, June 10, 2014.

70. Josh Rogin, "ISIS Video: America's Air Dropped Weapons Now in Our Hands," *Daily Beast*, October 21, 2014.

71. Peter Bergen and Emily Schneider, "Now ISIS Has Drones?" *CNN.com*, August 25, 2014.

72. Daniel Trombly and Yasir Abbas, "Who the U.S. Should Really Hit in ISIS," *Daily Beast*, September 23, 2014.

73. Ibid.

74. Nigel Inkster, "The Resurgence of ISIS," International Institute for Strategic Studies (IISS), June 13, 2014.

75. Charles Lister, "Profiling the Islamic State," Brookings Institution Doha Center Analysis Paper, No. 13, November 2014, p. 17.

76. Carter Malkasian, "If ISIS Has a 3-24 (II): Trying to Write the Field Manual of the Islamic State," *Foreign Policy*, October 7, 2014.

77. Daniel Byman and Jeremy Shapiro, "Homeward Bound? Don't Hype the Threat of Returning Jihadists," *Foreign Affairs*, September 30, 2014.

78. Caleb Weiss and Bill Roggio, "Islamic State Assaults City in Syrian Kurdistan," *The Long War Journal*, September 18, 2014.

79. James Dobbins, "Does ISIL Represent a Threat to the United States?" *The Hill*, October 3, 2014.

80. Yochi Dreazen, "From Electricity to Sewage, U.S. Intelligence Says the Islamic State Is Fast Learning How to Run a Country," *Foreign Policy*, August 18, 2014.

81. Matthew Levitt, "Show Me the Money: Targeting the Islamic State's Bottom Line," *Homeland Security Policy Institute*, October 1, 2014.

82. Frederic Wehrey, "To Beat ISIS, Exploit Its Contradictions," *CNN.com*, June 17, 2014.

83. John Nagl, "America Needs a More Aggressive Strategy Against ISIL. Now." *Politico*, October 12, 2014.

84. Andrew Shaver, "Turning the Lights Off on the Islamic State," *Washington Post* Monkey Cage Blog, October 16, 2014.

85. Brooke Satti, "Funding Terrorists: The Rise of ISIS," *Security Intelligence*, October 10, 2014.

86. Suliman Ali Zway and David D. Kirkpatrick, "Group Linked to ISIS Says It's Behind Assault on Libyan Hotel," *New York Times*, January 27, 2015.

87. Sami Yousafzai, "ISIS Targets Afghanistan Just as U.S. Quits," *Daily Beast*, December 19, 2014.

88. Reuters, "300 Chinese are Fighting Alongside ISIS in Iraq, Syria," December 15, 2014.

89. See Colin P. Clarke and Phil Williams, "The Islamic State of Iraq and Syria: Sustainable Insurgency or Paper Tiger?" in Lawrence Cline and Paul Shemella, eds., *The Future of Counterinsurgency: Contemporary Debates in Internal Security Strategy*, Santa Barbara, Calif.: ABC-CLIO, forthcoming 2015.

90. Daniel Trombly and Yasir Abbas, "Who the U.S. Should Really Hit in ISIS," *Daily Beast*, September 23, 2014.

91. Daniel Byman and Jeremy Shapiro, "Homeward Bound? Don't Hype the Threat of Returning Jihadists," *Foreign Affairs*, September 30, 2014.

92. Charles Lister, "Profiling the Islamic State," Brookings Institution Doha Center Analysis Paper, No. 13, November 2014, p. 17.

93. Ross Harrison, "Confronting the 'Islamic State:' Towards a Regional Strategy Contra ISIS," *Parameters*, Vol. 44, No. 3, Autumn 2014, p. 39.

94. Megan A. Stewart, "What's So New About the Islamic State's Governance?" *Washington Post* Monkey Cage Blog, October 7, 2014.

95. Rod Nordland, "Iraq's Sunni Militants Take to Social Media to Advance Their Cause and Intimidate," *New York Times*, June 28, 2014. For more on the group's use of social media, see Rita Katz, "Follow ISIS on Twitter: A Special Report on the Use of Social Media by Jihadists," *Insite Blog on Terrorism & Extremism*, June 26, 2014.

96. Jacob Siegel, "Has ISIS Peaked as a Military Power?" *Daily Beast*, October 22, 2014.

97. Terence McCoy, "How ISIS Leader Abu Bakr al-Baghdadi Became the World's Most Powerful Jihadist Leader," *The Washington Post*, June 11, 2014.

98. Tim Arango and Eric Schmitt, "U.S. Actions in Iraq Fueled the Rise of a Rebel," *The New York Times*, August 10, 2014.

99. For more on Shishani, see Will Cathcart, "The Secret Life of an ISIS Warlord," *Daily Beast*, October 27, 2014.

100. "The Anatomy of ISIS: How the 'Islamic State' is Run, from Oil to Beheadings," *CNN*, September 18, 2014.

101. Ben Hubbard and Eric Schmitt, "Military Skill and Terrorist Technique Fuel Success of ISIS," *The New York Times*, August 27, 2014.

102. "How ISIS Works," *The New York Times*, September 16, 2014.

103. Ben Hubbard and Eric Schmitt, "Military Skill and Terrorist Technique Fuel Success of ISIS," *The New York Times*, August 27, 2014. See also, Ruth Sherlock, "Inside the Leadership of Islamic State: How the New 'Caliphate' Is Run," *Daily Telegraph*, July 9, 2014.

104. David D. Kirkpatrick, "ISIS' Harsh Brand of Islam is Rooted in Austere Saudi Creed," *The New York Times*, September 24, 2014.

105. ISIS has been especially brutal in its treatment of women. Aki Peritz and Tara Maller, "The Islamic State of Sexual Violence," *Foreign Policy*, September 16, 2014.

106. David Motadel, "The Ancestors of ISIS," *New York Times*, September 23, 2014.

107. Daveed Gartenstein-Ross and Amichal Magen, "The Jihadist Governance Dilemma," *The Washington Post* Monkey Cage, July 18, 2014.

108. Lawrence Rubin, "Who's Afraid of an Islamic State," *Washington Post* Monkey Cage, October 2, 2014. See also, Ben Connable, "Defeating the Islamic State in Iraq," Congressional testimony presented before the Senate Foreign Relations Committee on September 17, 2014, RAND Corporation, CT-418, p. 9.

109. For more on the falling out between ISIS and Al Qaeda, see J.M. Berger, "The Islamic State vs. al Qaeda," *Foreign Policy*, September 2, 2014.

110. William McCants, "State of Confusion," *Foreign Affairs*, September 10, 2014.

111. David Ignatius, "The Manual That Chillingly Foreshadows the Islamic State," *Washington Post*, September 25, 2014.

112. Aaron Y. Zelin, "The Islamic State's First Colony in Libya," The Washington Institute for Near East Policy, Policy Watch 2325, October 10, 2014.

113. Aaron Y. Zelin, "The War Between ISIS and al-Qaeda for Supremacy of the Global Jihadist Movement," The Washington Institute for Near East Policy, No. 20, June 2014, p. 6.

114. Robin Simcox, "ISIS' Western Ambitions," *Foreign Affairs*, June 30, 2014.

115. Daniel Byman, "The State of Terror," *Slate*, June 13, 2014.

116. Aaron Y. Zelin, "ISIS is Dead, Long Live the Islamic State," *Foreign Policy*, June 30, 2014.

117. Graeme Wood, "What ISIS Really Wants," *The Atlantic,* March 2015.

118. "Islamic State Fighter Estimate Triples," *British Broadcasting Corporation (BBC)*, September 12, 2014.

119. Seth G. Jones, "Jihadist Sanctuaries in Syria and Iraq: Implications for the United States," presented to the Committee on Homeland Security Subcommittee on Counterterrorism and Intelligence, U.S. House of Representatives, July 24, 2014, p. 1.

120. The United States has been able to identify Americans fighting for ISIS and other Syrian insurgent organizations through analyzing intelligence collected from travel records, family members, intercepted electronic communications, social media postings and surveillance efforts of Americans living overseas who have expressed an interest in traveling to Syria. Eric Schmitt, "U.S. Is Trying to Counter ISIS' Efforts to Lure Alienated Young Muslims," *New York Times*, October 4, 2014.

121. "It Ain't Half Hot Here, Mum: Why and How Westerners Go to Fight in Syria and Iraq," August 30, 2014.

122. Somini Sengupta, "Nations Trying to Stop Their Citizens from Going to Middle East to Fight for ISIS," *New York Times*, September 12, 2014.

123. Jytte Klausen, "They're Coming: Measuring the Threat from Returning Jihadists," *Foreign Affairs*, October 1, 2014.

124. "Foreign Fighters Flow into Syria," *Washington Post*, October 11, 2014. As of late October 2014, more Tunisian foreign fighters had joined the Islamic State than fighters from any other country outside of Iraq and Syria. David D. Kirkpatrick, "New Freedoms in Tunisia Drive Support for ISIS," *New York Times*, October 21, 2014.

125. Peter Neumann, "Suspects into Collaborators," *London Review of Books*, Vol. 36, No. 7, April 3, 2014.

126. Tim Arango and Eric Schmitt, "Escaped Inmates from Iraq Fuel Syrian Insurgency," *New York Times*, February 12, 2014.

127. Kate Brannen, "Children of the Caliphate," *Foreign Policy*, October 27, 2014.

128. "The Anatomy of ISIS How the 'Islamic State' is Run, from Oil to Beheadings," *CNN*, September 18, 2014.

129. Aaron Y. Zelin, "When Jihadists Learn How to Help," *Washington Post* Monkey Cage, May 7, 2014.

130. Benjamin Bahney et al., *An Economic Analysis of the Financial Records of al-Qa'ida in Iraq*, Santa Monica, CA: RAND Corp., 2010; for more micro-level data on the group's financial bureaucracy, see Benjamin W. Bahney et al., "Insurgent Compensation: Evidence from Iraq," *American Economic Review*, Vol. 103, No. 3, 2013, pp. 518–522.

131. Howard J. Shatz, "To Defeat the Islamic State, Follow the Money," *Politico*, September 10, 2014.

132. Janine Davidson and Emerson Brooking, "ISIS Hasn't Gone Anywhere—And It's Getting Stronger," Council on Foreign Relations, Defense in Depth, July 24, 2014.

133. Mariam Karouny, "In Northeast Syria, Islamic State Builds a Government," *Reuters*, September 4, 2014.

134. For more, see Laura Ryan, "ISIS is Better Than Al-Qaeda at Using the Internet," *Defense One*, October 10, 2014.

135. Ali Fisher and Nico Prucha, "ISIS Is Winning the Online Jihad Against the West," *Daily Beast*, October 1, 2014.

136. Some of the hashtags promoted by ISIS included #AllEyesOnISIS and #OneBillionMuslimCampaigntoSupportIS.

137. Lorraine Ali, "Islamic State's Soft Weapon of Choice: Social Media," *Los Angeles Times*, September 22, 2014.

138. Ezzeldeen Khalil, "Gone Viral: Islamic State's Evolving Media Strategy," *Jane's Intelligence Review*, October 2014, p. 15.

139. Josh Kovensky, "ISIS's New Mag Looks Like a New York Glossy—With Pictures of Mutilated Bodies," *New Republic*, August 25, 2014. The name "Dabiq" was chosen for the magazine because Dabiq is a small village in Syria that is believed by some ISIS fighters to be the place where one of the final battles of the Islamic apocalypse will take place. See William McCants, "ISIS Fantasies of an Apocalyptic Showdown in Northern Syria," Brookings Institution, October 3, 2014.

140. Harleen K. Gambhir, "Dabiq: The Strategic Messaging of the Islamic State," *Institute for the Study of War*, August 15, 2014, p. 2.

141. James P. Farwell, "The Media Strategy of ISIS," *Survival*, Vol. 56, No. 6, December 2014/January 2015, pp. 49–55.

142. Marc Lynch et al., "Syria's Socially Mediated Civil War," United States Institute of Peace (USIP), Peaceworks No. 91, 2014, p. 15.

143. Scott Shane and Ben Hubbard, "ISIS Displaying a Deft Command of Varied Media," *New York Times*, August 30, 2014.

144. Philipp Holtmann, "The IS-Caliphate: What Should Be Done to Prevent It from Spinning Out of Control?" *Perspectives on Terrorism*, Vol. 8, No. 5, October 2014, pp. 127–128.

145. Keith Johnson and Jamila Trindle, "Treasury's War on the Islamic State," *Foreign Policy*, October 23, 2014.

146. Howard J. Shatz, "To Defeat the Islamic State, Follow the Money," *Politico*, September 10, 2014.

147. Charles Lister, "Cutting Off ISIS' Cash Flow," Brookings Institution, October 24, 2014.

148. Jamie Detmer, "How to Cut Off ISIS Terror Tycoons," *Daily Beast*, September 26, 2014.

149. Ibid.

150. Michael S. Schmidt, "U.S. Steps Up Fight to Block ISIS Volunteers," *New York Times*, October 8, 2014.

151. Marc Frey, "ISIS, Foreign Terrorist Fighters, and the Value of the Visa Waiver Program," *Center for Strategic & International Studies (CSIS)*, October 8, 2014.

152. Elizabeth Dickinson, "The Case Against Qatar," *Foreign Policy*, September 30, 2014.

153. Matthew Levitt, "Qatar's Not-So-Charitable Record on Terror Finance," *The Hill*, September 24, 2014.

154. Associated Press, "New Sanctions Proposed for the Islamic State Group Oil Trading," February 6, 2015.

155. Julie Hirschfeld Davis, "U.S. Strikes Cut Into ISIS Oil Revenues, Treasury Official Says," *New York Times*, October 23, 2014.

156. Austin Long, "The Anbar Awakening," *Survival*, Vol. 50, No. 2, April 2008, pp. 67–94.

157. Matthew Levitt, "Show Me the Money: Targeting the Islamic State's Bottom Line," *Homeland Security Policy Institute*, October 1, 2014.

158. Michael Eisenstadt, "Defeating ISIS: A Strategy for a Resilient Adversary and an Intractable Conflict," The Washington Institute for Near East Policy, No. 20, November 2014.

CHAPTER 9

1. Michael Freeman, "Introduction to Financing Terrorism: Case Studies," in Michael Freeman, *Financing Terrorism: Case Studies*, Farnham: Ashgate, 2012, p.3.

2. See Patrick B. Johnston, "Does Decapitation Work? Assessing the Effectiveness of Leadership Targeting in Counterinsurgency Campaigns," *International Security*, Vol. 36, No. 4, Spring 2012, pp. 47–79.

3. Sudarsan Raghavan, "As the U.S. Mission Winds Down, Afghan Insurgency Grows More Complex," *Washington Post*, February 13, 2015.

4. Victor Comras, "Al Qaeda Finances and Funding to Affiliated Groups," in Jeanne K. Giraldo and Harold A. Trinkunas, *Terrorism Financing and State Responses: A Comparative Perspective*, Stanford: Stanford University Press, 2007, p. 127.

5. Juan Miguel del Cid Gomez, "A Financial Profile of the Terrorism of Al-Qaeda and Its Affiliates," *Perspectives on Terrorism*, Vol. 4, No. 4, October 2010, p. 17.

6. Aaron Brantly, "Financing Terror Bit by Bit," *CTC Sentinel*, October 2014, Vol. 7, No. 10, p. 1.

7. Michael T. Flynn and Simone A. Ledeen, "Pay for Play: Countering Threat Financing," *Joint Forces Quarterly*, No. 56, 1st Quarter 2010, p. 123.

8. Tom Keatinge, "What Role Does CFT Play in International Security? Can It Be Deemed Effective?" Dissertation submitted to King's College London for MA in Intelligence & International Security, August 2012, p. 8.

9. Matthew Levitt, "Al-Qa'ida's Finances: Evidence of Organizational Decline?" *CTC Sentinel*, Vol. 1, No. 5, April 2008, p. 7.

10. Juan Miguel del Cid Gomez, "A Financial Profile of the Terrorism of Al-Qaeda and Its Affiliates," *Perspectives on Terrorism*, Vol. 4, No. 4, October 2010, p. 10.

11. Ibid., p. 7.

12. *The Al Qaeda Manual*, Department of Justice, p. 22.

13. Ibid., p. 18.

14. Keatinge, "What Role Does CFT Play?" p. 29.

15. Jacob N. Shapiro and David A. Siegel, "Underfunding in Terrorist Organizations," *International Studies Quarterly*, Vol. 51, No. 2, 2007, p. 408.

16. Angel Rabasa et al., *Beyond Al-Qaeda: The Global Jihadist Movement, Part I*, Santa Monica, CA: RAND Corp., 2006, pp. 60–61.

17. Juan Miguel del Cid Gomez, "A Financial Profile of the Terrorism of Al-Qaeda and Its Affiliates," *Perspectives on Terrorism*, Vol. 4, No. 4, October 2010, p. 15.

18. On Qatar in particular, see David Andrew Weinberg, "Qatar and Terror Finance, Part I: Negligence," Foundation for Defense of Democracies, Center on Sanctions & Illicit Finance, December 2014.

19. Angel Rabasa et al., *Beyond Al-Qaeda: The Global Jihadist Movement, Part I*, Santa Monica, CA: RAND Corp., 2006, p. 62.

20. Keatinge, "What Role Does CFT Play," pp. 33–34.

21. Ibid., p. 30. It is worth nothing that there is another interpretation, which is that the French or Germans had infiltrated this apartment building.

22. Juan C. Zarate, *Treasury's War: The Unleashing of a New Era of Financial Warfare*, New York: Public Affairs, 2013, p. 80.

23. Basile, p. 170.

24. Phil Williams, "From the New Middle Ages to the New Dark Ages: The Decline of the State and U.S. Strategy," United States Army War College Strategic Studies Institute, 2008, p. 13.

25. Rohan Kumar Gunaratna and Arabinda Acharya, "Terrorist Finance and the Criminal Underground," in Michael A. Innes, ed., *Denial of Sanctuary: Understanding Terrorist Safe Havens*, Westport, CT: Praeger Security International, 2007, p. 99.

26. David E. Kaplan, "Paying for Terror: How Jihadist Groups Are Using Organized Crime Tactics and Profits to Finance Attacks on Targets Around the Globe," *U.S. News & World Report*, November 27, 2005.

27. Timothy Wittig, *Understanding Terrorist Finance*, New York: Palgrave Macmillan, 2011, p. 190.

28. Moises Naim, "Mafia States: Organized Crime Takes Office," *Foreign Affairs*, May/June 2012, Vol. 91, No. 3, pp. 100–112.

29. "Challenges and Opportunities in Countering Threat Finance," Praescient Analytics, October 2012, p. 3.

30. Matthew Levitt and Michael Jacobson, "The Money Trail: Finding, Following, and Freezing Terrorist Finances," *The Washington Institute for Near East Policy*, Policy Focus #89, November 2008, pp. 38–39.

31. Diana L. Ohlbaum, "Terrorism, Inc.: How Shell Companies Aid Terrorism, Crime and Corruption," Open Society Foundations, October 2013, p. 1.

32. Richard H. Shultz, Jr. et al., "Armed Groups: A Tier One Security Priority," Institute for National Security Studies, United States Air Force, INSS Occasional Paper No. 57, September 2004.

33. Robert J. Bunker and John P. Sullivan, "Integrating Feral Cities and Third Phase Cartels/Third Generation Gangs Research: The Rise of Criminal (Narco) City Networks and BlackFor," *Small Wars & Insurgencies*, Vol. 22, No. 5, 2011, p. 765.

34. Juan Miguel del Cid Gomez, "A Financial Profile of the Terrorism of Al-Qaeda and Its Affiliates," *Perspectives on Terrorism*, Vol. 4, No. 4, October 2010, p. 11.

35. Thomas J. Bierstecker and Sue E. Eckert, eds., *Countering the Financing of Terrorism*, London: Routledge, 2008, p. 2.

36. Robert J. Bunker, "Fighting Irregular Fighters: Defeating Violent Non-State Actors," *Parameters*, Vol. 43, No. 4, Winter 2013–2014, p. 64.

37. Chad C. Serena, *It Takes More Than a Network: The Iraqi Insurgency and Organizational Adaptation*, Stanford: Stanford University Press, 2014, p. 143.

38. Even while terrorist attacks *can be* inexpensive, the author recognizes the difference between conducting a one-off attack and the more expensive aspects of terrorism, including training, preparation, transportation, and so on.

39. Angel Rabasa et al., *Beyond Al-Qaeda: The Global Jihadist Movement, Part I*, Santa Monica, CA: RAND Corp., 2006, p. 60.

40. Kevin D. Stringer, "Counter Threat Finance (CTF): Grasping the Eel," *Military Power Revue*, No. 2, 2013.

41. Moises Naim, *The End of Power: From Boardrooms to Battlefields and Churches to States, Why Being in Charge Isn't What It Used to Be*, New York: Basic, 2013, p. 107.

42. Emilie Oftedal, "The Financing of Jihadi Terrorist Cells in Europe," Norwegian Defence Research Establishment (FFI), January 2015, pp.3–7.

43. Data from Joshua Prober, "Accounting for Terror: Debunking the Paradigm of Inexpensive Terrorism," Washington Institute for Near East Policy, Policy Watch 1041, November 1, 2005.

44. Phil Williams, "In Cold Blood: The Madrid Bombings," *Perspectives on Terrorism*, June 2008, p. 22. For a more in-depth analysis of the Madrid bombings, see Phil Williams, "The Madrid Train Bombings," in Paul Shemella, ed., *Fighting Back: What Governments Can Do About Terrorism*, Stanford: Stanford University Press, 2011, pp. 298–316.

45. Bill Chappel, "ISIS Seen Profiting From Informal Money System in Spain," *NPR*, February 10, 2015. See also, Jose Maria Irujo, "Network of 250 Spanish Butchers and Phone Shops Funding Jihadists in Syria," *El Pais*, February 6, 2015.

46. Eric Schmitt, Mark Mazzetti and Rukmini Callimachi, "Disputed Claims Over Qaeda Role in Paris Attacks," *New York Times*, January 14, 2015.

47. Keatinge, "What Role Does CFT Play?" pp. 23–25.

48. Zarate, *Treasury's War*, p. 430.

49. Mark Rice-Oxley, "Why Terror Financing Is So Tough to Track Down," *The Christian Science Monitor*, March 8, 2006. See also, Keatinge, "What Role Does CFT Play?" p. 18.

50. Juan Miguel del Cid Gomez, "A Financial Profile of the Terrorism of Al-Qaeda and Its Affiliates," *Perspectives on Terrorism*, Vol. 4, Iss.4, October 2010, p. 3.

51. Randall Mikkelsen, "Bankers Say 'Derisking' Underway Amid Sanctions Crackdown; That's the Point, U.S. Regulators Say," *Reuters*, October 3, 2014.

52. "Hitting at Terrorists, Hurting Businesses," *The Economist*, June 14, 2014. See also, "Poor Correspondents," *The Economist*, June 14, 2014.

53. Tom Keatinge, "Breaking the Banks: The Financial Consequences of Counterterrorism," *Foreign Affairs*, June 26, 2014.

54. See Jennifer E. Carter, "Emerging DoD Role in the Interagency Counter Threat Finance Mission," U.S. Army War College Strategy Research Project, 2012; Matthew Levitt, "Follow the Money: Leveraging Financial Intelligence to Combat Transnational Threats," *Georgetown Journal of International Affairs*, Winter/Spring 2011, pp. 34–43; and J. Edward Conway, "Analysis in Combat: The Deployed Threat Finance Analyst," *Small Wars Journal*, July 4, 2012.

55. Perl, p. 255.

56. Laura K. Donohue, "Anti-Terrorist Finance in the United Kingdom and United States," *Michigan Journal of International Law*, Vol. 27, Winter 2006, p. 405.

57. Sue E. Eckert and Thomas J. Biersteker, "(Mis)Measuring Success in Countering the Financing of Terrorism," in Peter Andreas and Kelly M. Greenhill, eds., *Sex, Drugs, and Body Counts: The Politics of Numbers in Global Crime and Conflict*, Ithaca: Cornell University Press, 2010, p. 260.

58. Scott Helfstein with John Solomon, "Risky Business: The Global Threat Network and the Politics of Contraband," Combating Terrorism Center, May 2014, p. 29.

59. Timothy Wittig, *Understanding Terrorist Finance*, New York: Palgrave Macmillan, 2011, p. 112.

60. For more, see Douglas Farah's chapter, "Fixers, Super Fixers, and Shadow Facilitators: How Networks Connect," in Michael Miklaucic and Jacqueline Brewer, *Convergence: Illicit Networks and National Security in the Age of Globalization*, Washington, DC: National Defense University (NDU) Press, 2013.

61. Shima D. Keene, "Operationalizing Counter Threat Finance Strategies," *Letort Papers*, Carlisle, PA: Strategic Studies Institute (SSI) and United States Army War College (USAWC) Press, December 2014, p.21; see also, Shima D. Keene, *Threat Finance: Disconnecting the Lifeline of Organised Crime and Terrorism*, U.K.: Gower Publishing Co., 2013.

62. Juan Miguel del Cid Gomez, "A Financial Profile of the Terrorism of Al-Qaeda and Its Affiliates," *Perspectives on Terrorism*, Vol. 4, No. 4, October 2010, p. 17.

Bibliography

Aaron, David. *In Their Own Words: Voices of Jihad*, Santa Monica, Calif.: RAND Corp., 2008.

Aas, Katja Franko. *Globalization & Crime*, Los Angeles: Sage, 2013.

Abdullah, Ibrahim and Patrick Muana. "The Revolutionary United Front of Sierra Leone: A Revolt of the Lumpenproletariat," in Christopher Clapham, ed., *African Guerillas*, Oxford: James Currey, 1998.

Abocar, A. "Canada Police Say Tamil Gangs Funding Rebels," *Reuters*, March 28, 2000.

AbuKhalil, As'ad. "Ideology and Practice of Hizballah in Lebanon:" Islamization of Leninist Organizational Principles. pp. 390–403. *Middle Eastern Studies*, Vol. 27, No. 3, July 1991.

Achakzai, Matiullah. "Taliban Code of Conduct Seeks to Win Heart, Minds," *Associated Press*, August 3, 2010.

Acharya, Arabinda, Syed Adnan Ali Shah Bukhari, and Sadia Sulaiman. "Making Money in the Mayhem: Funding Taliban Insurrection in the Tribal Areas of Pakistan," *Studies in Conflict & Terrorism*, Vol. 32, No. 2, 2009, pp. 95–108.

Adams, James. *The Financing of Terror: How the Groups That Are Terrorizing the World Get the Money to Do It*, New York: Simon and Shuster, 1986.

Addis, Casey L. and Christopher M. Blanchard, Congressional Research Service (CRS) Report, January 3, 2011.

Ahram, Ariel I. "Can ISIS Overcome the Insurgency Resource Curse?" *Washington Post* Monkey Cage, July 2, 2014.

Ahram, Ariel I. "The Dangerous Mixture of Oil and Water in Iraq," *Political Violence @ a Glance*, August 18, 2014.

Alagha, Joseph. *The Shifts in Hizbullah's Ideology: Religious Ideology, Political Ideology, and Political Program*, Leiden: Amsterdam University Press, 2006.

Albanese, Jay S. *Transnational Crime and the 21st Century: Criminal Enterprise, Corruption, and Opportunity*, Oxford: Oxford University Press, 2011.

Albanese, Jay and Philip Reichel, eds. *Transnational Organized Crime: An Overview from Six Continents*, Los Angeles: Sage, 2014.

Ali, Lorraine. "Islamic State's Soft Weapon of Choice: Social Media," *Los Angeles Times*, September 22, 2014.

Alonso, Rogelio. "Irish Republican Thinking Toward the Utility of Violence," *Studies in Conflict and Terrorism*, Vol. 24, No. 2, 2001, pp. 131–144.

Andreas, Peter. *Blue Helmets and Black Markets: The Business of Survival in the Siege of Sarajevo*, Ithaca: Cornell University Press, 2008.

Anonymous, *Imperial Hubris: Why the West If Losing the War on Terror*, Washington, DC: Brassey's, Inc., 2004.

Appel, Yoav. "Israel: Bombers Tried to Use Cyanide," *Associated Press*, June 5, 2002.

Arango, Tim. "Uneasy Alliance Gives Insurgents an Edge in Iraq," *New York Times*, June 18, 2014.

Arango, Tim and Eric Schmitt. "Escaped Inmates from Iraq Fuel Syrian Insurgency," *New York Times*, February 12, 2014.

Arango, Tim and Eric Schmitt. "U.S. Actions in Iraq Fueled the Rise of a Rebel," *New York Times*, August 10, 2014.

Argo, Nichole. "The Role of Social Context in Terrorist Attacks," *Chronicle of Higher Education*, January 13, 2006.

Arias, Enrique D. "Understanding Criminal Networks, Political Order, and Politics in Latin America," in Anne L. Clunan and Harold A. Trinkunas, eds., *Ungoverned Spaces: Alternatives to State Authority in Era of Softened Sovereignty*, Stanford: Stanford University Press, 2010.

Aryasinha, Ravinatha. "Terrorism, the LTTE and the Conflict in Sri Lanka," *Conflict, Security, & Development*, Vol. 1, No. 2, 2001, pp. 25–50.

Asfar, Shahid et al. "The Taliban: An Organizational Analysis," *Military Review*, May/June 2008, pp. 58–73.

Bacon, Esther. "Balkan Trafficking in Historical Perspective," in Kimberley L. Thachuk, ed., *Transnational Threats: Smuggling and Trafficking in Arms, Drugs, and Human Life*, Westport, CT: Praeger Security International, 2007.

Bahney, Benjamin et al. *An Economic Analysis of the Financial Records of al-Qa'ida in Iraq*, Santa Monica, Calif.: RAND Corp., 2010.

Bahney, Benjamin W. et al. "Insurgent Compensation: Evidence from Iraq," *American Economic Review: Papers & Proceedings*, Vol. 103, No. 3, 2013, pp. 518–522.

Bajoria, Jayshree. *The Sri Lankan Conflict*, Council on Foreign Relations Backgrounder: May 18, 2009.

Balasingham, Adele S. *Liberation Tigers and Tamil Eelam Freedom Struggle*, Madras: Political Committee, LTTE, 1983.

Baracsky, Daniel. "The Evolutionary Path of Hamas: Examining the Role of Political Pragmatism in State Building and Activism," *Terrorism & Political Violence*, 2014, pp. 1–17.

Barfield, Thomas. *Afghanistan: A Cultural and Political History*, Princeton, NJ: Princeton University Press, 2010.

Basile, Mark. "Going to the Source: Why Al-Qaeda's Financial Network Is Likely to Withstand the Current War on Terrorist Financing," *Studies in Conflict & Terrorism*, Vol. 27, No. 3, 2004, pp. 169–185.

Bazzi, Mohamad. "Lebanon: Hezbollah's Way," *GlobalPost*, August 7, 2010.

Becker, Jo. "Beirut Bank Seen as a Hub of Hezbollah's Financing," *New York Times,* December 13, 2011.

Beecher, Lionel. "What Sri Lanka Can Teach Us about COIN," *Small Wars Journal,* August 27, 2010.

Beith, Malcolm. "HSBC Report Shows Difficulty of Stopping Money Launderers," *Daily Beast,* July 19, 2012.

Bell, J. Bowyer. "Revolutionary Dynamics: The Inherent Inefficiency of the Underground," *Terrorism and Political Violence,* Vol. 2, No. 4, 1990, pp. 193–211.

Bell, Stewart. "Canada a Key Source of Tamil Tiger Funding," *National Post,* July 20, 2009.

Berg Harpviken, Kristian. "The Transnationalization of the Taliban," *International Area Studies Review,* Vol. 15, No. 3, 2012, pp. 203–229.

Bergen, Peter. *Holy Terror, Inc.: Inside the Secret World of Osama bin Laden,* New York: Free Press, 2001.

Bergen, Peter and Emily Schneider. "Now ISIS Has Drones?" *CNN.com,* August 25, 2014.

Berger, James M. "The Islamic State vs. al Qaeda," *Foreign Policy,* September 2, 2014.

Bhasin, Tavishi and Maia C. Hallward. "Hamas as a Political Party: Democratization in the Palestinian Territories," *Terrorism and Political Violence,* Vol. 25, No. 1, 2013, pp. 75–93.

Bierstecker, Thomas J. and Sue E. Eckert, eds. *Countering the Financing of Terrorism,* London: Routledge, 2008.

Bishop, Patrick and Eamonn Mallie. *The Provisional IRA,* London: Corgi Books, 1992.

Blair, Dennis C. "Annual Threat Assessment of the US Intelligence Community," Testimony before the Senate Select Committee on Intelligence, February 2, 2010.

Blanford, Nicholas. *Warriors of God: Inside Hezbollah's Thirty-Year Struggle against Israel,* New York: Random House, 2011.

Bloom, Mia. *Dying to Kill: The Allure of Suicide Terror,* New York: Columbia University Press, 2005.

Boghardt, Lori P. "The Terrorist Funding Disconnect with Qatar and Kuwait," *Washington Institute for Near East Policy,* Policywatch 2247, May 2, 2014.

Boyle, Michael P. et al. "Expressive Responses to News Stories about Extremist Groups: A Framing Experiment," *Journal of Communication,* Vol. 56, No. 2, 2006, pp. 271–288.

Brachman, Jarret. "The Worst of the Worst," *Foreign Policy,* January 22, 2010.

Brahimi, Brahimi. "The Taliban's Evolving Ideology," London School of Economics Global Governance Working Paper, February 2010.

Brandt, Ben. "The Taliban's Conduct of Intelligence and Counterintelligence," *Combating Terrorism Center Sentinel,* Vol. 4, No. 6, June 2011, pp. 19–23.

Brannen, Kate. "Children of the Caliphate," *Foreign Policy,* October 27, 2014.

Brantly, Aaron. "Financing Terror Bit by Bit," *CTC Sentinel,* Vol. 7, No. 10, October 2014, pp. 1–5.

Brathwaite, Robert. "The Electoral Terrorist: Terror Groups and Democratic Participation," *Terrorism and Political Violence* Vol. 25, No. 1, 2013, pp. 53–74.

Bricknell, Samantha. "Misuse of the Nonprofit Sector for Money Laundering and Terrorist Financing," *Trends & Issues in Crime and Criminal Justice,* No. 424, September 2011, pp. 1–6.

Bronstein, Scott and Drew Griffin. "Self-Funded and Deep-Rooted: How ISIS Makes Its Millions," *CNN.com*, October 7, 2014.

Brooke, Steven. "Assumptions and Agendas in the Study of Islamic Social Service Provision," in *Islamist Social Services*, Project on Middle East Political Science (POMEPS), October 15, 2014.

Broschk, Florian. *Inciting the Believers to Fight: A Closer Look at the Rhetoric of the Afghan Jihad*, Afghanistan Analysts Network, February 2011.

Brown, Vahid and Don Rassler. *Fountainhead of Jihad: The Haqqani Nexus, 1973–2012*, Oxford: Oxford University Press, 2013.

Bunker, Robert J. "Fighting Irregular Fighters: Defeating Violent Non-State Actors," *Parameters*, Vol. 43, No. 4, Winter 2013–2014, pp. 57–65.

Bunker, Robert J. and John P. Sullivan. "Integrating Feral Cities and Third Phase Cartels/Third Generation Gangs Research: The Rise of Criminal (Narco) City Networks and BlackFor," *Small Wars & Insurgencies*, Vol. 22, No. 5, 2011, pp. 764–786.

Burke, Jason. *Al-Qaeda: The True Story of Radical Islam*, London: I.B. Tauris, 2003.

Byman, Daniel. *Deadly Connections: States that Sponsor Terrorism*, New York: Cambridge University Press, 2005.

Byman, Daniel. "Passive Sponsors of Terrorism," *Survival*, Vol. 47, No. 4, Winter 2005–2006, pp. 117–144.

Byman, Daniel. "Understanding Proto-Insurgencies," Santa Monica, Calif.: RAND Corp, 2007.

Byman, Daniel. "Talking with Insurgents: A Guide for the Perplexed," *Washington Quarterly*, Vol. 32, No. 2, 2009, pp. 125–137.

Byman, Daniel. *A High Price: The Triumphs & Failures of Israeli Counterterrorism*, Oxford: Oxford University Press, 2011.

Byman, Daniel. "The Lebanese Hezbollah and Israeli Counterterrorism," *Studies in Conflict and Terrorism*, Vol. 34, No. 12, 2011, pp. 917–941.

Byman, Daniel L. "Breaking the Bonds between Al-Qa'ida and Its Affiliate Organizations," Brookings Institution Analysis Paper, No. 27, August 2012.

Byman, Daniel. "Is Hamas Winning?" *Washington Quarterly*, Vol. 36, No. 3, Summer 2013, pp. 63–76.

Byman, Daniel. "The State of Terror," *Slate*, June 13, 2014.

Byman, Daniel and Kenneth M. Pollack. "Let Us Now Praise Great Men: Bringing the Statesman Back In," *International Security*, Vol. 25, No. 4, 2001, pp. 107–146.

Byman, Daniel and Jeremy Shapiro. "Homeward Bound? Don't Hype the Threat of Returning Jihadists," *Foreign Affairs*, September 30, 2014.

Byman, Daniel et al. *Trends in Outside Support for Insurgent Movements*, Santa Monica, Calif.: RAND Corp, 2001.

Byman, Daniel. "Appendix B: The LTTE's Military-Related Procurement," *Outside Support*, 2001, p. 121.

Callimachi, Rukmini. "Ransoming Citizens, Europe Becomes Al Qaeda's Patron," *New York Times*, July 29, 2014.

Cambanis, Thanassis. *A Privilege to Die: Inside Hezbollah's Legions and Their Endless War against Israel*, New York: Simon and Schuster, 2010.

Cambanis, Thanassis. "Stronger Hezbollah Emboldened for Fights Ahead," *New York Times*, October 6, 2010.

Carter, David B. "A Blessing or a Curse? State Support for Terrorist Groups," *International Organization,* Vol. 66, No. 1, January 2012, pp. 129–151.

Carter, Jennifer E. *Emerging DoD Role in the Interagency Counter Threat Finance Mission,* U.S. Army War College Strategy Research Project, 2012.

Casebeer, William D. and James A. Russell. "Storytelling and Terrorism: Towards a Comprehensive 'Counter-Narrative Strategy,'" *Strategic Insights,* Vol. IV, No. 3, March 2005.

Cathcart, Will. "The Secret Life of an ISIS Warlord," *Daily Beast,* October 27, 2014.

Chaim Levinson, "Shin Bet Probe Reveals Scope of Hamas Money Laundering through Chinese Banks," *Haaretz,* September 29, 2013.

Chalk, Peter. "Liberation Tigers of Tamil Eelam's (LTTE) International Organization and Operations—A Preliminary Analysis," Canadian Security Intelligence Service, Commentary No. 77, Winter 1999.

Chalk, Peter. "The Liberation Tigers of Tamil Eelam Insurgency in Sri Lanka," in Rajat Ganguly and Ian MacDuff, eds., *Ethnic Conflict and Secessionism in South and Southeast Asia,* London: Sage, 2003.

Chang, Jung. *Mao: The Unknown Story,* New York: Knopf, 2005.

Chivers, C.J. "Afghanistan's Hidden Taliban Government," *New York Times,* February 6, 2011.

Chivers, C.J. "After Retreat, Iraqi Soldiers Fault Officers," *New York Times,* July 1, 2014.

Chivers, C.J. "ISIS' Ammunition Is Shown to Have Origins in U.S. and China," *New York Times,* October 5, 2014.

Christia, Fotini and Michael Semple. "Flipping the Taliban: How to Win in Afghanistan," *Foreign Affairs,* Vol. 88, No. 4, July/August 2009, pp. 34–45.

Chung, Christian. "The Killer Tiger Roared: A Strategic Analysis of Sri Lankan 'Kinetic' Counterinsurgency and Its Theoretical Implications," *Small Wars Journal,* December 15, 2010.

Claessen, Erik A. "S.W.E.T. and Blood: Essential Services in the Battle between Insurgents and Counterinsurgents," *Military Review,* November/December 2007, pp. 91–98.

Clunan, Anne L. "U.S. and International Responses to Terrorist Financing," in Jeanne K. Giraldo and Harold A. Trinkunas, eds., *Terrorism Financing and State Responses: A Comparative Perspective,* Stanford: Stanford University Press, 2007.

Clunan, Anne L. and Harold A. Trinkunas, eds. *Ungoverned Spaces: Alternatives to State Authority in Era of Softened Sovereignty,* Stanford: Stanford University Press, 2010.

Clutterbuck, Richard. "Peru, Cocaine, Terrorism, and Corruption," *International Relations,* Vol. 12, No. 5, 1995, pp. 77–92.

Cockayne, James and Phil Williams. *The Invisible Tide: Towards an International Strategy to Deal with Drug Trafficking through West Africa,* New York: International Peace Institute, October 2009.

Coll, Steve. *Ghost Wars: The Secret History of the CIA, Afghanistan and Bin Laden from the Soviet Invasion to September 10, 2001,* New York: Penguin, 2004.

Collier, Paul and Anke Hoeffler. "Greed and Grievance in Civil War," *Oxford Economic Papers,* Vol. 56, 2004, pp. 563–595.

Collins, Catherine and Ashraf Ali. "Financing the Taliban: Tracking the Dollars behind the Insurgencies in Afghanistan and Pakistan," New America Foundation Counterterrorism Strategy Initiative Policy Paper April 2010.

Comras, Victor. "Al Qaeda Finances and Funding to Affiliated Groups," in Jeanne K. Giraldo and Harold A. Trinkunas, eds., *Terrorism Financing and State Responses: A Comparative Perspective*, Stanford: Stanford University Press, 2007.

Connable, Ben. "Defeating the Islamic State in Iraq," Congressional testimony presented before the Senate Foreign Relations Committee on September 17, 2014, RAND Corporation, CT-418.

Connable, Ben and Martin Libicki. *How Insurgencies End*, Santa Monica, Calif.: RAND Corp., 2010.

Conway, Edward J. "Analysis in Combat: The Deployed Threat Finance Analyst," *Small Wars Journal*, July 4, 2012.

Coogan, Tim Pat. *The IRA*, New York: Palgrave, 2000.

Cookman, Colin and Caroline Wadhams. *Governance in Afghanistan: Looking Ahead to What We Leave Behind*, Washington, DC: Center for American Progress, May 2010.

Cordesman, Anthony. *The Real Center of Gravity in the War against the Islamic State*, Center for Strategic and International Studies (CSIS), September 30, 2014.

Cordesman, Anthony H. et al. *Winning in Afghanistan: Creating Effective Afghan Security Forces*, Washington, DC: Center for Strategic and International Studies, May 2009.

Cornell, Svante. "Narcotics and Armed Conflict: Interaction and Implications," *Studies in Conflict & Terrorism*, Vol. 30, No. 3, 2007, pp. 207–227.

Cragin, R. Kim. "Early History of Al-Qa'ida," *Historic Journal*, Vol. 51, No. 4, December 2008, pp. 1047–1067.

Cragin, Kim. "Al Qaeda Confronts Hamas: Divisions in the Sunni *Jihadist* Movement and Its Implications for U.S. Policy," *Studies in Conflict & Terrorism*, Vol. 32, No. 7, 2009, pp. 576–590.

Cragin, Kim and Bruce Hoffman. *Arms Trafficking and Colombia*, Santa Monica, Calif.: RAND Corp., 2003.

Cragin, Kim et al. *The Dynamic Terrorist Threat: An Assessment of Group Motivations and Capabilities in a Changing World*, Santa Monica, Calif.: RAND Corporation, 2004.

Cragin, Kim et al. *Sharing the Dragon's Teeth: Terrorist Groups and the Exchange of New Technologies*, Santa Monica, Calif.: RAND Corp., 2007.

Croissant, Aurel and Daniel Barlow. "Following the Money Trail: Terrorist Financing and Government Responses in Southeast Asia," *Studies in Conflict & Terrorism*, Vol. 30, No. 2, 2007, pp. 131–156.

Cronin, Audrey K. "How al-Qaida Ends: The Decline and Demise of Terrorist Groups," *International Security*, Vol. 31, No. 1, Summer 2006, pp. 7–48.

Cruickshank, Paul. *The Militant Pipeline: Between the Afghanistan-Pakistan Border Region and the West*, Washington, DC: New America Foundation, February 2010.

Cumming-Bruce, Nick. "5,500 Iraqis Killed Since Islamic State Began Its Military Drive, U.N. Says," *New York Times*, October 2, 2014.

Dallal, Abboushi J. "Hezbollah's Virtual Civil Society," *Television and New Media*, Vol. 2, No. 4, 2001, pp. 367–372.

Daraghi, Borzou. "Afghan Intelligence Network Embraces the New," *Los Angeles Times*, April 13, 2011.

Davidson, Janine and Emerson Brooking. *ISIS Hasn't Gone Anywhere—And It's Getting Stronger*, Council on Foreign Relations, Defense in Depth, July 24, 2014.

Davis, Julie Hirschfeld. "U.S. Strikes Cut into ISIS Oil Revenues, Treasury Official Says," *New York Times*, October 23, 2014.

Dean, Aimen et al. "Draining the Ocean to Catch One Type of Fish: Evaluating the Effectiveness of the Global Counter-Terrorism Financing Regime," *Perspectives on Terrorism*, Vol. 7, No. 4, 2013.

DeGroot, Gerard. "The Enemy Below: Why Hamas Tunnels Scare Israel So Much," *Washington Post* Monkey Cage blog, July 25, 2014.

Denece, Eric and Alain Rodier. "The Security Challenges of West Africa," in OECD, ed., *Global Security Risks and West Africa: Development Challenges*, Paris, France: OECD Publishing, 2012.

Desai, Raj and Harry Eckstein. "The Transformation of Peasant Rebellion," *World Politics*, Vol. 42, No. 4, July 1990, pp. 441–465.

Detmer, Jamie. "How to Cut Off ISIS Terror Tycoons," *Daily Beast*, September 26, 2014.

DeYoung, Karen. "U.S. Trucking Funds Reach Taliban, Military-Led Investigation Concludes," *Washington Post*, July 24, 2011.

Di Giovanni, Janine et al. "How Does ISIS Fund Its Reign of Terror," *Newsweek*, November 6, 2014.

Dickinson, Elizabeth. *Playing with Fire: Why Private Gulf Financing for Syria's Extremist Rebels Risks Igniting Sectarian Conflict at Home*, Brookings Analysis Paper, No. 16, December 2014.

Dickinson, Elizabeth. "The Case against Qatar," *Foreign Policy*, September 30, 2014.

Dingley, James. *The IRA: The Irish Republican Army*, Santa Barbara: Praeger Security International, 2012.

Dishman, Chris. "Terrorism, Crime, and Transformation," *Studies in Conflict & Terrorism*, Vol. 24, No. 1, 2001, pp. 43–58.

Dishman, Chris. "The Leaderless Nexus: When Crime and Terror Converge," *Studies in Conflict & Terrorism*, Vol. 28, No. 3, 2005. pp. 237–252.

Dobbins, James F. *After the Taliban: Nation-Building in Afghanistan*, Washington, DC: Potomac, 2008.

Dobbins, James. "Does ISIL Represent a Threat to the United States?" *The Hill*, October 3, 2014.

Dolnik, Adam and Anjali Bhattacherjee. "Hamas: Suicide Bombings, Rockets, or WMD?" *Terrorism & Political Violence*, Vol. 14, No. 3, Autumn 2002, pp. 109–128.

Donohue, Laura K. "Anti-Terrorist Finance in the United Kingdom and United States," *Michigan Journal of International Law*, Vol. 27, Winter 2006, pp. 303–435.

Dreazen, Yochi. "From Electricity to Sewage, U.S. Intelligence Says the Islamic State Is Fast Learning How to Run a Country," *Foreign Policy*, August 18, 2014.

Drennan, Justine. "The Black Market Battleground," *Foreign Policy*, October 17, 2014.

Dressler, Jeffrey and Carl Forsberg. *The Quetta Shura Taliban in Southern Afghanistan: Organization, Operations, and Shadow Governance*, Washington, DC: Institute for the Study of War Backgrounder, December 21, 2009.

Edelstein, David M. "Occupational Hazards: Why Military Occupations Succeed or Fail," *International Security*, Vol. 29, No. 1, 2009, pp. 49–91.

Ehrenfeld, Rachel. *Funding Evil: How Terrorism Is Financed and How to Stop It*, Chicago: Bonus Books, 2003.

Eilstrup-Sangiovanni, Mette and Calvert Jones. "Assessing the Dangers of Illicit Networks," *International Security*, Vol. 33, No. 2, Fall 2008, pp. 7–44.

Eisenstadt, Michael. *Defeating ISIS: A Strategy for a Resilient Adversary and an Intractable Conflict*, The Washington Institute for Near East Policy, No. 20, November 2014. Washington, DC.

English, Richard. *Armed Struggle: The History of the IRA*, Oxford: Oxford University Press, 2004.

Ensign, Rachel Louise. "Will Anti-Money Laundering Efforts Work against the Islamic State?" *Wall Street Journal*, August 29, 2014.

Erlanger, Steven and Richard A. Oppel, Jr. "A Disciplined Hezbollah Surprises Israel with Its Training, Tactics, and Weapons," *New York Times*, August 7, 2006.

Ewi, Martin. "A Decade of Kidnappings and Terrorism in West Africa and the Trans-Sahel Region," *African Security Review*, Vol. 19, No. 4, 2010, pp. 64–71.

Exum, Andrew. *Hezbollah at War: A Military Assessment*, The Washington Institute for Near East Policy, Policy Focus #63, December 2006, Washington, DC.

Fair, C. Christine. *Urban Battlefields of South Asia: Lessons Learned from Sri Lanka, India, and Pakistan*, Santa Monica, Calif.: RAND Corp., 2004.

Fair, C. Christine and Bryan Shepherd. "Who Supports Terrorism? Evidence from Fourteen Muslim Countries," *Studies in Conflict & Terrorism*, Vol. 29, 2006, pp. 51–74.

Farah, Douglas. "Digging Up Congo's Dirty Gems," *Washington Post*, December 30, 2001.

Farah, Douglas. *Blood from Stones: The Secret Financial Network of Terror*, New York: Broadway Books, 2004.

Farrell, Theo and Antonio Giustozzi. "The Taliban at War: Inside the Helmand Insurgency, 2004–2012," *International Affairs*, Vol. 89, No. 4, 2013, pp. 845–871.

Farwell, James P. "The Media Strategy of ISIS," *Survival*, Vol. 56, No. 6, December 2014/January 2015, pp. 49–55.

Felbab-Brown, Vanda. "Kicking the Opium Habit? Afghanistan's Drug Economy and Politics Since the 1980s," *Conflict, Security, and Development*, Vol. 6, No. 2, Summer 2006, pp. 127–149.

Felbab-Brown, Vanda. *Shooting Up: Counterinsurgency and the War on Drugs*, Washington, DC: Brookings Institution Press, 2010.

Felbab-Brown, Vanda. "Fighting the Nexus of Organized Crime and Violent Conflict While Enhancing Human Security," in Phil Williams and Vanda Felbab-Brown, eds., *Drug Trafficking, Violence, and Instability*, Carlisle Barracks, PA: US Army War College Strategic Studies Institute, April 2012.

Ferland, Elisabeth. *Hezbollah and the Internet*, Center for Strategic and International Studies, March 4, 2010.

Fielden, Matthew and Jonathan Goodhand. "Beyond the Taliban? The Afghan Conflict and United Nations Peacemaking," *Conflict, Security & Development,* Vol. 1, No. 3, 2001, pp. 5–32.

Filkins, Dexter. "The Afghan Bank Heist," *New Yorker,* February 14, 2011.

Fisher, Ali and Nico Prucha. "ISIS Is Winning the Online Jihad against the West," *Daily Beast,* October 1, 2014.

Flanigan, Shawn T. "Charity as Resistance: Connections between Charity, Contentious Politics, and Terror," *Studies in Conflict and Terrorism,* Vol. 29, No. 7, 2006, pp. 641–655.

Flanigan, Shawn T. "Nonprofit Service Provision by Insurgent Organizations: The Cases of Hizballah and the Tamil Tigers," *Studies in Conflict & Terrorism,* Vol. 31, No. 6, 2008, pp. 499–519.

Flynn, Michael T. and Simone A. Ledeen, "Pay for Play: Countering Threat Financing," *Joint Forces Quarterly,* No. 56, 1st Quarter 2010, pp. 123–127.

Forest, James J.F. "Kidnapping by Terrorist Groups, 1970–2010 Is Ideological Orientation Relevant?" *Crime & Delinquency,* Vol. 58, No. 5, 2012, pp. 769–797.

Frampton, Martyn. *The Return of the Militants, Violent Dissident Republicanism,* International Centre for the Study of Radicalisation and Political Violence, 2010.

Freeman, Michael. "The Sources of Terrorist Financing: Theory and Typology," *Studies in Conflict & Terrorism,* Vol. 34, No. 6, 2011, pp. 461–475.

Freeman, Michael. "Introduction to *Financing Terrorism: Case Studies,*" in Michael Freeman, ed., *Financing Terrorism: Case Studies,* Farnham: Ashgate, 2012.

Frey, Marc. *ISIS, Foreign Terrorist Fighters, and the Value of the Visa Waiver Program,* Center for Strategic & International Studies (CSIS), October 8, 2014, Washington, DC.

Frisch, Hillel. "Strategic Change in Terrorist Movements: Lessons from Hamas," *Studies in Conflict & Terrorism,* Vol. 31, No. 12, 2009, pp. 1049–1065.

Fuller, Graham E. "The Hezbollah-Iran Connection: Model for Sunni Resistance," *Washington Quarterly,* Vol. 30, No. 1, Winter 2006/2007, pp. 139–150.

Galeotti, Mark. "Spirited Away—The Rise of Global Kidnapping Trends," *Jane's Intelligence Review,* April 27, 2010.

Gall, Carlotta. *The Wrong Enemy: America in Afghanistan, 2001–2014,* New York: Houghton Mifflin Harcourt, 2014.

Gambhir, Harleen K. *Dabiq: The Strategic Messaging of the Islamic State,* Institute for the Study of War, August 15, 2014. Washington, DC.

Gardner, Kathryn L. "Fighting Terrorism the FATF Way," *Global Governance,* Vol. 13, No. 3, July–Sept 2007, pp. 325–345.

Gartenstein-Ross, Daveed and Aaron Y. Zelin. "Uncharitable Organizations," *Foreign Policy,* February 26, 2013.

Gartenstein-Ross, David and Amichal Magen. "The Jihadist Governance Dilemma," *Washington Post* Monkey Cage, July 18, 2014.

Gettleman, Jeffrey and Nicholas Kulish. "Somali Militants Mixing Business and Terror," *New York Times,* September 30, 2013.

Giustozzi, Antonio. *Koran, Kalashnikov, and Laptop: The Neo-Taliban Insurgency in Afghanistan,* New York: Columbia University Press, 2008.

Giustozzi, Antonio, ed. *Decoding the New Taliban: Insights from the Afghan Field*, New York: Columbia University Press, 2009.

Giustozzi, Antonio. *Negotiating with the Taliban: Issues and Prospects*, New York: The Century Foundation, 2010.

Gohel, Saijan M. "Iran's Ambiguous Role in Afghanistan," *Combating Terrorism Center Sentinel*, Vol. 3, No. 3, March 2010, pp. 13–16.

Goldberg, Jeffrey. "A Reporter at Large: In the Party of God," Part II, *New Yorker*, October 28, 2002.

Gomez, Juan Miguel del Cid. "A Financial Profile of the Terrorism of Al-Qaeda and Its Affiliates," *Perspectives on Terrorism*, Vol. 4, No. 4, October 2010.

Gopal, Anand. "The Taliban in Kandahar," in Peter Bergen with Katherine Tiedemann, eds., *Talibanistan: Negotiating the Borders between Terror, Politics, and Religion*, Oxford: Oxford University Press, 2013.

Gormley, Dennis. "Silent Retreat: The Future of U.S. Nuclear Weapons," *Nonproliferation Review*, Vol. 14, No. 2, July 2007, pp. 183–206.

Grace, Robert and Andrew Mandelbaum. *Understanding the Iran-Hezbollah Connection*, United States Institute of Peace, September 2006.

Graham-Harrison, Emma. "Taliban Destroy Poppy Fields in Surprise Clampdown on Afghan Opium Growers," *The Guardian*, May 20, 2012.

Green, Jerrold. *Understanding Iran*, Santa Monica, Calif.: RAND Corp., 2008.

Greenhill, Kelly M. and Paul Staniland. "Ten Ways to Lose at Counterinsurgency," *Civil Wars*, Vol. 9, No. 4, 2007, pp. 402–419.

Grynkewich, Alexus G. "Welfare as Warfare: How Violent Non-State Groups Use Social Services to Attack the State," *Studies in Conflict and Terrorism*, Vol. 31, 2008.

Gunaratna, Rohan. *International and Regional Implications of the Sri Lankan Tamil Insurgency*, International Policy Institute for Counter-Terrorism, December 2, 1998. Herzliya, Israel.

Gunaratna, Rohan. "Sri Lanka: Feeding the Tamil Tigers," in Karen Ballentine and Jake Sherman, eds., *The Political Economy of Armed Conflict: Beyond Greed and Grievance*, Boulder: Lynne Rienner, 2003.

Gunaratna, Rohan. "The Post-Madrid Face of Al Qaeda," *Washington Quarterly*, Vol. 27, No. 3, 2004, pp. 91–100.

Gunaratna, Rohan and Anders Nielsen, "Al Qaeda in the Tribal Areas of Pakistan," *Studies in Conflict & Terrorism*, Vol. 31, No. 9, 2008, pp. 775–807.

Gunaratna, Rohan and Aviv Oreg. "Al Qaeda's Organizational Structure and Its Evolution," *Studies in Conflict & Terrorism*, Vol. 33, No. 12, 2010, pp. 1043–1078.

Gupta, Dipak K. and Kusum Mundra. "Suicide Bombing as a Strategic Weapon: An Empirical Investigation of Hamas and Islamic Jihad," *Terrorism and Political Violence*, Vol. 17, No. 4, 2005, pp. 573–598.

Haddad, Simon. "The Origins of Popular Support for Lebanon's Hezbollah," *Studies in Conflict and Terrorism*, Vol. 29, No. 1, 2006, pp. 21–34.

Hajjar, Sami G. *Hezbollah: Terrorism, National Liberation, or Menace?* New York: Diane Publishing, 2002.

Harik, Judith. "Syrian Foreign Policy and State/Resistance Dynamics in Lebanon," *Studies in Conflict & Terrorism*, Vol. 20, No. 3, 1997, pp. 249–265.

Harik, Judith Palmer. *Hezbollah: The Changing Face of Terrorism*, London: I.B. Tauris, 2004.

Harkins, Gina. "5 Things to Know about Islamic State's Military Capabilities," *Army Times*, September 16, 2014.

Harnden, Toby. *Bandit Country: The IRA & South Armagh*, London: Hodder & Stoughton, 2000.

Harris, Albert W. "Insurgency Decision-Making under Conditions of Risk," *International Journal of Psychological Studies*, Vol. 4, No. 3, 2012, pp. 43–47.

Harrison, Ross. "Confronting the 'Islamic State:' Towards a Regional Strategy Contra ISIS," *Parameters*, Vol. 44, No. 3, Autumn 2014, pp. 37–46.

Harte, Julia and R. Jeffrey Smith. "Where Does the Islamic State Get Its Weapons?" *Foreign Policy*, October 6, 2014.

Hasan, Harith. "Al Qaeda Sinks Roots in Mosul," *Al-Monitor*, October 24, 2013.

Haussler, Nicholas I. *Third Generation Gangs Revisited: The Iraq Insurgency*, Monterey, Calif.: Naval Postgraduate School, Thesis, September 2005.

Hegghammer, Thomas. "Terrorist Recruitment and Radicalization in Saudi Arabia," *Middle East Policy*, Vol. 13, No. 4, 2006, pp. 39–60.

Hegghammer, Thomas. *Saudi Militants in Iraq: Backgrounds and Recruitment Patterns*, Norwegian Defence Research Establishment (FFI), February 5, 2007. Kjeller, Norway.

Helfstein, Scott with John Solomon. *Risky Business: The Global Threat Network and the Politics of Contraband*, Combating Terrorism Center, May 2014.

Helmus, Todd. "Why and How Some People Become Terrorists," in Paul K. Davis and Kim Cragin, eds., *Social Science for Counterterrorism: Putting the Pieces Together*, Santa Monica, Calif.: RAND Corporation, 2009.

Hersh, Seymour. "Iran and the Bomb," *New Yorker*, June 6, 2011.

Hiro, Dilip. *Lebanon Fire and Embers: A History of the Lebanese Civil War*, New York: St. Martin Press, 1992.

Hobsbawm, Eric. *Primitive Rebels*, Manchester, England: Manchester University Press, 1959.

Hoffman, Bruce. "Al Qaeda Trends in Terrorism and Future Potentialities: An Assessment," paper presented at a meeting of the Council on Foreign Relations, Washington, DC Office, May 8, 2003.

Hoffman, Bruce. "The Changing Face of Al Qaeda and the Global War on Terrorism," *Studies in Conflict & Terrorism*, Vol. 27, No. 6, 2004, pp. 549–560.

Hoffman, Bruce. "The Myth of Grass-Roots Terrorism: Why Osama bin Laden Still Matters," *Foreign Affairs*, Vol. 87, No. 3, May–June 2008.

Hoffman, Bruce. "Al Qaeda's Uncertain Future," *Studies in Conflict & Terrorism*, Vol. 36, No. 8, 2013, pp. 635–653.

Holtmann, Philipp. "The IS-Caliphate: What Should Be Done to Prevent It from Spinning Out of Control?" *Perspectives on Terrorism*, Vol. 8, No. 5, October 2014.

Horgan, John and John F. Morrison. "Here to Stay? The Rising Threat of Violent Dissident Republicanism in Northern Ireland," *Terrorism and Political Violence*, Vol. 23, No. 4, 2011, pp. 642–669.

Horgan, John and Max Taylor, "The Provisional Irish Republican Army: Command and Functional Structure," *Terrorism and Political Violence*, Vol. 9, No. 3, 1997, pp. 1–32.

Horgan, John and Max Taylor. "Playing Green Card—Financing the Provisional IRA: Part I," *Terrorism and Political Violence,* Vol. 11, No. 2, Summer 1999, pp. 1–38.

Horgan, John and Max Taylor. "Playing the 'Green Card'—Financing the Provisional IRA: Part 2," *Terrorism and Political Violence,* Vol. 15, No. 2, Summer 2003, pp. 1–60.

Hubbard, Ben, Clifford Kraus and Eric Schmitt, "Rebels in Syria Claim Control of Resources," *New York Times,* January 28, 2014.

Hubbard, Ben and Eric Schmitt. "Military Skill and Terrorist Technique Fuel Success of ISIS," *New York Times,* August 27, 2014.

Hume, Jessica. "U.S. Seizes $150m from Hezbollah-linked Lebanese Canadian Bank," *Toronto Sun,* August 21, 2012.

Hussain, Jam H., "Son-in-Law of Gen Tariq Wins Freedom for Rs 300 m," *The Nation,* March 16, 2012.

Hutchinson, Steven and Pat O'Malley. "A Crime-Terror Nexus? Thinking Some on the Links between Terrorism and Criminality," *Studies in Conflict & Terrorism,* Vol. 30, No. 12, 2007, pp. 1095–1107.

Hylton, Hillary. "How Hezbollah Hijacks the Internet," *Time,* August 8, 2006.

Ignatius, David. "The Manual that Chillingly Foreshadows the Islamic State," *Washington Post,* September 25, 2014.

Ilardi, Gaetano Joe. "The 9/11 Attacks—A Study of Al Qaeda's Use of Intelligence and Counterintelligence," *Studies in Conflict & Terrorism,* Vol. 31, No. 1, 2009, pp. 171–187.

Ilardi, Gaetano Joe. "IRA Operational Intelligence: The Heartbeat of the War," *Small Wars & Insurgencies,* Vol. 21, No. 2, June 2010, pp. 331–358.

Inkster, Nigel. "The Resurgence of ISIS," *International Institute for Strategic Studies (IISS),* June 13, 2014.

Irish Republican Army. *Handbook for Volunteers of the Irish Republican Army: Notes on Guerrilla Warfare,* Boulder: Palladin Press, 1985.

Jaber, Hala. *Hezbollah: Born with a Vengeance,* New York: Columbia University Press, 1997.

Jackson, Brian. "Training for Urban Resistance: The Case of the Provisional Irish Republican Army," in James J.F. Forest, ed., *The Making of a Terrorist, Volume II: Training,* Santa Barbara: Praeger, 2005.

Jackson, Brian A. *Breaching the Fortress Wall: Understanding Terrorist Efforts to Overcome Defensive Technologies,* Santa Monica, Calif.: RAND Corp., 2007.

Jackson, Brian et al. *Aptitude for Destruction, Volume 2: Case Studies of Organizational Learning in Five Terrorist Groups,* Santa Monica, Calif.: RAND Corp., 2005.

Jenkins, Brian Michael. *Will Terrorists Go Nuclear?* New York: Prometheus Books, 2008.

Jenkins, Brian Michael. "The al Qaeda-Inspired Terrorist Threat: An Appreciation of the Current Situation," Testimony presented before the Canadian Senate Special Committee on Anti-terrorism on December 6, 2010.

Jenkins, Brian Michael. "Al Qaeda After Bin Laden: Implications for American Strategy," Testimony presented before the House Armed Services Committee, Subcommittee on Emerging Threats and Capabilities, June 22, 2011.

Jenkins, Brian Michael. *Stray Dogs and Virtual Armies,* Santa Monica, Calif.: RAND Corp., 2011.

Jenkins, Brian Michael. "Al Qaeda in Its Third Decade: Irreversible Decline or Imminent Victory?" Santa Monica, Calif.: RAND Corp., 2012.

Johnsen, Gregory. "A False Target in Yemen," *New York Times,* November 19, 2010.

Johnsen, Gregory D. *The Last Refuge: Yemen, Al Qaeda, and America's War in Arabia,* New York: W.W. Norton & Co., 2013.

Johnson, Thomas H. "Financing Afghan Terrorism," in Jeanne K. Giraldo and Harold A. Trinkunas, eds., *Terrorism Financing and State Responses: A Comparative Perspective,* Stanford: Stanford University Press, 2007.

Johnson, Thomas H. "On the Edge of the Big Muddy: The Taliban Resurgence in Afghanistan," *China and Eurasia Forum Quarterly,* Vol. 5, No. 2, 2007, pp. 93–129.

Johnson, Thomas H. "Taliban Adaptations and Innovations," *Small Wars & Insurgencies,* Vol. 24, No. 1, 2013, pp. 3–27.

Johnson, Thomas and Matthew C. Dupee. "Analyzing the New Taliban Code of Conduct (*Layeha*): An Assessment of Changing Perspectives and Strategies of the Afghan Taliban," *Central Asian Survey,* Vol. 31, No. 1, March 2012, pp. 77–91.

Johnson, Jeffrey M. and Carl Jensen. "The Financing of Terrorism," *The Journal of the Institute of Justice & International Studies,* No. 10, 2010.

Johnson, Thomas H. and M. Chris Mason. "Understanding the Taliban and Insurgency in Afghanistan," *Orbis,* Vol. 51, No. 1, Winter 2007, pp. 71–89.

Johnson, Thomas H. and M. Chris Mason, "All Counterinsurgency Is Local," *The Atlantic,* October 2008.

Johnson, Thomas H. and M. Chris Mason. "No Sign Until the Burst of Fire: Understanding the Pakistan-Afghanistan Frontier," *International Security,* Vol. 32, No. 4, Spring 2008, pp. 41–77.

Johnson, Keith and Jamila Trindle. "Treasury's War on the Islamic State," *Foreign Policy,* October 23, 2014.

Johnston, Patrick B. "Does Decapitation Work? Assessing the Effectiveness of Leadership Targeting in Counterinsurgency Campaigns," *International Security,* Vol. 36, No. 4, Spring 2012, pp. 47–79.

Johnston, Patrick B. and Benjamin Bahney. "Hit the Islamic State's Pocketbook," *Newsday,* October 5, 2014.

Jones, Clive. "'A Reach Greater Than the Grasp': Israeli Intelligence and the Conflict in South Lebanon, 1990–2000," *Intelligence and National Security,* Vol. 16, No. 3, 2001, pp. 1–26.

Jones, Seth. *Counterinsurgency in Afghanistan,* Santa Monica, Calif.: RAND Corporation, 2008.

Jones, Seth G. *In the Graveyard of Empires: America's War in Afghanistan,* New York: W.W. Norton & Co., 2009.

Jones, Seth G. "The Future of Al Qa'ida," Congressional Testimony, presented before the House Foreign Affairs Committee, Subcommittee on Terrorism, Nonproliferation and Trade, May 24, 2011.

Jones, Seth G. "Al Qaeda in Iran: Why Tehran Is Accommodating the Terrorist Group," *Foreign Affairs,* January 29, 2012.

Jones, Seth G. *Hunting in the Shadows: The Pursuit of Al Qaeda Since 9/11.* New York: W.W. Norton & Co., 2012.

Jones, Seth G. "Jihadist Sanctuaries in Syria and Iraq: Implications for the United States," presented to the Committee on Homeland Security Subcommittee on

Counterterrorism and Intelligence, U.S. House of Representatives, July 24, 2014.

Jones, Seth G. *A Persistent Threat: The Evolution of Al Qaida and Other Salafist Jihadists,"* Santa Monica, Calif.: RAND Corp., 2014.

Jones, Seth G. and Patrick B. Johnston. "The Future of Insurgency," *Studies in Conflict & Terrorism,* Vol. 36, No. 1, 2013, pp. 1–25.

Jonsson, Michael. "Following the Money: Financing the Territorial Expansion of Islamist Insurgents in Syria," Swedish Defense Research Agency, FOI Memo #4947, May 2014.

Jorisch, A. "Al-Manar: Hezbollah TV, 24.7," *Middle East Quarterly,* Winter 2004, pp. 17–31.

Joshi, Manoj. "On the Razor's Edge: The Liberation Tigers of Tamil Eelam," *Studies in Conflict and Terrorism,* Vol. 19, No. 1, 1996, pp. 19–42.

Kakar, Palwasha. *Tribal Law of Pashtunwali,* Harvard University School of Law.

Kanter, James and Jodi Rudoren. "European Union Adds Military Wing of Hezbollah to List of Terrorist Organizations," *New York Times,* July 22, 2013.

Kaplan, David E. "Paying for Terror: How Jihadist Groups Are Using Organized Crime Tactics and Profits to Finance Attacks on Targets around the Globe," *U.S. News & World Report,* November 27, 2005.

Karouny, Mariam. "In Northeast Syria, Islamic State Builds a Government," *Reuters,* September 4, 2014.

Katz, Rita. "Follow ISIS on Twitter: A Special Report on the Use of Social Media by Jihadists," *Insite Blog on Terrorism & Extremism,* June 26, 2014.

Katz, Yaakov and Yoaz Hendel. *Israel vs. Iran: The Shadow War,* Washington, DC: Potomac Books, 2012.

Keatinge, Tom. "What Role Does CFT Play in International Security? Can It Be Deemed Effective?" Dissertation submitted to King's College London for MA in Intelligence & International Security, August 2012.

Keatinge, Tom. "Breaking the Banks: The Financial Consequences of Counterterrorism," *Foreign Affairs,* June 26, 2014.

Keatinge, Tom. "How the Islamic State Sustains Itself: The Importance of the War Economy in Syria and Iraq," *RUSI Analysis,* August 29, 2014.

Keatinge, Tom. "The Importance of Financing in Enabling and Sustaining the Conflict in Syria," *Perspectives on Terrorism,* Vol. 8, No. 4, August 2014.

Keatinge, Tom. "The Price of Freedom: When Governments Pay Ransoms," *Foreign Affairs,* August 13, 2014.

Kenney, Michael. "Organizational Learning and Islamist Militancy," National Institute of Justice, NIJ Journal No. 265, 2010, pp. 18–21.

Khalidi, Khalidi. *Conflict and Violence in Lebanon: Confrontation in the Middle East,* Harvard University: Center for International Affairs, 1979.

Khalil, Ezzeldeen. "Gone Viral: Islamic State's Evolving Media Strategy," *Jane's Intelligence Review,* October 2014.

Khashan, Hilal. "Collective Palestinian Frustration and Suicide Bombings," *Third World Quarterly,* Vol. 24, No. 6, December 2003, pp. 1049–1067.

Kilcullen, David. *Out of the Mountains: The Coming Age of the Urban Guerilla,* Oxford: Oxford University Press, 2013.

Kirkpatrick, David D. "ISIS' Harsh Brand of Islam Is Rooted in Austere Saudi Creed," *New York Times,* September 24, 2014.

Kirkpatrick, David D. "New Freedoms in Tunisia Drive Support for ISIS," *New York Times,* October 21, 2014.

Kiser, Steve. *Financing Terror: An Analysis and Simulation for Affecting Al Qaeda's Financial Infrastructure,* RAND Pardee School dissertation, Santa Monica, Calif.: RAND Corporation, 2005.

Klausen, Jytte. "They're Coming: Measuring the Threat from Returning Jihadists," *Foreign Affairs,* October 1, 2014.

Klein, Joe. "The Hezbollah Project," *New York Times,* September 30, 2010.

Knickmeyer, Ellen. "Al Qaeda-Linked Groups Increasingly Funded by Ransom," *Wall Street Journal,* July 29, 2014.

Knudsen, Are. "Islamism in the Diaspora: Palestinian Refugees in Lebanon," *Journal of Refugee Studies,* Vol. 18, No. 2, 2005, pp. 216–234.

Kohlmann, Evan F. "The Real Online Terrorist Threat," *Foreign Affairs,* Vol. 85, No. 5, 2006.

Kohlmann, Evan F. *The Role of Islamic Charities in International Terrorist Recruitment and Financing,* Danish Institute for International Studies, DIIS Working Paper, 2006.

Kovensky, Josh. "ISIS's New Mag Looks Like a New York Glossy—With Pictures of Mutilated Bodies," *New Republic,* August 25, 2014.

Kramer, Martin. "The Moral Logic of Hezbollah," in I. Cronin, ed., *Confronting Fear: A History of Terrorism,* New York: Thunder's Mouth Press.

Lafraie, Najibullah. "Resurgence of the Taliban Insurgency in Afghanistan: How and Why?" *International Politics,* Vol. 46, No. 1, 2009, pp. 102–113.

Lake, Eli. "Meet Al Qaeda's New General Manager: Nasser al-Wuhayshi," *Daily Beast,* August 9, 2013.

Laub, Zachary. *Backgrounders: Al Qaeda in the Islamic Maghreb (AQIM),* Council on Foreign Relations, January 8, 2014.

Laub, Zachary. *The Taliban in Afghanistan,* Council on Foreign Relations Backgrounder, February 25, 2014.

Lee, Maggy. *Trafficking and Global Crime Control,* Los Angeles: Sage, 2011.

Lemieux, Frederic and Fernanda Prates. "Entrepreneurial Terrorism: Financial Strategies, Business Opportunities, and Ethical Issues," *Police Practice and Research: An International Journal,* Vol. 12, No. 5, 2011, pp. 368–382.

Levi, Michael and Peter Reuter. "Money Laundering," in Michael Tonry, ed., *The Oxford Handbook of Crime and Public Policy,* Oxford University Press, 2011.

Levitt, Matthew. *The Hezbollah Threat in Africa,* The Washington Institute, Policy-watch No. 283, January 2, 2004.

Levitt, Matthew. *Hezbollah Finances: Funding the Party of God,* The Washington Institute, February 2005.

Levitt, Matthew. "Hezbollah: Financing Terror through Criminal Enterprise," Testimony presented to United States Senate Committee on Homeland Security and Governmental Affairs, May 25, 2005.

Levitt, Matthew. *Palestinian Authority Minister of Economy Tied to Hamas?* Washington Institute for Near East Policy, Policy Watch #496, March 4, 2005.

Levitt, Matthew. *Hamas: Politics, Charity and Terrorism in the Service of Jihad,* New Haven, CT: Yale University Press, 2006.

Levitt, Matthew. "Could Hamas Target the West?" *Studies in Conflict & Terrorism*, Vol. 30, No. 11, 2007, pp. 925–945.

Levitt, Matthew. "Hezbollah Finances: Funding the Party of God," in Jeanne K. Giraldo and Harold A. Trinkunas, eds., *Terrorism Financing and State Responses: A Comparative Perspective*, Stanford: Stanford University Press, 2007.

Levitt, Matthew. "Al-Qa'ida's Finances: Evidence of Organizational Decline?" *CTC Sentinel*, Vol. 1, No. 5, April 2008.

Levitt, Matthew. "Foreign Fighters and Their Economic Impact: A Case Study of Syria and Al Qaeda in Iraq," *Perspectives on Terrorism*, Vol. 3, No. 3, 2009.

Levitt, Matthew. "Follow the Money: Leveraging Financial Intelligence to Combat Transnational Threats," *Georgetown Journal of International Affairs*, Winter/Spring 2011, pp. 34–43.

Levitt, Matthew. *Hezbollah: The Global Footprint of Lebanon's Party of God*, Washington, DC: Georgetown University Press, 2013.

Levitt, Matthew. "Hamas' Not-So-Secret Weapon," *Foreign Affairs*, July 9, 2014.

Levitt, Matthew. "Qatar's Not-So-Charitable Record on Terror Finance," *The Hill*, September 24, 2014.

Levitt, Matthew. *Show Me the Money: Targeting the Islamic State's Bottom Line*, Homeland Security Policy Institute, October 1, 2014.

Levitt, Matthew and Lori Plotkin Boghardt. *Funding ISIS*, The Washington Institute for Near East Policy, September 12, 2014.

Levitt, Matthew and Michael Jacobson. *The Money Trail: Finding, Following, and Freezing Terrorist Finances*, The Washington Institute for Near East Policy, Policy Focus #89, November 2008.

Lia, Brynjar and Ashild Kjok. *Islamist Insurgencies, Diaspora Support Networks, and Their Host States: The Case of the Algerian GIA in Europe 1993–2000*, Kjeller, Norway: Forsvartes Forskningsinstitutt, FFI/APPORT-2001/03789, August 8, 2001.

Libicki, Martin C. et al. *Byting Back: Regaining Information Superiority against 21st Century Insurgents*, Santa Monica, Calif.: RAND Corporation, 2007.

Lilja, Janine. "Trapping Constituents or Winning Hearts and Minds? Rebel Strategies to Attain Constituent Support in Sri Lanka," *Terrorism and Political Violence*, Vol. 21, No. 2, April 2009, pp. 306–326.

Lister, Charles. *Cutting Off ISIS' Cash Flow*, Brookings Institution, October 24, 2014.

Lister, Charles. *Profiling the Islamic State*, Brookings Institution Doha Center Analysis Paper, No. 13, November 2014.

Litvak, Meir. "Martyrdom Is Life: *Jihad* and Martyrdom in the Ideology of Hamas," *Studies in Conflict & Terrorism*, Vol. 33, No. 8, 2010, pp. 716–734.

Long, Austin. "The Anbar Awakening," *Survival*, Vol. 50, No. 2, April 2008, pp. 67–94.

Looney, Robert. "The Business of Insurgency: The Expansion of Iraq's Shadow Economy," *National Interest*, Vol. 81, Fall 2005, pp. 67–72.

Lormel, Dennis. "Identifying and Disrupting Funding Streams to Thwart Terrorist Financing and Organized Criminal Activities," *IPSA International*, 2009.

Lowther, William and Colin Freeman. "US Fund Terror Group to Sow Chaos in Iran," *The Telegraph*, February 25, 2007.

Lyall, Jason. "A (Fighting) Season to Remember in Afghanistan," *Washington Post* Monkey Cage blog, October 20, 2014.

Lynch, Marc. "Al Qaeda's Media Strategies," *National Interest*, Vol. 83, Spring 2006, pp. 50–56.

Lynch, Marc et al. *Syria's Socially Mediated Civil War*, United States Institute of Peace (USIP), Peaceworks No. 91, 2014.

Lynch, Marc. "Islamists and Their Charities," *Washington Post* Monkey Cage blog, October 15, 2014.

Lyons, Terrence and Peter Mandaville, eds. *Politics from Afar: Transnational Diasporas and Networks*, New York: Columbia University Press, 2012.

Maguire, Keith. "Fraud, Extortion and Racketeering: The Black Economy in Northern Ireland," *Crime, Law, and Social Change*, Vol. 20, No. 4, 1993, pp. 273–292.

Maguire, Keith. "Policing the Black Economy: The Role of C.13 of the R.U.C. in Northern Ireland," *Police Journal*, Vol. 66, No. 2, April–June 1993, pp. 127–135.

Mahendrarajah, Shivan. "Conceptual Failure, the Taliban's Parallel Hierarchies, and America's Strategic Defeat in Afghanistan," *Small Wars & Insurgencies*, Vol. 25, No. 1, 2014, pp. 91–121.

Makarenko, Tamara. "The Crime-Terror Continuum: Tracing the Interplay between Transnational Organized Crime and Terrorism," *Global Crime*, Vol. 6, No. 1, 2004, pp. 129–145.

Malka, Haim. "Forcing Choices: Testing the Transformation of Hamas," *Washington Quarterly*, Vol. 28, No. 4, 2005, pp. 37–53.

Malkasian, Carter. "If ISIS Has a 3-24 (II): Trying to Write the Field Manual of the Islamic State," *Foreign Policy*, October 7, 2014.

Mansfield, Don. "The Irish Republican Army and Northern Ireland," in Bard E. O'Neill, William R. Heaton, and Donald J. Alberts, eds., *Insurgency in the Modern World*, Boulder, CO: Westview Press, 1980.

Markey, Daniel S. *U.S. Strategy for Pakistan and Afghanistan*, Council on Foreign Relations Independent Task Force Report No. 65, November 2010.

Marks, Thomas. *Maoist Insurgency Since Vietnam*, Psychology Press, 1986.

Marks, Thomas. "Ideology of Insurgency: New Ethnic Focus or Old Cold War Distortions?" *Small Wars & Insurgencies*, Vol. 15, No. 1, Spring 2004, pp. 107–128.

Martin, John M. and Anne T. Romano. *Multinational Crime: Terrorism, Espionage, Drug & Arms Trafficking*, Los Angeles: Sage, 1992.

Matesan, Ioana Emy. "What Makes Negative Frames Resonant? Hamas and the Appeal of Opposition to the Peace Process," *Terrorism and Political Violence*, Vol. 24, No. 5, 2012, pp. 671–705.

McCallister, William S. "The Iraq Insurgency: Anatomy of a Tribal Rebellion," *First Monday*, Vol. 10, No. 3, March 2005.

McCants, William. *ISIS Fantasies of an Apocalyptic Showdown in Northern Syria*, Brookings Institution, October 3, 2014.

McCants, William. "State of Confusion," *Foreign Affairs*, September 10, 2014.

McCormick, G. H. and G. Gown. "Security and Coordination in Clandestine Organization," *Mathematical and Computer Modeling*, No. 31, 2000, pp. 175–192.

McCoy, Terence. "How ISIS Leader Abu Bakr al-Baghdadi Became the World's Most Powerful Jihadist Leader," *Washington Post*, June 11, 2014.

McCoy, Terrence. "ISIS Just Stole $425 Million, Iraqi Governor Says, And Became the 'World's Richest Terrorist Group.'" *Washington Post*, June 12, 2014.

McGartland, Matrin. *Fifty Dead Men Walking: The Heroic True Story of a British Secret Agent Inside the IRA*, London: John Blake, 2009.

McKenzie, Nick and Richard Baker. "Terrorists Taking Cut of Millions in Drug Money," *Canberra Times*, January 23, 2014.

Mickolous, Edward F. and Susan L. Simmons. *Terrorist List*, Santa Barbara: ABC-CLIO, 2011.

Mikkelsen, Randall. "Bankers Say 'Derisking' Underway Amid Sanctions Crackdown; That's the Point, U.S. Regulators Say," *Reuters*, October 3, 2014.

Millen, Raymond A. and Steven Metz. *Insurgency and Counterinsurgency in the 21st Century: Reconceptualizing Threat and Response*, Diane Publishing, 2004.

Milton-Edwards, Beverley. "Islamist Versus Islamist: Rising Challenge in Gaza," *Terrorism and Political Violence*, Vol. 26, No. 2, 2014, pp. 259–276.

Milton-Edwards, Beverley and Stephen Farrell. *Hamas: The Islamic Resistance Movement*, Cambridge: Polity Press, 2010.

Mishal, Shaul and Avraham Sela. *The Palestinian Hamas: Vision, Violence, and Coexistence*, New York: Columbia University Press, 2006.

Mitra, Anirudhya. "Rajiv Assassination: Conspiracy Surfaces" *India Today*, December 15, 1992.

Mockaitis, Thomas. *Resolving Insurgencies*, Strategic Studies Institute (SSI), U.S. Army War College, June 2011.

Moghdam, Assaf et al. "Say Terrorist, Think Insurgent: Labeling and Analyzing Contemporary Terrorist Actors," *Perspectives on Terrorism*, Vol. 8, No. 5, October 2014.

Moloney, Ed. *A Secret History of the IRA*, New York: WW Norton & Company, 2003.

Motadel, David. "The Ancestors of ISIS," *New York Times*, September 23, 2014.

Mozes, Tomer and Gabriel Weimann. "The E-Marketing Strategy of Hamas," *Studies in Conflict & Terrorism*, Vol. 33, No. 3, 2010, pp. 211–225.

Nader, Alireza and Joya Laha. *Iran's Balancing Act in Afghanistan*, Santa Monica, Calif.: RAND Corp., 2011.

Nagl, John. "America Needs a More Aggressive Strategy against ISIL. Now," *Politico*, October 12, 2014.

Naim, Moises. "Mafia States: Organized Crime Takes Office," *Foreign Affairs*, Vol. 91, No. 3, May/June 2012.

Naim, Moises. *The End of Power: From Boardrooms to Battlefields and Churches to States, Why Being in Charge Isn't What It Used to Be*, New York: Basic, 2013.

Nelson, Rick and Thomas M. Sanderson. *A Threat Transformed: Al Qaeda and Associated Movements in 2011*, Center for Strategic and International Studies (CSIS), February 2011.

Nesser, Petter. "Jihadism in Western Europe After the Invasion of Iraq: Tracing Motivational Influences from the Iraq War on Jihadist Terrorism in Western Europe," *Studies in Conflict & Terrorism*, Vol. 29, No. 4, 2006, pp. 323–342.

Neumann, Peter R. "Europe's Jihadist Dilemma," *Survival*, Vol. 48, No. 2, 2006, pp. 71–84.

Neumann, Peter R. *Old & New Terrorism*, Cambridge: Polity Press, 2009.

Neumann, Peter. "Suspects into Collaborators," *London Review of Books*, Vol. 36, No. 7, April 3, 2014.

Noe, Nicholas, ed. *Voice of Hezbollah: The Statements of Sayeed Hassan Nasrallah*, London: Verso, 2007.

Nordland, Rod. "Iraq's Sunni Militants Take to Social Media to Advance Their Cause and Intimidate," *New York Times*, June 28, 2014.

Norman, Paul. "The Terrorist Finance Unit and the Joint Action Group on Organised Crime: New Organisational Models and Investigative Strategies to Counter 'Organised Crime' in the UK," *Howard Journal*, Vol. 37, Number 4, November 1998, pp. 375–392.

Norton, Augustus Richard. *Extremist Ideals Versus Mundane Politics*, New York: Council on Foreign Relations, 1999.

Norton, Augustus R. "Hezbollah and the Israeli Withdrawal from Southern Lebanon," *Journal of Palestine Studies*, Vol. 30, No. 1, Autumn 2000, pp. 22–35.

Norton, Augustus R. "The Role of Hezbollah in Lebanese Domestic Politics," *International Spectator*, Vol. 42, No. 4, 2007, pp. 475–491.

Norton, Augustus R. *Hezbollah: A Short History*, Princeton: Princeton University Press, 2007.

O'Brien, Kevin A. "Assessing Hostile Reconnaissance and Terrorist Intelligence Activities: The Case for a Counter Strategy," *RUSI Journal*, Vol. 153, October 2008.

O'Brien, McKenzie. "Fluctuations between Crime and Terror: The Case of Abu Sayyaf's Kidnapping Activities," *Terrorism and Political Violence*, Vol. 24, No. 2, 2012, pp. 320–336.

O'Duffy, Brendan. "The Liberation Tigers of Tamil Eelam (LTTE): Majoritarianism, Self-Determination and Military-to-Political Transitions in Sri Lanka," in M. Heiburg, B. O'Leary, and J. Tirman, eds., *Terror, Insurgency and States*, Philadelphia, PA: University of Pennsylvania, 2007.

Ohlbaum, Diana L. *Terrorism, Inc.: How Shell Companies Aid Terrorism, Crime and Corruption*, Open Society Foundations, October 2013.

O'Neill, Bard E. *Insurgency and Terrorism: Inside Modern Revolutionary Warfare*, Washington, DC: Brassey's Inc., 1990.

Paley, Amit R. "Iraqis Joining Insurgency Less for Cause Than Cash," *Washington Post*, November 20, 2007.

Pall, Zoltan. *Kuwaiti Salafism and Its Growing Influence in the Levant*, Carnegie Endowment for International Peace, May 7, 2014.

Pape, Robert. *Dying to Win: The Strategic Logic of Suicide Terrorism*, New York: Random House, 2006.

Patrick, Stewart. "Weak States and Global Threats: Fact or Fiction?" *Washington Quarterly*, Vol. 29, No. 2, 2006, pp. 27–53.

Paul, Christopher. "How Do Terrorists Generate and Maintain Support?" in Paul K. Davis and Kim Cragin, eds., *Social Science for Counterterrorism: Putting the Pieces Together*, Santa Monica, Calif.: RAND Corporation, 2009.

Paul, Christopher. "As a Fish Swims in the Sea: Relationships between Factors Contributing to Support for Terrorist or Insurgent Groups," *Studies in Conflict and Terrorism*, Vol. 33, No. 6, 2010, pp. 488–510.

Paul, Christopher. *Counterinsurgency Scorecard: Afghanistan in Early 2011 Relative to the Insurgencies of the Past 30 Years*, Santa Monica, Calif.: RAND Corp., 2011.

Pedahzur, Ami. *Suicide Terrorism*, Cambridge, United Kingdom: Polity Press, 2005.

Peires, G.H. "Clandestine Transactions of the LTTE and the Secessionist Campaign in Sri Lanka," *Ethnic Studies Report*, Vol. 19, No. 1, 2001, pp. 1–38.

Peritz, Aki and Tara Maller. "The Islamic State of Sexual Violence," *Foreign Policy*, September 16, 2014.

Perl, Raphael. "Anti-Terror Strategy, The 9/11 Commission Report, and Terrorism Financing: Implications for U.S. Policymakers," in Jeanne K. Giraldo and Harold A. Trinkunas, eds., *Terrorism Financing and State Responses: A Comparative Perspective*, Stanford: Stanford University Press, 2007.

Perri, Frank S. and Richard G. Brody. "The Dark Triad: Organized Crime, Terror and Fraud," *Journal of Money Laundering Control*, Vol. 14, No. 1, 2011, pp. 44–59.

Perrin, Andrew. "Tiger Country: Whatever the Outcome of Peace Talks between Colombo and the Separatist Tigers, a Tamil Nation in All but Law Already Exists in Sri Lanka's Battle-Scarred Northeast," *Time*, September 16, 2002.

Peters, Gretchen. *Seeds of Terror: How Heroin Is Bankrolling the Taliban and Al Qaeda*, New York: MacMillian, 2010.

Peters, Gretchen. *Haqqani Network Financing: The Evolution of an Industry*, Combating Terrorism Center at West Point, Harmony Program, 2012.

Peters, Gretchen and Don Rassler. "Crime and Insurgency in the Tribal Areas of Afghanistan and Pakistan," Center for Combating Terrorism (CTC) at West Point, 2010.

Philippes, Brian J. "Terrorist Group Cooperation and Longevity," *International Studies Quarterly*, Vol. 58, No. 2, 2014, pp. 336–347.

Philippone, Doug. "Hezbollah: The Organization andIts Finances," in Michael Freeman, ed., *Financing Terrorism: Case Studies*, Surrey: Asghate, 2012.

Pollack, Kenneth M. *The Persian Puzzle: The Conflict between Iran and America*, New York: Random House, 2004.

Poole, Patrick. "Mortgage Fraud Funding Jihad?" *Front Page Magazine*, April 11, 2007.

Post, Jerrold M. *The Mind of the Terrorist: The Psychology of Terrorism from the IRA to al-Qaida*, New York: Palgrave Macmillan, 2007.

Prober, Joshua. *Accounting for Terror: Debunking the Paradigm of Inexpensive Terrorism*, Washington Institute for Near East Policy, Policy Watch 1041, November 1, 2005.

Prusher, Ilene R. "Through Charity, Hezbollah Charms Lebanon," *Christian Science Monitor*, April 19, 2000.

Qaseem, Naim. *Hizbullah: The Story from Within*, trans. D. Khalil, London: Saqi, 2005.

Qazi, Shehzad H. "Rebels of the Frontier: Origins, Organization, and Recruitment of the Pakistani Taliban," *Small Wars & Insurgencies*, Vol. 22, No. 4, October 2011, pp. 574–602.

Rabasa, Angel et al. *Beyond al-Qaeda, Pat II: The Outer Rings of the Terrorist Universe*, Santa Monica, Calif.: RAND Corp., 2006.

Rabasa, Angel et al. *Beyond Al-Qaeda: The Global Jihadist Movement, Part I*, Santa Monica, Calif.: RAND Corp., 2006.

Rabasa, Angel et al. *Ungoverned Territories: Understanding and Reducing Terrorism Risks*, Santa Monica, Calif.: RAND Corp., 2007.

Rana, Asim Qadeer. "Mullah Omar Wars Taliban Leaders of Action Over Abductions," *The Nation*, April 3, 2013.

Ranstorp, Magnus. *Hizb'Allah in Lebanon*, New York: St. Martin's Press, 1997.

Ranstorp, Magnus. "The Strategy and Tactics of Hezbollah's Current 'Lebanonization Process,'" *Mediterranean Politics*, Vol. 3, No. 1, Summer 1998, pp. 103–134.

Ranstorp, Magnus. "The Hezbollah Training Camps of Lebanon," in James J.F. Forest, ed., *The Making of a Terrorist, Volume II: Training*, Santa Barbara: Praeger, 2005.

Rashid, Ahmed. *Taliban*, New Haven: Yale University Press, 2001.

Rashid, Ahmed. *Descent into Chaos: How the War against Islamic Extremism Is Being Lost in Pakistan, Afghanistan, and Central Asia*, London: Allen Lane, 2008.

Rassler, Don et al. *Letters from Abbottabad: Bin Laden Sidelined*, Combating Terrorism Center (CTC) at West Point, 2012.

Reese, Justin Y. "Financing the Taliban," in Michael Freeman, ed., *Financing Terrorism: Case Studies*, Surrey: Ashgate, 2012.

Revill, James. *Militancy in the FATA and the NWFP*, Pakistan Security Research Unit, Brief No. 23, November 19, 2007.

Rice-Oxley, Mark. "Why Terror Financing Is So Tough to Track Down," *Christian Science Monitor*, March 8, 2006.

Richardson, Louise. *What Terrorists Want*, New York: Random House, 2006.

Robinson, Jeffrey. "The Money Trail: How Petty Crime Funds Terror," *New York Times*, August 13, 2004.

Rogin, Josh. "America's Allies Are Funding ISIS," *Daily Beast*, June 14, 2014.

Rogin, Josh. "ISIS Video: America's Air Dropped Weapons Now in Our Hands," *Daily Beast*, October 21, 2014.

Rollins, John and Liana Sun-Wyler. *Terrorism and Transnational Crime: Foreign Policy Issues for Congress*, Congressional Research Service (CRS), October 19, 2012.

Rosenau, William. "Understanding Insurgent Intelligence Operations," *Marine Corps University Journal*, Vol. 2, No. 1, Spring 2011, pp. 1–33.

Rosett, Claudia. "Can We Give to Gaza Without Giving to Hamas?" *Forbes*, March 5, 2009.

Ross, Michael L. "How Do Natural Resources Influence Civil War? Evidence from Thirteen Cases," *International Organization*, Vol. 58, No. 1, Winter 2004, pp. 35–67.

Ross, Michael L. "What Do We Know about Natural Resources and Civil War?" *Journal of Peace Research*, Vol. 41, No. 3, 2004, pp. 337–356.

Roston, Aram. "How the US Army Protects Its Trucks—By Paying the Taliban," *The Guardian*, November 12, 2009.

Roston, Aram. "How the US Funds the Taliban," *The Nation*, November 11, 2009.

Rotberg, Robert I. ed. *Creating Peace in Sri Lanka: Civil War & Reconciliation*, Washington, DC: Brookings Institution Press, 2005.

Roth, John et al. *Monograph on Terrorist Financing*, Staff Report to the National Commission on Terrorist Attacks Upon the United States, Washington, DC: U.S. Government Printing Office, 2004.

Roule, Triffin J. "Post- 911 Financial Freeze Dries Up Hamas Funding," *Jane's Intelligence Review*, April 19, 2002.

Rowayheb, Marwan G. "Political Change and the Outbreak of Civil War: The Case of Lebanon," *Civil Wars*, Vol. 13, No. 4, 2011, pp. 414–436.

Roy, Sara. *Hamas and Civil Society in Gaza: Engaging the Islamist Social Sector*, Princeton: Princeton University Press, 2011.

Rubin, Barnett R. "The Political Economy of War and Peace in Afghanistan," *World Development*, Vol. 28, No. 10, 2000, pp. 1789–1803.

Rubin, Alissa J. "U.S. Patrols Smuggling Routes to Macedonia: Balkans: American Peacekeepers in Kosovo Intercept Weapons on Way to Rebels," *Los Angeles Times*, August 20, 2001.

Rubin, Alissa J. "Taliban Causes Most Civilian Deaths in Afghanistan," *New York Times*, March 9, 2011.

Rubin, Alissa J. "Taliban Say Offensive Will Begin Sunday," *New York Times*, April 30, 2011.

Rubin, Lawrence. "Who's Afraid of an Islamic State," *Washington Post* Monkey Cage, October 2, 2014.

Rudoren, Jodi. "Tunnels Lead Right to the Heart of Israeli Fear," *New York Times*, July 28, 2014.

Rudoren, Jodi and Ben Hubbard. "Despite Gains, Hamas Sees a Fight for Its Existence and Presses Ahead," *New York Times*, July 27, 2014.

Ruttig, Thomas. *The Battle for Afghanistan: Negotiations with the Taliban: History and Prospects for the Future*, New America Foundation, National Security Studies Program Policy Paper, May 2011.

Ryan, Laura. "ISIS Is Better Than Al-Qaeda at Using the Internet," *Defense One*, October 10, 2014.

Saab, Bilal Y. "Rethinking Hezbollah's Disarmament," *Middle East Policy*, Vol. 15, No. 3, 2008, pp. 93–106.

Saad, Hwaida and Rick Gladstone. "Syrian Insurgents Claim to Control Large Hydropower Dam," *New York Times*, February 11, 2013.

Saad-Ghorayeb, Amal. *Hizbu'llah: Politics and Religion*, London: Pluto Press, 2002, p. 43.

Salama, Ahmad. "Kidnapping and Construction: Al Qaeda Turns to Big Business, Mafia-Stylye," *Niqash*, April 6, 2011.

Sanderson, Thomas M. "Transnational Terror and Organized Crime: Blurring the Lines," *SAIS Review*, Vol. 24, No. 1, Winter-Spring 2004, pp. 49–61.

Sanger, David E. and Julie H. Davis. *Struggling to Starve ISIS of Oil Revenue, U.S. Seeks Assistance from Turkey*, September 13, 2014.

Sanin, Francisco Gutierrez and Antonio Giustozzi. "Networks and Armies: Structuring Rebellion in Colombia and Afghanistan," *Studies in Conflict & Terrorism*, Vol. 33, No. 9, 2010, pp. 836–853.

Satti, Brooke. "Funding Terrorists: The Rise of ISIS," *SecurityIntelligence*, October 10, 2014.

Savage, Charlie. "Iranians Accused of a Plot to Kill Saudis' U.S. Envoy," *New York Times*, October 11, 2011.

Sayers, Eric. *The Islamic Emirate of Waziristan and the Bajaur Tribal Region: The Strategic Threat of Terrorist Sanctuaries*, The Center for Security Policy, No. 19, February 2007.

Sayigh, Yezid. *Hamas Rule in Gaza: Three Years On*, Brandeis University Crown Center for Middle East Studies, Middle East Brief No. 41, March 2010.

Scheuer, Michael. *Al Qaeda's Media Doctrine*, The Jamestown Foundation; Vol. 4, Iss. 15, May 30, 2007.

Schleifer, Ron. "Psychological Operations: A New Variation on an Age Old Art: Hezbollah versus Israel," *Studies in Conflict and Terrorism*, Vol. 29, No. 1, 2006, pp. 1–19.

Schmidt, Farhana. "From Islamic Warriors to Drug Lords: The Evolution of the Taliban Insurgency," *Mediterranean Quarterly*, Vol. 21, No. 2, Spring 2010, pp. 61–77.

Schmidt, Michael S. "U.S. Steps up Fight to Block ISIS Volunteers," *New York Times*, October 8, 2014.

Schmitt, Eric. "U.S. Is Trying to Counter ISIS' Efforts to Lure Alienated Young Muslims," *New York Times*, October 4, 2014.

Seelke, Clare R. et al. *Latin America and the Caribbean: Illicit Drug Trafficking and U.S. Counterdrug Programs*, Congressional Research Service (CRS), May 12, 2011.

Seib, Philip. "The Al-Qaeda Media Machine," *Military Review*, May/June 2008, pp. 74–80.

Semple, Kirk and Eric Schmitt. "Missiles of ISIS May Pose Peril for Aircrews," *New York Times*, October 26, 2014.

Sengupta, Somini. "Take Aid from China and Take a Pass on Human Rights," *New York Times*, March 9, 2008.

Sengupta, Somini. "Nations Trying to Stop Their Citizens from Going to Middle East to Fight for ISIS," *New York Times*, September 12, 2014.

Serena, Chad C. *It Takes More than a Network: The Iraqi Insurgency and Organizational Adaptation*, Stanford: Stanford University Press, 2014.

Shane, Scott and Ben Hubbard. "ISIS Displaying a Deft Command of Varied Media," *New York Times*, August 30, 2014.

Shapiro, Jacob. "Bureaucratic Terrorists: Al-Qa'ida in Iraq's Management and Finances," in Brian Fishman, ed., *Bombers, Bank Accounts & Bleedout: Al Qa'ida's Road In and Out of Iraq*, West Point, NY: Combating Terrorism Center (CTC), 2008.

Shapiro, Jacob N. and David A. Siegel. "Underfunding in Terrorist Organizations," *International Studies Quarterly*, Vol. 51, No. 2, 2007, pp. 405–429.

Shatz, Adam. "In Search of Hezbollah," *New York Review of Books*, April 29, 2004.

Shatz, Howard J. "How ISIS Funds Its Reign of Terror," *New York Daily News*, September 8, 2014.

Shatz, Howard J. "To Defeat the Islamic State, Follow the Money," *Politico*, September 10, 2014.

Shaver, Andrew. "Turning the Lights Off on the Islamic State," *Washington Post* Monkey Cage Blog, October 16, 2014.

Sheffer, Gabriel. "Diasporas and Terrorism," in Louise Richardson, ed., *The Roots of Terrorism*, London: Routledge, 2006.

Shelley, Louise I. *Dirty Entanglements: Corruption, Crime and Terrorism*, New York: Cambridge University Press, 2014.

Shelley, Louise. "Blood Money: How ISIS Makes Bank," *Foreign Affairs*, November 30, 2014.

Shelley, Louise I. and John T. Picarelli. "Methods Not Motives: Implications of the Convergence of International Organized Crime and Terrorism," *Police Practice and Research*, Vol. 3, No. 4, 2002, pp. 305–318.

Sherlock, Ruth. "Inside the Leadership of Islamic State: How the New 'Caliphate' Is run," *Daily Telegraph*, July 9, 2014.

Shinn, James and James Dobbins. *Afghan Peace Talks: A Primer*, Santa Monica, Calif.: RAND Corp., 2011.

Short, Philip. *Mao: A Life*, New York: Holt, 1999.

Shukla, Paraag. "ISW in Brief: Jailbreak Spurs Attacks in Kandahar City," *Institute for the Study of War*, May 12, 2011.

Shultz, Richard H. Jr. and Andrea J. Dew. *Terrorists, Insurgents, and Militias: The Warriors of Contemporary Combat*, New York: Columbia University Press, 2007.

Shultz, Richard H. Jr. et al. *Armed Groups: A Tier One Security Priority*, Institute for National Security Studies, United States Air Force, INSS Occasional Paper No. 57, September 2004.

Shulz, Helena L. with Juliane Hammer. *The Palestinian Diaspora: Formation of Identities and Politics of Homeland*, London: Routledge, 2003.

Shurkin, Michael. *Subnational Government in Afghanistan*, Santa Monica, Calif.: RAND Corp., 2011.

Siegel, Jacob. "Has ISIS Peaked as a Military Power?" *Daily Beast*, October 22, 2014.

Simcox, Robin. "ISIS' Western Ambitions," *Foreign Affairs*, June 30, 2014.

Simon, Steven and Jonathan Stevenson. "Al-Qaeda's New Strategy: Less Apocalypse, More Street Fighting," *Washington Post*, October 10, 2010.

Simpson, Cam. "The Banality of the Islamic State: How ISIS Corporatized Terror," *Bloomberg Business Week*, November 20, 2014.

Smith, Niel A. "Understanding Sri Lanka's Defeat of the Tamil Tigers," *Joint Forces Quarterly*, No. 59, 4th quarter, 2010, pp. 40–44.

Snyder, Richard. "Does Lootable Wealth Breed Disorder? A Political Economy of Extraction Framework," *Comparative Political Studies*, Vol. 39, No. 8, October 2006, pp. 943–968.

Stanekzai, Mohammad M. *Thwarting Afghanistan's Insurgency: A Pragmatic Approach toward Peace and Reconciliation*, United States Institute of Peace, September 2008. Washington, DC.

Staniland, Paul. "Defeating Transnational Insurgencies: The Best Offense Is a Good Fence," *Washington Quarterly*, Vol. 29, No. 1, 2005, pp. 21–40.

Staniland, Paul. "Caught in the Muddle: America's Pakistan Strategy," *Washington Quarterly*, Winter 2011, pp. 133–148.

Staniland, Paul. "Between a Rock and a Hard Place: Insurgent Fratricide, Ethnic Defection, and the Rise of Pro-State Paramilitaries," *Journal of Conflict Resolution*, Vol. 56, No. 1, 2012, pp. 16–40.

Stenersen, Anne. *The Taliban Insurgency in Afghanistan—Organization, Leadership, and Worldview*, Norwegian Defense Research Establishment (FFI), February 5, 2010.

Stewart, Megan A. "What's So New about the Islamic State's Governance?" *Washington Post* Monkey Cage blog, October 7, 2014.

Stokke, Kristian. "Building the Tamil Eelam State: Emerging State Institutions and Forms of Governance in LTTE-controlled Areas in Sri Lanka," *Third World Quarterly*, Vol. 27, No. 6, 2006, pp. 1021–1040.

Stringer, Kevin D. "Tackling Threat Finance: A Labor for Hercules or Sisyphus" *Parameters*, Vol. 41, No. 1, Spring 2011, pp. 101–119.

Stringer, Kevin D. *Counter Threat Finance (CTF): Grasping the Eel*, Military Power Revue, No. 2, 2013.

Sullivan, Daniel P. "Tinder, Spark, Oxygen, and Fuel: The Mysterious Rise of the Taliban," *Journal of Peace Research*, Vol. 44, No. 1, January 2007, pp. 93–108.

Tanner, Stephen. *Afghanistan: A Military History from Alexander the Great to the War against the Taliban*, revised edition, Philadelphia, PA: De Capo Press, 2009.

Taylor, Peter. *Provos: The IRA & Sinn Fein*, London: Bloomsbury, 1997.

Tekwani, Shyam. *The LTTE's Online Network and Its Implications for Regional Security*, Singapore: Institute of Defense and Strategic Studies, January 2006.

Thomas, Timothy L. "Al Qaeda and the Internet: The Danger of 'Cyberplanning,'" *Parameters*, Spring 2003, pp. 112–123.

Thompson, Edwina A. "An Introduction to the Concept and Origins of *Hawala*," *Journal of the History of International Law*, Vol. 10, No. 1, 2008, pp. 83–118.

Thompson, John C. and Jon Turlej. *Other People's Wars: A Review of Overseas Terrorism in Canada*, Toronto: The Mackenzie Institute, 2003.

Thruelsen, Peter D. "The Taliban in Southern Afghanistan: A Localized Insurgency with a Local Objective," *Small Wars & Insurgencies*, Vol. 21, No. 2, June 2010, pp. 259–276.

Torres, Manuel R. et al. "Analysis and Evolution of Global Jihadist Media Propaganda," *Terrorism & Political Violence*, Vol. 18, No. 3, 2006, pp. 399–421.

Treverton, Gregory F. et al. *Film Piracy, Organized Crime, and Terrorism*, Santa Monica, Calif.: RAND Corp., 2009.

Trombly, Danie and Yasir Abbas. "Who the U.S. Should Really Hit in ISIS," *Daily Beast*, September 23, 2014.

Tsfati, Yariv and Gabriel Weimann, "www.terrorism.com: Terror on the Internet," *Studies in Conflict and Terrorism*, Vol. 25, No. 5, 2006, pp. 317–332.

Tuck, Christopher. "Northern Ireland and the British Approach to Counter-Insurgency," *Defense & Security Analysis*, Vol. 23, No. 2, 2007, pp. 165–183.

Van de Voorde, Cecile. "Sri Lankan Terrorism: Assessing and Responding to the Threat of the Liberation Tigers of Tamil Eelam," *Police Practice and Research*, Vol. 6, No. 2, 2005, pp. 181–199.

Vaughan-Williams, Nick. *Border Politics: The Limits of Sovereign State Power*, Edinburgh: Edinburgh University Press, 2012.

Vick, Alan et al. *Airpower in the New Counterinsurgency Era: The Strategic Importance of USAF Advisory and Assist Missions*, Santa Monica, Calif.: RAND Corp., 2007.

Vittori, Jodi. "Idealism Is Not Enough: The Role of Resources in the Autonomy and Capability of Terrorist Groups," Ph.D. dissertation, University of Denver, June 2008.

Vittori, Jodi. *Terrorist Financing and Resourcing*, New York: Palgrave Macmillan, 2011.

Wagemakers, Joas. "Legitimizing Pragmatism: Hamas' Framing Efforts from Militancy to Moderation and Back?" *Terrorism and Political Violence*, Vol. 22, No. 3, 2010, pp. 357–377.

Waldmann, Peter K. *Radicalisation in the Diaspora: Why Muslims in the West Attack Their Host Countries*, Real Instituto Elcano Working Paper, September 2010.

Walt, Vivienne. "How Guns and Oil Net ISIS $1 Million A Day," *Fortune*, July 24, 2014.

Wannenburg, Gail. "Organised Crime in West Africa," *African Security Review*, Vol. 14, No. 4, 2005, pp. 5–16.

Warrick, Joby. "Attack on Israeli Tourists Prompts Fears of Escalating 'Shadow War,'" *Washington Post*, July 19, 2012.

Watson, Paul and Mubashir Zaidi. "Militants Flourish in Plain Sight," *Los Angeles Times*, January 25, 2004.

Wehrey, Frederic. "A Clash of Wills: Hezbollah's Psychological Campaign against Israel in South Lebanon," *Small Wars and Insurgencies*, Vol. 13, No. 2, 2001, pp. 53–74.

Wehrey, Frederic. "To Beat ISIS, Exploit Its Contradictions," *CNN.com*, June 17, 2014.

Wehrey, Frederic et al. *Dangerous but not Omnipotent: Exploring the Reach and Limitations of Iranian Power in the Middle East*, Santa Monica, Calif.: RAND Corp., 2009.

Wehrey, Frederic et al. *The Rise of the Pasdaran: Assessing the Domestic Roles of Iran's Islamic Revolutionary Guards Corps*, Santa Monica, Calif..: RAND Corp., 2009.

Weimann, Gabriel. "Hezbollah Dot Com: Hezbollah's Online Campaign," in *New Media and Innovative Technologies*, Ben-Gurion University Press, 2008.

Weinberg, David Andrew. *Qatar and Terror Finance, Part I: Negligence*, Foundation for Defense of Democracies, Center on Sanctions & Illicit Finance, December 2014.

Weintraub, Sidney. "Disrupting the Financing of Terrorism," *Washington Quarterly*, Vol. 25, No. 1, Winter 2002, pp. 53–60.

Weiss, Gordon. *The Cage: The Fight for Sri Lanka and the Last Days of the Tamil Tigers*, London: Bodley Head, 2011.

Weiss, Caleb and Bill Roggio. "Islamic State Assaults City in Syrian Kurdistan," *Long War Journal*, September 18, 2014.

Welsh, Declan and Eric Schmitt. "Drone Strike Killed No. 2 in Al Qaeda U.S. Officials Say," *New York Times*, June 5, 2012.

Williams, Brian G. "Mullah Omar's Missiles," *Middle East Policy*, Vol. 15, No. 4, Winter 2008, pp. 26–46.

Williams, Phil. "The Nature of Drug-Trafficking Networks," *Current History*, April 1998, pp. 154–159.

Williams, Phil. "Crime, Illicit Markets, and Money Laundering," in P. J. Simmons and Chantel Ouderen, eds., *Challenges in International Governance*, Washington, DC: Carnegie Endowment for International Peace, 2001.

Williams, Phil. "Transnational Criminal Enterprises, Conflict and Instability," in Chester A. Crocker, Fen O. Hampson, and Pamela Aal, eds., *Turbulent Peace: The Challenges of Managing International Conflict*, Washington, DC: United States Institute of Peace Press, 2001.

Williams, Phil. "Warning Indicators and Terrorist Financing," in Jeanne K. Giraldo and Harold A. Trinkunas, eds., *Terrorism Financing and State Responses: A Comparative Perspective*, Stanford: Stanford University Press, 2007.

Williams, Phil. "Terrorist Financing and Organized Crime: Nexus, Appropriation, or Transformation?" in Thomas J. Biersteker and Sue E. Eckert, eds., *Countering the Financing of Terrorism*, New York: Routledge, 2008.

Williams, Phil. *Criminals, Militias, and Insurgents: Organized Crime in Iraq*, Carlisle, PA: US Army War College Strategic Studies Institute (SSI), June 2009.

Williams, Phil. "Terrorist Financing," in Paul Shemella, ed., *Fighting Back: What Governments Can Do about Terrorism*, Stanford: Stanford University Press, 2011.

Williams, Phil. "Insurgencies and Organized Crime," in Phil Williams and Vanda Felbab-Brown, eds., *Drug Trafficking, Violence, and Instability*, Carlisle Barracks, PA: U.S. Army War College Strategic Studies Institute, April 2012.

Williams, Phil and Colin P. Clarke. "Terrorist Financing and Organized Crime," in Amit Kumar and Dennis Lormel, eds., *Understanding and Combating Terrorist Financing*, London: Taylor and Francis, *forthcoming*.

Winer, Jonathan M and Trifin J. Roule. "Fighting Terrorist Finance," *Survival*, Vol. 44, No. 3, 2002, pp. 87–104.

Wittig, Timothy. *Understanding Terrorist Finance*, New York: Palgrave Macmillan, 2011.

Worth, Robert F. "Hezbollah Seeks to Marshal the Piety of the Young," *New York Times*, November 20, 2008.

Wright, Lawrence. *The Looming Tower*, New York: Random House, 2006.

Young, William et al. *Spillover from the Conflict in Syria: An Assessment of the Factors that Aid and Impede the Spread of Violence*, Santa Monica, Calif.: RAND Corporation, 2014.

Yousafzai, Sami. "For the Taliban, A Crime that Pays," *Daily Beast*, September 5, 2008.

Zarate, Juan C. *Treasury's War: The Unleashing of a New Era of Financial Warfare*, New York: Public Affairs, 2013.

Zavis, Alexandrea. "Foreign Fighters in Iraq Seek Recognition, US Says," *Los Angeles Times*, March 17, 2008;

Zelin, Aaron Y. "ISIS Is Dead, Long Live the Islamic State," *Foreign Policy*, June 30, 2014.

Zelin, Aaron Y. *The Islamic State's First Colony in Libya*, The Washington Institute for Near East Policy, Policy Watch 2325, October 10, 2014.

Zelin, Aaron Y. *The War between ISIS and al-Qaeda for Supremacy of the Global Jihadist Movement*, The Washington Institute for Near East Policy, No. 20, June 2014.

Zelin, Aaron, Y. "When Jihadists Learn How to Help," *Washington Post* Monkey Cage, May 7, 2014.

ARTICLES WITH NO LISTED AUTHOR

The Al Qaeda Manual, Department of Justice.

"The Anatomy of ISIS: How the 'Islamic State' Is Run, from Oil to Beheadings," *CNN*, September 18, 2014.

"Arms Windfall for Insurgents as Iraq City Falls," *New York Times*, June 10, 2014.

"Attacking ISIL's Foundation," Remarks of Under Secretary for Terrorism and Financial Intelligence David S. Cohen at The Carnegie Endowment for International Peace, October 23, 2014.

British Broadcasting Corporation (BBC), "Religions: Islam," *BBC.com*, 2009.

"Challenges and Opportunities in Countering Threat Finance," *Praescient Analytics*, October 2012.

Department of Defense Report on Progress toward Stability and Security in Afghanistan: United States Plan for Sustaining the Afghan National Security Forces, April 2012.

"Did Islamic State Militants Use Bitcoin to Fund Their English-Language Website?" *Radio Free Europe/Radio Liberty,* October 13, 2014.

The Engagement of the Syrian Diaspora in Germany in Peacebuilding, United Nations University Migration Network, IS Academy Policy Brief, No. 13.

"European Union Must Respond to Hezbollah's Attack in Bulgaria," *Washington Post,* February 5, 2013.

"Fighting Terrorism in Africa," Testimony of Douglas Farah, Committee on International Relations, Subcommittee on Africa, United States House of Representatives, April 1, 2004.

Financial Action Task Force (FATF) IX Special Recommendations, October 2001. These recommendations were significantly revised again in 2012.

"Foreign Fighters Flow into Syria," *Washington Post,* October 11, 2014.

"Gaza Banks Close in Protest at Hamas Cash Seizure," *Reuters,* reprinted online in the *Jerusalem Post,* March 3, 2011.

Global Surveillance of Dirty Money: Assessing Assessment of Regimes to Control Money Laundering and Combat the Financing of Terrorism, Center on Law & Globalization, January 30, 2014.

"Hamas Extortion Ring Uncovered in Israel," *Xinhua,* September 24, 2012.

"Hamas Leaders Worth Millions of Dollars from Allegedly Skimming Donations and Extortion: Is Anyone Surprised?" *Inquisitr,* July 18, 2014.

Headquarters, U.S. Department of the Army, and Headquarters, U.S. Marine Corps, *Counterinsurgency Field Manual,* Field Manual 3-24/Marine Corps Warfighting Publication 3-33.5, Chicago, Ill.: University of Chicago Press, 2007.

Hearing of the House Permanent Select Committee on Intelligence, *Annual Worldwide Threat Assessment,* February 7, 2008.

"Hezbollah: Financing Terror through Criminal Enterprise," Testimony of Matthew Levitt, Committee on Homeland Security and Government Affairs, United States Senate, May 25, 2005.

"Hitting at Terrorists, Hurting Businesses," *The Economist,* June 14, 2014.

Hizbollah: Rebel without a Cause? International Crisis Group Middle East Briefing Paper, July 30, 2003.

"How ISIS Works," *New York Times,* September 16, 2014.

IHS Jane's World Terrorism and Insurgency, "Liberation Tigers Tamil Eelam."

International Crisis Group Report, *Taliban Propaganda: Winning the War of Words?* Asia Report No. 158, July 24, 2008.

Irregular Warfare Joint Operating Concept, 2007.

"ISIS Selling Iraq's Artifacts in Black Market: UNESCO," *Al Arabiya News,* September 30, 2014.

"Islamic State Ammunition in Iraq and Syria: Analysis of Small-Calibre Ammunition Recovered from Islamic State Forces in Iraq and Syria," London: Conflict Armament Research, October 2014, p. 5.

"Islamic State Fighter Estimate Triples," *British Broadcasting Corporation (BBC),* September 12, 2014.

"It Ain't Half Hot Here, Mum: Why and How Westerners Go to Fight in Syria and Iraq," August 30, 2014.

"A New Focus on Foreign Fighters," *New York Times*, September 24, 2014.

"Pakistan's Tribal Areas," Council on Foreign Relations, October 26, 2007.

"Pakistan's Tribal Areas: Appeasing the Militants," (*International Crisis Group*, Asia Report No. 125, 12/11/2006.

"Poor Correspondents," *The Economist*, June 14, 2014.

Reuters, "Saudi Says Arrests Qaeda Suspects Planning Attacks," *Washington Post*, March 3, 2008.

"Risk of Terrorist Abuse in Non-Profit Organizations," Report of the Financial Action Task Force (FATF), June 2014.

"Sri Lanka: Sri Lanka's Rebels Involved in Trafficking Human Cargo," *Xinhua News Agency*, April 7, 2000.

Terrorist Financing, Council on Foreign Relations, Report of an Independent Task Force, 2002.

Terrorist Financing, Financial Action Task Force, February 29, 2008.

U.S. Comptroller General, *Money Laundering: Extent of Money Laundering through Credit Cards Is Unknown*, Washington, DC: U.S. Government Accountability Office (GAO), 2002.

Warlord Inc.: Extortion and Corruption along the U.S. Supply Chain in Afghanistan, Report of the Majority Staff, Subcommittee on National Security and Foreign Affairs, U.S. House of Representatives, June 2010.

Index

274   Index